T0183562

Lecture Notes in Computer Science 12244

More information about this subseries at http://www.springer.com/series/7410

Guido Marco Bertoni · Francesco Regazzoni (Eds.)

Constructive Side-Channel Analysis and Secure Design

11th International Workshop, COSADE 2020
Lugano, Switzerland, April 1–3, 2020
Revised Selected Papers

 Springer

Editors
Guido Marco Bertoni
RD
Security Pattern SRL
Brescia, Italy

Francesco Regazzoni
AlaRI
Università della Svizzera italiana
Lugano, Switzerland

ISSN 0302-9743   ISSN 1611-3349   (electronic)
Lecture Notes in Computer Science
ISBN 978-3-030-68772-4   ISBN 978-3-030-68773-1   (eBook)
https://doi.org/10.1007/978-3-030-68773-1

LNCS Sublibrary: SL4 – Security and Cryptology

This Springer imprint is published by the registered company Springer Nature Switzerland AG
The registered company address is: Gewerbestrasse 11, 6330 Cham, Switzerland

Preface

It is our pleasure to welcome you to COSADE 2020, the 11th edition of the International Workshop on Constructive Side-Channel Analysis and Secure Design. The conference was originally planned in Lugano, Switzerland, April 1–3, 2020. However, the physical version of the conference had to be canceled due to COVID-19, and the conference was turned into a virtual event. Since 2010, COSADE has provided a well-established international platform for researchers, academics, and industry participants to present their work and their current research topics in implementation attacks, secure implementation, implementation attack-resilient architectures and schemes, secure design and evaluation, and practical attacks, test platforms, and open benchmarks.

COSADE 2020 was organized by Università della Svizzera italiana. This year, we received 36 papers, each of which was assigned to 4 reviewers. All the submissions went through a rigorous double-blind peer-review process. The Program Committee included 35 members from 15 countries, selected among experts from academia and industry in the areas of secure design, side channel attacks and countermeasures, and architectures and protocols. Overall, the program committee returned 176 reviews. During the decision process, 15 papers were selected for publication. These manuscripts are contained in these proceedings and the corresponding presentations were part of the COSADE 2020 program. We would like to express our gratitude to the program committee members and the 32 subreviewers for their reviews and for their active participation in the paper discussion phase.

In addition to the 15 presentations of selected papers, the program of COSADE 2020 was completed by 2 keynotes and one industrial session. The first keynote was titled "Tracking a Three Billion Dollar Bug with Electromagnetic Fault Injection" and was given by Colin O'Flynn from NewAE Technology Inc. and Dalhousie University. The talk explored a product safety incident through the lens of a hardware security researcher using tools with which hardware security researchers are familiar. The second keynote was titled "Security Aspects of CPSs: a Dive into Threat Modelling" and was given by Davide Ariu from Pluribus One. The talk provided an introduction to Threat Modeling, surveying possible Threat Modeling methodologies that can be applied to Cyber-Physical Systems of Systems and discussing the main challenges related to their application. The industrial session included three talks from Secure-IC ("Catalyzr tool: an environment to get your software secure; application to Post-Quantum Cryptography"), from Riscure ("Riscure tooling; 'we love FI'"), and from FortifyIQ ("Applying the best security and development practices to HW security").

We would like to thank the general chairs, Alberto Ferrante and Subhadeep Banik, and the local organizers, Liliana Sampietro and Nadia Ruggiero-Ciresa, from Università della Svizzera italiana, for the local organization. We would also like to thank the two Web administrators, Helmut Häfner and Lothar Hellmeier of the

University of Stuttgart, for maintaining the COSADE website for 2020. We are very grateful for the financial support received from our generous sponsors Hasler Stiftung, FortiyfIQ, NewAE Technology Inc., Riscure, Secure-IC, PQShield, and Rambus Cryptography Research.

October 2020   Guido Marco Bertoni
                                                            Francesco Regazzoni

Organization

Steering Committee

Jean-Luc Danger   Télécom Paris, France
Werner Schindler   Bundesamt für Sicherheit in der Informationstechnik
                         (BSI), Germany

General Chairs

Alberto Ferrante   ALaRI - USI, Switzerland
Subhadeep Banik   EPFL, Switzerland

Program Committee Chairs

Guido Marco Bertoni   Security Pattern, Italy
Francesco Regazzoni   ALaRI - USI, Switzerland

Program Committee

Divya Arora   Intel, USA
Reza Azarderakhsh   Florida Atlantic University, USA
Josep Balasch   KU Leuven, Belgium
Goerg T. Becker   ESMT, Germany
Sonia Belaïd   CryptoExperts, France
Davide Bellizia   UCL Crypto Group, Belgium
Shivam Bhasin   Nanyang Technological University, Singapore
Elke De Mulder   Rambus Cryptography Research, USA
Fabrizio De Santis   Siemens AG, Germany
Baris Ege   Riscure, The Netherlands
Wieland Fischer   Infineon Technologies, Germany
Samaneh Ghandali   Google, USA
Jorge Guajardo   Bosch, USA
Sylvain Guilley   Secure-IC, France
Tim Güneysu   Ruhr-Universität Bochum, Germany
Annelie Heuser   CNRS, IRISA, France
Naofumi Homma   Tohoku University, Japan
James Howe   PQShield, UK
Jens-Peter Kaps   George Mason University, USA
Michael Kasper   Fraunhofer Singapore, Singapore
Elif Bilge Kavun   The University of Sheffield, UK
Osnat Keren   Bar-Ilan University, Israel
Roel Maes   Intrinsic ID, The Netherlands

Pedro Massolino	Radboud University, The Netherlands
Marcel Medwed	NXP Semiconductors, Austria
Debdeep Mukhopadhyay	IIT Kharagpur, India
Makoto Nagata	Kobe University, Japan
Paolo Palmieri	University College Cork, Ireland
Colin O'Flynn	NewAE Technology Inc., Canada
Gerardo Pelosi	Politecnico di Milano, Italy
Ilia Polian	Universität Stuttgart, Germany
Kazuo Sakiyama	The University of Electro-Communications, Japan
Johanna Sepúlveda	Airbus, Germany
Patrick Schaumont	Worcester Polytechnic Institute, USA
Georg Sigl	TU Munich, Germany
Marc Stöttinger	Continental AG, Germany
Ruggero Susella	STMicroelectronics, Italy

Additional Reviewers

Abubakr Abdulgadir
Manaar Alam
Florian Bache
Jakub Breier
Olivier Bronchain
Lauren De Meyer
William Diehl
Farnoud Farahmand
Michael Gruber
Dirmanto Jap
Pantea Kiaei
Kris Kwiatkowski
Yohei Hori
Yang Li
Silvia Mella
Julien Montmasson

Thorben Moos
Adriaan Peetermans
Jan Richter-Brockmann
Sayandeep Saha
Thomas Schamberger
Tobias Schneider
Hermann Seuschek
Hadi Soleimany
Patrick Struck
Lars Tebelmann
Jan Thoma
Rei Ueno
Florian Unterstein
Gilles Van Assche
Ville Yli-Mäyry
Fan Zhang

Contents

Fault and Side Channel Attacks

Persistent Fault Analysis with Few Encryptions

Sébastien Carré[1,2], Sylvain Guilley[1,2,3(✉)], and Olivier Rioul[2]

[1] Secure-IC S.A.S., Think Ahead Business Line, Paris, France
`sylvain.guilley@secure-ic.com`
[2] LTCI, Télécom Paris, Institut Polytechnique de Paris, Palaiseau, France
[3] DIENS, École normale supérieure, CNRS, PSL University, Paris, France

Abstract. Persistent fault analysis (PFA) consists in guessing block cipher secret keys by biasing their substitution box. This paper improves the original attack of Zhang *et al.* on AES-128 presented at CHES 2018. By a thorough analysis, the exact probability distribution of the ciphertext (under a uniformly distributed plaintext) is derived, and the maximum likelihood key recovery estimator is computed exactly. Its expression is turned into an attack algorithm, which is shown to be twice more efficient in terms of number of required encryptions than the original attack of Zhang *et al.* This algorithm is also optimized from a computational complexity standpoint. In addition, our optimal attack is naturally amenable to key enumeration, which expedites full 16-bytes key extraction. Various tradeoffs between data and computational complexities are investigated.

Keywords: Persistent fault analysis · Substitution box · Maximum likelihood distinguisher · Key enumeration

1 Introduction

Cryptographic algorithms are generally "mathematically secure". As an example, the current best mathematical attack on AES cryptosystem is the biclique attack [4] that has a complexity of $2^{254.4}$ for AES-256. However, the implementation of a cryptographic algorithm can leak information that can greatly reduce the complexity of attacks. For example, any implementation for which the encryption time or the power consumption depends on the secret key gives the attacker some sensitive information about that key. Attacks exploiting physical leakages are known as *side-channel attacks*. Another class of attacks, known as *fault attacks* [1,5,7,12], deliberately creates errors in the cryptographic algorithm to help the attacker find the secret key. There are many types of fault attacks. Differential fault attacks [3,8,16,18,21] compare a faulted ciphertext with a correct one. Statistical fault attacks [10] perform multiple faulted encryptions to get sensitive information through statistical tools. Persistent fault attacks [6,20,23] consist in making a fault that remains persistent during the whole encryption

© Springer Nature Switzerland AG 2021
G. M. Bertoni and F. Regazzoni (Eds.): COSADE 2020, LNCS 12244, pp. 3–24, 2021.
https://doi.org/10.1007/978-3-030-68773-1_1

and across several consecutive encryptions. Persistent fault injection can be performed in various ways: laser injection [19], which requires a local access and which is possibly expensive; RowHammer attack [2,9,11,14,17] or Plunder-Volt [13] which can be triggered remotely and which do not require any expensive laboratory equipment. Combining fault attacks with side-channel attacks subsequently gives an attacker the ability to break a cryptosystem in a very efficient way.

1.1 Zhang *et al.*'s Attack

The attack of Zhang *et al.* [23] focuses on injecting a fault in the SBOX of AES that is used to perform the SubBytes operation. Such a fault eliminates an element y_- of the SBOX and creates a new one $y_+ \neq y_-$ instead. As a consequence, the element y_+ appears twice in the SBOX after the fault injection. This results in a bias on the output of the SubBytes operation: Assuming a uniformly distributed input, the value y_- cannot be observed at all as the output, while the value y_+ is observed with a higher probability of $2/256$; other values are observed with an unchanged probability of $1/256$. The resulting output probability distribution D is then

$$D : \mathbb{P}(y) = \begin{cases} 0 & \text{if } y = y_-, \\ 2/256 & \text{if } y = y_+, \\ 1/256 & \text{otherwise.} \end{cases} \tag{1}$$

The attack of Zhang *et al.* [23] requires enough encryptions to obtain an empirical distribution where only *one* element per byte is *not* observed, as shown in Fig. 1. From such never observed byte value x_-, the key byte can be obtained as $k = x_- \oplus y_-$.

Because each AES round gives a 16-byte output and consumes a 16-byte key, there are 16 possible biased distributions for an AES output, which only differ by the key byte value. In Fig. 1, each subplot represents one byte distribution among the 16 bytes of an AES ciphertext.

Thus, for the attack of Zhang *et al.* to work, the number of required encryptions should be such that all values are observed but one. This is an instance of the *coupon collector* problem. Figure 2 shows the success rate of the reproduced Zhang *et al.* [23] attack to recover a full 128 bits AES key. Their attack typically requires more than 2500 encryptions to obtain the AES master key with probability $\geq 80\%$.

1.2 Contributions

The Zhang *et al.* [23] attack assumes a *uniform* distribution at the input of the last round SBOX. Since the faulted SBOX is used in each AES round, it is not obvious that this uniformity assumption actually holds. In this paper, we assume that the fault location and the fault value are known by the attacker. We first give a formal proof of uniformity at the input of the last round SBOX, thanks

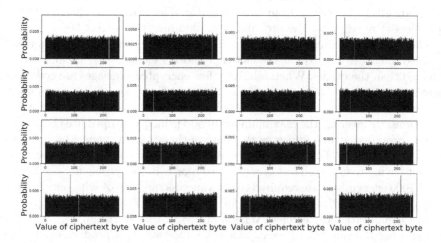

Fig. 1. Empirical distributions for each byte of the ciphertext. The bias depends on the last round key value.

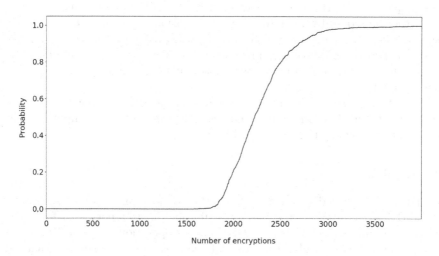

Fig. 2. Success rate of the Zhang *et al.* attack over 1000 retries to recover the complete AES key. With such a strategy, the attacker needs at least 2500 encryptions to obtain the AES master key with probability $\geq 80\%$.

to a property of the MixColumns operation. Then, under this assumption, the maximum likelihood estimator for n encryptions is determined and an efficient attack algorithm is derived from this estimator. The maximum likelihood principle aims at maximizing the probability of obtaining the correct key.

The attack of Zhang *et al.* only exploits the only element x_- that is never observed, but does not exploit the fact that another element is more likely to be observed than the others. When relatively few encrypted messages are collected, there may be more than one element not observed. Therefore, there are as many key candidates as unobserved elements, which are equally likely. To prevent these limitations, we leverage the maximum likelihood principle to optimize the attack.

The proposed attack improves the state-of-the-art performance by reducing the required number of encryptions. Less encryptions can still give the correct key without having to use a full instance of the coupon collector problem. Specifically, about 1000 encryptions are required to get a success rate of 80% with our strategy compared to about 2500 encryptions for the attack of Zhang *et al.* Besides, we detail a computationally efficient version of the attack algorithm.

Reducing the number of encryptions is important in a product evaluation context that uses, for instance, the Common Criteria (ISO/IEC 15408) since it influences the quotation. Indeed, in Common Criteria parlance, the quotation is a score which results from a combination of different factors, including time for trace collection and time for analysis.

More important, our result allows to calibrate one countermeasure against a persistent fault analysis: We derive a lower bound on the number of encryptions to successfully extract the correct key and the designer can simply refresh the key more frequently than this bound to avoid such attack. The number of encryptions can further be reduced thanks to a key enumeration algorithm. Our analysis is very amenable to such enumeration since it provides likelihoods to each subkey.

This paper also improves the proposed attack using various techniques such as key byte enumeration and key combination, exploring multiple strategies for each technique.

The attack presented in this paper is optimal for full key recovery since it is optimal at byte level in term of number of traces and also computationally optimal at the combination level of all bytes.

1.3   Outline

This paper is organized as follows. Section 2 mathematically shows that, even if the SubBytes operation gives a biased distribution due to a persistent fault, this bias is eventually cancelled by the MixColumns operation. Section 3 improves Zhang *et al.* attack: An algorithm to find the most probable key for each last round key is developed in Subsect. 3.1. Then, multiple combination strategies are discussed in Subsects. 3.2 and 3.3 in order to find the complete last round key and eventually the master key. Subsection 3.4 compares the success rate of our approaches compared to the one of Zhang *et al.* Section 4 concludes and gives some perspectives.

2 Bias Cancelling Effect of MixColumns

The attack of Zhang *et al.* is possible provided the distribution of the last round SubBytes operation is uniformly distributed. This assumption is not obvious since the output of SBOX in each AES round is not uniformly distributed due to the persistent fault which biases the SBOX. Proposition 1 shows that, in the context of this paper, the MixColumns operation returns a uniform distribution even for a biased input (output of corrupted SubBytes). Therefore, as AES consists in alternations between SubBytes and MixColumns (and other functions such as ShiftRows and AddRoundKey which do not change the distributions), provided the plaintext is uniformly distributed, so is the output of each Mix-Columns at every round.

Lemma 1 (Convolutional Identity). *For any $u \in \mathbb{F}_{256}$, we have*

$$\sum_{b \in \mathbb{F}_{256}} D(b)D(u-b) = \frac{1}{256}\Big(1 + D(u+y_+) - D(u+y_-)\Big). \tag{2}$$

where y_- and y_+ were defined in Subsect. 1.1.

Proof. Observe that (1) writes $D(b) = \frac{1}{256}(1 + \mathbb{1}_{\{y_+\}}(b) - \mathbb{1}_{\{y_-\}}(b))$. Therefore

$$256 \sum_{b \in \mathbb{F}_{256}} D(b)D(u-b) = \sum_{b \in \mathbb{F}_{256}} (1 + \mathbb{1}_{\{y_+\}}(b) - \mathbb{1}_{\{y_-\}}(b))D(u-b)$$

$$= \sum_{b \in \mathbb{F}_{256}} D(u-b) + D(u+y_+) - D(u+y_-)$$

$$= 1 + D(u+y_+) - D(u+y_-)$$

□

Lemma 2 (Uniformity of the AES State Bytes). *If the plaintext is uniformly distributed, then any intermediate variable in the AES algorithm is also uniformly distributed.*

Proof. AES being a Substitution-Permutation Network (SPN), each operation is bijective on the states. Therefore, uniformity property is maintained from the plaintext down to any intermediate state. □

Corollary 1 (Uniformity Implies Independence). *Provided the AES plaintext is uniformly distributed, all bits or bytes at any stage of the algorithm are mutually independent.*

Therefore, under the hypothesis of plaintext uniformity, the input bytes of the MixColumns operation are independent.

Proposition 1 (Bias Cancelling Effect of MixColumns). *Let $y_-, y_+ \in \mathbb{F}_{256}$ and distribution D be defined by Eq. (1). Let $B_0, B_1, B_2, B_3 \in \mathbb{F}_{256}$ be four bytes representing an AES state column before a MixColumns operation, independent and identically distributed according to distribution D. Then each byte $Z_0, Z_1, Z_2, Z_3 \in \mathbb{F}_{256}$ representing an AES state column after a MixColumns operation is uniformly distributed.*

Proof. For any $z \in \mathbb{F}_{256}$, given the assumed independence of B_0, B_1, B_2, B_3:

$$\mathbb{P}(Z_0 = z) = \mathbb{P}(02B_0 + 03B_1 + B_2 + B_3 = z)$$

$$= \sum_{b_0,b_1,b_2 \in \mathbb{F}_{256}} \mathbb{P}(02b_0 + 03b_1 + b_2 + B_3 = z | B_0 = b_0, B_1 = b_1, B_2 = b_2) D(b_0) D(b_1) D(b_2)$$

$$= \sum_{b_0 \in \mathbb{F}_{256}} D(b_0) \sum_{b_1 \in \mathbb{F}_{256}} D(b_1) \sum_{b_2 \in \mathbb{F}_{256}} D(b_2) \mathbb{P}(B_3 = z - 02b_0 - 03b_1 - b_2)$$

$$= \sum_{b_0 \in \mathbb{F}_{256}} D(b_0) \sum_{b_1 \in \mathbb{F}_{256}} D(b_1) \sum_{b_2 \in \mathbb{F}_{256}} D(b_2) D(z - 02b_0 - 03b_1 - b_2). \tag{3}$$

where the $+$ (XOR) sign denotes addition (same as subtraction) in $\mathbb{F}_{256}$. Using Lemma 1, Eq. (3) is simplified by collapsing the sums using Eq. (2). Each sum (lefthand-side of Eq. (2)) generates three terms (righthand-side of Eq. (2)), and the first constant term further simplifies by noting that $\sum_{b \in \mathbb{F}_{256}} D(u - b) = 1$.

After three recursive applications of Eq. (2), Eq. (3) becomes:

$$\mathbb{P}(Z_0 = z) = \frac{1}{256} + \frac{1}{256^3} \begin{bmatrix} D(z + 02y_+ + 03y_+ + y_+) - D(z + 02y_- + 03y_+ + y_+) \\ - D(z + 02y_+ + 03y_- + y_+) - D(z + 02y_+ + 03y_+ + y_-) \\ + D(z + 02y_- + 03y_- + y_+) + D(z + 02y_- + 03y_+ + y_-) \\ + D(z + 02y_+ + 03y_- + y_-) - D(z + 02y_- + 03y_- + y_-) \end{bmatrix}$$

where we observe that the terms in D pairwise cancel, as per:

$$
\begin{aligned}
D(z + 02y_+ + 03y_+ + y_+) = & \quad D(z + 0) & = D(z + 02y_- + 03y_- + y_-), \\
D(z + 02y_- + 03y_+ + y_+) = & \ D(z + 02(y_+ + y_-)) & = D(z + 02y_+ + 03y_- + y_-), \\
D(z + 02y_+ + 03y_- + y_+) = & \ D(z + 03(y_+ + y_-)) & = D(z + 02y_- + 03y_+ + y_-), \\
D(z + 02y_- + 03y_- + y_+) = & \quad D(z + y_+ + y_-) & = D(z + 02y_+ + 03y_+ + y_-).
\end{aligned}
$$

Hence $\mathbb{P}(Z_0 = z) = 1/256$, the uniform distribution. $\square$

The independence hypothesis in Proposition 1 assumes the rounds prior to the last round are executing the genuine AES, so that Lemma 2 applies, and yields the independence between any tuple of bytes in an AES intermediate state.

This proposition considerably simplifies the modeling of the problem, and allows us to derive exact results in the sequel. Additionally, the obtained uniformity at the output of the MixColumns operation, despite SubBytes is not uniform (after persistent fault), makes it possible to prove that, provided the plaintext is uniformly distributed, all configurations are explored, hence attack success rate does reach 100% asymptotically.

This proposition also shows that only one MixColumns operation is required to cancel the bias. This is confirmed by taking many observations and building the empirical distribution from these observations as shown in Fig. 3 where each element indeed appears to have the same probability to be observed. This means that one can consider the input of the last round as being uniformly distributed, no matter where the persistent fault occurred.

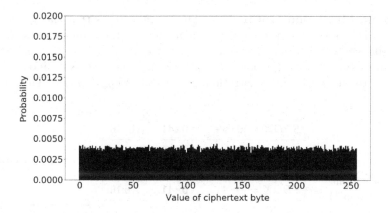

Fig. 3. Empirical distribution of a byte of an AES state after a MixColumns operation that takes a small biased input given by distribution D of Proposition 1.

3 Improvement Using Maximum Likelihood

This section explains how the Zhang *et al.* attack can be improved. First of all, the most likely key value for each byte of the last round key is extracted. In this step, each key per byte of the last round key is ranked from the most to the least probable. Then, a combination strategy is used to guess each byte of the last round key in a complete 128-bit last round key. Eventually, the correct master AES key is extracted from that last round key. Note that the value of the last round key is not necessarily the correct one, typically when the key schedule uses the faulted SBOX. This situation can be considered marginal, since most of the time, the keys are scheduled once, then reused multiple times. Hence, if the permanent fault in the SBOX occurs after the key is scheduled, then the round keys are correct, and the master key can be recovered from the last round key. Otherwise, the key schedule can also be inverted, although with some uncertainty: when a key byte is equal to y_+, then the two antecedents shall be considered when inversing the round of the key schedule. The number of possible master keys is in the order of $\frac{2}{256} \times 16 \times 10$ (< 2), which is manageable to enumerate.

3.1 Optimal Distinguisher

In this section, n AES encryptions are used to find the most probable key. For pedagogical reasons, only the first byte of an AES ciphertext is considered in this section, but other bytes are treated in a similar way. For the same reason, only the first byte of the last round key is considered. In this section, the term *key* refers to one byte of the last round key of AES. Precisely, this section focuses on the extraction of the last round key. From these n encryptions, n bytes $x_1, \ldots, x_n$, that can be viewed as elements of $\mathbb{F}_{256}$, are observed.

Maximum Likelihood Optimality. This section shows that the application of the MLE is optimal in the sense that it maximizes the attack success rate in a Bayesian context.

Figure 4 summarizes the idea of the attack until the success to find one byte of the last round key. In this illustration, $y_- = 0x63$ and $y_+ = 0x41$. This section

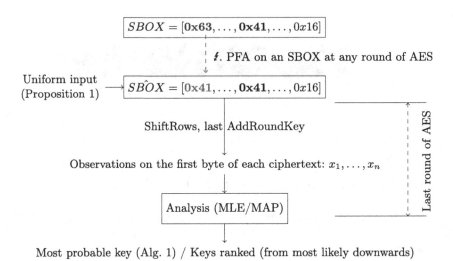

Fig. 4. Fault model and attack principle for this paper (with $y_- = \mathbf{0x63}$, $y_+ = 0x41$).

first assumes that each possible key is equally probable before any observation, meaning that $\mathbb{P}(k) = 1/256$ for each of the 256 possible keys k. Note that the fault also alters the round keys since the key scheduler uses SBOX. However, the biased output of an SBOX in the key scheduler is added to a uniform random variable in $\mathbb{F}_{256}$ before to output a round key. This eventually gives uniformly distributed round keys. Thus, even with the fault, it makes sense to assume a uniform distributed key for each of the AES round before any observations. Then, these probabilities are updated after the observations. This is then a Bayesian context of statistical inference in which this paper is written.

Finding the most probable key k means finding the key that maximizes the conditional probability $\mathbb{P}(k \mid x_1, \ldots, x_n)$ for observations $x_1, \ldots, x_n$. This is a well known problem in a Bayesian context known as *Maximum a posteriori (MAP)* estimator that is a generalisation of *Maximum Likelihood Estimator (MLE)*. These estimators are defined in the Definition 1.

Definition 1 (MAP and MLE). *Given a joint distribution of $k, x_1, \ldots, x_n$ of such distribution, we define two estimators:*

– *Maximum A Posteriori (MAP) estimator* $\hat{k}_{MAP} = \arg\max_k \mathbb{P}(k \mid x_1, \ldots, x_n)$.
– *Maximum Likelihood Estimator (MLE)* $\hat{k}_{MLE} = \arg\max_k \mathbb{P}(x_1, \ldots, x_n \mid k)$.

For uniformly distributed key hypotheses the estimators coincide:

Lemma 3 (MAP=MLE for Uniform Distribution). *In a Bayesian context, $\hat{k}_{MAP} = \hat{k}_{MLE}$ for a uniform a priori distribution of k.*

Lemma 3 is a classical result but we include its proof for completeness.

Proof. MAP is defined as $\hat{k}_{MAP} = \arg\max_{k} \mathbb{P}(k \mid x_1, \ldots, x_n)$. By Bayes' formula, this also writes

$$\hat{k}_{MAP} = \arg\max_{k} \frac{\mathbb{P}(x_1, \ldots, x_n \mid k)\mathbb{P}(k)}{\mathbb{P}(x_1, \ldots, x_n)} = \arg\max_{k} \mathbb{P}(x_1, \ldots, x_n \mid k)\mathbb{P}(k)$$

since $\mathbb{P}(x_1, \ldots, x_n)$ does not depend on k. Moreover, for a uniform a priori distribution, $\mathbb{P}(k)$ is constant and, therefore,

$$\hat{k}_{MAP} = \arg\max_{k} \mathbb{P}(x_1, \ldots, x_n \mid k) = \hat{k}_{MLE}.$$

$\square$

Since we assume that, before any observation, each possible key has the same probability, MLE is used to compute the MAP and find the most probable key. The choice of using MLE instead of directly computing MAP is motivated by the fact that, since observations are independent, computing $\mathbb{P}(x_1, \ldots, x_n \mid k)$ is much easier that computing $\mathbb{P}(k \mid x_1, \ldots, x_n)$, since the former simplifies to a product $\mathbb{P}(x_i \mid k) = D(x_i \oplus k)$ for all $1 \leq i \leq n$. This distribution can be extended for multiple observations. Such distribution is given in the Lemma 4.

Lemma 4 (Computation of the Likelihoods). *Given $k, y_-, y_+ \in \mathbb{F}_{256}, y_- \neq y_+$,*

$$\mathbb{P}(x_1, \ldots, x_n \mid k) = \begin{cases} 0 & \text{if } \exists i, 1 \leq i \leq n \mid x_i \oplus k = y_-, \\ 2^{m_{k,2}-8n} & \text{otherwise} \end{cases}$$

where $m_{k,2} = \#\{i \in \{1, \ldots, n\} \mid x_i \oplus k = y_+\}$.

Proof. Since the observations are conditionally independent given k, one has $\mathbb{P}(x_1, \ldots, x_n \mid k) = \prod_{i=1}^{n} \mathbb{P}(x_i \mid k) = \prod_{i=1}^{n} D(x_i \oplus k)$. This product is equal to zero if at least one $D(x_i \oplus k)$ is equal to zero. For a given k, there is only one element x_i for which $D(x_i \oplus k) = 0$ since it can only happen when $x_i \oplus k = y_-$ where y_- is the only element that is never observed at the output of the SBOX due to the fault. If no such term is equal to zero, then there are two options:

- if $x_i \oplus k = y_+$, then $D(x_i \oplus k) = \frac{2}{256}$ since y_+ appears twice at the output of the faulted SBOX;
- otherwise, $x_i \oplus k \neq y_+$ and $x_i \oplus k \neq y_-$. Thus $x_i \oplus k$ only appears exactly once in the faulted SBOX and $D(x_i \oplus k) = \frac{1}{256}$, which happens for 254 SBOX unique outputs.

Thus, $\mathbb{P}(x_1, \ldots, x_n \mid k)$ is equal to

$$\prod_{i=1}^{n} \mathbb{P}(x_i \mid k) = \left(\prod_{i \mid x_i \oplus k = y_-} 0 \right) \left(\prod_{i \mid x_i \oplus k = y_+} \frac{2}{256} \right) \left(\prod_{i \mid x_i \oplus k \notin \{y_-, y_+\}} \frac{1}{256} \right)$$

$$= (0)^{m_{k,0}} \left(\frac{1}{256} \right)^{m_{k,1}} \left(\frac{2}{256} \right)^{m_{k,2}} = \begin{cases} 0 & \text{if } \exists i \mid x_i \oplus k = y_-, \\ \left(\frac{1}{256} \right)^{m_{k,1}} \left(\frac{2}{256} \right)^{m_{k,2}} & \text{otherwise} \end{cases}$$

where we have noted $m_{k,0} = \#\{i \mid x_i \oplus k = y_-\}$, , and $m_{k,2} = \#\{i \mid x_i \oplus k = y_+\}$. Note that $m_{k,0} + m_{k,1} + m_{k,2} = n$. Moreover, when $\mathbb{P}(x_1, \ldots, x_n \mid k) \neq 0$, one has $m_{k,0} = 0$, thus $m_{k,1} = n - m_{k,2}$. Therefore, when there is no i, $1 \leq i \leq n$, such that $x_i \oplus k = y_-$, one has

$$\mathbb{P}(x_1, \ldots, x_n \mid k) = \left(\frac{1}{256} \right)^{n - m_{k,2}} \left(\frac{2}{256} \right)^{m_{k,2}} = \frac{1}{256^n} 2^{m_{k,2}} = 2^{m_{k,2} - 8n}.$$

$\square$

From Lemma 4, a two-step strategy is developed to find the correct key:

1. Eliminate keys that have the value $x \oplus y_-$ for each observation x since the probability to observe such element is null;
2. Among the remaining keys, declare the most likely key to be the one that has the value $x_+ \oplus y_+$, for an observation x_+ that appears the most often among all the observations. Indeed, x_+ is the value that should appear the largest number of times, owing to Lemma 4.

This strategy is optimal in the sense that it maximizes the likelihood. We now go one step further by applying the strategy without actually computing the probabilities. The computationally efficient strategy is exposed in our Proposition 2.

Proposition 2 (Operational MLE Computation for PFA). *Consider n observations of ciphertext bytes $\{x_1, \ldots, x_n\}$, and known PFA characteristic values $y_-, y_+ \in \mathbb{F}_{256}, y_- \neq y_+$. Define*

$$\mathcal{A} = \{x \oplus y_- \mid x \in \mathbb{F}_{256} - \{x_1, \ldots, x_n\}\}$$
$$\mathcal{B}_j = \{i \in \{1, \ldots, n\} \mid x_i = j \text{ and } x_i \oplus y_+ \in \mathcal{A}\} \qquad (0 \leq j \leq 255)$$

We have $\hat{k}_{MLE} \in \mathcal{A}$, and $\hat{k}_{MLE}$ is the index of $\mathcal{B}_j$ which is the largest set, i.e., $\hat{k}_{MLE} = \arg\max_j(\#\{\mathcal{B}_j\})$.

Proof. First, note that $\{x \in \mathbb{F}_{256} - \{x_1, \ldots, x_n\}\}$ and $\{x \in \{x_1, \ldots, x_n\}\}$ are complementary sets. This implies that $\mathcal{A}$ and are complementary. Since $\mathbb{P}(x_j \mid k) = 0$ for $x_j \oplus k = y_-$, then value $k \neq x_j \oplus y_-$. Thus, $\hat{k}_{MLE} \in \mathcal{A}$.

For the second point, we note that $\mathcal{B}_m$ contains the element that is the most often observed for which the condition $x_m \oplus y_+ \in \mathcal{A}$ holds. In other word, x_m is the most often observed value after removing elements x_i such that $x_i \oplus y_- = k$.

The proof then consists in showing that the maximum likelihood estimator is given by eliminating values k such that $x_i \oplus k = y_-$ and for which x_i appears the most often. Let $\hat{k} = \arg\max_k \mathbb{P}(x_1, \ldots, x_n \mid k)$ be the maximum likelihood estimator. The values of k such as $x_i \oplus k = y_-$ for at least one observation give $\mathbb{P}(x_1, \ldots, x_n; k) = 0$. Such keys can then be eliminated from the maximization. Since $m \mapsto 2^{m-8n}$ is strictly increasing in variable $m \in \mathbb{N}$, we have that $\arg\max_k 2^{m_{k,2}-8n} = \arg\max_k m_{k,2}$, i.e., the most likely key values are the values k that maximize $m_{k,2}$ (amongst k values which have not been ruled out).   □

Note that the set $\mathcal{A}$ contains all the possible keys. Thus, all impossible keys have been eliminated to get this set. This is the first remarkable point of our strategy. The elements contained in each class $\mathcal{B}_j$ are chosen in such a way that they match with a possible key. For the correct key, one observation has to appear the most often compared to the others. This observation can then be found by taking the class $\mathcal{B}_j$ that has the maximum number of elements. This is the second peculiarity of our strategy.

Based on Proposition 2, Algorithm 1 consists in eliminating the impossible keys and selecting the most likely one through the most observed value. Note that line 5 of this algorithm counts the number of times a key, related to an observation, can be observed and also takes care to only select possible keys by using the term $A[x_i \oplus y_-]$ that is equal 0 for the key $k = x_i \oplus y_-$. At line 2, the algorithm discards a key candidate if the value $k = x_i \oplus y_-$ is not already in set $\mathcal{A}$. Therefore, the set of impossible keys is increasing with respect to the inclusion. When all the 255 unique values of the ciphertexts x_i have been seen, the set $\mathcal{A}$ has cardinality 255, and the algorithm returns the key (in a singleton). As a corollary, when the correct key is found, more ciphertexts do not alter the outcome of the attack. This behavior differs from that of side-channel attacks where the measurements are noisy (e.g., powerline attacks, etc.).

Algorithm 1: Algorithm to extract the most likely key

---

input : The SBOX erased value $y_- \in \{0, \ldots, 255\}$, the SBOX duplicated value $y_+ \neq y_-$, and n observations $(x_1, \ldots, x_n)$ of ciphertext bytes.

output: Most likely key

---

1 $h[256] \leftarrow 0, \ldots, 0$ `// Histogram storing the occurrence count of a` `possible key. Notice that` $h[j] = \#\{\mathcal{B}_j\}$ `as per proposition 2`

2 $A[256] \leftarrow 1, \ldots, 1$ `// Indicator of the set of possible keys.` $A[k] = 1$ `if` k `is a possible key, otherwise` $A[k] = 0$

3 **for** $i \in \{1, \ldots, n\}$ **do**   `// Iterating on the observations`

4      $A[x_i \oplus y_-] \leftarrow 0$ `// Eliminate impossible key` $x_i \oplus y_-$`. This builds the` `set` $\mathcal{A}$ `of proposition 2`

5      $h[x_i \oplus y_+] \leftarrow A[x_i \oplus y_+] \times (h[x_i \oplus y_+] + 1)$ `// Among the remaining keys,` `count the ones that appear the most`

6 **return** $\arg\max_j h[j]$ `// Returns a list in case of` *ex æquo* `keys`

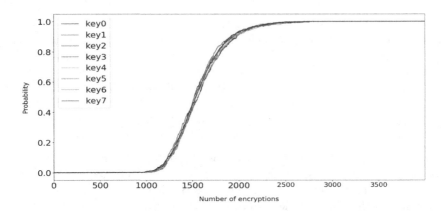

Fig. 5. $\mathbb{P}(\hat{k} = k)$ for one byte of multiple last round key of AES, averaged over 1 000 tries.

In our case, k is an AES last round key and an observation is a byte resulting from an encryption. We evaluate the number of required encryptions for all of the 256 possible keys. Figure 5 gives the success rate. The maximum likelihood estimator is known to be consistent. Thus, $\mathbb{P}(\hat{k} = k) = 1$ for enough observations, where k is the correct key. For clarity, only 7 keys are represented in this figure. However, the 256 possible keys follow the same trend.

Figure 6 shows how many key bytes remain, averaged over 1000 set of plaintexts, possible as a function of the number of encryptions by considering only the keys that are eliminated from the first figure or the keys that maximize the likelihood. Note that, some keys have the same likelihood and, thus, multiple key can maximize the likelihood. Note that the number of keys that maximizes the likelihood can locally increase but will eventually decrease down to 1. For less than 800 encryptions, the figure shows that more than 15 keys byte candidates are possible.

A Note About Guessing Entropy. Another approach to find a key k such as $\mathbb{P}(x_1, \ldots, x_n \mid k)$ is maximal from n observations is to use the guessing entropy defined as $GE = \sum_{i=1}^{256} k\mathbb{P}(x_1, \ldots, x_n \mid k)$ where $\{\mathbb{P}(x_1, \ldots, x_n \mid k)\}$ are sorted in decreasing order. Due to this sort, the guessing entropy is approximately equal to 1 if $\mathbb{P}(x_1, \ldots, x_n \mid k)$ is the biggest probability and other are small relatively to it. We thus estimate the number of observations required to get $GE = 1$ and observe that the guessing entropy becomes equal to 1 between 1200 and 1400 observations meaning that we require between 1200 and 1400 observations to be able to get the AES master key. This mean that, between 1200 to 1400 encryptions are required to get the correct key.

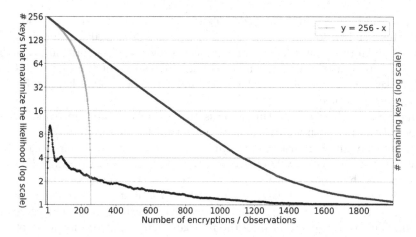

Fig. 6. Remaining values of one byte of last round keys after eliminating impossible keys (blue) and remaining values of one byte of last round keys that maximize the likelihood (black), averaged over 1000 tries. The line $y = 256 - x$ is represented as a reference, to illustrate the optimistic situation where one values of one byte of a last round key hypothesis is ruled out at each new encryption (never twice the same ciphertext byte).

3.2 Key Byte Ranking

Algorithm 1 returns not one unique value of a byte of the last round key, but a set of values of a byte of the last round key (since there are possibly ties in the likelihood values). Full 128 bits key can be reconstructed using key ranking algorithms, such as [22]. Indeed, one byproduct of our attack is that, in addition to be optimal, it is based on MLE, hence can sort out key candidates based on probabilities. Therefore, key ranking algorithms apply in a straightforward manner. In most cases, this requires to modifying Algorithm 1 so that instead of returning the most probable value of a byte of the last round key (the $\arg\max_j h[j]$ at line 6), it returns the most probable value of a byte of the last round key sorted with decreasing probabilities.

3.3 Combination of Several Key Bytes to Reconstruct the Full Key

In case not enough observations are available, the key byte ranking (Sect. 3.2) can fail to rank the keys correctly. In order to get around this limitation, a combination algorithm is given in this section.

The complete last round key can be recovered by combining key byte candidates in an empirical algorithm consisting in 16 imbricated loops. The first loop (outer loop) iterates over the candidates of the first key byte. The second loop iterates over the candidates for the second key byte and so on. Noting N_i the number of candidates for the last round key byte i, the total number of candidates for the whole last round key is $N = \prod_{i=1}^{16} N_i$. This product can be very large and can induce a high time complexity of the attack. For instance, for 100 candidates per byte of the last round key, we have $N = 100^{16}$ last round key candidates. More specifically, assuming the key byte rank algorithm gives the correct key byte as the first candidate for key bytes except the first one, then the attacker has to test between 2×100^{15} and 100^{16} last round key candidates which is not practical.

One strategy to mitigate this issue is to only test a predefined maximum number of key byte candidates. This assumes that the key byte rank algorithm is efficient enough. For instance, assuming that the key byte rank algorithm always rank the correct key byte between the first and the third rank, the time complexity is then reduced from $N = 100^{16}$ to $N = 3^{16}$. While this assumption is not always met, for each key byte candidate, the first key byte candidate is often the correct one and only very few key byte candidates are not correctly ranked. Thus we can consider only the first key byte candidate for most of the bytes and only iterate over the few other bytes. Due to this observation, our strategy consists in building the last round key candidates through 16 stages.

The first stage consists in trying all possibilities for only one byte over the 16 bytes. This gives a maximum of $16 \times 256 = 4096$ possibilities. At this stage, each of the 15 other key byte candidates is fixed to the first candidate. Those 15 bytes are called *small varying bytes*. If the full 128 bits key is not found, the second stage is used.

The second stage consists in trying all possibilities for two bytes among all combinations of two bytes among the 16 bytes. This gives a maximum number of testing key equal to $16 \times 15 \times 256^2$. At this stage, each of the 14 other key byte candidates is fixed to the first candidate. Those 14 bytes are called *small varying byte*. If the full 128 bits key is not found, the third stage is used.

All stages are built along the same scheme for at most $\sum_{k=1}^{n=16} \frac{16!}{(16-k)!} 256^k$ keys to test. Even if this appears to be a huge number, in practice the correct key is found in the first stages. To reduce again the time complexity, we can limit the number of byte candidates to p_i for byte i instead of 256. The parameter p_i is chosen experimentally to optimize the time it takes to perform the attack can be performed in a relatively short time.

For each stage, the *small varying bytes* were fixed to the first candidates. A more general strategy consists in choosing the first n candidates instead of the first. In such case, the maximum number of tested key is $\frac{16!}{(16-i)!} p_i^i \alpha_i^{16-i}$ per stage where α_i is the value of the *small varying bytes*.

Table 1 gives the time required to perform the attack and get the AES master key, according to the number of stages and the number of *small varying bytes*. The rows describe the number of stages that is used to perform the attack. The stages are used in order. For example, for 3 stages, the stage 1, 2 and 3 are used one after the other. The columns describe the value of the *small varying bytes*. For a *small varying byte* equal to 1, we used $p_1 = 256$, $p_2 = 256$, $p_3 = 108$, $p_4 = 17$, $p_5 = 6$, $p_6 = 3$ and $p_7 = 1$. For a *small varying byte* equal to 2 we used $p_1 = 256$, $p_2 = 33$, $p_3 = 5$ in the same idea to not test an excessive number of keys. For the same reason, the stage 4 to 7 is not used in this case. For a *small*

Table 1. Time, expressed in second, required to perform the attack and get the 16-bytes AES-128 master key, as a function of the number of stages used (in rows) and the value of the *small varying byte* (in columns).

	1	2	3
1	256/0.005 s	256/0.291 s	18/7.652 s
2	256/0.067 s	33/4.376 s	–
3	108/2.424 s	5/5.947 s	–
4	17/2.887 s	–	–
5	6/2.975 s	–	–
6	3/2.993 s	–	–
7	2/3.022 s	–	–

varying byte count equal to 3, we use only one stage with $p_1 = 18$. Each cell of the table reminds p_i before the time t_i in the format p_i/t_i.

Figure 7 gives a comparison of success rates, according to the number of stages and the value of the *small varying byte* in the same configuration given by Table 1. Only two stages is quite efficient compared to the success rate illustrated in Fig. 2. The figure shows that the best curve in term of number of encryption is for *small varying byte* equal to 2 with only 3 stages with 1371 encryptions.

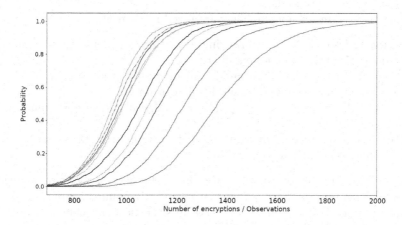

Fig. 7. Our MLE attacks for the complete last round key of AES— Comparison of success rates, according to the number of used stages. The value of *small varying bytes* is taken equal to 1 (plain line), 2 (dotted line), and 3 (semi dotted line). One color by number of stage is used, respectively red, green, blue, black, yellow, cyan, purple for 1, 2, 3, 4, 5, 6, 7 stages. Note that the result of stages six and seven are almost identical. (Color figure online)

3.4   Efficiencies of Key Byte Rank and Combination Algorithms

In order to test the efficiency of the key byte rank and combination algorithms, we compare multiple strategies that are combinations of three tactics:

1. Using the key byte algorithm or not. If the key byte algorithm is not used, the key byte candidates are tested in the order of the non observed values.
2. Getting ciphertexts until the histograms are full, meaning that all possible values are observed, or not. If we do not require the histograms to be full, we limit the number of candidates and stages with the better strategy discussed before that consists in using only three stages.
3. Using the combination algorithm or not.

This leads to $2^3 = 8$ possible strategies. However, there are $2^2 = 4$ strategies, for which we get enough encryption to fill the empirical histograms, that yield the same results. Indeed, in such cases, there is only one key byte candidate and then testing all candidates is the same than testing only one candidate. Moreover, and for the same reason, using the key byte rank algorithm necessarily gives the same results whether used or not. This reduces 4 strategies to only 1 and thus only 5 strategies remain.

We also note that, if we do not use the key byte rank algorithm and if we do not ensure a full histogram, then the success rate does not depend whether we use the combination algorithm or not. This shows the importance of a key byte rank and it is also due to the fact that our combination algorithm relies on the results of this key byte rank.

Thus four strategies remain. They are listed hereafter:

Strategy 1. Use the key byte ranking algorithm; Do not require to fill histograms; Use the combination algorithm.
Strategy 2. Use the key byte ranking algorithm; Do not require to fill histograms; Do not use the combination algorithm.
Strategy 3. Do not use the key byte ranking algorithm; Do not require to fill histograms.
Strategy 4. Require to fill histograms. As far as we understand, this strategy is the one used by Zhang *et al.* [23].

Figure 8 (top) gives the success rates over 1000 tries of the four strategies. The last one, in blue, is the worst since it necessarily requires more encryptions to fill histograms. The best one, in black color, is the most efficient one and is also the one that uses the key byte rank algorithm and the combination algorithm. Not using the combination algorithm is less efficient as shown by the red curve, but is still better than the green curve that shows the strategy that does not use the key byte ranking algorithm. One can note that the combination algorithm greatly improves the efficiency.

Each curve of the top figure of 8 is obtained by computing an average over 1000 curves where each of the 1000 curves describes a success rate for a given plaintext. For each of those 1000 curves, the success rate becomes equal to one more or less rapidly. The repartition of when the success rate is equal to 1

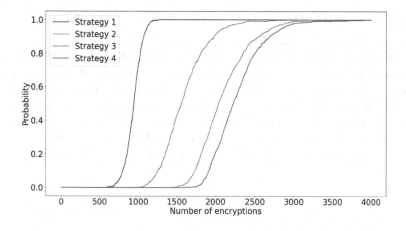

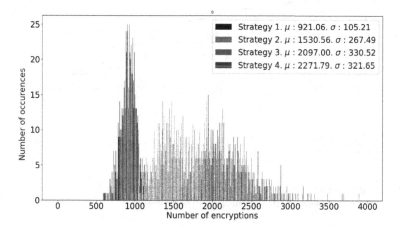

Fig. 8. Our MLE attacks for the complete last round key of AES—Success rates of strategies 1 to 4 over 1000 tries (top). Distribution of minimum number of encryptions over 1000 tries (bottom). Less than 1000 encryptions are required with the first strategy whereas more than 2000 are required for the last one. The smallest dispersion is reached for the first strategy whereas the worst one is reached by strategy four where no ranking algorithm is used.

over those 1000 curves are given by the bottom of the Fig. 8 that shows the distribution of minimum number of encryptions over 1000 tries. On this figure, mean μ and standard deviation σ are also given. Less than 1000 encryptions are required with the first strategy whereas more than 2000 are required for the last one. Also the best dispersion is reached for the first strategy and the worst one is reached on strategy four where no ranking algorithm is used. Strategy 1 is thus relevant to go further than the theoretical number encryption induced by the Coupon Collector Problem and discussed by Zhang *et al.* [23].

3.5   Comparison with the Tool of Veyrat-Charvillon *et al.* [22]

Our methodology to combine bytes can be compared to the C++ tool of Veyrat-Charvillon *et al.*, which implements the maximum likelihood algorithm to give the rank of the full 16-byte key based on the distribution of each individual key byte. This tool is pessimistic, in that, in case of ties (recall black curve in Fig. 6), it provides the largest rank. While the tool of Veyrat-Charvillon *et al.* is generally more efficient, our strategy focuses in reducing the time for small number of encryptions. For instance, getting the AES last round key with 893 encryptions requires about 20 min where the tool of Veyrat-Charvillon *et al.* takes about 3 h.

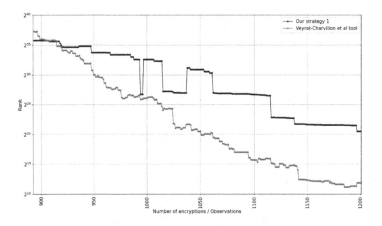

Fig. 9. Comparison between the combination algorithm described in paper with the tool of Veyrat-Charvillon *et al.* for one trace (no average)

Figure 9 shows the rank of the correct key estimated by the tool of Veyrat-Charvillon *et al.* and our method. For less than 903 encryptions our method gives the correct key at a lower rank compared to the tool of Veyrat-Charvillon *et al.*

4   Conclusion and Perspectives

4.1   Conclusion

In this paper, we revisited the fault attack that makes a permanent fault in the AES SBOX and we improve it by using multiple techniques including estimation theory, rank and key combination algorithms. With enough observations, if one focuses on the most observed value x_+, the most likely key will be $k = x_+ \oplus y_+$. Some observations can have exactly or approximately the same number of occurrences among the overall observations. In such case, since an observation x cannot be equal to $k \oplus y_-$, one can eliminate some keys. The strategy developed in this paper, and derived from the maximum likelihood analysis, to find the correct key therefore consists in two steps:

1. eliminate keys that have the value $x \oplus y_-$ for each observation x;
2. declare the most likely key among the remaining keys to be the one that has the value $x_+ \oplus y_+$, for an observation x_+, that appears the most often.

The key byte rank algorithm uses maximum likelihood estimation and guessing entropy. Various techniques have been experimented to build combination algorithms such as using imbricated loops, truncating the number of key byte candidates or to a more specific strategy that uses so-called *stages*.

After recalling some basics about how AES encryption works and how AES round keys are derived from the master key, the paper shows how a single byte fault can affect the final ciphertext. This fault can be stepped on at any time of the encryption. The attacker can also permanently fault the SBOX before or after key scheduling. The fault is only assumed to be persistent for all encryptions. The paper first assumes that an attacker can encrypt any messages, that are not necessarily chosen, in order to get an ideal empirical distribution for each of the 16 bytes of the ciphertext. In the state-of-the-art, more than 2000 encryptions were required to get such ideal distribution for each byte of the last round key. The attack in this paper works because the MixColumns operation is performed on all of the AES rounds but the last one. From those distributions, the paper explains how an attacker can find the last round of AES by analysing only the ciphertexts. Since the fault can affect the key scheduler, this last round key can be wrong but the paper shows that an attacker can still get the correct master key from a wrong last round key, and then derives the correct round keys.

The attack was further improved by considering non ideal empirical distributions. This was done by using a key rank algorithm for multiple key candidates with a combination algorithm that combines each potential byte of the last round key to get a complete round key. On average, less than 922 encryptions to get the AES master key with a high probability was necessary. In order to check whether the correct key is found, one can decrypt a ciphertext and check whether the resulting plaintext does make sense.

4.2 Perspectives

TBOX. In this paper, we focused on the faults on AES SBOX. Some implementations of AES use tables called TBOX to perform jointly the SubBytes and the MixColumns operations [15, Sec. 5.2.1, page 18]. Cryptographic libraries that implement AES with TBOX uses 4 tables of 256 elements. Each of those elements has 4 bytes size and those tables are used for all AES rounds except the last one since it does not require the MixColumns operation. For the last round, some implementations use a fifth table whereas others, like OpenSSL, mask 3 of the 4 bytes of the TBOX elements in order to only use the SubBytes operation out of the TBOX. In cryptographic libraries that use TBOX, two cases are possible to perform the attack described in this paper. These two cases are discussed here for future works.

In the first case, an attacker can try to target the SubBytes operation implemented by the TBOX. To reach this aim on implementations that uses 5 tables, an attacker can only target the fifth table that does not implement the Mix-Columns operation. For implementations that only use 4 tables, an attacker can only target 1/4 of the tables. Note that for implementations that only uses 4 tables, one fault per table has to be made in order to get the same effect with a single fault on an SBOX table. If one only targets one table it actually only targets one column of an AES state and thus, 4 bytes of a key.

In the second case, an attacker targets the MixColumns operation implemented by the TBOX. In such cases, we do not observe any bias for all of the bytes of the ciphertexts. However, we observe a bias on column of an AES states. The attack described in this document could then be adapted at column-level instead of byte-level. However, since a column represents 2^{32} possible values instead of 2^8 for a byte, more encryptions are required. If we assume that the number of encryptions is proportional to the number of values, and since we need 1371 encryption for an analysis at a byte level, we then need $1371 \times 2^{32}/2^8 = 23001563136$ encryptions. We could also need a more efficient key rank algorithm since we will have to test more keys.

Knowledge About the Fault. This paper considers that the location of the fault in the SBOX and also the value of the fault are known. In other words, it is assumed that the values y_- and y_+ are known by the attacker. Based on this assumption, if uniform byte values were submitted to each sbox, then the attack would converge in 255 plaintexts (because, at each newly observed byte c, the attacker knows that $c \oplus y_-$ is not a valid key byte). This is depicted by the curve $y = 256 - x$ in Fig. 6. This assumption was originally accepted in the case of a rowhammer attacker on a shared SBOX where the attacker can read the fault in memory. This assumption is invalid on some implementations, such as the AES-NI instruction set, where the SBOX is not exposed to the user (it can for instance be some firmware). Without the knowledge of y_- and y_+, one can still use a ranking algorithm to get the most likely value of $y_+ \oplus y_-$. Only 256 guess values are required to guess y_-, and y_+ will directly follow from the most likely value of $y_+ \oplus y_-$ when analyzing the ciphertext distribution.

4.3   Note Added After Revision of the Accepted Paper

We became aware of the recent work "Persistent Fault Attack in Practice" [24]. This paper elaborates on the attack converge speed and attributes it to MLE. Our work does further in that we mathematically derive the attack from the MLE. Besides, we show the merit of exploiting the likelihood for each key candidate to enumerate them by decreasing probability, thereby further speeding up the attack. This results in "strategy 1", whereas [24] consists in the strategy we called "strategy 2".

References

1. Bar-El, H., Choukri, H., Naccache, D., Tunstall, M., Whelan, C.: The Sorcerer's apprentice guide to fault attacks. Proc. IEEE **94**(2), 370–382 (2006)
2. Bhattacharya, S., Mukhopadhyay, D.: Curious case of rowhammer: flipping secret exponent bits using timing analysis. In: Gierlichs, B., Poschmann, A.Y. (eds.) CHES 2016. LNCS, vol. 9813, pp. 602–624. Springer, Heidelberg (2016). https://doi.org/10.1007/978-3-662-53140-2_29
3. Biham, E., Shamir, A.: Differential fault analysis of secret key cryptosystems. In: Kaliski, B.S. (ed.) CRYPTO 1997. LNCS, vol. 1294, pp. 513–525. Springer, Heidelberg (1997). https://doi.org/10.1007/BFb0052259
4. Bogdanov, A., Khovratovich, D., Rechberger, C.: Biclique cryptanalysis of the full AES. In: Lee, D.H., Wang, X. (eds.) ASIACRYPT 2011. LNCS, vol. 7073, pp. 344–371. Springer, Heidelberg (2011). https://doi.org/10.1007/978-3-642-25385-0_19
5. Boneh, D., DeMillo, R.A., Lipton, R.J.: On the importance of checking cryptographic protocols for faults. In: Fumy, W. (ed.) EUROCRYPT 1997. LNCS, vol. 1233, pp. 37–51. Springer, Heidelberg (1997). https://doi.org/10.1007/3-540-69053-0_4
6. Caforio, A., Banik, S.: A study of persistent fault analysis. In: Bhasin, S., Mendelson, A., Nandi, M. (eds.) SPACE 2019. LNCS, vol. 11947, pp. 13–33. Springer, Cham (2019). https://doi.org/10.1007/978-3-030-35869-3_4
7. Carré, S., Desjardins, M., Facon, A., Guilley, S.: OpenSSL Bellcore's protection helps fault attack. In: Novotný, M., Konofaos, N., Skavhaug, A. (eds.) 21st Euromicro Conference on Digital System Design, DSD 2018, Prague, Czech Republic, 29–31 August 2018, pp. 500–507. IEEE Computer Society (2018)
8. Dusart, P., Letourneux, G., Vivolo, O.: Differential fault analysis on A.E.S. In: Zhou, J., Yung, M., Han, Y. (eds.) ACNS 2003. LNCS, vol. 2846, pp. 293–306. Springer, Heidelberg (2003). https://doi.org/10.1007/978-3-540-45203-4_23
9. Gruss, D., Maurice, C., Mangard, S.: Rowhammer.js: a remote software-induced fault attack in JavaScript. In: Caballero, J., Zurutuza, U., Rodríguez, R.J. (eds.) DIMVA 2016. LNCS, vol. 9721, pp. 300–321. Springer, Cham (2016). https://doi.org/10.1007/978-3-319-40667-1_15
10. Jain, S., Agrawal, V.D.: Statistical fault analysis. IEEE Design Test Comput. **2**(1), 38–44 (1985)
11. Kim, Y., et al.: Flipping bits in memory without accessing them: an experimental study of dram disturbance errors. SIGARCH Comput. Archit. News **42**(3), 361–372 (2014)
12. Li, Y., Sakiyama, K., Gomisawa, S., Fukunaga, T., Takahashi, J., Ohta, K.: Fault sensitivity analysis. In: Mangard, S., Standaert, F.-X. (eds.) CHES 2010. LNCS, vol. 6225, pp. 320–334. Springer, Heidelberg (2010). https://doi.org/10.1007/978-3-642-15031-9_22
13. Murdock, K., Oswald, D., Garcia, F.D., Van Bulck, J., Gruss, D., Piessens, F.: Plundervolt: software-based fault injection attacks against Intel SGX. Tracked as CVE-2019-11157 (2020)
14. Mutlu, O., Kim, J.S.: Rowhammer: a retrospective (2019). arXiv:1904.09724 [cs.CR]
15. NIST. AES Proposal: Rijndael (now FIPS PUB 197), 9 April 2003. http://csrc.nist.gov/archive/aes/rijndael/Rijndael-ammended.pdf. Accessed 19 Apr 2020

16. Piret, G., Quisquater, J.-J.: A differential fault attack technique against SPN structures, with application to the AES and KHAZAD. In: Walter, C.D., Koç, Ç.K., Paar, C. (eds.) CHES 2003. LNCS, vol. 2779, pp. 77–88. Springer, Heidelberg (2003). https://doi.org/10.1007/978-3-540-45238-6_7

17. Razavi, K., Gras, B., Bosman, E., Preneel, B., Giuffrida, C., Bos, H.: Flip Feng Shui: hammering a needle in the software stack. In: 25th USENIX Security Symposium (USENIX Security 16), pp. 1–18. USENIX Association, Austin, August 2016

18. Rivain, M.: Differential fault analysis on DES middle rounds. In: Clavier, C., Gaj, K. (eds.) CHES 2009. LNCS, vol. 5747, pp. 457–469. Springer, Heidelberg (2009). https://doi.org/10.1007/978-3-642-04138-9_32

19. Roscian, C., Dutertre, J.M., Tria, A.: Frontside laser fault injection on cryptosystems - application to the AES' last round. In: 2013 IEEE International Symposium on Hardware-Oriented Security and Trust (HOST), pp. 119–124, June 2013

20. Schmidt, J.M., Hutter, M., Plos, T.: Optical fault attacks on AES: a threat in violet. In: 2009 Workshop on Fault Diagnosis and Tolerance in Cryptography (FDTC), pp. 13–22, September 2009

21. Tunstall, M., Mukhopadhyay, D., Ali, S.: Differential fault analysis of the advanced encryption standard using a single fault. In: Ardagna, C.A., Zhou, J. (eds.) WISTP 2011. LNCS, vol. 6633, pp. 224–233. Springer, Heidelberg (2011). https://doi.org/10.1007/978-3-642-21040-2_15

22. Veyrat-Charvillon, N., Gérard, B., Standaert, F.-X.: Security evaluations beyond computing power. In: Johansson, T., Nguyen, P.Q. (eds.) EUROCRYPT 2013. LNCS, vol. 7881, pp. 126–141. Springer, Heidelberg (2013). https://doi.org/10.1007/978-3-642-38348-9_8

23. Zhang, F., et al.: Persistent fault analysis on block ciphers. IACR Trans. Cryptogr. Hardware Embed. Syst. **2018**(3), 150–172 (2018)

24. Zhang, F., et al.: Persistent fault attack in practice. IACR Trans. Cryptogr. Hardware Embed. Syst. **2020**(2), 172–195 (2020)

A Template Attack to Reconstruct the Input of SHA-3 on an 8-Bit Device

Shih-Chun You and Markus G. Kuhn[(⊠)]

Department of Computer Science and Technology, University of Cambridge,
Cambridge CB3 0FD, UK
{scy27,mgk25}@cl.cam.ac.uk

Abstract. We present an enumeration procedure based on a template attack to recover the complete input text of a SHA-3 implementation on an 8-bit microprocessor from a single trace of a power-analysis side channel. This attack targets 600 bytes of triple-redundant internal state in each invocation of the permutation used by SHA-3. We first build templates that can generate for each of these bytes a rank table of all 256 candidates. The templates we obtained for our 8-bit target CPU nearly identified the correct value of most target bytes directly, rather than just gathering information about their Hamming weights. We then search the full intermediate state of the Keccak permutation to eliminate remaining uncertainties about the recovered byte values. From the resulting intermediate states we finally reconstruct both the input and output of SHA-3 and verify the output. In our experimental evaluation of this procedure we achieved success rates higher than 99%.

Keywords: Template attack · SHA-3 · Keccak · Enumeration trees

1 Introduction

In 2015, the National Institute of Standards and Technology (NIST) standardized *Secure Hash Algorithm 3* (SHA-3) [16], which is based on the Keccak sponge function and the Keccak-f permutation designed by Bertoni et al. [2,3]. Keccak-f consists of multiple rounds, each of which consists of five steps known as θ, ρ, π, χ and ι. The Keccak-f permutation is not only the main building block of the SHA-3 family of hash functions, but is also used in the SHAKE family of extendable-output functions, and can be used in many other contexts, such as key-derivation functions, message-authentication codes, and key-agreement schemes (e.g., NewHope [1]), where either its inputs or outputs can be confidential data for which side-channel attacks may be a concern.

Previous papers discussed side-channel attacks to recover keys used in the generation of Keccak-based message authentication codes (MAC-Keccak). Taha and Schaumont mainly used Differential Power Analysis (DPA) to attack step θ

S.-C. You—Supported by the Cambridge Trust and the Ministry of Education, Taiwan.

G. M. Bertoni and F. Regazzoni (Eds.): COSADE 2020, LNCS 12244, pp. 25–42, 2021.
https://doi.org/10.1007/978-3-030-68773-1_2

to recover a fixed-length key and discussed the relationship between key-length and the DPA resilience of MAC-Keccak [23]. They later applied similar attacks to recovering MAC-Keccak keys with arbitrary length [22]. Luo et al. modified this attack to determine the intermediate state after a complete round of Keccak-f [10], applying DPA after the non-linear step χ.

Such DPA-style attacks can effectively recover a MAC-Keccak key K, but they do not extend to other applications where there is no fixed key K, as they require leakage traces of many thousand repeated executions of SHA-3($K\|M$) with known variable input message M. For example, a DPA-style attack could not reconstruct the complete input of MAC-Keccak. Instead, we focus here on attacking a *single* invocation of Keccak-f in order to reconstruct both its input and output. To achieve this, we require a template attack (TA) [4]. We then use this capability to demonstrate recovery of a complete SHA-3 input given a single power trace and then verify the results with the given output of SHA-3. Our technique therefore not only can recover MAC-Keccak keys of arbitrary length without prior knowledge of the message M. It naturally also extends to other Keccak-f applications with confidential inputs or outputs, such as random-bit generation.

Since each step of the Keccak-f permutation is invertible, given its full output state we can calculate the input state of the step. Likewise, if we can determine a complete intermediate state, we can calculate from that both the input and output of the entire permutation. Having reconstructed the output of one Keccak-f invocation and the input of the next, we merely have to XOR these together in order to reconstruct one block of input of a SHA-3 execution.

We first tried to use the template attack to determine the value of every byte in a single full intermediate state. However, there is no room for mistakes: the diffusion of Keccak-f means that even a single bit error will result in a completely different input or output. Therefore, we combined a kind of template attack with an enumeration technique around the mathematical structure of Keccak-f to correct errors. We first use a template attack to estimate the likelihood of each of the 256 possible values of each byte in *three* consecutive intermediate states. Since the state of Keccak-f contains 200 bytes (1600 bits), there will be 200 per-byte rank tables associated with each observed intermediate state, that is 600 rank tables in total. In a pair of (nearly) consecutive intermediate states, each byte will only depend on a small number of bytes in neighboring states: the avalanche effect takes multiple rounds to come into effect. This makes it possible to eliminate errors by combining likelihood information from neighboring intermediate states and using the result to build rank tables for combinations of bytes. We repeat this until we obtain the (top of the) rank table for the entire state.

In this paper, we discuss the details of the template attack we performed on SHA-3 to obtain rank tables of all bytes of three consecutive intermediate states (Sect. 4), and then present the search procedure we used to recover the complete intermediate states (Sect. 5). Finally, we evaluate the success probability of recovering the inputs of SHA-3 by this method (Sect. 5.4).

2 Preliminaries and Notation

2.1 Keccak-f[1600] and SHA-3

Our terminology and notation related to SHA-3 and the Keccak-f permutation closely follow NIST FIPS 202 [16]. The SHA-3 algorithm is based on the Keccak-f[1600] permutation, which consists of a sequence of five steps that iterates 24 times on a 1600-bit state.

Each of the steps θ, ρ, π, χ and ι results in an intermediate state of 1600 bits. In this paper, we refer to these intermediate states as α_ω, α'_ω, β_ω and β'_ω as follows:

$$\textbf{Input} \xrightarrow{\theta} \alpha_0 \xrightarrow{\rho,\pi} \alpha'_0 \xrightarrow{\chi} \beta_0 \xrightarrow{\iota} \beta'_0 \xrightarrow{\theta} \alpha_1 \xrightarrow{\rho,\pi} \cdots \xrightarrow{\chi} \beta_{23} \xrightarrow{\iota} \textbf{Output}$$

The round index ω runs from 0 to 23 in Keccak-f[1600]. We use the term *intermediate byte* to refer to one of the 200 bytes in an intermediate state of Keccak-f[1600]. The SHA-3 standard describes these states as a $5 \times 5 \times 64$-bit cube with an x, y and z axis. Since we used an 8-bit processor in our experiments, we refer to the 64 bits along the z axis as 8 bytes. For example, we describe an intermediate byte in state α_0 as $\alpha_0[i, j, k]$, where i, j, k are the x, y, z coordinates with $0 \le i \le 4$, $0 \le j \le 4$, $0 \le k \le 7$. The least significant bit in this byte we denote by $\alpha_0[i, j, k][0]$ and its most significant bit by $\alpha_0[i, j, k][7]$. We call the five bytes with the same y and z coordinates a *byte row*, and the 25 bytes with the same z coordinate a *byte slice*.

All five steps in a Keccak-f[1600] round are practical to invert [2] and the Keccak team provides C++ implementations of the corresponding inverse functions [9]. In other words, the input, output, and all intermediate states of a Keccak-f[1600] execution can be converted into each other efficiently.

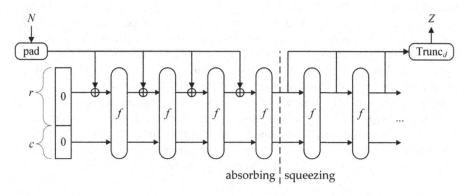

Fig. 1. The diagram of the Keccak sponge function from NIST FIPS 202 [16]. In this diagram, N is the arbitrary-length input sequence and Z is the d-bit output sequence.

The Keccak[c](N, d) function is based on the Keccak-f[1600] permutation [16]. It first "absorbs" an arbitrary-length input bit sequence into its internal state and then can "squeeze" out an arbitrary-length output bit sequence, and so is described as a "sponge function". Figure 1 shows how Keccak$[c](N, d)$ absorbs the input bit string N and squeezes out a d-bit result. Input message N is first padded and then split into blocks of $r = 1600 - c$ bits, where parameter c is called the *capacity* and parameter r the *rate*. The input and output of Keccak-$f[1600]$ each consist of $r + c = 1600$ bits, which we denote accordingly by $\mathbf{R} \| \mathbf{C}$. After all r-bit blocks have been absorbed, in the squeezing stage the output sequence is generated by concatenating the $\mathbf{R}$ fragment being output by each iteration of Keccak-$f[1600]$ until the concatenated sequence is at least of the required length d, and it is then truncated to d bits.

The SHA-3 family is finally defined for input messages M using Keccak$[c]$ for the output sizes $d \in \{224, 256, 384, 512\}$ bits as

$$\mathbf{SHA3\text{-}}d(M) = \mathbf{Keccak}[2d](M\|01, d).$$

In addition, SHA-3 defines two extendable-output functions (XOFs) as

$$\mathbf{SHAKE128}(M, d) = \mathbf{Keccak}[256](M\|1111, d)$$
$$\mathbf{SHAKE256}(M, d) = \mathbf{Keccak}[512](M\|1111, d)$$

where users have free choice over the output length d.

We ran all experiments in this paper on $\mathbf{SHA3\text{-}512}(M)$ because this is the SHA-3 algorithm with the largest capacity c, i.e. the largest security margin. The technique works equally well on the other SHA-3 algorithms.

2.2   Template Attack

The Traditional Template Attack. Chari et al. introduced a powerful side-channel exploitation technique called Template Attack (TA) [4]. It consists of two stages, profiling and attack. During profiling, we build templates that model the leakage traces of different candidate secrets from traces recorded while a known secret is processed. Then, we record an attack trace while an unknown secret is processed. We compare that with all the templates, and predict the secret as the candidate with the template most similar to the attack trace.

In this approach, attackers need to collect a sizable number of profiling traces. These will be separated into subsets according to the secret value targeted. If we target one intermediate byte, the number of subsets will be 256. From the trace subset corresponding to intermediate byte b, we construct a template consisting of an expected trace $\bar{\mathbf{x}}_b \in \mathbb{R}^m$ and a covariance matrix $\mathbf{S}_b \in \mathbb{R}^{m \times m}$, as

$$\bar{\mathbf{x}}_b = \frac{1}{n_b} \sum_{t=1}^{n_b} \mathbf{x}_{b,t}, \quad \mathbf{S}_b = \frac{1}{n_b - 1} \sum_{t=1}^{n_b} (\mathbf{x}_{b,t} - \bar{\mathbf{x}}_b)(\mathbf{x}_{b,t} - \bar{\mathbf{x}}_b)^\mathsf{T},$$

where n_b is the number of profiling traces in this subset, and $\mathbf{x}_{b,t}$ is the tth profiling trace with corresponding intermediate byte b, each trace containing m points in time.

Later, when we obtain an attack trace $\mathbf{x_a}$, we can calculate as a likelihood function a probability-density value for each template with

$$f(\mathbf{x_a}|\bar{\mathbf{x}}_b, \mathbf{S}_b) = \frac{1}{\sqrt{(2\pi)^m|\mathbf{S}_b|}} \exp\left(-\frac{1}{2}(\mathbf{x_a} - \bar{\mathbf{x}}_b)^\mathsf{T}\mathbf{S}_b^{-1}(\mathbf{x_a} - \bar{\mathbf{x}}_b)\right).$$

Then we can sort the 256 results into a rank table, where the top entry is the most likely candidate.

The Template Attack with Stochastic Models. The previous approach, where the arithmetic mean of the traces in *each* subset is used to estimate their expected value, needs a large total number of profiling traces. Based on the stochastic model $\mathcal{F}_9$ by Schindler et al. [19], Choudary and Kuhn used an alternative solution [6]. They treat each bit, $b[0]$ to $b[7]$, in the targeted intermediate byte as an independent variable and then use multivariate linear regression to calculate coefficients c_0 to c_7 and a constant c_8 for predicting the expected values of single points on a trace as $\hat{x}_b = \sum_{l=0}^{7}(b[l] \cdot c_l) + c_8$ and equivalently as

$$\hat{\mathbf{x}}_b = \sum_{l=0}^{7}(b[l] \cdot \mathbf{c}_l) + \mathbf{c}_8$$

for an entire trace, where $\mathbf{c}_0, \ldots, \mathbf{c}_8 \in \mathbf{R}^m$ are the vectors of coefficients and constants previously estimated by multivariate linear regression.

They also modified the way to calculate the covariance matrices $\mathbf{S}_b$ as

$$\mathbf{S}_b = \frac{1}{n_b - 1}\sum_{t=1}^{n_b}(\mathbf{x}_{b,t} - \hat{\mathbf{x}}_b)(\mathbf{x}_{b,t} - \hat{\mathbf{x}}_b)^\mathsf{T}, \quad \mathbf{S}_{\text{pooled}} = \frac{1}{\sum_{b=0}^{255}n_b}\sum_{b=0}^{255}(n_b - 1)\mathbf{S}_b.$$

Instead of a different $\mathbf{S}_b$ in each template, they used one single *pooled* covariance matrix estimate, $\mathbf{S}_{\text{pooled}}$, which is the weighted average of the $\mathbf{S}_b$, because previous studies [8,17] had suggested this is a more effective estimate when the actual covariance matrix can be assumed to be independent of the targeted value b. The function to calculate the probability density value then becomes

$$f(\mathbf{x_a}|\hat{\mathbf{x}}_b, \mathbf{S}_{\text{pooled}}) = \frac{1}{\sqrt{(2\pi)^m|\mathbf{S}_{\text{pooled}}|}} \exp\left(-\frac{1}{2}(\mathbf{x_a} - \hat{\mathbf{x}}_b)^\mathsf{T}\mathbf{S}_{\text{pooled}}^{-1}(\mathbf{x_a} - \hat{\mathbf{x}}_b)\right).$$

Data Compression with Linear Discriminant Analysis. Choudary and Kuhn also integrated Fisher's Linear Discriminant Analysis (LDA), as proposed by Standaert and Archambeau [20], into their approach [6]. This is a procedure to project the traces onto a subspace with higher signal-to-noise ratio (SNR), as determined by two covariance matrices $\mathbf{B}$ and $\mathbf{\Sigma}$, where $\mathbf{B}$ is the inter-class scatter representing the signal, while $\mathbf{\Sigma}$ is the total intra-class scatter representing the noise. When recovering 8-bit secrets, these two matrices can be calculated from the profiling traces as

$$\mathbf{B} = \frac{1}{\sum_{b=0}^{255} n_b} \sum_{b=0}^{255} n_b (\hat{\mathbf{x}}_b - \bar{\mathbf{x}})(\hat{\mathbf{x}}_b - \bar{\mathbf{x}})^\mathsf{T},$$

$$\mathbf{\Sigma} = \frac{1}{\sum_{b=0}^{255} n_b} \sum_{b=0}^{255} \sum_{t=1}^{n_b} (\mathbf{x}_{b,t} - \hat{\mathbf{x}}_b)(\mathbf{x}_{b,t} - \hat{\mathbf{x}}_b)^\mathsf{T} = \mathbf{S}_{\mathrm{pooled}},$$

where $\bar{\mathbf{x}} = 256^{-1}\sum_{b=0}^{255} \hat{\mathbf{x}}_b = \mathbf{c}_8 + \frac{1}{2}\sum_{l=0}^{7} \mathbf{c}_l$ is the arithmetic mean of the expected values $\hat{\mathbf{x}}_b$.

We then build a matrix $\mathbf{A} \in \mathbb{R}^{m \times m'}$ where the columns are the m' normalized eigenvectors of the matrix $\mathbf{\Sigma}^{-1}\mathbf{B}$ corresponding to its m' largest eigenvalues (see also [7, footnote 6]). The LDA projection of a raw trace $\mathbf{x}_a$ onto the resulting m'-dimensional subspace is then $\mathbf{x}_{\mathrm{proj}} = \mathbf{A}^\mathsf{T}\mathbf{x}_a$.

In our experiments, we follow Choudary and Kuhn's approach [6] as outlined above, firstly using multivariate linear regression to build matrices $\mathbf{\Sigma}$ and $\mathbf{B}$, secondly calculating the projection matrix $\mathbf{A}$, then using that to project all profiling traces onto the subspace with high SNR. From these projected traces, we then build very compact templates, again using multivariate linear regression. The resulting template information consists of a new covariance matrix $\mathbf{S}_{\mathrm{proj}} \in \mathbb{R}^{m' \times m'}$, 256 new expected traces $\hat{\mathbf{x}}_{b,\mathrm{proj}} \in \mathbb{R}^{m'}$, along with $\mathbf{A}$.

2.3 Combining Multiple Likelihood Tables

With ideal templates, attackers should find the full state of a secret by simply taking the most likely candidate from each part of the secret and concatenating them. However, template attacks are noise sensitive, so the correct candidate will not always top the rank table. Therefore, Veyrat-Charvillon et al. introduced an optimal key enumeration algorithm to search the correct key across several ranked likelihood tables of the sub-keys of AES [24]. Given two rank tables in descending order of likelihood, each with 2^8 values, there will be 2^{16} possible combinations. Their approach searches the 2^{16} possible combinations in descending order of their joint likelihood until the correct combination is found, without calculating the joint likelihoods of all 2^{16} combinations. They generalized this method using a recursive tree structure that combines two tables at a time to combine the results of more than two rank tables. With this algorithm, it becomes practical to search the correct combination of the sub-keys when correct candidates do not top the tables. This increases the noise resiliency of the attack significantly.

We applied their method in our experiments to enumerate the intermediate states instead of any key. We will refer to their tree-structured algorithm as an *enumeration tree* in this paper.

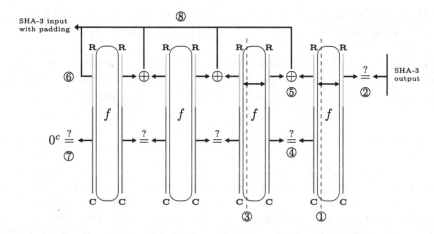

Fig. 2. The procedure to reconstruct SHA-3 inputs by template attack: ① reconstruct an intermediate state of the last Keccak-f[1600] permutation and calculate its input and output; ② verify the correctness by checking whether the first 512 bits in the output match the SHA3-512 output; ③ repeat ① on other permutations but ④ verify the correctness by checking whether the **C** of the output matches that of the input in the following permutation; ⑤ XOR the **R** of the two consecutive permutations to calculate each part of the SHA-3 input; ⑥ in the special case of the first r bits of the SHA-3 input, that part is identical to the **R** part of the input of the first Keccak-f[1600] permutation and ⑦ the **C** part of that permutation should be c 0 bits; ⑧ concatenate each part to form the complete SHA-3 input with padding.

3   Attack Strategy

Because of the invertibility of every step in Keccak, attackers can access not only the output but also the input of a Keccak-f[1600] permutation once they obtain any intermediate state. Figure 2 depicts how we can use this to recover an input of SHA3-512.

First, we use template attacks to reconstruct all the bytes in an intermediate state of the last Keccak-f[1600] permutation. After, for example, state α_0' is reconstructed, we can calculate the inverses of π, ρ, and θ to find out the input of this Keccak-f[1600] permutation, and then its output. We can verify the correctness of the latter by checking whether its first 512 bits match the SHA3-512 output.

Second, we can repeat what we have done on the last Keccak-f[1600] permutation for its predecessor, and verify the correctness of its output by checking whether its last $c = 1024$ bits **C** match those of the input of its successor. The input of the first Keccak-f[1600] permutation has **C** equal to an all-zero string.

Third, we can calculate each part of the SHA-3 input by XOR-ing the **R** part of the input and the output of two consecutive Keccak-f[1600] permutations. In the special case of the first r bits of the SHA-3 input, that is identical to the **R** part of the input of the first Keccak-f[1600] permutation. Finally, after concatenating all the parts and removing the padding, the input of SHA3-512 is recovered.

To target SHAKE128 or SHAKE256, we only need to attack permutations in the absorbing stage, as the squeezing stage fully depends on the output of the former, and recall that SHAKE uses slightly different padding.

4   Template Attack on SHA-3

Now the problem remains how to successfully recover at least one intermediate state in each invocation of the Keccak-f[1600] permutation in the SHA3-512 procedure by template attack. We chose the intermediate states α_0', β_0, and α_1 to build our templates, in order to cover a non-linear step (χ) while limiting the dependency on bits from other slices. (Any other choice of target round should work equally well.)

4.1   Target Hardware Device and Measurement Setup

Our SHA3-512 implementation is based on the Keccak-f[1600] implementation in the official C reference code, the Extended Keccak Code Package [25]. We ran it on a power-analysis test board designed by Choudary [5, Section 2.2.2].

The target processor is the 8-bit microcontroller ATxmega256A3U [12]. We supply it with an 2 MHz square wave clock signal generated by a National Instruments PXIe-5423 [15] wave generator that is configured to use the same reference clock as the NI PXIe-5160 [14] oscilloscope that we used to record the traces of power consumption. This way, with a sampling rate of 250 MHz, each clock cycle contains exactly 125 data points, with phase jitter about 8 ps standard deviation. The power supply was an NI PXI-4110 [13].

We recorded 32 000 profiling traces and 1000 evaluation traces of the Keccak-f[1600] permutation with random inputs to build the templates and evaluate their quality. For testing, we also recorded two sets of SHA3-512 traces. The first one contains 1000 random inputs with length shorter than 71 bytes, so it needs one Keccak-f[1600] permutation to absorb the input. The second set contains 1000 random inputs whose lengths range from 216 to 287 bytes, so they need four Keccak-f[1600] permutations to be absorbed. Since our target states are α_0', β_0, and α_1, we only recorded the traces covering the power consumption of the first two rounds of one Keccak-f[1600] permutation, and each raw trace contained 40 000 clock cycles or 5 000 000 samples.

4.2   Interesting Clock Cycle Detection

Since our raw traces were too long for building templates directly, we first determined the clock cycles that contain information about the targeted intermediate states, which in the Keccak-f[1600] permutation each contain 200 intermediate bytes. We tested each clock cycle to find out whether it is related to any of the intermediate bytes we target. We used the 8 bits in the intermediate bytes as 8 binary variables in a multivariate linear regression to analyze their correlation with the peak current in each clock cycle.

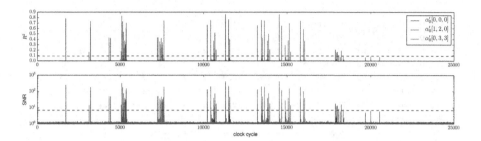

Fig. 3. Comparison of the highest R^2 coefficient and SNR value in each clock cycle.

We decided whether the correlation is sufficiently high via the coefficient of determination (R^2), as estimated by the regression. The clock cycles with R^2 higher than a threshold were added to the set of interesting clock cycles. Since traditionally the interval $-0.3 < R < 0.3$ indicates a variable of low correlation, we selected clock cycles based on the threshold $R^2 > 0.09$. The multivariate linear regression and R^2 were calculated using the `LinearRegression` class in the Python library `scikit-learn` [18]. Figure 3 shows the resulting highest R^2 value occuring in each clock cycle, along with SNR value [11]

$$\text{SNR}(s) = \frac{\sum_{b=0}^{255} n_b (\bar{\mathbf{x}}_b[s] - \bar{\mathbf{x}}[s])^2}{\sum_{b=0}^{255} \sum_{t=0}^{n_b} (\mathbf{x}_{b,t}[s] - \bar{\mathbf{x}}_b[s])^2}$$

at each per-clock-cycle peak time s. (Our $R^2 > 0.09$ threshold is approximately equivalent to an SNR > 7 threshold.)

Let $\mathcal{A}'_{0,[i,j,k]}$ be the set of interesting clock cycles for intermediate byte $\alpha'_0[i,j,k]$, $\mathcal{B}_{0,[i,j,k]}$ that of $\beta_0[i,j,k]$, and $\mathcal{A}_{1,[i,j,k]}$ that of $\alpha_1[i,j,k]$. The clock cycles that leak these $3 \times 200 = 600$ intermediate bytes should be sufficient for building working templates, but we found a method to consider more clock cycles at the same time. Between the intermediate states α_0 and α'_0 are the steps ρ and π, which are both transposition steps. We give an example here how the eight bits in $\alpha'_0[2,1,1]$ match those from up to two bytes in α_0:

$$\alpha'_0[2,1,1][0] = \alpha_0[0,2,0][5], \qquad \alpha'_0[2,1,1][1] = \alpha_0[0,2,0][6],$$
$$\alpha'_0[2,1,1][2] = \alpha_0[0,2,0][7], \qquad \alpha'_0[2,1,1][3] = \alpha_0[0,2,1][0],$$
$$\alpha'_0[2,1,1][4] = \alpha_0[0,2,1][1], \qquad \alpha'_0[2,1,1][5] = \alpha_0[0,2,1][2],$$
$$\alpha'_0[2,1,1][6] = \alpha_0[0,2,1][3], \qquad \alpha'_0[2,1,1][7] = \alpha_0[0,2,1][4].$$

Therefore we extend the set of interesting clock cycles for $\alpha'_0[2,1,1]$ from $\mathcal{A}'_{0,[2,1,1]}$ to $\mathcal{A}'_{0,[2,1,1]} \cup \mathcal{A}_{0,[0,2,0]} \cup \mathcal{A}_{0,[0,2,1]}$. This similarly applies to the intermediate state α_1, but the other way round.

Table 1. The number of interesting clock cycles for each byte in $\alpha'_0[i,j,k]$ (left) and $\beta_0[i,j,k]$ (right). The numbers for α_1 (omitted here) look similar to those for α'_0.

(i,j)	k							
	0	1	2	3	4	5	6	7
(0, 0)	36	38	33	33	32	33	42	33
(1, 0)	112	114	102	96	100	109	98	106
(2, 0)	107	103	96	96	98	103	94	98
(3, 0)	115	122	103	84	78	89	92	103
(4, 0)	134	124	82	74	74	87	95	100
(0, 1)	110	116	102	94	80	91	93	105
(1, 1)	109	117	95	83	77	88	97	102
(2, 1)	107	87	75	75	72	82	94	108
(3, 1)	109	109	96	93	97	102	92	100
(4, 1)	118	112	97	93	88	106	122	121
(0, 2)	90	75	75	73	69	70	84	97
(1, 2)	113	99	82	73	77	85	98	110
(2, 2)	86	86	94	85	70	69	76	81
(3, 2)	50	38	35	33	32	30	51	37
(4, 2)	103	99	87	71	65	72	80	100
(0, 3)	99	101	98	91	82	88	91	97
(1, 3)	108	112	104	99	95	97	97	103
(2, 3)	110	99	77	73	70	78	89	96
(3, 3)	127	114	79	70	73	87	89	99
(4, 3)	44	44	45	41	46	45	60	45
(0, 4)	127	119	104	98	97	112	127	125
(1, 4)	117	109	98	92	96	110	112	111
(2, 4)	115	110	100	103	94	89	94	98
(3, 4)	87	88	88	87	98	95	86	83
(4, 4)	93	87	89	83	72	80	90	104

(i,j)	k							
	0	1	2	3	4	5	6	7
(0, 0)	34	39	34	31	30	29	37	33
(1, 0)	25	26	23	23	30	26	32	27
(2, 0)	28	28	25	29	27	24	31	30
(3, 0)	26	32	30	25	27	24	34	28
(4, 0)	29	38	24	25	24	24	31	30
(0, 1)	27	25	25	27	24	24	34	29
(1, 1)	27	29	23	25	23	24	34	29
(2, 1)	27	28	23	25	24	27	36	37
(3, 1)	26	30	25	26	28	29	34	31
(4, 1)	30	29	24	27	28	22	34	35
(0, 2)	27	27	23	24	23	23	35	34
(1, 2)	30	24	22	24	21	21	29	30
(2, 2)	27	28	28	25	21	21	30	28
(3, 2)	32	24	23	24	23	23	30	31
(4, 2)	28	28	21	23	21	23	29	29
(0, 3)	28	26	26	29	26	26	33	28
(1, 3)	25	25	22	26	27	28	32	28
(2, 3)	32	26	23	25	25	25	35	33
(3, 3)	31	36	22	28	24	25	35	30
(4, 3)	30	29	25	27	29	29	45	34
(0, 4)	28	36	23	27	24	26	36	36
(1, 4)	27	32	25	25	27	29	42	30
(2, 4)	28	32	26	31	31	25	35	30
(3, 4)	27	29	25	30	28	22	35	28
(4, 4)	26	33	26	30	56	32	35	40

Table 1 lists the number of interesting clock cycles selected for each intermediate byte after that extension. In state α'_0, the numbers in lanes $(0,0)$, $(3,2)$, and $(4,3)$ are smaller because step ρ rotates the bits in these lanes by multiples of eight. For example, we always have $\alpha'_0[3,2,0] = \alpha_0[4,3,7]$, which implies that $\mathcal{A}'_{0,[3,2,0]} = \mathcal{A}_{0,[4,3,7]} = \mathcal{A}'_{0,[3,2,0]} \cup \mathcal{A}_{0,[4,3,7]}$, and that does not extend the set of clock cycles.

4.3 Building Templates

Pre-processing. When targeting a specific byte, we select only the samples in the interesting clock cycle set of this byte. For example, when building the template for $\alpha'_0[2,1,1]$, the profiling traces reassembled this way cover 87 clock cycles with $87 \times 125 = 10875$ samples.

Since the 125 samples per clock cycle still lead to too long execution times for building the templates, we reduced the sampling rate further by a factor 5, averaging five consecutive samples into a new sample.

Templates with LDA Compression. After the detection and pre-processing steps, we now have shorter traces for building templates for each of 600 bytes. We apply Choudary et al.'s method [6] (see Sect. 2.2). In the LDA compression, we chose only the first $m' = 8$ eigenvectors to form the projection matrices since the other eigenvalues are negligible. Besides the projection matrices, our templates therefore contain 8×8 covariance matrices and 8-point expected traces.

4.4 Evaluating the Quality of Templates

Having built the templates, we use the 1000 evaluation traces to estimate template quality, resulting in 600 rank tables for each evaluation trace.

As figures of merit, we use both the first-order success rate and the guessing entropy as defined by Standaert et al [21]. Table 2 shows the resulting success rates for states α'_0 and β_0, i.e. the fraction of these 1000 evaluation where the correct candidate topped the rank table. Table 3 shows the guessing entropy for each byte of states α'_0 and β_0, i.e. the average rank of the correct candidates in these 1000 evaluations (top rank = 1).

5 Searching the Correct Intermediate States

The results of the template evaluations show that it is improbable that all 200 bytes of an intermediate state can be directly recovered by combining only the top-ranking candidates. Therefore attackers will need a search scheme to find the

Table 2. Success rates on $\alpha'_0[i, j, k]$ (left) and $\beta_0[i, j, k]$ (right). The rates for α_1 (omitted here) look similar to those for α'_0.

(i, j)	k								(i, j)	k							
	0	1	2	3	4	5	6	7		0	1	2	3	4	5	6	7
(0, 0)	0.924	0.924	0.598	0.749	0.485	0.542	0.946	0.931	(0, 0)	0.803	0.872	0.718	0.587	0.413	0.528	0.801	0.677
(1, 0)	0.995	0.994	0.931	0.957	0.971	0.965	0.999	0.991	(1, 0)	0.530	0.654	0.255	0.226	0.354	0.274	0.522	0.314
(2, 0)	0.993	0.978	0.937	0.936	0.963	0.918	0.981	0.992	(2, 0)	0.487	0.592	0.334	0.262	0.263	0.355	0.475	0.351
(3, 0)	0.999	0.997	0.983	0.787	0.771	0.878	0.967	0.969	(3, 0)	0.529	0.683	0.309	0.220	0.294	0.275	0.498	0.355
(4, 0)	0.999	0.999	0.769	0.736	0.669	0.831	0.979	0.995	(4, 0)	0.526	0.651	0.299	0.207	0.235	0.351	0.490	0.353
(0, 1)	1.000	1.000	0.982	0.956	0.846	0.780	0.999	0.986	(0, 1)	0.373	0.365	0.286	0.305	0.274	0.306	0.536	0.483
(1, 1)	0.995	0.997	0.931	0.905	0.794	0.903	0.984	0.991	(1, 1)	0.293	0.348	0.327	0.280	0.272	0.376	0.608	0.449
(2, 1)	1.000	0.925	0.811	0.819	0.655	0.879	0.987	0.998	(2, 1)	0.259	0.353	0.262	0.240	0.291	0.298	0.596	0.533
(3, 1)	0.997	0.978	0.923	0.946	0.995	0.949	0.988	0.988	(3, 1)	0.290	0.346	0.290	0.267	0.352	0.376	0.544	0.485
(4, 1)	1.000	0.975	0.877	0.921	0.896	0.943	0.998	1.000	(4, 1)	0.358	0.385	0.295	0.390	0.362	0.259	0.619	0.437
(0, 2)	0.998	0.951	0.829	0.803	0.657	0.695	0.999	1.000	(0, 2)	0.277	0.300	0.340	0.322	0.200	0.263	0.569	0.325
(1, 2)	0.998	0.997	0.836	0.726	0.669	0.838	0.995	0.998	(1, 2)	0.289	0.300	0.309	0.354	0.216	0.259	0.553	0.341
(2, 2)	0.972	0.989	0.984	0.853	0.719	0.664	0.969	0.990	(2, 2)	0.224	0.299	0.339	0.358	0.197	0.258	0.541	0.281
(3, 2)	0.998	0.816	0.642	0.536	0.579	0.616	0.973	0.991	(3, 2)	0.275	0.244	0.327	0.269	0.233	0.270	0.508	0.341
(4, 2)	0.997	0.977	0.810	0.679	0.677	0.747	0.984	0.997	(4, 2)	0.284	0.230	0.236	0.293	0.173	0.263	0.530	0.315
(0, 3)	1.000	1.000	0.968	0.945	0.816	0.846	0.994	0.980	(0, 3)	0.301	0.252	0.291	0.289	0.444	0.319	0.638	0.374
(1, 3)	0.990	0.996	0.941	0.979	0.959	0.945	0.988	0.994	(1, 3)	0.312	0.256	0.260	0.257	0.438	0.344	0.700	0.336
(2, 3)	0.999	0.942	0.823	0.728	0.703	0.658	0.986	1.000	(2, 3)	0.383	0.225	0.274	0.268	0.347	0.328	0.661	0.396
(3, 3)	0.999	1.000	0.732	0.715	0.632	0.834	0.964	0.994	(3, 3)	0.379	0.285	0.270	0.265	0.311	0.307	0.695	0.340
(4, 3)	0.911	0.878	0.791	0.759	0.850	0.972	0.997	0.987	(4, 3)	0.337	0.262	0.260	0.247	0.425	0.340	0.696	0.401
(0, 4)	1.000	1.000	0.897	0.889	0.880	0.961	1.000	1.000	(0, 4)	0.351	0.413	0.241	0.225	0.256	0.326	0.612	0.474
(1, 4)	1.000	0.998	0.879	0.895	0.896	0.978	1.000	0.991	(1, 4)	0.338	0.393	0.260	0.216	0.228	0.332	0.593	0.332
(2, 4)	0.992	0.996	0.935	0.984	0.984	0.749	0.970	0.991	(2, 4)	0.299	0.350	0.282	0.299	0.302	0.318	0.616	0.493
(3, 4)	0.982	0.939	0.905	0.977	0.992	0.832	0.972	0.989	(3, 4)	0.303	0.326	0.271	0.290	0.253	0.262	0.649	0.400
(4, 4)	0.991	0.947	0.914	0.959	0.727	0.768	0.999	1.000	(4, 4)	0.319	0.783	0.528	0.516	0.828	0.601	0.587	0.670

Table 3. Guessing entropy on $\alpha_0'[i,j,k]$ (left) and $\beta_0[i,j,k]$ (right). The entropy for α_1 (omitted here) look similar to those for α_0'.

(i,j)	k							
	0	1	2	3	4	5	6	7
(0, 0)	1.095	1.109	2.336	1.616	3.215	2.592	1.074	1.096
(1, 0)	1.005	1.006	1.085	1.049	1.033	1.048	1.001	1.009
(2, 0)	1.007	1.024	1.074	1.070	1.044	1.102	1.022	1.008
(3, 0)	1.001	1.003	1.018	1.377	1.424	1.185	1.035	1.034
(4, 0)	1.001	1.001	1.452	1.575	1.680	1.297	1.028	1.005
(0, 1)	1.000	1.000	1.021	1.053	1.255	1.440	1.002	1.014
(1, 1)	1.005	1.003	1.084	1.127	1.353	1.147	1.020	1.009
(2, 1)	1.000	1.089	1.325	1.347	1.756	1.208	1.014	1.002
(3, 1)	1.003	1.022	1.092	1.066	1.006	1.056	1.013	1.012
(4, 1)	1.000	1.027	1.187	1.107	1.158	1.076	1.002	1.000
(0, 2)	1.003	1.057	1.294	1.377	1.833	1.819	1.001	1.000
(1, 2)	1.002	1.003	1.275	1.565	1.670	1.269	1.005	1.002
(2, 2)	1.031	1.012	1.020	1.274	1.625	1.947	1.035	1.010
(3, 2)	1.002	1.341	2.042	2.546	2.370	2.100	1.027	1.009
(4, 2)	1.003	1.026	1.395	1.709	1.832	1.508	1.019	1.003
(0, 3)	1.000	1.000	1.035	1.075	1.297	1.294	1.008	1.026
(1, 3)	1.010	1.004	1.068	1.024	1.053	1.072	1.012	1.008
(2, 3)	1.001	1.072	1.355	1.575	1.710	1.812	1.015	1.000
(3, 3)	1.001	1.000	1.594	1.618	1.959	1.324	1.050	1.006
(4, 3)	1.121	1.194	1.443	1.525	1.301	1.054	1.003	1.013
(0, 4)	1.000	1.000	1.140	1.175	1.156	1.054	1.000	1.000
(1, 4)	1.000	1.002	1.216	1.177	1.142	1.024	1.000	1.009
(2, 4)	1.010	1.005	1.083	1.020	1.022	1.491	1.030	1.009
(3, 4)	1.023	1.078	1.131	1.028	1.008	1.318	1.032	1.012
(4, 4)	1.009	1.060	1.122	1.052	1.652	1.492	1.001	1.000

(i,j)	k							
	0	1	2	3	4	5	6	7
(0, 0)	1.296	1.178	1.622	2.351	3.931	2.629	1.391	1.715
(1, 0)	2.643	1.954	7.313	9.001	5.537	7.692	2.752	5.906
(2, 0)	2.675	2.241	4.973	8.000	6.842	4.567	2.914	4.949
(3, 0)	2.371	1.778	7.058	8.803	6.444	6.724	2.959	5.089
(4, 0)	2.433	1.794	6.284	9.404	6.959	4.883	3.105	5.764
(0, 1)	4.583	5.037	6.780	7.534	5.965	6.288	2.697	3.360
(1, 1)	6.258	5.443	5.074	7.012	7.183	4.046	2.053	3.480
(2, 1)	6.325	5.132	7.682	8.731	6.660	6.622	2.468	2.980
(3, 1)	6.103	5.088	6.765	7.806	5.521	4.701	2.317	3.210
(4, 1)	5.267	4.972	6.526	5.000	4.129	7.227	2.214	3.897
(0, 2)	7.704	6.183	5.059	5.273	9.640	7.801	2.431	6.919
(1, 2)	5.800	7.270	6.671	4.691	9.212	6.722	2.723	5.457
(2, 2)	8.800	7.315	5.902	4.676	9.164	7.875	2.852	7.929
(3, 2)	6.875	8.534	6.677	6.691	8.061	8.670	2.906	6.216
(4, 2)	7.238	8.397	8.326	6.095	9.477	9.050	2.687	7.163
(0, 3)	5.747	7.825	6.600	6.936	3.231	5.893	2.140	4.747
(1, 3)	5.547	8.029	7.555	7.707	3.502	5.444	1.716	5.898
(2, 3)	4.549	8.766	7.473	6.990	4.631	5.860	1.899	3.982
(3, 3)	4.746	6.739	7.764	7.300	5.486	6.208	1.648	5.044
(4, 3)	5.313	8.414	8.048	7.751	3.531	5.413	1.796	4.470
(0, 4)	5.294	3.874	7.979	9.418	8.310	6.139	2.309	3.309
(1, 4)	5.309	3.939	7.766	8.770	7.162	6.030	2.335	5.722
(2, 4)	5.261	4.359	6.343	6.365	6.494	6.079	2.259	3.364
(3, 4)	6.766	4.995	7.510	7.268	7.313	7.794	1.929	4.508
(4, 4)	5.753	1.355	2.426	3.045	1.295	2.164	2.393	2.405

correct combination of high-ranking candidates. One obvious choice is to build an enumeration tree [24] to successively combine the rank tables for individual target bytes into tables for larger byte sequences, until the high-ranking combinations of all 200 bytes of an intermediate state are determined. While this approach is practical to search for moderately-sized states (e.g., 16-byte AES keys), we found that, when it comes to our much larger 200-byte states, it would still require unrealistically accurate templates for the search time to be tolerable.

To avoid directly combining the rank tables of our 200 target bytes, we built a three-layer scheme that can gradually combine the probabilistic information available about these bytes into a full state. In addition, rather than targeting just 200 bytes, our scheme actually takes 600 rank tables into consideration, to consider per-byte likelihoods from three intermediate states: α_0', β_0, and α_1. At the bottom, Layer 1 first merges the rank tables associated with five bytes in the same byte row, updates the likelihood of each combination, and then generates in total 40 new rank tables that cover entire byte rows. Layer 2 then combines five byte rows in the same byte slice, updates their likelihood values, and then generates eight new rank tables for byte slices. Finally, Layer 3 just concatenates the eight top candidates from each byte-slice rank table, and verifies the correctness of the resulting full intermediate state.

5.1 Layer 1: Generating Tables for Byte Rows

Between the intermediate states α_0' and β_0 is step χ. It can be calculated within a byte row, without any influence from other byte rows, which allows us to split the combination of these intermediate states into 40 mutually independent parts. Therefore we can combine per-byte rank tables using a practical enumeration tree that covers only five bytes at a time. We use the first byte row ($j = 0, k = 0$) here to demonstrate this.

First, we initialize the number T of combinations we want to collect in the resulting byte-row rank table to $T = 2500$. The five bytes of state α_0' in the first byte row are $\alpha_0'[0,0,0]$, $\alpha_0'[1,0,0]$, $\alpha_0'[2,0,0]$, $\alpha_0'[3,0,0]$, $\alpha_0'[4,0,0]$, and we use the five variables $A_0', A_1', A_2', A_3', A_4'$ to represent their values. As likelihood functions we use the Gaussian multivariate probability-density values provided by the template attack: $\mathcal{L}(\alpha_0'[0,0,0] = A_0') = f_{\alpha_0'[0,0,0]}(\mathbf{x}_{\text{proj}}|\hat{\mathbf{x}}_{A_0'}, \text{proj}, \mathbf{S}_{\text{proj}})$, etc. With the rank tables of these five bytes, we build an enumeration tree to search the first T combinations in descending order of joint likelihood of a byte row. Assuming independence, our first estimate of their joint likelihood is

$$\mathcal{L}_{\text{row}}(\alpha_0'[\cdot, 0, 0] = (A_0', A_1', A_2', A_3', A_4')) := \prod_{i=0}^{4} \mathcal{L}(\alpha_0'[i, 0, 0] = A_i').$$

Now the top-T combinations and their corresponding joint likelihoods form a truncated rank table for this byte row.

For these T combinations, we calculate the values of state β_0 in this byte row as

$$(B_0, B_1, B_2, B_3, B_4) = \chi(A_0', A_1', A_2', A_3', A_4').$$

Since we also have ranked likelihood tables for all bytes in state β_0, we now can similarly calculate the likelihood for any combination $(B_0, B_1, B_2, B_3, B_4)$, and update the above top-T joint likelihoods by multiplying with the likelihood of β_0, that is

$$\mathcal{L}_{\text{row}}^{\text{new}}(\alpha_0'[\cdot, 0, 0] = (A_0', A_1', A_2', A_3', A_4')) :=$$

$$\prod_{i=0}^{4} \mathcal{L}(\alpha_0'[i, 0, 0] = A_i')\mathcal{L}(\beta_0[i, 0, 0] = B_i).$$

Then, we sort these T combinations again in descending order of their updated joint likelihood, and obtain the new rank table of this byte row.

5.2 Layer 2: Generating Tables for Byte Slices

We then use a method similar to Layer 1 to combine five byte-row rank tables into a byte-slice rank table. We use here the first byte slice ($k = 0$) to demonstrate this. Let R_j' represent a byte row value of state $\alpha_0'[\cdot, j, 0]$ in this byte slice, such that it contains five bytes, where $R_j' = (A_{0,j}', A_{1,j}', A_{2,j}', A_{3,j}', A_{4,j}')$.

We use the rank tables of the five byte rows again to build an enumeration tree, and search the first T combinations in descending order of joint likelihood of a byte slice. Number T is as in Layer 1. Our initial joint likelihood estimate for a byte slice is

$$\mathcal{L}_{\text{slice}}(\alpha_0'[\cdot,\cdot,0] = (R_0', R_1', R_2', R_3', R_4')) :=$$

$$\prod_{j=0}^{4} \mathcal{L}_{\text{row}}^{\text{new}}(\alpha_0'[\cdot,j,0] = R_j') = \prod_{j=0}^{4}\prod_{i=0}^{4} \mathcal{L}(\alpha_0'[i,j,0] = A_{i,j}')\mathcal{L}(\beta_0[i,j,0] = B_{i,j}).$$

Similar as in Layer 1, we now update these joint likelihoods by taking the rank tables of α_1 into account. We use variable $A_{i,j}$ to represent the candidates of intermediate byte $\alpha_1[i,j,0]$, and with $R_j = (A_{0,j}, A_{1,j}, A_{2,j}, A_{3,j}, A_{4,j})$ have

$$(R_0, R_1, R_2, R_3, R_4) = \theta^*(\iota_{0,k}^*(\chi(R_0'), \chi(R_1'), \chi(R_2'), \chi(R_3'), \chi(R_4')), \tau),$$

where $\iota_{0,k}^*$ is ι in round 0 with input and output truncated to byte slice k, and $\theta^*(\ldots,\tau)$ is θ applied to just one byte slice, where $\tau \in \{0,1\}^5$ represents the five bits of column-parity information taken by θ from the previous byte slice. Since step χ operates within a byte row, it will not use any data outside the byte slice. Likewise, step ι XORs with a round constant, so it too is independent of other byte slices. However, when executing step θ on only a byte slice, we will lack information about five bits, because bit rotations are involved in step θ and hence these five bits come from another byte slice. Without that information τ, step θ^* on only one byte slice will have 32 possible outcomes. It is reasonable to choose the combination τ that maximizes the joint likelihood of $\alpha_1[\cdot,\cdot,0]$, which is

$$\max_{\tau \in \{0,1\}^5} \prod_{j=0}^{4}\prod_{i=0}^{4} \mathcal{L}(\alpha_1[i,j,0] = A_{i,j}).$$

Then, we can update the joint likelihood of this byte slice by multiplying with the joint likelihood of α_1, that is

$$\mathcal{L}_{\text{slice}}^{\text{new}}(\alpha_0'[\cdot,\cdot,0] = (R_0', R_1', R_2', R_3', R_4')) :=$$

$$\prod_{j=0}^{4}\prod_{i=0}^{4} \mathcal{L}(\alpha_0'[i,j,0] = A_{i,j}')\mathcal{L}(\beta_0[i,j,0] = B_{i,j})\mathcal{L}(\alpha_1[i,j,0] = A_{i,j}).$$

We then again sort these T combinations in descending order of the updated joint likelihoods to form a new rank table for this byte slice.

5.3 Layer 3: Consistency Checking

In Layer 3, we could again form an enumeration tree to combine the top-T entries in the eight byte-slice rank tables from Layer 2 into a single top-T rank table of the full 200-byte state. In practice, however, we found that this was never necessary, as in all our experiments if a byte-slice rank table contained the correct combination, it was already ranked top. Therefore, Layer 3 actually only needed to concatenate the top-ranked combinations from all eight byte-slice tables together and then can calculate the corresponding input and output of the Keccak-f[1600] permutation. Then, we can check consistency of these with available SHA-3 data, as described in Sect. 3 and Fig. 2.

If the top combination fails that consistency check, most likely the correct candidate was already missing in the tables produced by layers 1 or 2. Therefore we quadruple T and restart the search from Layer 1 in such cases (see Fig. 4). (In our experiments, we gave up after still not finding a correct solution with $T = 640\,000$, but this limit can of course be raised given sufficient computing resources.)

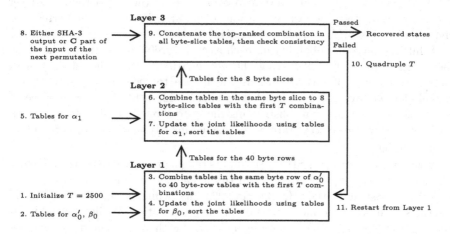

Fig. 4. The procedure to combine a full state from 600 tables.

5.4 Results

SHA3-512 with Only One Keccak-f[1600] Invocation. We first evaluated our attack using 1000 test traces of SHA3-512 executions, each with a random input shorter than 72 bytes. This is the simplest case, where a SHA3-512 execution invokes Keccak-f[1600] only once to digest the input. We only need to apply the template attack here to obtain the 600 rank tables of intermediate bytes in that one Keccak-f[1600] invocation, apply our three-layer search to find the correct combination, and calculate the input and output of the Keccak-f[1600] invocation. Its correctness can be verified by checking whether the first 512 bits of the output match the SHA-3 output and whether the last 1024 bits of the input are all zero. If both checks pass, the input of SHA-3 can be reconstructed by removing the padding from the first 576 bits of the recovered Keccak-f[1600] input.

In these 1000 tests, we successfully reconstructed the SHA3-512 input 999 times, while we failed to recover one remaining one even with $T = 640\,000$.

The number of additional traces for which we recovered the correct input was
for each T value

T	2500	10 000	40 000	160 000	640 000	failed
new traces recovered	873	77	33	11	5	1
cumulative %age	87.3	95.0	98.3	99.4	99.9	100
CPU time avr. [s]	8.20	24.98	90.53	431.35	2605.88	N/A
CPU time std. [s]	0.23	0.44	1.70	7.65	23.86	N/A

SHA3-512 with Multiple Keccak-f[1600] Invocations. Generally, where
the input is longer than 72 bytes, it takes multiple Keccak-f[1600] invocations to
digest. There we need to use the templates to obtain the 600 rank tables of the
three intermediates states in every invocation, and we then start the three-layer
search for each, from the last invocation to the first. We verify the correctness
and calculate the SHA-3 input as described in Sect. 3.

While the success probability for each Keccak-f[1600] invocation is the same,
the success rate of reconstructing the entire SHA-3 input should drop with
increasing number of invocations, as the failure to recover the state of any
Keccak-f[1600] invocation means that two SHA-3 input blocks cannot be recovered. If the success rate of reconstructing the state of one Keccak-f[1600] permutation is p, then the success rate of reconstructing SHA3-512 inputs of L bytes
length will be $p^{\lceil \frac{L+1}{72} \rceil}$.

We also tried to recover SHA3-512 inputs ranging from 216 bytes to 287 bytes,
where Keccak-f[1600] was invoked four times. Of 1000 attempted traces, we successfully reconstructed the SHA-3 input 999 times, while in the only unsuccessful
one the search failed for one invocation of the permutation. While we would normally expect the success rate of attacking SHA-3 with shorter input to be higher
than with longer inputs, in these experiments the success rates were both too
close to 1 to be distinguishable.

6   Discussion and Conclusion

Search time and success rate may be optimized further by adjusting the rank-
table length T for each byte row or slice separately, depending on the relative
likelihoods involved. So far we used the same T for all 40 byte rows in Layer 1
and all eight byte slices. From the numbers in Table 2, it is evident that the
success rates are much better for some byte locations, and for these, smaller
initial values of T may lead to a faster hit.

Our method could be extended by also building templates of intermediate
states in later rounds, such as a combination of α_1', β_1, α_2. When attackers
fail to recover the state in the first round, they could then try to search other
rounds and do a similar search as they have done in the first round. Although ι
is different in each round, there may be scope for reusing at least some templates
across rounds. In total there should be 23 combinations of intermediate states
that attackers could target using our search method.

With our method, we demonstrated that it is practical to reconstruct the inputs of an unprotected SHA-3 software implementation on an ATxmega256A3U 8-bit microcontroller using a template attack, even where the templates fail to rank some correct bytes highest. In future work, we hope to extend this attack procedure to work on 32-bit devices, where the success rates of templates can be far worse.

References

1. Alkim, E., et al.: NewHope: Algorithm specifications and supporting documentation (2019). https://newhopecrypto.org/
2. Bertoni, G., Daemen, J., Peeters, M., Van Assche, G.: The Keccak reference (2011)
3. Bertoni, G., Daemen, J., Peeters, M., Van Assche, G.: Keccak. In: Johansson, T., Nguyen, P.Q. (eds.) EUROCRYPT 2013. LNCS, vol. 7881, pp. 313–314. Springer, Heidelberg (2013). https://doi.org/10.1007/978-3-642-38348-9_19
4. Chari, S., Rao, J.R., Rohatgi, P.: Template attacks. In: Kaliski, B.S., Koç, K., Paar, C. (eds.) CHES 2002. LNCS, vol. 2523, pp. 13–28. Springer, Heidelberg (2003). https://doi.org/10.1007/3-540-36400-5_3
5. Choudary, M.O.: Efficient multivariate statistical techniques for extracting secrets from electronic devices. Technical Report, UCAM-CL-TR-878, PhD thesis, University of Cambridge (2015)
6. Choudary, M.O., Kuhn, M.G.: Efficient stochastic methods: profiled attacks beyond 8 bits. In: Joye, M., Moradi, A. (eds.) CARDIS 2014. LNCS, vol. 8968, pp. 85–103. Springer, Cham (2015). https://doi.org/10.1007/978-3-319-16763-3_6
7. Choudary, M.O., Kuhn, M.G.: Efficient, portable template attacks. IEEE Trans. Inf. Forensics Secur. **13**(2), 490–501 (2018)
8. Choudary, O., Kuhn, M.G.: Efficient template attacks. In: Francillon, A., Rohatgi, P. (eds.) CARDIS 2013. LNCS, vol. 8419, pp. 253–270. Springer, Cham (2014). https://doi.org/10.1007/978-3-319-08302-5_17
9. KeccakTools. https://github.com/KeccakTeam/KeccakTools
10. Luo, P., Fei, Y., Fang, X., Ding, A.A., Kaeli, D.R., Leeser, M.: Side-channel analysis of MAC-Keccak hardware implementations. In: Proceedings of the Fourth Workshop on Hardware and Architectural Support for Security and Privacy (HASP 2015). Association for Computing Machinery (2015)
11. Mangard, S.: Hardware countermeasures against DPA – a statistical analysis of their effectiveness. In: Okamoto, T. (ed.) CT-RSA 2004. LNCS, vol. 2964, pp. 222–235. Springer, Heidelberg (2004). https://doi.org/10.1007/978-3-540-24660-2_18
12. Microchip: ATxmega256A3U. Accessed Feb 2020, https://www.microchip.com/wwwproducts/en/atxmega256a3u
13. National Instruments: PXI-4110 programmable power supply. http://www.ni.com/en-gb/support/model.pxi-4110.html
14. National Instruments: PXIe-5160 oscilloscope. http://www.ni.com/en-gb/support/model.pxie-5160.html
15. National Instruments: PXIe-5423 waveform generator. http://www.ni.com/en-gb/support/model.pxie-5423.html
16. NIST: SHA-3 standard: permutation-based hash and extendable-output functions (2015). http://dx.doi.org/10.6028/NIST.FIPS.202, FIPS PUB 202

17. Oswald, D., Paar, C.: Breaking Mifare DESFire MF3ICD40: power analysis and templates in the real world. In: Preneel, B., Takagi, T. (eds.) CHES 2011. LNCS, vol. 6917, pp. 207–222. Springer, Heidelberg (2011). https://doi.org/10.1007/978-3-642-23951-9_14

18. Pedregosa, F., Varoquaux, G., Gramfort, A., Michel, V., Thirion, B., Grisel, O., Blondel, M., Prettenhofer, P., Weiss, R., Dubourg, V., et al.: Scikit-learn: machine learning in Python. J. Mach. Learn. Res. **12**, 2825–2830 (2011)

19. Schindler, W., Lemke, K., Paar, C.: A stochastic model for differential side channel cryptanalysis. In: Rao, J.R., Sunar, B. (eds.) CHES 2005. LNCS, vol. 3659, pp. 30–46. Springer, Heidelberg (2005). https://doi.org/10.1007/11545262_3

20. Standaert, F.-X., Archambeau, C.: Using subspace-based template attacks to compare and combine power and electromagnetic information leakages. In: Oswald, E., Rohatgi, P. (eds.) CHES 2008. LNCS, vol. 5154, pp. 411–425. Springer, Heidelberg (2008). https://doi.org/10.1007/978-3-540-85053-3_26

21. Standaert, F.-X., Malkin, T.G., Yung, M.: A unified framework for the analysis of side-channel key recovery attacks. In: Joux, A. (ed.) EUROCRYPT 2009. LNCS, vol. 5479, pp. 443–461. Springer, Heidelberg (2009). https://doi.org/10.1007/978-3-642-01001-9_26

22. Taha, M., Schaumont, P.: Differential power analysis of MAC-Keccak at any key-length. In: Sakiyama, K., Terada, M. (eds.) IWSEC 2013. LNCS, vol. 8231, pp. 68–82. Springer, Heidelberg (2013). https://doi.org/10.1007/978-3-642-41383-4_5

23. Taha, M., Schaumont, P.: Side-channel analysis of MAC-Keccak. In: 2013 IEEE International Symposium on Hardware-Oriented Security and Trust (HOST), pp. 125–130. IEEE (2013)

24. Veyrat-Charvillon, N., Gérard, B., Renauld, M., Standaert, F.-X.: An optimal key enumeration algorithm and its application to side-channel attacks. In: Knudsen, L.R., Wu, H. (eds.) SAC 2012. LNCS, vol. 7707, pp. 390–406. Springer, Heidelberg (2013). https://doi.org/10.1007/978-3-642-35999-6_25

25. Extended Keccak code package. https://github.com/XKCP/XKCP, Accessed April 2019, lib/low/KeccakP-1600/Compact64/KeccakP-1600-compact64.c

Single-Trace Side-Channel Analysis on Polynomial-Based MAC Schemes

Rei Ueno[1]([✉]), Kazuhide Fukushima[2], Yuto Nakano[2], Shinsaku Kiyomoto[2], and Naofumi Homma[1]

[1] Research Institute of Electrical Communication, Tohoku University,
2–1–1 Katahira, Aoba-ku, Sendai-shi 980-8577, Japan
{ueno,homma}@riec.tohoku.ac.jp
[2] KDDI Research, Inc., Ohara 2-1-15, Fujimino-shi, Saitama 356-8502, Japan

Abstract. This paper presents the first side-channel analysis (SCA) on polynomial-based message authentication code (MAC) schemes which is applicable to Poly1305. Typical SCAs (e.g., simple power analysis (SPA) and differential power analysis (DPA)) and conventional attacks on GCM/GMAC that focus on the first multiplication result in the universal hashing (i.e., polynomial evaluation) cannot be applied to Poly1305 owing to one-time keys and the structure of prime-field multiplication. On the other hand, the proposed attack retrieves the hash key from a single side-channel trace (e.g., a power/EM trace given by one execution) with a non-negligible probability and is applicable to polynomial-based MAC schemes implemented on an 8-bit micro-controller. The proposed attack allows the attacker to forge the authentication tag even if the hash key is a one-time key. The basic idea of the proposed attack is to exploit the addition in polynomial-based MAC schemes. Since the output or one input of the addition in these MAC schemes is known, we can efficiently estimate the unknown operands of addition, and then retrieve the hash key by the polynomial factorizations with the estimated candidates. This study also shows a cost-effective countermeasure for ChaCha20-Poly1305 using a combination of a lightweight masked Poly1305 and first-order mask conversion from Boolean to arithmetic.

Keywords: ChaCha20-Poly1305 · Polynomial hash function · Message authentication code · Authenticated encryption · Side-channel analysis

1 Introduction

Authenticated encryption (AE) has been widely deployed in many cryptographic protocols and secure systems. AE is a kind of symmetric cryptography that securely combines a symmetric encryption with message authentication code (MAC) for checking its integrity. The use of AE makes it possible not only to prevent eavesdropping on the common communication channel but also to detect any malicious or accidental modification of messages. While some conventional encryption schemes without authenticity are not robust to ciphertext

© Springer Nature Switzerland AG 2021
G. M. Bertoni and F. Regazzoni (Eds.): COSADE 2020, LNCS 12244, pp. 43–67, 2021.
https://doi.org/10.1007/978-3-030-68773-1_3

tampering, AE can achieve higher security thanks to the capability of authenticity verification. AE is expected to be implemented on even resource-constrained devices assumed to be used for Internet-of-Things (IoT) applications. Notably, the new version of Transport Layer Security (TLS) [Res18], which is a representative cryptographic protocol, no longer employs symmetric encryption without authenticity owing to the existence of numerous attacks on TLS exploiting the CBC-related modes (e.g., CBC_HMAC) such as BEAST and Lucky Thirteen [DR11, AFP13]. Thus, it is increasingly important to implement AEs efficiently and securely.

Many AEs use a symmetric encryption and tag generation function (i.e., MAC) in a combination. Many modern MAC schemes follow the Wegman-Carter construction: the message is first converted to a short hash value using universal hashing with a secret key [WC81]. Especially, universal hashing based on polynomial evaluation over a Galois Field (GF), namely, the polynomial hash function is known to be useful for constructing an efficient MAC. AES-GCM [MV05] and ChaCha20-Poly1305 [Lan15] are typical AEs that use a polynomial hash function for the tag generation. AES-GCM is the de facto standard AE specified by the National Institution of Standards and Technology (NIST) [Dwo07]. ChaCha20-Poly1305, which is based on a stream cipher ChaCha20 [Ber18] and a MAC based on a polynomial hash function over $GF(2^{130} - 5)$ (i.e., Poly1305) [Ber05], is now popular and is used in, for example, TLS and Google Chrome. While AES-GCM can achieve a high throughput using hardware acceleration, including AES-NI equipped on many Intel and AMD processors, ChaCha20-Poly1305 can be efficiently implemented with a constant time on low-end and/or application-specific processors without AES-NI (e.g., low-end ARM and AVR micro-controllers). This is because ChaCha20 is an ARX cipher and Poly1305 is basically implemented using arithmetic operations without carry-less multiplication (CLMUL) instruction set. In the CAESAR project [Cry16] and NIST Lightweight Cryptography (LWC) [NIS19], which are an international competition involving AE, the constructions of AES-GCM and ChaCha20-Poly1305 have a significant impact on CAESAR candidates. Thus, implementation studies on such AEs using polynomial hash function are important from both practical and academic perspectives.

The above AEs are currently considered to be secure against the existing cryptanalyses. [HP08, IOM12, PC15]. On the other hand, there is a possibility of side-channel analysis (SCA) [KJJ99] on these AEs. In particular, it is quite likely that ChaCha20-Poly1305 could be deployed in many embedded systems, including smart cards, which can be a major target of SCA. Therefore, the evaluation of SCA resistance/vulnerability is essential, and the development of SCA-resistant ChaCha20-Poly1305 modules is required. Until now, some differential power analyses (DPAs) and correlation power analysis (CPA) on ChaCha20 have been reported [JB17, AFM17], and several SCA-resistant modules for ARX ciphers including ChaCha20 have also been studied [BSMG17, JPS18]. On the other hand, to the best of the authors' knowledge, there has been no report of SCA on Poly1305. Although the ciphertext cannot be decrypted using the keys of Poly1305 alone, an attacker who retrieves the keys can forge authentication tags, which can be a critical vulnerability in the context of AEs. Thus, the evaluation of the SCA security of Poly1305 is essential.

This study presents the first single-trace SCA on polynomial-based MACs, successfully retrieving hash keys of Poly1305 and forging its authentication tag. While some attacks on the tag generation of AES-GCM (i.e., GMAC) have been proposed [BFG+14,BCF+15,OUHA18], these attacks are not applicable to Poly1305 owing to the difference between GFs used in these MACs (i.e., binary field $GF(2^{128})$ and prime field $GF(2^{130} - 5)$). In addition, since ChaCha20-Poly1305 uses one-time keys for tag generation, it is essentially difficult to apply conventional SCAs using a statistical mean including DPAs and the above attacks on GCM/GMAC [BFG+14,BCF+15,OUHA18] to Poly1305. On the other hand, the proposed attack retrieves the hash key of Poly1305 from side-channel information during one computation of Poly1305. The new algorithms exploit side-channel information of the final addition of a hash value and a key or the addition of an intermediate value and input block. The proposed algorithms efficiently estimate the candidates of intermediate value by exploiting the conditions of existence and non-existence of carry-propagation/generation. A notable feature of the proposed attack is its applicability to other known polynomial-based MAC schemes such as GCM/GMAC, hash127 [Ber99], CWC-HASH [KVW03], and Sophie Germain Counter Mode (SGCM) [Saa11] in principle. We demonstrate the feasibility of the attack through simulations. In this study, we assume the implementation of Poly1305 on an 8-bit low-end microcontroller without AES-NI, As in [HS13], ChaCha20-Poly1305 is likely to be implemented on such an embedded microprocessor for applications others than TLS because of its advantage on performance, while TLS is not much frequently implemented on embedded microprocessors. The results show that the hash key of ChaCha20-Poly1305 can be retrieved with a practical level of computational complexity and non-negligible probability. Finally, we present a cost-effective countermeasure against the proposed attack. Assuming that symmetric cipher encryption is protected by masking if Poly1305 is protected, the presented countermeasure employs a combination of a lightweight masked Poly1305 inspired by a masked GMAC in [OUHA18] and a first-order mask conversion from Boolean to arithmetic masking [Gou01]. This can be efficiently computed with 128-bit random number generation and only seven elementary operations.

2 Preliminaries and Related Works

2.1 Basic Notation

Mathematical notation in this paper for Poly1305 and MAC of AES-GCM (i.e., GMAC) is defined as follows. H, S, and T denote the 16-byte hash key, key for final addition, and output tag, respectively. $\mathcal{A}$ denotes the input to MAC and consists of 16-byte input blocks given by $A_1, A_2, \ldots, A_i, \ldots, A_n$, where n is the number of input blocks. Let $X_i = A_1 H^i + A_2 H^{i-1} + \cdots + A_i H$ be the i-th intermediate value in polynomial evaluation. Let $W_i = (2^{128} + A_i) + X_{i-1}$ be the output of the i-th addition. In addition, let U be the output of polynomial evaluation (i.e., $U = X_n$). Finally, let h_j, s_j, t_j, $a_{i,j}$, $x_{i,j}$, $w_{i,j}$, and u_j be the j-th byte of H, S, T, A_i, X_i, W_i, and U, respectively. Here, each variable denoted by uppercase letter is basically an element of the prime field $GF(2^{130} - 5)$ and binary field $GF(2^{128})$ for Poly1305 and GMAC, respectively, and the addition of 2^{128} to A_i in Poly1305 is omitted if it is not essential.

2.2 Authenticated Encryptions Based on Polynomial Hash Function

AEs are typically constructed on the basis of generic composition (GC), which combines a symmetric encryption (e.g., block cipher mode of operation and additive stream cipher) with a MAC for tag generation [BN00,BN08,BN18]. While an AE based on a composition of an encryption and a MAC (i.e., GC) formally uses two distinct keys for symmetric encryption and MAC, a key for the MAC is frequently generated from symmetric encryption using another key in many practical AEs, including ChaCha20-Poly1305, AES-GCM, and many CAESAR candidates. Here, ChaCha20-Poly1305 and AES-GCM employ a MAC based on polynomial hash function, where the output (authentication) tag T is described as

$$T = S \star U, \tag{1}$$

$$U = \sum_{i=1}^{n} A_i H^{n-i+1}, \tag{2}$$

where H, S, and A_i are the hash key, key for final addition, and i-th input block, respectively. Here, the operator $\star$ in Eq. (1) denotes an Abelian group operation (e.g., bit-parallel-XOR and addition modulo 2^α (where α is an integer) or a prime) and Eq. (2) is applied over a field. For its practical implementation, U in Eq. (2) is usually rewritten in the recurrence form as follows:

$$U = X_n, \tag{3}$$
$$X_i = (A_i + X_{i-1})H \ (1 \leq i \leq n), \tag{4}$$
$$X_0 = 0. \tag{5}$$

In the following, we describe the algorithmic overview of ChaCha20-Poly1305. ChaCha20-Poly1305 is an AE based on a composition of an encryption and a MAC, that uses an ARX stream cipher ChaCha20 as encryption and a polynomial-based MAC Poly1305 for tag generation. Algorithm 1 is its algorithmic description, where $\mathcal{D}$, $\mathcal{P}$, and $\mathcal{C}$ denote the associated data, plaintext, and ciphertext, respectively. In addition, P_l and C_l $(1 \leq l \leq m)$ denote the l-th 256-bit block of $\mathcal{P}$ and $\mathcal{C}$, respectively, where m is the number of 256-bit blocks of $\mathcal{P}$. ChaCha20 consists of a 256-byte state and updates the state using the QuarterRound function. The initial state is defined by a secret key, an initial vector (given a as nonce), and a counter value l, ChaCha20 generates a 256-bit key stream after applying QuarterRound to the state 20 times. At Line 3, we

Algorithm 1. ChaCha20-Poly1305

Input: Associated data $\mathcal{D}$, plaintext $\mathcal{P}$, 256-bit secret key K, 96-bit initial vector V
Output: Ciphertext $\mathcal{C}$, authentication tag T
1: **Function** CHACHA20-POLY1305($\mathcal{D}, \mathcal{P}, K, V$)
2:    int $l \leftarrow 0$;
3:    $(H, S) \leftarrow$ ChaCha20-core(K, V, l);
4:    $l \leftarrow l + 1$;
5:    **while** $l \leq m$ **do**
6:        $C_l \leftarrow P_l \oplus$ ChaCha20-core(K, V, l);
7:        $l \leftarrow l + 1$;
8:    **end while**
9:    $\mathcal{A} \leftarrow (\mathcal{D}, \mathcal{C}, (\text{len}(\mathcal{D})||\text{len}(\mathcal{C})))$;
10:    $T \leftarrow$ Poly1305($\mathcal{A}, H, S$);
11:    **return** $(\mathcal{D}, \mathcal{C}, T)$;
12: **end Function**

---

generate the first key stream (H, S) used for Poly1305. The following key streams generated at Lines 5–8 are XORed with plaintext and ciphertext during encryption and decryption, respectively. This means that both H and S are one-time keys in ChaCha20-Poly1305, unlike AES-GCM. At Line 9, we format $\mathcal{D}$ and $\mathcal{C}$ for the input (i.e., $\mathcal{A}$) of Poly1305, where $(\text{len}(\mathcal{D})||\text{len}(\mathcal{C}))$ is a value derived by concatenating the lengths of $\mathcal{D}$ and $\mathcal{C}$ (each of which is given by eight bytes). Note that each block of $\mathcal{A}$ is a 16-byte value while that of $\mathcal{C}$ is a 32-byte value. Next, the tag T is computed from $\mathcal{A}$, H, and S by Poly1305.

Algorithm 2 describes Poly1305, which generates an authentication tag T from input message blocks $A_1, A_2, \ldots, A_n$, H, and S based on polynomial evaluation over $GF(2^{130} - 5)$. In Poly1305, H is first masked (i.e., bit-parallel-ANDed) with 0x0ffffffc0ffffffc0ffffffc0fffffff, which indicates that the 29th–34th, 61st–66th, 93rd–98th, and 125th–128th bits of H are fixed to zero and H is considered as a 106-bit value. At Lines 4–6, we perform polynomial evaluation over $GF(2^{130} - 5)$ as represented by Eqs. (3)–(5). Here, each 16-byte input block is padded to 17 bytes by appending 0x01 to the most significant byte[1], which corresponds to the addition of 2^{128} at Line 5. After computing X_n, T is generated by the sum of X_n and S modulo 2^{128}. Note that this final addition is not over $GF(2^{130} - 5)$.

2.3   The Problem of Unforgeability

For preserving unforgeability, both the hash key H and the key S should be secret. If the attacker retrieves either of these keys, she can forge the authentication tag, which can be a critical vulnerability for AEs. For example, with AES-GCM, it is known that an attacker can make victims perform a compromised HTTPS authentication that redirects to malicious websites by deceiving the authentication provided by TLS [BZD+16]. In addition, if the encryption is

---

[1] In the case of ChaCha20-Poly1305, if the final blocks of $\mathcal{D}$ and $\mathcal{C}$ are given with b bytes shorter than 16 bytes, 0x01 is appended to the $(b + 1)$-th byte and the rest is padded with zeros.

Algorithm 2. Poly1305

Input: Message $\mathcal{A}$, hash key H, key S
Output: Authentication tag T
1: **Function** POLY1305($\mathcal{A}, H, S$)
2:     $H \leftarrow H$ & 0x0ffffffc0ffffffc0ffffffc0fffffff;
3:     $X_0 \leftarrow 0$;
4:     **for** i from 1 to n **do**
5:         $X_i \leftarrow ((2^{128} + A_i) + X_{i-1})H \bmod 2^{130} - 5$; $\triangleright$ $GF(2^{130} - 5)$ polynomial evaluation
6:     **end for**
7:     $T \leftarrow (S + X_n) \bmod 2^{128}$; $\triangleright$ Final addition (not over $GF(2^{130} - 5)$)
8:     **return** T;
9: **end Function**

---

given as a block cipher in CTR-mode or stream cipher, the adversary can control the difference between the correct and forged plaintexts [PC15]. Therefore, AE modules should never expose H and S in addition to the root secret key in symmetric encryption.

To preserve the secrecy of H, another key S should be a nonce and should not be reused. Otherwise, Joux's forbidden attack, which was originally proposed for GCM and used to retrieve H by exploiting nonce reuse, is a threat [Jou06]. If the attacker observes authentication tags for two different messages generated by an identical S, she can immediately retrieve H as follows. Let T and T' be the tags for messages $A_1, A_2, \ldots, A_n$ and $A'_1, A'_2, \ldots, A'_n$ generated using H and S. The attacker first computes the difference between two tags as

$$T - T' = \sum_{i=1}^{n}(A_i - A'_i)H^{n-i+1}. \tag{6}$$

Here, Eq. (6) contains only H as an indeterminate variable. Because there are at most n roots over the GF, the attacker reduces the number of candidates for H to at most n if she solves this univariate equation.

In the case of AES-GCM, since S is generated from the AES encryption result of the initial vector, the initial vector should be a nonce and should not be reused. Otherwise, once the attacker retrieves H, she can perform universal forgery (i.e., forge tags for any messages) because H is fixed for the same root secret key. Such universal forgery is catastrophic for an AE. On the other hand, this attack is infeasible and is not a threat if the system is correctly implemented with respect to nonce. In addition, this attack is far less effective for ChaCha20-Poly1305 because H is a one-time key, which indicates that retrieving H in ChaCha20-Poly1305 makes sense only for the reused nonce. Thus, an attack using only one computation result can be a greater threat, which allows forging tags without the above limitation.

2.4 Conventional SCAs on Polynomial Hash Function

ChaCha20-Poly1305 and AES-GCM consist of symmetric encryption and MAC schemes. So far, many SCAs on ChaCha20 and AES and their countermeasures have been studied. On the other hand, only a few SCAs on GCM are known as attacks on polynomial-based MAC schemes [BFG+14, BCF+15, OUHA18].

The state-of-the-art attacks [BCF+15, OUHA18] focus on the first multiplication of GMAC (i.e., $X_1 = A_1 H$) for many different A_1. The attacker constructs a system of equations with errors over $GF(2)$ (i.e., a learning parity with noise (LPN) problem) with 128 variables (i.e., bits of H) from Hamming weight (HW) of X_1 estimated from side-channel information and solves the LPN problem to obtain H. However, this attack is not applicable to Poly1305 for the following reasons. Such attacks require many traces to construct an LPN problem that can be solved with a practical level of computational complexity. Since the hash key of ChaCha20-Poly1305 is used only once, in contrast to AES-GCM, an attacker cannot construct such an LPN problem. Though the attacker may be able to obtain the HWs of many different X_1 from a fixed H if Poly1305 is combined with a 128-bit block cipher mode of operation such as Poly1305-AES [Ber05], Even if the attacker obtains the HWs of different X_1 in Poly1305, it is impossible to construct the LPN problem from multiplication over the prime field $GF(2^{130} - 5)$. Instead, she may construct a univariate learning with error (LWE) problem over $GF(2^{130} - 5)$; however, there is no known method/tool for solving such problems over a large GF.

Other conventional SCAs such as simple power analysis (SPA) and DPA are also inapplicable to Poly1305. There is basically no branch that can be an SPA-leakage during polynomial evaluation. DPAs are not appropriate owing to its one-time hash key. In addition, since a GF multiplication diffuses a hash key to a whole intermediate value, the divide-and-conquer approach of DPAs is not available. Although there is more sophisticated SCAs on symmetric keys such as algebraic SCA (ASCA) [RS09, RSVC09], and soft analytical SCA (SASCA) [VCGS14], their applicability to and effectiveness on Poly1305 are unknown. In fact, existing SAT solvers would have difficulty in handling the logical expression of such large multipliers [Dre04].

3 Proposed Attack on ChaCha20-Poly1305

3.1 Attack Description

This section presents the proposed side-channel analysis (SCA) on ChaCha20-Poly1305 implemented on low-end micro-controllers. The proposed SCA uses only one trace of Poly1305 computation and therefore can adapt the use case of ChaCha20-Poly1305 in practice. In this attack, we employ the HW model as a leakage model under the assumption that the attacker accurately obtains the byte-wise HWs of intermediate values, H, and S by side-channel information, from the target 8-bit micro-controller. This assumption has been used and experimentally validated in many previous works [Man03, RS09, RSVC09, CMW14, KUH+17, OUHA18], especially for low-end micro-controllers. For example, according to [OUHA18], the side-channel information from a low-end smart card can be observed with a good signal-to-noise ratio (SNR) of 107.9 in a laboratory setting.

In contrast to the previous attack on GCM, the proposed attack focuses on the final addition of S and U ($= X_n$) or the intermediate addition of $W_i = (2^{128} + A_i) + X_{i-1}$ during polynomial evaluation. We first observe side-channel information (i.e., single power/EM trace) as an online step. We then perform the following three offline steps: (a) obtain candidates for U or X_i using the new algorithm exploiting byte-wise HWs of intermediate values, (b) compute the hypothetical H corresponding to each candidate of U using a polynomial factorization, and (c) check whether the hypothetical H is correct. At (a), we can reduce byte-wise candidates of intermediate value to approximately 50 in average. Then, at (b), we can further reduce the byte-wise candidates to around 20 on the basis of the proposed algorithm. At (c), we finally obtain the 130-bit-wise candidates by combining the byte-wise candidates in a non-redundant manner according to another algorithm.

3.2 Side-Channel Analysis on Final Addition

In Step (a), our attack is performed in a slightly different way depending on whether we focus on final addition or intermediate addition during polynomial evaluation. We first describe the attack focusing on the final addition, where we obtain possible candidates of U using the byte-wise HWs of S and U obtained from side-channel information. Since the attacks on final and intermediate addition is almost same, see Appendix for the description of the attack on intermediate addition. The basic idea is to inversely compute the HW of S from guessed U and the output of final addition (i.e., T) which is observable to the attacker, and compare the hypothetical HW of S with the estimated one from side-channel information. Thus, the attacker makes a set of lists containing possible byte-wise candidates. However, we cannot observe the existence/non-existence of carry signals in the final addition. In other words, we should consider all cases of carry-in and/or carry-out propagation at the j-th byte addition. Therefore, it is difficult to sufficiently reduce the candidate space unless the existence/non-existence of carry propagations is appropriately considered. To handle the existence/non-existence of carry-in and carry-out propagation efficiently, we introduce the following proposition.

Proposition 1 *Let u_j and s_j ($0 \le s_j < 2^8$ and $0 \le u_j < 2^8$) be the two input operands of j-th byte addition, and let t_j ($0 \le t_j < 2^8$) be the j-th byte output. When there is no carry-in signal to the j-th byte, the carry-out signal to the $(j+1)$-th byte occurs if and only if $t_j < u_j$.*

Proof. Let us consider the case in which the carry-out signal to the $(j+1)$-byte occurs (i.e., the value of the carry-out signal is 1). In this case, the addition is represented by $u_j + s_j = t_j + 2^8$, which is followed by $s_j = t_j - u_j + 2^8$. With the range of s_j, the above equation is rewritten to an inequality of $0 \le t_j - u_j + 2^8 < 2^8$, and therefore, $t_j - u_j < 0$, which means $t_j < u_j$. We then consider the case in which the carry-out signal does not occur (i.e., the value of the carry-out signal is 0). In this case, the addition is represented by $u_j + s_j = t_j$. Similarly to the above, we derive $0 \le t_j - u_j < 2^8$, and therefore, $t_j \ge u_j$.

We derive a similar proposition when there is the carry-in signal (i.e., the value of the carry-in signal is 1) from the representations of $u_j + s_j + 1 = t_j + 2^8$ and $u_j + s_j + 1 = t_j$, except for the case in which $t_j = 0$. If $t_j = 0$, then the carry-out signal always occurs because $u_j + s_j + 1$ should be greater than 0. By means of Proposition 1, we can distinguish the existence/non-existence of carry signals at the $(j + 1)$-th byte from t_j and a guessed u_j, and finally derive the candidate for U without any redundancy.

Algorithm 3 derives the list of candidates for U from T and side-channel information, where $\mathcal{L}(S)$ and $\mathcal{L}(U)$ indicates the side-channel information of S and U, respectively. Lines 2 and 3 first obtain the byte-wise HWs of U and S from the corresponding side-channel information, respectively. Note that U is a 17-byte value over $GF(2^{130} - 5)$. In Algorithm 3, $HW(x)$ denotes the HW of x. Line 4 initializes $\Omega_{0,0}$, $\Omega_{0,1}$, $\Omega_{1,0}$, and $\Omega_{1,1}$, each of which is a list of lists for candidates for U. The j-th list of $\Omega_{y,z}$ contains candidates for the j-th byte of U, where the carry-in signal from the $(j - 1)$-th byte and the carry-out signal to the $(j + 1)$-th byte are assumed to be y and z ($y, z \in \{0, 1\}$), respectively. Such classification is used for eventually deriving the candidates for U by the combination of byte-wise candidates.

The main loop at Lines 5–39 is performed 16 times. In this loop, Line 6 initializes lists $\Omega_{0,0}^{(j)}$, $\Omega_{0,1}^{(j)}$, $\Omega_{1,0}^{(j)}$, and $\Omega_{1,1}^{(j)}$, storing the candidates for the j-th byte of U at the j-th loop. The lists correspond to the j-th elements of $\Omega_{0,0}$, $\Omega_{0,1}$, $\Omega_{1,0}$, and $\Omega_{1,1}$, respectively. Lines 7–11 calculate t_j' corresponding to $u_j + s_j$ when the carry-in signal is 1. Basically t_j' is given by $t_j - 1$. If $t_j = 0$, then t_j' becomes 255 because $u_j + s_j + 1$ should not be less than zero.

Lines 12–37 inversely calculate $HW(s_j)$ from t_j (or t_j') and the guessed u_j and then obtain the candidates of u_j by comparing the hypothetical $HW(s_j)$ and the estimated one from side-channel information, where $\{d \in \mathbb{Z} \mid HW(d) = HW(u_j) \text{ and } 0 \le d < 2^8\}$ at Line 12 denotes a set containing all possible integers whose HW equals $HW(u_j)$ (e.g., if $HW(u_j) = 1$, it is given by $\{1, 2, 4, 8, 16, 32, 64, 128\}$). Lines 13–16, 17–21, 23–30, and 31–34 acquire the candidates when the (carry-in value, carry-out value) is (0, 1), (0, 0), (1, 1), and (1, 0), respectively. Here, $\Omega_{y,z}^{(j)}$.append(g) indicates an operation adding an element g to the end of list $\Omega_{y,z}^{(j)}$. Note that $\Omega_{1,1}^{(1)}$ and $\Omega_{1,0}^{(1)}$ should be empty lists because the carry-in value to the first byte should be 0. In addition, Lines 27–30 correspond to the aforementioned special case of $t_j = 0$ with a carry-in signal. After filtering the all-guessed u_j according to $HW(s_j)$, the resulting list of candidates (i.e., $\Omega_{y,z}^{(j)}$) is the j-th element of $\Omega_{y,z}$.

Finally, Line 40 combines the byte-wise candidates and obtains the resulting list of candidates for U. Here, we should use this combination with considering carry-generations and propagations at each byte. Figure 1 shows the trellis diagram of the combination of byte-wise lists considering carry-generations and propagations. We should combine $\Omega_{0,0}^{(j-1)}$ and $\Omega_{1,0}^{(j-1)}$ with $\Omega_{0,0}^{(j)}$ and $\Omega_{0,1}^{(j)}$ as denoted by solid arrows which represent that neither carry-generation nor propagation occurs between the $(j - 1)$-th and j-th bytes. On the other hand, $\Omega_{0,1}^{(j-1)}$

Algorithm 3. Side-channel analysis on final addition

Input: Authentication tag T, side-channel informations $\mathcal{L}(U)$ and $\mathcal{L}(S)$
Output: List Ω (containing candidates for U)
1: **Function** DERIVECANDIDATESFROM($T, \mathcal{L}(U), \mathcal{L}(S)$)
2:      list of int $[HW(u_1), HW(u_2), \ldots, HW(u_{17})] \leftarrow$ EstimateByteWiseHWsFrom($\mathcal{L}(U)$);
3:      list of int $[HW(s_1), HW(s_2), \ldots, HW(s_{16})] \leftarrow$ EstimateByteWiseHWsFrom($\mathcal{L}(S)$);
4:      list of list $\Omega_{0,0} \leftarrow []$; list of list $\Omega_{0,1} \leftarrow []$; list of list $\Omega_{1,0} \leftarrow []$; list of list $\Omega_{1,1} \leftarrow []$;
5:      **for** j from 1 to 16 **do**
6:          list of int $\Omega_{0,0}^{(j)} \leftarrow []$; list of int $\Omega_{0,1}^{(j)} \leftarrow []$; list of int $\Omega_{1,0}^{(j)} \leftarrow []$; list of int $\Omega_{1,1}^{(j)} \leftarrow []$;
7:          **if** $t_j = 0$ **then**
8:              int $t'_j \leftarrow 2^8 - 1$;
9:          **else**
10:              int $t'_j \leftarrow t_j - 1$;
11:          **end if**
12:          **for each** $g \in \{d \in \mathbb{Z} \mid HW(d) = HW(u_j) \text{ and } 0 \leq d < 2^8\}$ **do**
13:              **if** $g > t_j$ **then**   ▷ If carry-in is 0 and carry-out is 1
14:                  **if** $HW(t_j - g + 2^8) = HW(s_j)$ **then**
15:                      $\Omega_{0,1}^{(j)}$.append(g);
16:                  **end if**
17:              **else**   ▷ If carry-in is 0 and carry-out is 0
18:                  **if** $HW(t_j - g) = HW(s_j)$ **then**
19:                      $\Omega_{0,0}^{(j)}$.append(g);
20:                  **end if**
21:              **end if**
22:              **if** $j \neq 1$ **then**
23:                  **if** $g > t'_j$ **then**   ▷ If carry-in is 1 and carry-out is 1
24:                      **if** $HW(t'_j - g + 2^8) = HW(s_j)$ **then**
25:                          $\Omega_{1,1}^{(j)}$.append(g);
26:                      **end if**
27:                  **else if** $t'_j = 255$ **then**
28:                      **if** $HW(t'_j - g) = HW(s_j)$ **then**
29:                          $\Omega_{1,1}^{(j)}$.append(g);
30:                      **end if**
31:                  **else**   ▷ If carry-in is 1 and carry-out is 0
32:                      **if** $HW(t'_j - g) = HW(s_j)$ **then**
33:                          $\Omega_{1,0}^{(j)}$.append(g);
34:                      **end if**
35:                  **end if**
36:              **end if**
37:          **end for**
38:          $\boldsymbol{\Omega}_{0,0}$.append($\Omega_{0,0}^{(j)}$); $\boldsymbol{\Omega}_{0,1}$.append($\Omega_{0,1}^{(j)}$); $\boldsymbol{\Omega}_{1,0}$.append($\Omega_{1,0}^{(j)}$); $\boldsymbol{\Omega}_{1,1}$.append($\Omega_{1,1}^{(j)}$);
39:      **end for**
40:      list of int $\Omega \leftarrow$ CombineByteWiseCandidates($\boldsymbol{\Omega}_{0,0}, \boldsymbol{\Omega}_{0,1}, \boldsymbol{\Omega}_{1,0}, \boldsymbol{\Omega}_{1,1}, HW(s_{17})$);
41:      **return** Ω;
42: **end Function**

---

and $\Omega_{1,1}^{(j-1)}$ should be combined with $\Omega_{1,0}^{(j)}$ and $\Omega_{1,1}^{(j)}$ as denoted by dashed arrows which represent that either carry-generation or carry-propagation occurs at the $(j-1)$-th byte.

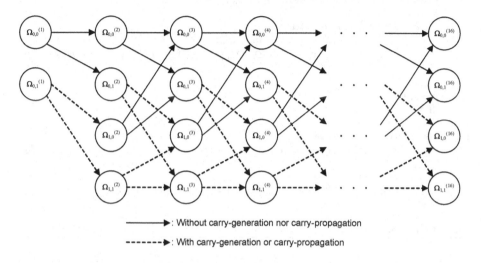

———▶ : Without carry-generation nor carry-propagation

------▶ : With carry-generation or carry-propagation

Fig. 1. Trellis diagram for combining byte-wise candidates.

Algorithm 4 combines the lists of byte-wise candidates as a list of candidate integers on the basis of Fig. 1. Lines 2–6 correspond to the aforementioned combination of byte-wise candidates, where $\Omega_{z'} \times \Omega_{y,z}^{(j)}$ denotes the direct product ($z' \in \{0,1\}$). Since the candidates for U are computed from the first byte (i.e., $j = 1$) in ascending order, Line 2 sets $\Omega_{0,0}^{(1)}$ and $\Omega_{0,1}^{(1)}$ as the initial list of intermediate buffer lists Ω_0 and Ω_1, respectively. In the j-th loop at Lines 3–8, $\Omega_{z'}$ corresponds to the list of candidate integers given from the first to the j-th bytes such that the carry-out value to the $(j+1)$-th byte should be z'. In other words, Lines 5 and 6 correspond to the computation flow given by solid and dashed arrows in Fig. 1, respectively. Since the carry-in value to first byte should always be 0, two intermediate buffers Ω_0 and Ω_1 are enough to combine the byte-wise candidates in accordance with Fig. 1. In addition, while U is a 130-bit (i.e., 17-byte) value, we can know the value of 17-th byte according to $HW(u_{17})$ as Lines 10–16. If $HW(u_{17})$ is 0 or 2, u_{17} should be determined as 0x00 or 0x03, respectively. Therefore, when $u_{17} = 0\text{x}03$, $2^{128} + 2^{129}$ is added to each candidate of Ω_0 and Ω_1 at Line 15. If $HW(u_{17}) = 1$, u_{17} should be either 0x01 or 0x02, which is represented by adding either 2^{128} or 2^{129} to the candidates at Line 13.

The computational complexity of Algorithm 3 is evaluated with the number of byte-wise guesses at the main loop (i.e., Lines 5–39). The number of elements in $\{d \in \mathbb{Z} \mid HW(d) = HW(u_j) \text{ and } 0 \leq d < 2^8\}$ at Line 12 is less than 2^8. Since the byte-wise guesses are performed for 16 bytes, we perform the guesses at most $2^8 \cdot 16 = 2^{12}$ times, which is a trivial number. On the other hand,

---

Algorithm 4. Derive list of candidates of U from byte-wise candidates

---

Input: Lists of byte-wise candidates $\mathbf{\Omega}_{0,0}, \mathbf{\Omega}_{0,1}, \mathbf{\Omega}_{1,0}, \mathbf{\Omega}_{1,1}$, HW of 17th byte $HW(u_{17})$
Output: List of candidates for U
1: **Function** CombineByteWiseCandidates($\mathbf{\Omega}_{0,0}, \mathbf{\Omega}_{0,1}, \mathbf{\Omega}_{1,0}, \mathbf{\Omega}_{1,1}, HW(u_{17})$)
2:   List of int $\Omega_0 \leftarrow \Omega_{0,0}^{(1)}$; List of int $\Omega_1 \leftarrow \Omega_{0,1}^{(1)}$;
3:   **for** j from 2 to 16 **do**
4:     list of int $\Omega_0^{(j)}$; list of int $\Omega_1^{(j)}$;
5:     $\Omega_0^{(j)} \leftarrow \{e_0 + 2^{8j} \cdot e_{0,0}^{(j)} \mid (e_0, e_{0,0}^{(j)}) \in \Omega_0 \times \Omega_{0,0}^{(j)}\} \cup \{e_1 + 2^{8j} \cdot e_{1,0}^{(j)} \mid (e_1, e_{1,0}^{(j)}) \in \Omega_1 \times \Omega_{1,0}^{(j)}\}$;
6:     $\Omega_1^{(j)} \leftarrow \{e_0 + 2^{8j} \cdot e_{0,1}^{(j)} \mid (e_0, e_{0,1}^{(j)}) \in \Omega_0 \times \Omega_{0,1}^{(j)}\} \cup \{e_1 + 2^{8j} \cdot e_{1,1}^{(j)} \mid (e_1, e_{1,1}^{(j)}) \in \Omega_1 \times \Omega_{1,1}^{(j)}\}$;
7:     $\Omega_0 \leftarrow \Omega_0^{(j)}$; $\Omega_1 \leftarrow \Omega_1^{(j)}$;
8:   **end for**
9:   list of int Ω;
10:   **if** $HW(u_{17}) = 0$ **then**
11:     $\Omega \leftarrow \Omega_0 \cup \Omega_1$;
12:   **else if** $HW(u_{17}) = 1$ **then**
13:     $\Omega \leftarrow \{e_0 + 2^{128} \mid e_0 \in \Omega_0\} \cup \{e_0 + 2^{129} \mid e_0 \in \Omega_0\} \cup \{e_1 + 2^{128} \mid e_1 \in \Omega_1\} \cup \{e_1 + 2^{129} \mid e_1 \in \Omega_1\}$;
14:   **else if** $HW(u_{17}) = 2$ **then**
15:     $\Omega \leftarrow \{e_0 + 2^{128} + 2^{129} \mid e_0 \in \Omega_0\} \cup \{e_1 + 2^{128} + 2^{129} \mid e_1 \in \Omega_1\}$;
16:   **end if**
17:   **return** Ω;
18: **end Function**

---

although the computational complexity of Algorithm 4 heavily depends on the resulting number of candidates for U, it does not matter in Step (a) because the candidates for U can be combined from the list of byte-wise candidates in Steps (b) and (c) on-the-fly. The resulting number of candidates is evaluated below.

3.3 Exhaustive Polynomial Factorization

In Step (b), we perform the polynomial factorization of $A_1 H^{i-1} + A_2 H^{i-2} + \cdots + A_{i-1} H - X_{i-1}$ $(2 \leq i \leq n+1)$ over $GF(2^{130} - 5)$ for all candidates for X_{i-1} in order to derive the corresponding hypothetical key(s) H, like in Joux's forbidden attack. Here, $i = n+1$ corresponds to the attack on final addition. We here choose i such that the number of remaining candidates for X_{i-1} is the smallest. Finally, in Step (c), we check whether the hypothetical H is the correct key, which can be done by computing the intermediate values $X_1, X_2, \ldots, X_n$ with the hypothetical H and compare their HWs with the corresponding HWs estimated from side-channel information. Thus, we can determine the only correct key H, if the exhaustive polynomial factorization in Step (b) is feasible.

3.4 Feasibility Evaluation

The feasibility of the proposed attack is evaluated through an experimental simulation. We first evaluate the candidates for U obtained from Algorithm 3, which is equal to the (worst-case) number of required polynomial factorizations in Step (b). We generate 10,000,000 authentication tags with random messages and keys and obtain the byte-wise HWs of each pair of S and U by a simulation.

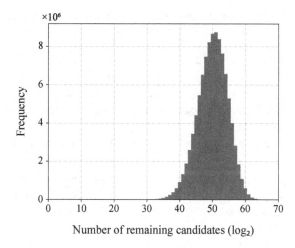

Fig. 2. Histogram of number of remaining candidates.

Figure 2 shows the resulting histogram, where the horizontal axis denotes the number of candidates of U remaining after Step (a) on a logarithmic scale and the vertical axis denotes the frequency. In addition, Table 1 displays the frequency. The number of candidates for each byte of U is reduced to approximately 20 in average. The number of resulting candidates for U combined based on Fig. 1 is less than just a product of the number of byte-wise candidates because we appropriately consider the condition of carry-propagation and generation in Algorithms 3 and 4. We confirmed that we can obtain the similar result for X_{i-1} by using Algorithm 7. We then randomly generate 1,000 $(i-1)$-th degree polynomials whose coefficients are in the form of Poly1305 in order to evaluate the required time for polynomial factorizations for Step (b). Table 2 shows the average time for factoring an $(i-1)$-th degree polynomial. Here, we used an open-source computer algebra software Risa/Asir [asi] on a Linux PC with an Intel Xeon Gold 6144 processor and 384GB of memory to perform the polynomial factorization.

From Fig. 2 (Table 1) and Table 2, we can estimate the expected time for the proposed attack because the computational time of Algorithm 3 and Step (c) is trivial compared to the exhaustive polynomial factorization of Step (b). For example, if $i-1=2$, the polynomial factorization using a single core is completed within about 24 min for 2^{20} candidates and 13 h for 2^{25} candidates. In addition, the attacker can perform the exhaustive polynomial factorization in parallel using multi-cores. Hence, the time required for the attack is given by (time per polynomial factorization) × (number of remaining candidates after Step (a))/(number of cores for polynomial factorization). Roughly, 2^{10}–2^{20} cores are currently available for (a cluster of) commercial/off-the-shelf high-end servers or cloud servers provided in a machine-as-a-service (MaaS) such as Amazon EC2 and Google GCP. Therefore, the attack would be feasible using high-end servers

Table 1. Frequency of number of remaining candidates (number of candidates is given in $\log_2$)

# Candidates	0–23	24	25	26	27	28	29	30
Frequency	2*	4	10	24	40	105	195	461
# Candidates	31	32	33	34	35	36	37	38
Frequency	825	1,568	2,803	5,045	8,900	14,959	24,731	39,105
# Candidates	39	40	41	42	43	44	45	46
Frequency	60,474	91,598	133,605	188,692	259,208	344,179	441,076	546,027
# Candidates	47	48	49	50	51	52	53	54
Frequency	652,036	747,325	822,649	866,532	874,554	838,187	763,422	656,229
# Candidates	55	56	57	58	59	60	61	62
Frequency	529,021	400,212	282,278	184,218	109,778	60,218	29,115	12,994
# Candidates	63	64	65	66	67	68	69	70–128
Frequency	5,097	1,790	535	133	31	8	2	0*

* In total

Table 2. Average time for factoring $(i-1)$-th degree polynomial

Degree of polynomial $i-1$	2	4	8	16	32	64	128
Average time (ms)	1.4	3.0	6.8	20.0	76.4	327.5	1,180

even if 2^{40}–2^{45} candidates remain after Step (a), respectively. In this sense, according to Table 1, the probabilities of successful tag forgery using a high-end server at a computational cost of less than 2^{30} for a core is given by approximately 2.5% and 52.5% if the number of available cores is 2^{10} and 2^{20}, respectively. This probability is non-negligible because this probability is considered for the all addition in one Poly1305 computation. More precisely, we can retrieve the correct hash key if we find an attackable X_{i-1} among $1 \leq i \leq n$. In addition, the attacker may observe the side-channel information many times until she finds an attackable one, although our attack uses only one trace. Let v be the number of observation of side-channel information of Poly1305 tag generation and let $\bar{n}$ be the average of the input block length among v tags. The expected probability p_{success} for at least one success of the proposed attack within e factorizations during v observations is expressed by

$$p_{\text{success}} = 1 - (1 - \mathbf{cmf}(e))^{v\bar{n}}, \tag{7}$$

where $\mathbf{cmf}(e)$ denotes the probability that the acceptable number of candidates after the side-channel analysis on final or intermediate addition should be less-than e, and $\mathbf{cmf}(e)$ is derived as the cumulative mass function corresponding to Fig. 2 (and Table 1). Table 3 illustrates the relation between the success probability, $\mathbf{cmf}(e)$ (related to the computational cost), and $v\bar{n}$ (related to the number of observation of addition in Poly1305). From Table 3, we can confirm that we successfully perform forgery at least one tag of Poly1305 via the proposed side-channel attack with practical computational cost and probability. For example,

Table 3. Success probability p_{success} for various e and $v\bar{n}$ (%)

		$v\bar{n}$				
		10	100	1,000	10,000	100,000
e	2^{25}	$<7.00 \times 10^{-4}$	$<7.00 \times 10^{-3}$	$<7.00 \times 10^{-2}$	5.98×10^{-1}	5.82
	2^{30}	3.80×10^{-2}	3.79×10^{-1}	3.72	31.6	97.8
	2^{35}	1.10	10.5	67.0	>99.9	>99.9
	2^{40}	14.8	79.9	>99.9	>99.9	>99.9
	2^{45}	71.4	>99.9	>99.9	>99.9	>99.9
	2^{50}	99.7	>99.9	>99.9	>99.9	>99.9

if we can observe more than 1,000 additions in Poly1305, 2^{30} and 2^{35} polynomial factorizations would be sufficient to forge at least one tag with probabilities of more than 3.72% and 67.0%, respectively. Given that the polynomial factorization is parallelizable as mentioned before, we can confirm that the proposed attack is feasible within a practical span of time with non-negligible probability.

3.5 Application to Open-Source Poly1305 Implementation

In this subsection, we consider the application of the proposed attack to an open-source Poly1305 implementation. In this paper, we refer to μNaCl (micro Networking and Cryptography library) [HS19], which is an open-source library of cryptographic software including Poly1305 and is involved in a publication of [HS13].

In the implementation, the reduction by $2^{130} - 5$ after multiplication is in a lazy manner for an efficient computation. An integer $F \in [0, (2^{130} - 5)^2)$ is equal to $5F_1 + F_0$ modulo $2^{130} - 5$, where F_1 and F_0 are integer in the range of $[0, 2^{130})$ such that $F = 2^{130}F_1 + F_0$. Let F_1' and F_0' be 17- and 16-byte integers such that $F = 2^{128}F_1' + F_0'$, respectively. According to the above property, the reduction of F by $2^{130} - 5$ is efficiently calculated by $F_0 + F_1'' + (F_1'' \gg 2)$ on 8-bit micro-controllers, where F_1'' is an integer satisfying $4\lfloor F_1'/4 \rfloor \; (= 4F_1)$ and $(F_1'' \gg 2)$ denotes a two-bit shift to right. Since the reduction result is given as a 133-bit integer (and the result of following addition becomes 134-bit), another reduction to $[0, 2^{130} - 5)$ should be performed before the final addition (called "freeze" operation).

Our attack on final addition can be applied to this implementation, because the generated tag should be fully reduced regardless of the representation of intermediate values. In addition, our attack on intermediate addition can be also available with an additional computational cost of 2^2–2^3 as described in Appendix. Thus, our attack can be still practical and can be performed with a non-negligible complexity according to Eq. (7) (and Table 3).

4   Discussion

4.1   Noise Tolerance

Our attack requires a good signal-to-noise ratio (SNR) for the observation such that the HWs of the bytes of interest is correctly estimated. Many previous works [Man03, RS09, RSVC09, CMW14, KUH+17, OUHA18] showed that the side-channel information of low-end micro-controllers can be observed with such SNR values; and therefore, the HWs of values stored in registers are accurately estimated, which implies that our single-trace attack is practical and realistic.

On the other hand, there is a possibility that the attack is feasible even if the HWs observed from side-channel information include some noise. The use of likelihood estimation for HWs at Lines 2 and 3 in Algorithm 3 (resp. Algorithm 7) would be a possible extension for improving the noise tolerance [RS09]. More concretely, the byte-wise HWs of U and S (resp. X_{i-1} and W_i) are ranked using the maximum likelihood estimation, and the proposed attack is iterated in accordance with the rank until the correct H is found. For example, according to [OUHA18], the side-channel information from a low-end smart card can be observed with an SNR of 107.9 in a laboratory setting. This SNR is good enough to perform the proposed attack, because the correct HWs of U and S (resp. X_{i-1} and W_i) would be highly ranked.

Another possible extension for improving the noise tolerance may be based on a belief propagation technique which derives the candidates for U or X_{i-1} as a probability mass function. In the attack on final addition, we first derive the distribution of byte-wise candidates for U and S from side-channel information [VCGS14]. Like [PPM17], we then perform a belief propagation from the byte-wise U and S to T by replacing Lines 14–16, 18–20, 23–30, and 32–34 in Algorithm 3 with a belief propagation for byte-wise candidate, and inversely propagate the distribution of T to U with a known value T. Thus, we derive the probability mass function representing U. The attack on the i-th intermediate addition may be also extended in the same manner. However, straightforward belief propagation for larger-than 128-bit adders would be infeasible because there are many conditional probability calculations owing to the existence/nonexistence of carry-generation/propagation (i.e., intersections) as shown in Fig. 1, while a method approximating the conditional probability calculation might be available. Establishing and evaluating a concrete algorithm based on such a belief propagation technique for the 128-bit adder, which can be a noise-tolerant alternative of Algorithms 3 and 7, could be a future research avenue.

4.2   Applicability and Generality of the Proposed Attack

Our attack can be extended and applied to other known polynomial-based MAC schemes in principle, where the final addition is basically given by an Abelian group operation or polynomial evaluation is performed over a GF. This Abelian operation is typically defined as addition modulo 2^α (e.g., Poly1305), bit-parallel-XOR (e.g., GCM/GMAC), or addition over a prime field (e.g., SGCM).

SGCM has the same structure as GCM and Poly1305, except that GF is replaced with a prime field $GF(p)$ where $p \ (= 2^{128} + 12451)$ is the prime corresponding to a Sophie Germain prime $(p-1)/2 = 2^{127} + 6225$. While the authenticated tag of SGCM is given by the sum of U and S modulo p, Algorithms 3, 4, and 7 are sufficiently applicable to SGCM that we can easily consider the existence/non-existence of reduction of modulo p by means similar to Proposition 1.

On the other hand, the proposed attack requires the assembly-level information of the target software in order to estimate HWs of interest from side-channel information. However, there are many devices running open-source software and the attacker can easily obtain the assembly code of target software with cross compilation. Thus, the scenario of our attack is sufficiently realistic, especially in the context of the IoT.

Another important assumption of the proposed attack is that the attack in this study focuses on an 8-bit micro-controller as the attack target. Proposition 1 and Algorithms 3, 4, and 7 themselves are easily extended to an attack on 16- and 32-bit micro-controllers, where we employ the 16-bit- and 32-bit-wise HW models (and "EstimateByteWiseHWsFrom" at Lines 2 and 3 is accordingly changed), change the unit of each data value (i.e., 2^8 is replaced with 2^{16} and 2^{32}), and change the number of iterations of j from 16 $(= 128/8)$ to 8 $(= 128/16)$ and 4 $(= 128/32)$, respectively. In such cases, the computational complexities (i.e., the total number of 16-bit- and 32-bit-wise guesses) is given by $2^{16} \cdot 8 = 2^{19}$ and $2^{32} \cdot 4 = 2^{34}$, respectively. However, it seems difficult to reduce the candidates for U and X_{i-1} to less than 2^{64} using Algorithm 3 because the side-channel information from such micro-controllers (i.e., the 16-bit- and 32-bit-wise HWs) is less informative than that from 8-bit micro-controllers (i.e., 8-bit-wise HWs). More precisely, the number of remaining candidates is distributed mainly at around 2^{75} and 2^{100} when attacking 16-bit and 32-bit micro-controllers, respectively. In addition, measurement with a good SNR from 16-bit and 32-bit micro-controllers is more difficult than that from 8-bit micro-controllers. In summary, the proposed attack is infeasible for micro-controllers larger than 8-bit ones so far, and such extensions remain for future work.

4.3   Countermeasures

Conventional software masking schemes can be applied to polynomial-based MAC schemes to prevent the proposed attack if the polynomial evaluation and final addition employ an identical GF. In this case, the Ishai-Sahai-Wagner (ISW) scheme [ISW03], domain-oriented masking (DOM) [GMK16], and unified masking approach (UMA) [GM18] are typical examples. However, the applications of such masking schemes require large overheads in the case of schemes over a large GF. In addition, when we apply the above additive masking schemes to polynomial-based MAC schemes, calculation of unmask value would require a large computational cost because the secret hash key is multiplied to intermediate values, while the secret key is added in most symmetric ciphers.

A possible cost-effective masking-based countermeasure for GCM/GMAC was proposed in [OUHA18]. It uses masking for intermediate values (but not for H), precomputation of unmasked value, and an offset of $S - SH$ and its correction. It was shown that the masking scheme can protect GCM/GMAC from SCAs with overheads of $1 + \log_2(n)$ multiplications and $n + 1$ additions over $GF(2^{128})$ and a 128-bit random value as the initial randomness. However, the above masking scheme cannot be applied to Poly1305 because Poly1305 employs polynomial evaluation over $GF(2^{130} - 5)$ and final addition modulo 2^{128}. This indicates that the mask and offset values should be converted from $GF(2^{130} - 5)$ to $\mathbb{Z}/2^{128}\mathbb{Z}$, while such a conversion algorithm is not known.

Addressing the above issues, we discuss a cost-effective countermeasure applicable directly to Poly1305. The proposed attack on final addition cannot be applied if either S or U is protected as the attack using only U ($= X_n$) or S is infeasible. Masking either S or U is sufficient for protecting the final addition of Poly1305. Here, we assume that ChaCha20 should be protected when protecting Poly1305, and therefore the output of ChaCha20 (i.e., H and S) is masked. QuarterRound of ChaCha20 performs the operations in the order of modular addition, bit-parallel-XOR, and rotation. This indicates that S is generated with a Boolean mask if masking is applied to ChaCha20. Therefore, we consider a countermeasure using the mask of S from a masked ChaCha20 and Boolean-to-arithmetic mask conversion [Gou01, BCZ18] for the final addition and a masked polynomial evaluation to prevent the attack on the i-th addition.

Algorithm 5 is the algorithmic description of a masking-based ChaCha20-Poly1305 resistant to the proposed attack, where $H^{(\mathbb{B})}$, $S^{(\mathbb{B})}$, and $C_l^{(\mathbb{B})}$ denote H, S, and C_l masked with $M_H^{(\mathbb{B})}$, $M_S^{(\mathbb{B})}$, and $M_{C_l}^{(\mathbb{B})}$, respectively (i.e., $H^{(\mathbb{B})} = H \oplus M_H^{(\mathbb{B})}$ and the same for S and C_l). In contrast, $S^{(\mathbb{Z})}$ and $T^{(\mathbb{Z})}$ denote S and T with arithmetic masks $M_S^{(\mathbb{Z})}$ and $M_T^{(\mathbb{Z})}$ (i.e., $S^{(\mathbb{Z})} = S + M_S^{(\mathbb{Z})} \bmod 2^{128}$ and $T^{(\mathbb{Z})} = T + M_T^{(\mathbb{Z})} \bmod 2^{128}$), respectively. Here, $M_T^{(\mathbb{Z})} = M_S^{(\mathbb{Z})}$ because $T^{(\mathbb{Z})} = S^{(\mathbb{Z})} + U = S + U + M_S^{(\mathbb{Z})} = T + M_S^{(\mathbb{Z})} \bmod 2^{128}$. In Algorithm 5, we use masked ChaCha20 (e.g., based on [JPS18]) for generating $H^{(\mathbb{B})}$, $S^{(\mathbb{B})}$, and key stream for encryption with a Boolean mask. While $H^{(\mathbb{B})}$ and $C_l^{(\mathbb{B})}$ are immediately unmasked, the pair of $S^{(\mathbb{B})}$ and $M_S^{(\mathbb{B})}$ is converted to the pair of $S^{(\mathbb{Z})}$ and $M_S^{(\mathbb{Z})}$, that is, the arithmetic-masked S. After computing the arithmetic-masked tag $T^{(\mathbb{Z})}$ using a masked Poly1305 with $S^{(\mathbb{Z})}$ instead of S, the output tag T is finally generated by unmasking $T^{(\mathbb{Z})}$ with $M_T^{(\mathbb{Z})}$ ($= M_S^{(\mathbb{Z})}$).

Algorithm 6 displays the proposed masked Poly1305. Here, $X_0^{(\mathbb{F})}$ and $X_n^{(\mathbb{F})}$ denotes the masked X_0 and X_n with a prime-field mask $M_{X_0}^{(\mathbb{F})}$ and $M_{X_n}^{(\mathbb{F})}$, respectively. At Line 4, we generate an initial prime-field mask $M_{X_0}^{(\mathbb{F})}$. At Line 5, we apply the prime-field mask to the first intermediate value X_0. In Lines 6–8, we perform the masked polynomial evaluation over $GF(2^{130} - 5)$, where X_{i-1} (and W_i) is always masked with $M_{X_0}^{(\mathbb{F})} H^i$ (i.e., $X_{i-1}^{(\mathbb{F})} = X_i + M_{X_0}^{(\mathbb{F})} H^i$); and therefore, the proposed attack on the i-th addition cannot be applied. After the masked polynomial evaluation, at Line 9, we calculate an unmask value $M_{X_n}^{(\mathbb{F})}$ directly from $M_{X_0}^{(\mathbb{F})}$ and H, without computing unmask values for intermediate values $X_1, X_2, \ldots, X_{n-1}$. Such a method is known to be useful for efficient unmask value

---

Algorithm 5. Masked ChaCha20-Poly1305

Input: Associated data $\mathcal{D}$, plaintext $\mathcal{P}$, 256-bit secret key K, 96-bit initial vector V
Output: Ciphertext $\mathcal{C}$, authentication tag T
1: **Function** MASKEDCHACHA20-POLY1305($\mathcal{D}, \mathcal{P}, K, V$)
2:     int $l \leftarrow 0$;
3:     $((H^{(\mathbb{B})}, M_H^{(\mathbb{B})}), (S^{(\mathbb{B})}, M_S^{(\mathbb{B})})) \leftarrow$ MaskedChaCha20-core(K, V, l);
4:     $H \leftarrow H^{(\mathbb{B})} \oplus M_H^{(\mathbb{B})}$;   ▷ Unmask $H^{(\mathbb{B})}$
5:     $l \leftarrow l + 1$;
6:     **while** $l \leq m$ **do**
7:         $(C_l^{(\mathbb{B})}, M_{C_l}^{(\mathbb{B})}) \leftarrow P_l \oplus$ MaskedChaCha20-core(K, V, l);
8:         $C_l \leftarrow C_l^{(\mathbb{B})} \oplus M_{C_l}^{(\mathbb{B})}$;   ▷ Unmask $C_l^{(\mathbb{B})}$
9:         $l \leftarrow l + 1$;
10:     **end while**
11:     $\mathcal{A} \leftarrow (\mathcal{D}, \mathcal{C}, (\text{len}(\mathcal{D}) || \text{len}(\mathcal{C})))$;
12:     $(S^{(\mathbb{Z})}, M_S^{(\mathbb{Z})}) \leftarrow$ BooleanToArithmeticMaskConversion($S^{(\mathbb{B})}, M_S^{(\mathbb{B})}$)
13:     $T^{(\mathbb{Z})} \leftarrow$ MaskedPoly1305($\mathcal{A}, H, S^{(\mathbb{Z})}$);
14:     $T \leftarrow (T^{(\mathbb{Z})} + M_T^{(\mathbb{Z})}) \mod 2^{128}$;   ▷ Unmask T with $M_T^{(\mathbb{Z})} = M_S^{(\mathbb{Z})}$
15:     **return** $(\mathcal{D}, \mathcal{C}, T)$;
16: **end Function**

Algorithm 6. Masked Poly1305

Input: Message $\mathcal{A}$, hash key H, masked key $S^{(\mathbb{Z})}$
Output: Masked authentication tag $T^{(\mathbb{Z})}$
1: **Function** MASKEDPOLY1305($\mathcal{A}, H, S^{(\mathbb{Z})}$)
2:     $H \leftarrow H$ & 0x0ffffffc0ffffffc0ffffffc0fffffff;
3:     $X_0 \leftarrow 0$;
4:     $M_{X_0}^{(\mathbb{F})} \xleftarrow{\$} GF(2^{130} - 5)$;   ▷ Initial prime-field mask generation
5:     $X_0^{(\mathbb{F})} \leftarrow X_0 - M_{X_0}^{(\mathbb{F})}$;   ▷ Initial masking over $GF(2^{130} - 5)$
6:     **for** i from 1 to n **do**
7:         $X_i^{(\mathbb{F})} \leftarrow ((2^{128} + A_i) + X_{i-1}^{(\mathbb{F})})H \mod 2^{130} - 5$;   ▷ Masked polynomial evaluation over $GF(2^{130} - 5)$
8:     **end for**
9:     $M_{X_n}^{(\mathbb{F})} \leftarrow M_{X_0}^{(\mathbb{F})} H^n$;   ▷ Unmask value calculation
10:     $X_n \leftarrow X_n^{(\mathbb{F})} + M_{X_n}^{(\mathbb{F})}$;   ▷ Unmask X_n
11:     $T^{(\mathbb{Z})} \leftarrow (S^{(\mathbb{Z})} + X_n) \mod 2^{128}$;   ▷ Masked final addition (not over $GF(2^{130} - 5)$)
12:     **return** $T^{(\mathbb{Z})}$;
13: **end Function**

---

calculation with $1 + \log_2(n)$ multiplications by the left-to-right binary method. In addition, this method erases the joint leakage of masked and unmask values, which might be exploited[2]. We then unmask X_n and compute the masked authentication tag $T^{(\mathbb{Z})}$ from the masked key $S^{(\mathbb{Z})}$ and X_n. The proposed attack on final addition is also impossible thanks to the masked key.

In Algorithm 5, the overhead of the protection of Poly1305 (excluding that of ChaCha20) is given by the cost of mask conversion from Boolean to $\mathbb{Z}/2^{128}\mathbb{Z}$

---

[2] On the other hand, if it is required to prevent side-channel leakage of H^i during the computation of H^n, we should compute $M_{X_n}^{(\mathbb{F})}$ in the order of $M_{X_0}^{(\mathbb{F})} H, M_{X_0}^{(\mathbb{F})} H^2, \ldots, M_{X_0}^{(\mathbb{F})} H^n$, which is realized by n multiplications.

(i.e., arithmetic) and the overhead of masked Poly1305. The Boolean-to-arithmetic mask conversion is efficiently computed in the case of a small number of shares (i.e., security order) even if the bit length is large. In particular, in first-order security, the mask conversion from Boolean to arithmetic can be performed only with a 128-bit random number, five bit-parallel-XORs, and two subtractions [Gou01]. Since first-order protection should be enough for preventing the proposed attack, the overhead for protecting S is small and negligible compared to the ChaCha20-Poly1305 computation itself. Even if a higher-order masking is applied to ChaCha20, the first-order mask conversion should be performed for the sake of efficient computation because the attacker cannot perform DPAs on the conversion in the scenario of ChaCha20-Poly1305. On the other hand, the proposed masked Poly1305 requires an overhead of a 130-bit random number generation, one addition, one subtraction, and $1+\log_2(n)$ multiplications over $GF(2^{130} - 5)$. This overhead is meaningfully smaller for a large GF than the aforementioned common masking schemes as described in [OUHA18]. The countermeasure is also available if Poly1305 is combined with another symmetric encryption scheme which is not ChaCha20.

The proposed countermeasure is also resistant to higher-order-like attacks which combine the leakage of some $X_i^{(\mathbb{F})}$'s. Each X_i should be masked with a distinct mask $M_{X_0}^{(\mathbb{F})} H^i$. Since i is unique for X_i and computation of intermediate unmask values (i.e., $M_{X_i}^{(\mathbb{F})}$) is avoidable, we cannot cancel the effect of $M_{X_0}^{(\mathbb{F})}$ by any combination of leakage of $X_i^{(\mathbb{F})}$ without knowledge of H. Note that we cannot discuss the resistance of our countermeasure to other type of attacks (e.g.., DPA) because no other side-channel attack applicable Poly1305 has been known so far.

5   Conclusion

In this study, we proposed the first single-trace SCA on the polynomial-based MAC schemes that is applicable to Poly1305. While the conventional attacks on GCM/GMAC cannot be applied to Poly1305 due to their one-time keys and the difference of GFs, the proposed attack retrieves the hash key from a single-trace with a non-negligible probability, allowing the attacker to forge the authentication tag. The proposed attack focuses on the final addition or the intermediate addition during polynomial evaluation. Because the output of final addition or one input operand of the intermediate addition is observable to the attacker, our new algorithms can efficiently estimate the operands of these additions. We also presented a cost-effective countermeasure using a combination of the first-order mask conversion from Boolean to arithmetic masking and new masked Poly1305.

A further reduction of computational complexity including noise tolerance remains for future work, which should makes it feasible to apply our attack to other larger platform and major scenarios (e.g., TLS). It is also interesting to investigate the applications of the new algorithm to other schemes.

Appendix: Side-Channel Analysis on Intermediate Addition

We then describe the attack focusing on the i-th intermediate addition of X_{i-1} and A_i (i.e., $W_i = (2^{128} + A_i) + X_{i-1}$). In contrast to final addition, while the output of i-th addition (i.e., W_i) is a secret value, the attacker knows A_i. Therefore, similarly to Algorithm 3, we can make a list of candidates for X_{i-1} by calculating $HW(w_{i,j})$ from $a_{i,j}$ and guessed $x_{i-1,j}$ and comparing the hypothetical $HW(w_{i,j})$ with the estimated one from side-channel information. Algorithm 7 calculates a list of candidates for X_{i-1}. Algorithm 7 is basically derived by inverting the sign of g and 2^8 in Algorithm 3 since Algorithm 7 is considered as a variant of Algorithm 3 where $W_i - X_{i-1} = A_i$ corresponds $S + U = T$. In addition, the special case $a_{i,j} = 0$ is removed because $a'_{i,j}$ at Line 7, which is a value representing that carry-in value is one, is calculated by adding one, but not by subtracting one. At Lines 29–38, we perform the loop for 17th byte. The 17th loop should be simplified because the 17th bytes of X_i and W_i should have limited value represented by only two bits and there should be no carry-propagation/generation to the 18th byte. At Line 39, we combine byte-wise candidates for X_{i-1} by "CombineByteWiseCandidatesEval," which basically performs Algorithm 4, but the output is given by $\Omega_0 \cup \Omega_1$ and Lines 10–16 are skipped because the addition is performed upto the 17th byte. Note that the main loop in Algorithm 7 and CombineByteWiseCandidatesEval is performed until $j = 17$, but the computational cost of Algorithm 7 is almost equal to Algorithm 3.

Major concern about attacking the i-th addition is that the addition is performed over $GF(2^{130} - 5)$, namely, reduction by $2^{130} - 5$ may be applied to the result of addition and we cannot correctly estimate W_i. However, our attack can be still applied to many practical implementation where a reduction is applied only to the multiplication result, but not to the addition result. (Actually, the reduction is not always applied to the result of addition in many practical implementation.)

In addition, some implementation employs an efficient reduction exploiting the property of Mersenne-like prime after multiplication, which indicates that multiplication result is reduced in a kind of lazy manner and X_{i-1} is given by more-than 130 bits. Let us consider the open-source implementation in [HS19] as well as Section 3.5. The implementation employs a lazy reduction and 133- and 134-bit representation for intermediate values. More precisely, the multiplication result is not fully reduced by $2^{130} - 5$, X_{i-1} is not given as a 130-bit value as described in Sect. 3.5, but is 133-bit (and W_i is 134-bit). Our algorithms are still applied to this implementation by modifying the upper bound of d at Line 33 to 2^5, because Algorithm 7 only assumes that X_{i-1} and W_i are 17-byte values and there should be no carry-propagation/generation to 18-th byte. Due to the redundancy, the number of candidates for X_{i-1} after applying Algorithm 7 may be greater than the evaluation in Sect. 3.4 (i.e., Fig. 2 and Table 1). However, we confirmed that the number of candidates is only about 2^2–2^3 times greater than that given in Sect. 3.4 in average case by a simulation. Thus, our attack can be

Algorithm 7. Side-channel analysis on i-th addition

Input: The i-th input block A_i, side-channel informations $\mathcal{L}(X_{i-1})$ and $\mathcal{L}(W_i)$
Output: List Ω (containing candidates for X_{i-1})

1: **Function** DeriveCandidatesFrom($A_i, \mathcal{L}(X_{i-1}), \mathcal{L}(W_i)$)
2:     **list of int** $[HW(x_{i-1,1}), \ldots, HW(x_{i-1,17})] \leftarrow$ EstimateByteWiseHWsFrom($\mathcal{L}(X_{i-1})$);
3:     **list of int** $[HW(w_{i,1}), \ldots, HW(w_{i,17})] \leftarrow$ EstimateByteWiseHWsFrom($\mathcal{L}(W_i)$);
4:     **list of list** $\Omega_{0,0} \leftarrow []$; **list of list** $\Omega_{0,1} \leftarrow []$; **list of list** $\Omega_{1,0} \leftarrow []$; **list of list** $\Omega_{1,1} \leftarrow []$;
5:     **for** j from 1 to 16 **do**
6:         **list of int** $\Omega_{0,0}^{(j)} \leftarrow []$; **list of int** $\Omega_{0,1}^{(j)} \leftarrow []$; **list of int** $\Omega_{1,0}^{(j)} \leftarrow []$; **list of int** $\Omega_{1,1}^{(j)} \leftarrow []$;
7:         **int** $a'_{i,j} \leftarrow a_{i,j} + 1$;
8:         **for each** $g \in \{d \in \mathbb{Z} \mid HW(d) = HW(x_{i-1,j}) \text{ and } 0 \leq d < 2^8\}$ **do**
9:             **if** $a_{i,j} + g \geq 2^8$ **then**   ▷ If carry-in is 0 and carry-out is 1
10:                 **if** $HW(a_{i,j} + g - 2^8) = HW(w_{i,j})$ **then**
11:                     $\Omega_{0,1}^{(j)}$.append(g);
12:                 **end if**
13:             **else**   ▷ If carry-in is 0 and carry-out is 0
14:                 **if** $HW(a_{i,j} + g) = HW(w_{i,j})$ **then**
15:                     $\Omega_{0,0}^{(j)}$.append(g);
16:                 **end if**
17:             **end if**
18:             **if** $j \neq 1$ **then**
19:                 **if** $a'_{i,j} + g \geq 2^8$ **then**   ▷ If carry-in is 1 and carry-out is 1
20:                     **if** $HW(a'_{i,j} + g - 2^8) = HW(w_{i,j})$ **then**
21:                         $\Omega_{1,1}^{(j)}$.append(g);
22:                     **end if**
23:                 **else**   ▷ If carry-in is 1 and carry-out is 0
24:                     **if** $HW(a'_{i,j} + g) = HW(w_{i,j})$ **then**
25:                         $\Omega_{1,0}^{(j)}$.append(g);
26:                     **end if**
27:                 **end if**
28:             **end if**
29:         **end for**
30:         $\Omega_{0,0}$.append($\Omega_{0,0}^{(j)}$); $\Omega_{0,1}$.append($\Omega_{0,1}^{(j)}$); $\Omega_{1,0}$.append($\Omega_{1,0}^{(j)}$); $\Omega_{1,1}$.append($\Omega_{1,1}^{(j)}$);
31:     **end for**
32:     **list of int** $\Omega_{0,0}^{(17)} \leftarrow []$; **list of int** $\Omega_{1,0}^{(17)} \leftarrow []$;   ▷ 17th loop
33:     **for each** $g \in \{d \in \mathbb{Z} \mid HW(d) = HW(x_{i-1,17}) \text{ and } 0 \leq d < 2^2\}$ **do**
34:         **if** $HW(g + 1) = HW(w_{i,17})$ **then**   ▷ If carry-in is 0
35:             $\Omega_{0,0}^{(17)}$.append(g);
36:         **end if**
37:         **if** $HW(g + 2) = HW(w_{i,17})$ **then**   ▷ If carry-in is 1
38:             $\Omega_{1,0}^{(17)}$.append(g);
39:         **end if**
40:     **end for**
41:     $\Omega_{0,0}$.append($\Omega_{0,0}^{(17)}$); $\Omega_{1,0}$.append($\Omega_{1,0}^{(17)}$);
42:     **list of int** $\Omega \leftarrow$ CombineByteWiseCandidatesEval($\Omega_{0,0}, \Omega_{0,1}, \Omega_{1,0}, \Omega_{1,1}$);
43:     **return** Ω;
44: **end Function**

---

still practical and can be performed with a non-negligible complexity according to Eq. (7) (and Table 3).

References

AFM17. Adomnicai, A., Fournier, J.J.A., Masson, L.: Bricklayer attack: a side-channel analysis on the ChaCha quarter round. In: Patra, A., Smart, N.P. (eds.) INDOCRYPT 2017. LNCS, vol. 10698, pp. 65–84. Springer, Cham (2017). https://doi.org/10.1007/978-3-319-71667-1_4

AFP13. Al Fardan, N.J., Paterson, K.G.: Lucky thirteen: breaking the TLS and DTLS record protocols. In: IEEE Symposium on Security and Privacy (S&P), pp. 526–540. IEEE (2013)

asi. Risa/Asir (Kobe distribution) download page. http://www.math.kobe-u.ac.jp/Asir/asir.html

BCF+15. Belaïd, S., Coron, J.-S., Fouque, P.-A., Gérard, B., Kammerer, J.-G., Prouff, E.: Improved side-channel analysis of finite-field multiplication. In: Güneysu, T., Handschuh, H. (eds.) CHES 2015. LNCS, vol. 9293, pp. 395–415. Springer, Heidelberg (2015). https://doi.org/10.1007/978-3-662-48324-4_20

BCZ18. Bettale, L., Coron, J.-S., Zeitoun, R.: Improved high-order conversion from Boolean to arithmetic masking. IACR Trans. Cryptogr. Hardware Embed. Syst. (TCHES) 22–45 (2018)

Ber99. Bernstein, D.J.: Guaranteed message authentication faster than MD5 (1999). http://cr.yp.to/antiforgery/hash127-abs.pdf

Ber05. Bernstein, D.J.: The Poly1305-AES message-authentication code. In: Gilbert, H., Handschuh, H. (eds.) FSE 2005. LNCS, vol. 3557, pp. 32–49. Springer, Heidelberg (2005). https://doi.org/10.1007/11502760_3

Ber18. Bernstein, D.J.: ChaCha, a variant of Salsa20, October 2018. http://cr.yp.to/chacha/chacha-20080128.pdf

BFG+14. Belaïd, S., Fouque, P.-A., Gérard, B.: Side-channel analysis of multiplications in $GF(2^{128})$. In: Sarkar, P., Iwata, T. (eds.) ASIACRYPT 2014. LNCS, vol. 8874, pp. 306–325. Springer, Heidelberg (2014). https://doi.org/10.1007/978-3-662-45608-8_17

BN00. Bellare, M., Namprempre, C.: Authenticated encryption: relations among notions and analysis of the generic composition paradigm. In: Okamoto, T. (ed.) ASIACRYPT 2000. LNCS, vol. 1976, pp. 531–545. Springer, Heidelberg (2000). https://doi.org/10.1007/3-540-44448-3_41

BN08. Bellare, N., Namprempre, C.: Authenticated encryption: relations among notations and analysis of the generic composition paradigm. J. Cryptol. 21(4), 469–491 (2008)

BN18. Bellare, N., Namprempre, C.: Authenticated encryption: Relations among notations and analysis of the generic composition paradigm (full version), October 2018. https://cseweb.ucsd.edu/~mihir/papers/oem.pdf

BSMG17. Bache, F., Schneider, T., Moradi, A., Güneysu, T.: SPARX–a side-channel protected processor for ARX-based cryptography. In: Design, Automation and Test in Europe Conference and Exhibition (DATE), pp. 990–995. IEEE (2017)

BZD+16. Böck, H., Zauner, A., Devlin, S., Somorovsky, J., Jovanovic, P.: Nonce-disrespecting adversaries: practical forgery attacks on GCM in TLS. In: 10th USENIX Workshop on Offensive Technologies (WOOT 2016), pp. 1–13. USENIX Association (2016)

CMW14. Clavier, C., Marion, D., Wurcker, A.: Simple power analysis on AES key expansion revisited. In: Batina, L., Robshaw, M. (eds.) CHES 2014. LNCS, vol. 8731, pp. 279–297. Springer, Heidelberg (2014). https://doi.org/10.1007/978-3-662-44709-3_16

Cry16. Cryptographic competitions. CAESAR: Competition for authenticated encryption: Security, applicability, and robustness (2016). https://competitions.cr.yp.to/caesar.html

DR11. Duong, T., Rizzo, J.: Here come the $\oplus$ ninjas (2011). https://www.nist.gov/

Dre04. Drechsler, R. (ed.): Advanced Formal Verification. Kluwer Academic Publishers, Amsterdam (2004)

Dwo07. Dworlin, M.: NIST special publication 800–38D–recommendation for block cipher modes of operation: Galois/Counter Mode (GCM) and GMAC. Technical report, National Institute of Standards and Technology (NIST) (2007). http://dl.acm.org/citation.cfm?id=2206251

GM18. Gross, H., Mangard, S.: A unified masking approach. J. Cryptogr. Eng. 8(2), 109–124 (2018). https://doi.org/10.1007/s13389-018-0184-y

GMK16. Gross, H., Mangard, S., Korak, T.: Domain-oriented masking: compact masked hardware implementations with arbitrary protection order. In: ACM Workshop on Theory of Implementation Security, p. 3 (2016)

Gou01. Goubin, L.: A sound method for switching between Boolean and arithmetic masking. In: Koç, Ç.K., Naccache, D., Paar, C. (eds.) CHES 2001. LNCS, vol. 2162, pp. 3–15. Springer, Heidelberg (2001). https://doi.org/10.1007/3-540-44709-1_2

HP08. Handschuh, H., Preneel, B.: Key-recovery attacks on universal hash function based MAC algorithms. In: Wagner, D. (ed.) CRYPTO 2008. LNCS, vol. 5157, pp. 144–161. Springer, Heidelberg (2008). https://doi.org/10.1007/978-3-540-85174-5_9

HS13. Hutter, M., Schwabe, P.: NaCl on 8-Bit AVR microcontrollers. In: Youssef, A., Nitaj, A., Hassanien, A.E. (eds.) AFRICACRYPT 2013. LNCS, vol. 7918, pp. 156–172. Springer, Heidelberg (2013). https://doi.org/10.1007/978-3-642-38553-7_9

HS19. Hutter, M., Schwabe, P.: μNaCl–the networking and cryptography library for microcontrollers, May 2019. https://munacl.cryptojedi.org/index.shtml

IOM12. Iwata, T., Ohashi, K., Minematsu, K.: Breaking and repairing GCM security proofs. In: Safavi-Naini, R., Canetti, R. (eds.) CRYPTO 2012. LNCS, vol. 7417, pp. 31–49. Springer, Heidelberg (2012). https://doi.org/10.1007/978-3-642-32009-5_3

ISW03. Ishai, Y., Sahai, A., Wagner, D.: Private circuits: securing hardware against probing attacks. In: Boneh, D. (ed.) CRYPTO 2003. LNCS, vol. 2729, pp. 463–481. Springer, Heidelberg (2003). https://doi.org/10.1007/978-3-540-45146-4_27

JB17. Jungk, B., Bhasin, S.: Don't fall into a trap: physical side-channel analysis of ChaCha20-Poly1305. In: Design, Automation and Test in Europe Conference and Exhibition (DATE), pp. 1110–1115. IEEE (2017)

Jou06. Joux, A.: A authentication failures in NIST version of GCM (2006). http://csrc.nist.gov/groups/ST/toolkit/BCM/documents/comments/800-38_Series-Drafts/GCM/Joux_comments.pdf

JPS18. Jungk, B., Petri, R., Stöttinger, M.: Efficient side-channel protections of ARX ciphers. IACR Trans. Cryptogr. Hardware Embed. Syst. (TCHES) 627–653 (2018)

KJJ99. Kocher, P., Jaffe, J., Jun, B.: Differential power analysis. In: Wiener, M. (ed.) CRYPTO 1999. LNCS, vol. 1666, pp. 388–397. Springer, Heidelberg (1999). https://doi.org/10.1007/3-540-48405-1_25

KUH+17. Kawai, W., Ueno, R., Homma, N., Aoki, T., Fukushima, K., Kiyomoto, S.: Practical power analysis on KCipher-2 software on low-end microcontrollers. In: IEEE European Symposium on Security and Privacy Workshops (EuroSPW) on Secuity for Embedded and Mobile Systems (SEMS), pp. 113–121 (2017)

KVW03. Kohno, T., Viega, J., Whiting, D.: CWC: A high-performance conventional authenticated encryption mode. IACR ePrint Archives: Report 2003/106 (2003). https://eprint.iacr.org/2003/106

Lan15. Langley, A.: RFC 7539 - ChaCha20 and Poly1305 for IETF protocols - IETF tools (2015). https://tools.ietf.org/html/rfc7539

Man03. Mangard, S.: A simple power-analysis (SPA) attack on implementations of the AES key expansion. In: Lee, P.J., Lim, C.H. (eds.) ICISC 2002. LNCS, vol. 2587, pp. 343–358. Springer, Heidelberg (2003). https://doi.org/10.1007/3-540-36552-4_24

MV05. McGrew, D.A., Viega, J.: The Galois/Counter Mode of operation (GCM) (2005). http://csrc.nist.gov/groups/ST/toolkit/BCM/documents/gcm-revised-spec.pdf

NIS19. NIST: Lightweight cryptography (2019). https://csrc.nist.gov/projects/lightweight-cryptography

OUHA18. Oshida, H., Ueno, R., Homma, N., Aoki, T.: On masked Galois-field multiplication for authenticated encryption resistant to side channel analysis. In: Fan, J., Gierlichs, B. (eds.) COSADE 2018. LNCS, vol. 10815, pp. 44–57. Springer, Cham (2018). https://doi.org/10.1007/978-3-319-89641-0_3

PC15. Procter, G., Cid, C.: On weak keys and forgery attacks against polynomial-based MAC schemes. J. Cryptol. **28**(4), 769–795 (2015)

PPM17. Primas, R., Pessl, P., Mangard, S.: Single-trace side-channel attacks on masked lattice-based encryption. In: Fischer, W., Homma, N. (eds.) CHES 2017. LNCS, vol. 10529, pp. 513–533. Springer, Cham (2017). https://doi.org/10.1007/978-3-319-66787-4_25

Res18. Rescorla, E.: The Transport Layer Security (TLS) protocol version 1.3. Internet Engineering Task Force (IETF), RFC 8446, October 2018. https://datatracker.ietf.org/doc/rfc8446/

RS09. Renauld, M., Standaert, F.-X.: Algebraic side-channel attacks. In: Bao, F., Yung, M., Lin, D., Jing, J. (eds.) Inscrypt 2009. LNCS, vol. 6151, pp. 393–410. Springer, Heidelberg (2010). https://doi.org/10.1007/978-3-642-16342-5_29

RSVC09. Renauld, M., Standaert, F.-X., Veyrat-Charvillon, N.: Algebraic side-channel attacks on the AES: why time also matters in DPA. In: Clavier, C., Gaj, K. (eds.) CHES 2009. LNCS, vol. 5747, pp. 97–111. Springer, Heidelberg (2009). https://doi.org/10.1007/978-3-642-04138-9_8

Saa11. Saarinen, M.-J.O.: SGCM: The Sophie Germain counter mode. IACR ePrint Archives: Report 2011/326 (2011). https://eprint.iacr.org/2011/326

VCGS14. Veyrat-Charvillon, N., Gérard, B., Standaert, F.-X.: Soft analytical side-channel attacks. In: Sarkar, P., Iwata, T. (eds.) ASIACRYPT 2014. LNCS, vol. 8873, pp. 282–296. Springer, Heidelberg (2014). https://doi.org/10.1007/978-3-662-45611-8_15

WC81. Wegman, M.N., Lawrence Carter, J.: New hash functions and their use in authentication and set equality. J. Comput. Syst. Sci. **22**(3), 265–279 (1981)

Side-Channel Analysis Methodologies

Wavelet Scattering Transform
and Ensemble Methods
for Side-Channel Analysis

Gabriel Destouet[1,2]($\boxtimes$), Cécile Dumas[1], Anne Frassati[1], and Valérie Perrier[2]

[1] Univ. Grenoble Alpes, CEA, LETI, DSYS, CESTI, 38000 Grenoble, France
`{gabriel.destouet,cecile.dumas,anne.frassati}@cea.fr`
[2] Univ. Grenoble Alpes, CNRS, Grenoble INP, LJK, 38000 Grenoble, France
`valerie.perrier@univ-grenoble-alpes.fr`

Abstract. Recent works in side-channel analysis have been fully relying on training classification models to recover sensitive information from traces. However, the knowledge of an attacker or an evaluator is not taken into account and poorly captured by solely training a classifier on signals. This paper proposes to inject prior information in preprocessing and classification in order to increase the performance of side-channel attacks (SCA). First we propose to use the Wavelet Scattering Transform, recently proposed by Mallat, for mapping traces into a time-frequency space which is stable under small translation and diffeomorphism. That way, we address the issues of desynchronization and deformation generally present in signals for SCA. The second part of our paper extends the canonical attacks over byte and Hamming weight by introducing a more general attack. Classifiers are trained on different labelings of the sensitive variable and combined by minimizing a cross-entropy criterion so as to find the best labeling strategy. With these two key ideas, we successfully increase the performance of Template Attacks on artificially desynchronized traces and signals from a jitter-protected implementation.

Keywords: Side-channel analysis · Time-frequency analysis · Wavelet Scattering Transforms · Machine learning · Ensemble methods · Template Attack

1 Introduction

The signal analysis of current consumption and electromagnetic radiations (EM) from electronic components can leak compromising information. A whole research area and an industry have been developed around the task of assessing the security of electronic devices. Since the first attacks, the countermeasures

---

Univ. Grenoble Alpes, CNRS, Grenoble INP—Institute of Engineering Univ. Grenoble Alpes.

G. M. Bertoni and F. Regazzoni (Eds.): COSADE 2020, LNCS 12244, pp. 71–89, 2021.
https://doi.org/10.1007/978-3-030-68773-1_4

and conversely the attacks have been constantly improved in order to cut the leak of sensitive information to potential eavesdropper. In the community of side-channel analysis (SCA), profiled-attacks make use of open-samples so as to derive an optimal strategy to retrieve information on similar devices.

These attacks are critical when cryptographic algorithms are involved. It has been shown with the first Template Attacks [1], known in machine learning as Quadratic Discriminant Analysis (QDA) [2], that cryptographic keys can be recovered by training a QDA on traces acquired during an algorithm execution. From a machine learning perspective, the attacker would like to maximize his chance to retrieve the right cryptographic key, or at least to lower the time-cost of a brute force attack by ordering potential keys according to their likelihood. He would have to choose a classification model that links signals with a sensitive information depending on the key, and to train this classifier on the open-sample with the hope that the model will generalize well on other devices with unknown keys. The training requires a search for parameters of the classifier, e.g. covariances matrices and means in the case of a QDA, or weights for neural networks. This search is usually driven by optimizing a criterion that evaluates the performance of the classifier and can be helped by any prior information about the device (i.e the physical phenomena involved, a leakage model, etc.) which constraints the space of parameters or structurally modifies how the criterion is evaluated.

Given a classification model, we are interested in ways of increasing the performance of attacks by injecting prior information either during preprocessing with time-frequency analyses or during classification.

The main motivation for pushing time-frequency preprocessing is to consider bases of analysis in which traces are represented in terms of elementary signals whose characteristics are closer to emanations from physical phenomena. The usual raw temporal representation from the acquisition phase, i.e the projection of the analogous signal on a dirac basis, is inconsistent with the duration of transients in electric currents. In the case of SCA, we do not know a priori neither what form the signals leaking sensitive information have, nor at which time scales the sensitive variable are manipulated. However we know that the physical processes involved are non-stationary and lasting in time, e.g. the current consumption of a CMOS during a switch. Thus it seems reasonable to analyze signals with a basis of functions which at least respect these properties. Decomposing traces into elementary signals is an intuitive process, it is usually performed in signals realignment by intercorrelating traces with selected patterns. This procedure is a projection on a basis composed of translated versions of these patterns and is a particular case of time-frequency analysis by using a custom basis of functions. But this usually needs a know-how and it becomes difficult to select patterns in deformed and translated traces from jitter-protected implementation.

In order to improve the performance of profiled attacks, most recent works have been comparing different machine learning methods for the classification of traces in SCA but only few of them have considered time-frequency preprocessing. Historically Templates attacks from [1] fit multivariate Gaussian distributions to clusters of fixed temporal points of interest. With the introduction of neural networks, most deep learning based works such as [3–5] presented networks trained on temporal representations, with the exception of the paper [6] in which a convolutional neural network is trained on 2D spectrograms. Other methods such as [7] make use of histograms of amplitudes of temporal points in order to characterize patterns for realignment and attacks. This method requires a correct filtering of signals since the presence of a low frequency noise can produce a shift in histograms and do not take into account deformations of patterns. It has been early shown by [8] that EM signals of various cryptographic implementations can be analyzed (by-hand) in the Fourier domain and differential electromagnetic attacks (DEMA) can be successfully carried with carefully chosen frequency bands. Non-profiled attacks, which usually need a theoretical leakage model so as to replace the profiling phase, have proven efficiency when considering time-frequency representation. The spectrogram representation used in Differential Frequency Analysis in [9–11] transposes Differential Power analysis in the time-frequency domain: these works showed that sensitive information is more easily retrieved by decomposing traces into temporally localized Fourier atoms. Discrete wavelet transform has been used in [12] for compressing traces and improving DPA attacks with synchronized traces. The authors of [13] used it to realign traces with a simulated annealing method. The work of [14] and [15] improved it by providing more efficient methods inspired by speech recognition methods and image analysis. However, the main difficulties with spectrogram and wavelet transform are their instability respectively under small deformation and translation.

The first idea of this paper is to use the wavelet scattering transform by Mallat in [16,17] to tackle these issues. This transform maps signals in a time-frequency space, stable under small time-shifts and deformations. This preprocessing provides an in-depth analysis of signals while being formally established to address these problems.

Side-channel attacks also depend on the classification goal we fixed for the classifier. Generally, it is not clear how a sensitive variable from a cryptographic algorithm leaks into traces and if the classifier is able to recover it.

Most works in SCA usually consider only one specific leakage model, historically the Hamming weight of sensitive variables or the variable itself. However it is known that bits are actually leaking dissymmetrically, suggesting that the leak is of complex nature, for example *Suzuki et al.* in [18] proposed leakage models that consider operations on bits in CMOS logic circuits to explain biases in power consumption. *Schindler et al.* in [19] make a linear regression of the leakage model by assuming that the deterministic part of signals can be approximated by a weighted sum of a basis of functions defined on the algorithm variables. More generally the leakage is an unknown function of the manipulated sensitive variables.

Consequently, the second idea is to act on the goal we fixed for the classifier: we propose to target partitions of the sensitive information in order to find the best strategy of attack. By combining clues retrieved on different partitions, we can reduce the number of likely values and recover the sensitive variable. The attack becomes less dependent to a specific leakage model while giving information about how subsets of values are leaking in traces. This involves combining probabilities from classifiers and refers to Ensemble method [20] in machine learning.

Contribution

First, we propose to use the Wavelet Scattering Transform as preprocessing so as to provide a stable representation for analyzing misaligned and deformed signals, to the best of our knowledge this transform has not been used before in SCA. Then we develop a combination procedure of classifiers trained on partitions of the sensitive variable's values so as to compare and find efficient strategies of attacks.

These two approaches can be used with any type of classifiers, whose relations with traces can be arbitrary complex. We demonstrate that these steps successfully increase the performance of Template Attacks on the ASCAD database and on a jitter-protected SoC.

The paper is organized as follow: in Sect. 2 the problem of profiled side-channel attacks is reminded, the Wavelet Scattering Transform and its properties are introduced for preprocessing traces in SCA in Sect. 3, a combination procedure for finding the leakage model is developed Sect. 4 and finally attack results on ASCAD and traces from jitter-protected SoC are presented in Sect. 5.

2   Problem Statement

A procedure g is computing a sensitive variable Z with a plaintext E and a key K. During its execution, the procedure is leaking signals X, or traces, e.g. EM or current consumption signals. Traces have a finite size noted d, thus $X \in \mathbb{R}^d$. From the perspective of the attacker, all of these variables are considered as random and written uppercase. In the following, calligraphic letters such as $\mathcal{X}$ refers to the set of possible values of the random variable X. Realizations of random variable is noted with lowercase letter, thus x is a realization of X.

The procedure $g(\,.\,,K) : \mathcal{E} \to \mathcal{Z}$ is assumed to be bijective and maps the set of plaintexts $\mathcal{E}$ to the set of sensitive variables $\mathcal{Z}$. A *profiled attack* consists of training a classifier y on signals X to recover Z, which gives clues on K given E. The training requires a set of observations labelized with their associated sensitive variable, we notes $\mathcal{D}_t$ the set of data acquired from the open-sample which consists of tuple $\mathcal{D}_t = \{(x_1, z_1), \dots, (x_{N_t}, z_{N_t})\}$ with N_t being the size of the training set. An attack set $\mathcal{D}_a = \{x_1, \dots, x_{N_a}\}$ of size N_a has a fixed key k^* and allows us to evaluate the performance of the classifier. Here it is assumed that plaintexts are always known, thus for each realization $(x_i, z_i) \in \mathcal{D}_t$ or $x_i \in \mathcal{D}_a$ a plaintext e_i is associated. The classifier y is trained on $\mathcal{D}_t$ in order to have an approximation of $\mathbb{P}(Z|X)$. During an attack, we can get an estimation of the target key k^* with a realization $x_i \in \mathcal{D}_a$:

$$\mathbb{P}(K = k | X = x_i) = \mathbb{P}(Z = g(e_i, k) | X = x_i) \tag{1}$$

However, if the quality of estimations are too poor, one-shot estimation of the key k is in general not enough, i.e given an observation x_i, $k^* \neq \mathrm{argmax}_{\hat{k}}\, \mathbb{P}(K = \hat{k}|X = x_i)$. Thus the attacker has to use many observations to obtain better predictions:

$$\mathbb{P}(K = k|\mathcal{D}_a) = \prod_{i=1}^{N_a} \mathbb{P}(Z = g(e_i, k)|X = x_i) \qquad (2)$$

After sorting $\{\mathbb{P}(K = k_j|\mathcal{D}_a)\}_{k_j \in \mathcal{K}}$ in decreasing order, the rank is defined as the position of $\mathbb{P}(K = k^*|\mathcal{D}_a)$ in the sorted list $\mathbb{P}(K = k_i|\mathcal{D}_a) > ... > \mathbb{P}(K = k_j|\mathcal{D}_a)$. In the following, the guessing entropy [21] is estimated by taking the empirical mean of rank values obtained for many attacks. Note that the less attack data N_a is required to have a low rank, the better is the attack.

The attack involves the task of estimating the posterior $\mathbb{P}(Z|X)$ or the likelihood $\mathbb{P}(X|Z)$ from the data. It requires a preprocessing of the observed traces X and a statistical learning algorithm to learn $\mathbb{P}(Z|X)$.

3 Time-Frequency Analysis with the Wavelet Scattering Transform

In this section, we will present common Time-Frequency transformations used for preprocessing traces in SCA, their limits in the case of deformed and misaligned signals, and we will introduce the Wavelet Scattering Transform of Mallat [16,17]. In the following, we assume that the attacker acquired traces in the form of vectors $x \in \mathbb{R}^d$, where d is the number of temporal points.

3.1 Some Time-Frequency Representations

Analysis in a Dirac Basis (i.e the Raw Temporal Representation). The sampled trace x from the analogous signal x_a, $x(p) = x_a(pT)$ with T the sampling period, can be represented as follow, for each time index p we have:

$$x(p) = \int x_a(t)\delta(t - pT)dt \qquad (3)$$

This is the projection of x_a on a Dirac basis $\{\delta_{pT}\}_{0 \leq p \leq d-1}$. The continuous approximation $\tilde{x}$ of x_a can be represented as a sum of weighted Dirac functions:

$$\tilde{x} = \sum_p x(p)\delta_{pT} \qquad (4)$$

This approximation is completely characterized by $\{x(p)\}_{0 \leq p \leq d-1}$ which are assumed to be infinitely concentrated at time pT where $F_s = 1/T$ is the sampling rate. In the following, we equivalently use either the continuous form $\tilde{x}$ or the vector x to formulate Time-Frequency transformations.

Discrete Fourier Transform. With the canonical inner product on $\mathbb{C}^d$, the Discrete Fourier Transform is the projection on periodic signals $\{e^{2i\pi k/d}\}_{0 \le k \le d-1}$ and reverses the analysis made in a Dirac basis, i.e instead of considering x as a sum of time-concentrated signals, the discrete Fourier Transform interprets x as being composed of periodic signals with an infinitely small frequency bandwidth. If we note $\hat{x}$ the Discrete Fourier Transform of x we have for each time index p and frequency k:

$$\hat{x}(k) = (x|e^{2i\pi k/d}) = \sum_p x(p)e^{-2i\pi kp/d} \tag{5}$$

$$x(p) = \frac{1}{d}\sum_k (x|e^{2i\pi k/d})e^{2i\pi kp/d} = \frac{1}{d}\sum_k \hat{x}(k)e^{2i\pi kp/d} \tag{6}$$

Dirac and Fourier bases interpret x as being composed of signals concentrated respectively in time and in frequency. However, the sensitive information in SCA's traces are contained in transient patterns, which are not well captured by these two transforms. Thus we would like to use this prior knowledge and to interpret x with elementary signals of finite duration and frequency bandwidth.

Short Time Fourier Transform. Time-frequency representations such as the short-time Fourier transform (STFT) analyze signals with a basis $\{w_m e^{2i\pi p/d}\}_{m,p}$ composed of modulated versions of a window function $w_m(n) = w(n-m)$, where n is the time index and m a translation coefficient. The temporal scale and the frequency bandwidth of the window function w give the precision of analysis in the time-frequency space. It concentrates the signal energy into time-frequency boxes of fix area $a(t,f) = \sigma_t \sigma_f$ where σ_t and σ_f are the temporal and frequency supports of w and remain constant (see Fig. 2). Gabor transforms [22] optimize the concentration of the signal energy into time-frequency boxes by using Gaussian windows.

Wavelet Transform. The basis used in Wavelet Transform (WT) $\{\psi_{u,s}\}_{u,s}$ is composed of scaled and translated versions $\psi_{u,s}(t) = \frac{1}{\sqrt{s}}\psi(\frac{t-u}{s})$ of a mother wavelet ψ, where respectively u and s are translation and dilation coefficients. In order to compute the projection over all translation coefficients u and for a given dilation coefficient s, the signal $\tilde{x}$ is convoluted with $\psi_s = \frac{1}{\sqrt{s}}\psi(\frac{t}{s})$. To facilitate notation, we formulate the projection on the continuous approximation $\tilde{x}$:

$$(\tilde{x}|\psi_{u,s}) = \int \tilde{x}(t)\frac{1}{\sqrt{s}}\psi^*(\frac{t-u}{s})dt = \tilde{x} * \overline{\psi_s}(u) \tag{7}$$

where x^* is the complex conjugate of x, $\overline{x}(t) = x^*(-t)$, $*$ is the convolutional operator and the inner product is defined on $\mathbf{L}^2(\mathbb{C})$. In order to pave the time-frequency plane, the dilation coefficient has to be varied and is usually sampled on a dyadic scale $s = 2^{-j}$ with $j \in \mathbb{N}$. If we note f_0 the center frequency of the mother wavelet, the center frequency of its j-th dilated version is approximately at $f_0/2^j$. This is due to the scaling property of the Fourier Transform:

$$\mathcal{FT}(\psi_s)(f) = \sqrt{s}\mathcal{FT}(\psi)(sf) \qquad (8)$$

where $\mathcal{FT}$ is the Fourier Transform. When changing the dilation coefficient s the bandwidth σ_f inversely varies with the temporal support σ_t, thus allowing variations of the shape of the area $a(t,f) = \sigma_t(t)\sigma_f(f)$ across the time-frequency plane.

Translation Invariance and Stability Under Diffeomorphism. In the case of SCA, where a device can produce distorted traces and misalignment due to countermeasures such as jitter effects, we claim that a good representation Φx of the traces x should be stable under small translation and deformation.

Let x_1, x_2 be two acquired traces, we say that x_1 is a *deformed* version of x_2 if there exists a diffeomorphism $\tau(t)$ (an invertible transformation) such that $x_1(t) = x_2(\tau(t))$.

A practical example in SCA is given Fig. 1 where two patterns from EM signals are plotted. Although both signals contain the same cryptographic information, we notice a translation of the temporal and frequency structures. In fact, the transformations presented above are unstable for temporal translation $\delta_\tau > \sigma_t/2$ and frequency variation $\delta_f > \sigma_f/2$, where σ_t and σ_f are respectively the temporal and frequency widths covered by an element of a basis. In Fig. 2, we have illustrated the time-frequency space coverage of the bases used in WT and STFT. WT is robust to small deformations but not translation invariant, while the spectrogram is translation invariant but not stable by deformations.

Identifying a diffeomorphism between traces is a difficult task and we better find an operator Φ that makes the two signals "collide" in the sense that $\Phi x \approx \Phi L_\tau x$ where L_τ denotes the deformation operator induced by the diffeomorphism τ. According to [16], the operator Φ should be designed with respect to the two following properties:

- Φ is *translation invariant*, i.e for $c \in \mathbb{R}$ and $L_c x(t) = x(t - c)$:

$$\Phi x = \Phi L_c x$$

- Moreover, Φ is *stable by diffeomorphism*, i.e it is Lipschitz continuous to the action of a C^2-diffeomorphism τ. For $\tau \in \mathcal{C}^2(\mathbb{R})$, $L_\tau x(t) = x(t - \tau(t))$ and $C \in \mathbb{R}^+$:

$$\|\Phi x - \Phi L_\tau x\| \leq C\|x\|(\ \|\frac{\partial\tau}{\partial t}\|_\infty + \|\frac{\partial^2\tau}{\partial t^2}\|_\infty\ ) \qquad (9)$$

Wavelet Scattering transforms proposed in [16] provide these useful mathematical properties we claim relevant to analyze signals in SCA, it will be extensively used in our experiments and are presented hereafter.

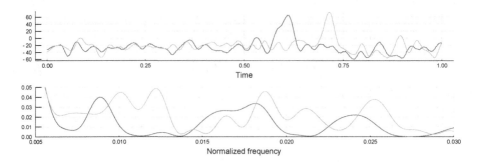

Fig. 1. Jitter effect and deformation taken from Jit signals (see Sect. 5.2). Two temporal patterns are plotted on the top with their associated Fourier Transform on the bottom. The deformation between these patterns is characterized here by a frequency shift of some components (e.g. at frequency = 0.026) in the Fourier spectrum.

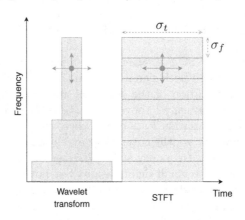

Fig. 2. Illustration of WT and STFT, the black spot is the frequency component we would like to capture. Under the action of translation the spot moves horizontally and under small dilation it moves vertically. Each box is a time-frequency area sized by each elementary signal of the transform.

3.2 The Wavelet Scattering Transform

In order to have such properties, Mallat proposes in [16,17] cascading continuous wavelet transforms defined here in continuous form with $x \in \mathbf{L}^2(\mathbb{R})$, $\psi \in \mathbf{L}^2(\mathbb{C})$ by:

$$W[\lambda]x(u) = x * \overline{\psi_\lambda} = \int x(t)\frac{1}{\sqrt{\lambda}}\psi^*(\frac{u-t}{\lambda})dt \qquad (10)$$

where $*$ is the convolutional operator and ψ is a mother wavelet (a zero mean function). Each wavelet ψ_λ parametrized with scales λ is followed by a non-linear operation $|.|$ and averaged on a time domain of 2^J samples with $A_J x = x * \phi_{2^J}$. The windowed scattering transform S_J of a signal x over a path $p = (\lambda_1, ..., \lambda_m)$ with $\lambda_i > 2^{-J}$ is defined by:

$$S_J[p]x = |||x * \psi_{\lambda_1}| * \psi_{\lambda_2}|... * \psi_{\lambda_m}| * \phi_{2^J}$$
$$= |W[\lambda_m]| ... |W[\lambda_2]| |W[\lambda_1]x||| * \phi_{2^J}$$
$$= A_J |W[\lambda_m]| ... |W[\lambda_2]| |W[\lambda_1]x|||$$
$$= A_J U[\lambda_m] ... U[\lambda_2]U[\lambda_1]x \qquad (11)$$

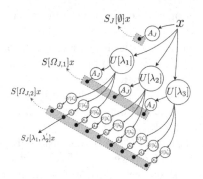

Fig. 3. A two-level wavelet scattering transform

With $U[\lambda]x = |W[\lambda]x| = |x * \psi_\lambda|$ and $A_J x = x * \phi_{2^J}$. In practice the windowed scattering transform is calculated on a path subset $\Omega_{J,m}$ for which a maximum length m of paths $p \in \Omega_{J,m}$ is set and with scales $\lambda > 2^{-J}$, meaning that the Wavelet Transform only captures frequencies superior than 2^{-J} and the remaining spectral energy will be captured by ϕ_{2^J}. An example of scattering is displayed on Fig. 3.

While wavelet transforms provide stability under the action of small diffeomorphism, the nonlinear operation and the integration over time give translation invariance. Cascading wavelet transforms allows to recover high frequencies lost when averaging the absolute values of coefficients of previous wavelet transforms.

Depending on the spectral richness of signals we use wavelets on dyadic scales $2^{-j}, 0 \le j < J$ or on intermediate scales $2^{-j/Q}, 0 \le j < JQ$ where Q defines the number of wavelets used by octave of frequencies. In the following, the Wavelet Scattering Transform are implemented with the python software proposed in [23]. Morlet wavelets are used for the first and second levels, and the whole transform is characterized by three parameters: the scale 2^J of averaging $J \ge 2, J \in \mathbb{N}$, the number of wavelets by octave $Q \ge 1, Q \in \mathbb{N}$ and the number of levels of the scattering transform $m \in \{1, 2\}$. To tune such parameters, we propose the following rules of thumb: choose J proportionally with the amount of translation (i.e jitter) present in signals, Q in proportion to the desired discrimination at high frequency. If J is set too high, a second level $m=2$ is required to retrieve the information lost.

4 A Combination Procedure for Ensemble Methods in SCA

For the task of classification in SCA, one label is usually considered to provide an estimation of a sensitive variable Z. Here we focus on the space of targeted class values with multiple classifiers trained on L different labelings $\{C_l\}_{1 \le l \le L}$, each labeling giving clues on the sensitive variable z with a probability $\mathbb{P}(Z = z | C_l = c_l)$.

Classification of the sensitive variables considered in SCA lends itself well to partition our target space $Z \in \mathcal{Z}$ in complementary regions. We denote β_l the partition function that associates each z to a label $c_l \in \mathcal{C}_l$, such that $\beta_l(z) = c_l$ and $\boldsymbol{\beta}(z) = (c_1, ..., c_L) = \boldsymbol{c} \in \mathcal{C}$. For example, if z is the byte 0x12 and $\boldsymbol{\beta}$ is composed of labelings respectively over $\mathbb{Z}_8$, Hamming weight and the first big-endian bit value, then $\boldsymbol{\beta}(0x12) = (0x12, 2, 0)$.

Here we consider the labelings C_l to be conditionally independent and note Θ the global classifier over all C_l we have: $\mathbb{P}(C = \boldsymbol{c} | X = x, \Theta) = \prod_l \mathbb{P}(C_l = c_l | X = x, \Theta)$. For clarity's sake, we will drop the notation for the conditional dependence over the model and keep a simplified notation $\mathbb{P}(C = \boldsymbol{c} | X = x)$ instead of $\mathbb{P}(C = \boldsymbol{c} | X = x, \Theta)$.

We assume here that $\boldsymbol{\beta}$ is bijective. Given a signal x, an estimation for z is given by:

$$\log(\mathbb{P}(Z = z | X = x)) = \log(\mathbb{P}(C = \boldsymbol{\beta}(z) | X = x)) \tag{12}$$

$$= \sum_l \log \mathbb{P}(C_l = \beta_l(z) | X = x)) \tag{13}$$

A set of L classifiers $\{y_1, \ldots, y_L\}$ are trained accordingly to partitions β_l and give predictions $\mathbb{P}(C_l = \beta_l(z) | X = x)$. Once each classifier is trained, their predictions can be naively summed, in which case a *soft voting* (SV) is performed; or a classifier-specific weight can be applied to each classifier depending on its performance, that is a *weighted soft voting* (WSV). Remark that SV is a particular case of WSV where weights are all equal. If we note $y_l(z, x) = \log(\mathbb{P}(C_l = \beta_l(z) | X = x))$ the vote accorded to the classifier l for the value z of Z, and $y(z, x) = \sum_l w_l y_l(z, x)$ the weighted vote with $w_l \in \mathbb{R}$. We can iteratively find a weight vector $\boldsymbol{w} \in \mathbb{R}^L$ such that the following cross-entropy loss is minimized:

$$L_{\text{wsv}}(X, Z) = -\frac{1}{N_t} \sum_{(x_i, z_i) \in \mathcal{D}_t} \mathbb{P}(Z = z_i) y(z_i, x_i) \tag{14}$$

$$= -\frac{1}{N_t} \sum_{(x_i, z_i) \in \mathcal{D}_t} \sum_l w_l \mathbb{P}(Z = z_i) \log(\mathbb{P}(C_l = \beta_l(z_i) | x = x_i)) \tag{15}$$

To illustrate our approach, we consider the case where signals x are Gaussian distributed with the same covariance matrix. This is equivalent to choosing Linear Discriminant Analysis as classifiers [2], we have:

$$y_l(z, x) = \log(\frac{1}{R} e^{(x - \mu_l(z))^t \Sigma(x - \mu_l(z))})$$

With R the normalization factor, $\mu_l(z)$ the mean value of signals for the labeling l and the label value z, and Σ the inverse covariance matrix. We assume a balanced dataset, i.e $\mathbb{P}(Z=z_i) = p$ is constant, and constraint weights such that $\sum_l w_l = 1$, we get:

$$L_{\text{wsv}}(X, Z) = -\frac{p}{N_t} \sum_{(x_i,z_i) \in \mathcal{D}} \sum_l w_l \left((x_i - \mu_l(z_i))^t \Sigma(x_i - \mu_l(z_i)) - \log(R)\right) \quad (16)$$

$$= -\frac{p}{N_t} \sum_{(x_i,z_i) \in \mathcal{D}} \left((x_i - \mu^*(z_i))^t \Sigma(x_i - \mu^*(z_i)) + c_\mu(z_i) - \log(R)\right) \quad (17)$$

$$\propto \log\left(\prod_{(x_i,z_i) \in \mathcal{D}} \frac{1}{R} e^{(-(x_i - \mu^*(z_i))^t \Sigma(x_i - \mu^*(z_i)))} \right) \quad (18)$$

where $\mu^* = \sum_l w_l \mu_l$ and $c_\mu = \sum_l w_l \mu_l^t \Sigma \mu_l - \sum_{l,k} w_l w_k \mu_l^t \Sigma \mu_k$ that depends on estimated means μ_l, on weights w_l and on the inverse covariance matrix Σ. In the Gaussian distributed case with a fixed covariance matrix, we can see that the minimization of $L_{\text{wsv}}(X, Z)$ is equivalent to minimizing $(x_i - \sum_l w_l \mu_l(z_i))^t \Sigma(x_i - \sum_l w_l \mu_l(z_i))$ which is a simple linear regression with parameters w.

Our combination procedure can be seen as a generalization of the Linear Regression Analysis of *Schindler et al.* [19] where no assumption is made on the linearity of the leakage model. Arbitrary complex classifiers can be used to draw relations between signals and labels and the relevance of such relation can be evaluated by minimizing the cross-entropy criterion, i.e classifiers with the highest weights are the most relevant. To obtain the overall estimation, log probabilities are linearly summed according to a simple Bayes rule, in case classifiers output scores, a logistic regression layer [2] can be added and trained to get probabilities.

As remarked Zhou in [20, Chap 4.3.5.2] the global score obtained after minimization can be worse than considering the best classifier in the model. This procedure is interesting when no knowledge about the leakage model is available and can be iteratively improved by removing bad classifiers, i.e when their weights are too low.

In practice, classifiers are individually trained on their associated labeling C_l and their predictions are combined after minimizing (15) with the weight vector w.

5   Experiments

In this section, we integrate the two previous methods presented Sects. 3 and 4 to perform attacks on desynchronized traces from ASCAD and signals from jitter-protected SoC. Attack results are compared with other preprocessings: raw temporal signals and spectrogram of traces. We also study the effect of optimizing the weights of the combination procedure (15) on attack results.

5.1   Method Used

We propose the method displayed on Fig. 4. First, traces are preprocessed with
the Wavelet Scattering Transform (WST), then a PCA is applied to reduce the
dimension and finally QDA classifiers trained on predefined labelings C_l outputs
predictions which are merged with a Weighted Soft Voting (WSV) (15).

The set of classifiers is trained on canonical partitions, i.e identity on z,
Hamming weight and bit values:

$$\{\text{Id} : z \to z, \ \text{HW} : z \to \text{HW}(z), \ \text{Bit}_i : z \to (z \gg i) \ \& \ 1 \ \forall i \in \{0, 1, \ldots, 7\}\}$$

The optimal weights of the combination procedure are found by iterating a
state of the art gradient descent algorithm AMSGrad [24].

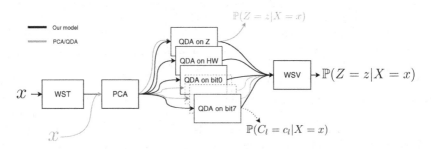

Fig. 4. Illustration of the global method in black with the Wavelet Scattering Transform (WST) and the Weighted Soft Voting (WSV) from Sects. 3 and 4. We also depicted
in green a standard Template Attack with PCA. We replace the WST with the modulus
of a Short-Time Fourier Transform (see Sect. 3.1) when comparing with Spectrogram
preprocessing.

5.2   Datasets

The ASCAD dataset [5] is composed of EM traces emitted from a device running
a masked AES implementation, an artificial jitter is simulated by randomly
translating traces with an uniformly distributed random variable $\delta_N \sim \mathcal{U}\{0, N\}$.
Three sets of traces are available, the first one ASCAD_0 is composed of aligned
traces while ASCAD_{50} and ASCAD_{100} are desynchronized respectively with δ_{50}
and δ_{100}. We tested our model on all three sets but for purpose of clarity we
present results with δ_{100} and δ_0. The targets are the outputs of the third SBox
processing of the first round of AES. Each set consists of $60,000$ traces of 700
points.

The second dataset noted Jit is composed of traces acquired from an AES
hardware implementation on a modern secure smartcard with a strong jitter.
The Sboxes are processed sequentially and all traces start with the processing of
the first byte while the rest of the SBox processing is misaligned. In total $160,000$
traces of $8,192$ points were acquired, $150,000$ (or $75,000$) traces have random

keys and are used for the training set. 10,000 traces with a fix key are used for the attack set. The targets are the output from the second SBox processing. An example of deformations and translation in Jit signals is displayed on Fig. 1.

5.3   Choosing the Parameters

Hyperparameters for the preprocessing with Wavelet Scattering Transform and Spectrogram are chosen accordingly to the dataset and attack results.

For ASCAD, we used 54,000 traces for the training set and 6,000 traces for the attack set. For the scattering transform, traces are first upsampled to 1,024 points, we fixed $Q = 1$ since a fine resolution between high frequency bands is not required. We obtained good results with time scales $J = 3$ and $J = 7$, and limited the scattering transform to one layer $m = 1$. For Spectrogram preprocessing, traces are also upsampled to 1,024. The best result in terms of guessing entropy is obtained with a sliding window of 128 points which corresponds to a time scale of 88 in the original traces, the overlap was set to 64.

For Jit, we considered a restrained dataset of 75,000 traces since spectrogram and raw representation had too many features to fit the whole dataset in memory and to perform the PCA based dimension reduction. We managed to fit traces preprocessed with WST in memory when considering the whole training set of size 150,000. For WST, we expected the Jit dataset to have a strong jitter so we set the following parameters $J = 10$, $Q = 8$, $m = 2$ which gave preprocessed traces of size 2,992. For spectrogram, we used a sliding window of size 1,024 with an overlap of 512 which gave spectrogram of 7,680 features.

For each dataset we limited the PCA to 50 components which corresponds to the number of components used for SoA template attack combined with a PCA on aligned temporal traces. When minimizing the loss function (15), we stopped the gradient descent after 200 iterations.

5.4   Results

In order to evaluate our model, we performed our attack on 3 folds. For each fold an intermediate guessing entropy (GE) measure [21] is calculated by averaging 100 rank curves obtained by shuffling the order of traces in Eq. (2). The final guessing entropy is obtained by averaging the guessing entropy of the three folds.

In the following we use the following notations: SV and WSV (15) when respectively a soft voting and weighted soft voting is applied with all the classifiers, SumBits a soft voting with the classifiers on bits, Z when considering only the classification on the byte and HW with the hamming weight. "Temp", "Spec" and "Scat" respectively denote the raw temporal representation, the Spectrogram preprocessing and the Wavelet Scattering Transform. Attack results on SumBits, Z, HW and SV are used to characterize the performance of each preprocessing. The rank gap between SV and WSV indicates the efficiency of the combination procedure (15) for merging prediction of differently performing classifiers. We displayed on Table 1, the weights obtained after optimizing the WSV and the number of attack traces required to have a guessing entropy of 40 (NGE_{40}) when considering classifier individually (Z and HW), with SumBits, SV and WSV.

Results for ASCAD are displayed Fig. 5 and on Table 1. When no desynchronization is present, preprocessings with a small time scale of analysis perform the best: attack results on SumBits are almost identical when considering WST with $J = 3$, spectrograms and raw temporal traces; the same WST performs slightly better for Z and SV. Intriguingly the effect of desynchronization on attack results in ASCAD_{100} strongly varies with labelings. The large scale WST with $J = 7$ performs the best on Z and SV and shows its robustness to desynchronization; the attack on SumBits is better with spectograms and might be due to the overlap between frames of analysis. The combination procedure resulted differently: it decreased the rank of SV of $2,000$ with spectograms preprocessing and of only 5 with WST. Globally, as expected the WSV is better than SV and makes all models converge to rank 1 except for temporal attacks on ASCAD_{100}.

In presence of a strong jitter and deformations in Jit, spectrogram and temporal attacks indubitably fail for any classifier while preprocessing with WST provides better attack results and becomes possible on SumBits (see Fig. 6 and Table 1). On Jit, the WSV performed well and decreased the rank of SV for WST of approximately $1,600$.

The weights of the WSV seem to be correlated with the guessing entropy of classifiers, e.g. when considering temporal attacks we see that weights on bits are higher than weights on H or Z. On ASCAD, the weights for the WST seem to be more distributed among classifiers and could explain why the weighted soft voting did not converged as well as for Spectrogram preprocessing where the classifier over Z was heavily penalized. In other words, the iterative optimization of WSV seems to be facilitated with classifiers of unbalanced performance. We also notice the fact that bits are leaking dissymmetrically as proposed by *Suzuki et al.* in [18], e.g. on ASCAD the classifier on bit0 has a higher weight than the average on bits (SumBits), while on Jit the weight on bit7 is higher when considering successful models (Scattering with Jit 75k and 150k).

From our results on these datasets and given QDAs as classification models, Z and HW leakage models are globally disadvantaged when looking at the guessing entropy and the weights associated. The WSV has approximated a leakage model that relies more on individual bits. The difference of performance between Sumbits, Z and HW is also explained by the number of samples required to estimate the parameters of QDAs, which makes attacks on individual bits more stable since less parameters are required. Thus a trade-off has to be made on the number of components for the PCA: while a high number of components increases the number of parameters to estimate, the attack results can be improved by selecting more eigenvectors with lower eigenvalues and better discriminating power.

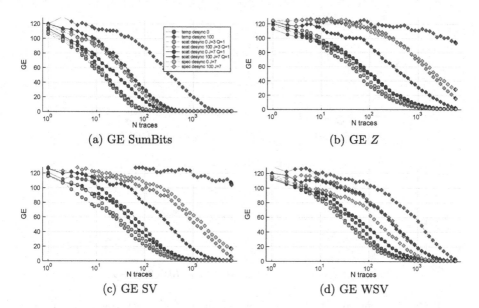

Fig. 5. Guessing entropy as a function of the number of attack traces on ASCAD with classifiers trained on Z, SumBits, with naive combination of prediction (SV) and with WSV.

5.5 Visualizing Leakages

We previously showed results in terms of guessing entropy. Now, one could wonder how does the leakage look like in traces from the point of view of the QDA classifiers. We propose here an easy computation of a SNR score on the preprocessed traces by taking into account the covariances and means estimated during training. It is also possible to compute a SNR score without considering classifiers with an analysis of variance (ANOVA). For each classifier l we compute a SNR score in the subspace induced by the PCA with a projection $P \in \mathbb{R}^{d \times p}$, where p is the number of components chosen for the PCA and d is the original dimension.[1] Each QDA classifier is defined by means $\mu_{l,i} \in \mathbb{R}^p$ and covariances matrices $\Sigma_{l,i} \in \mathbb{R}^{p \times p}$ for each label values $c_{l,i}$, $\forall i$. We note $\mathrm{SNR}_l^s \in \mathbb{R}^p$ and $\mathrm{SNR}_l^o \in \mathbb{R}^d$ respectively the SNR in the subspace and in the original space before the PCA, we have:

$$\mathrm{SNR}_l^s[r] = \frac{\mathrm{Var}_i\left[\mu_{l,i}[r]\right]}{\mathbb{E}_i\left[\mathrm{Diag}(\Sigma_{l,i})[r]\right]} \quad , \quad r = 1, \ldots, p$$

$$\mathrm{SNR}_l^o = (P\,\mathrm{SNR}_l^s).\hat{} 2 \tag{19}$$

where $.\hat{}$ defines the entry-wise power. This score (19) gives some indication on the temporal and frequency aspects of the leakage. We computed some visual-

---

[1] After preprocessing, wavelet scattering transform and spectrogram representations are vectorized before the PCA.

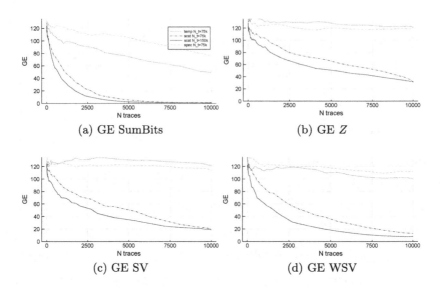

(a) GE SumBits   (b) GE Z

(c) GE SV   (d) GE WSV

Fig. 6. Guessing entropy as a function of the number of attack traces on Jit with classifiers for Z, SumBits, with naive combination of prediction (SV) and with WSV. N_t is the number of traces used for training.

Table 1. For each preprocessing: number of traces for a guessing entropy of 40 (NGE_{40}) when considering individual classifiers with labeling over Z and H, with a soft voting over bits noted SumBits, with a overall Soft Voting SV and finally with a Weighted Soft Voting. We also indicated the weights of the classifiers obtained after optimizing the WSV for classifiers over Z, H, some individual bits and their average for SumBits. For ASCAD_{100}: we displayed the results obtained with a WST with J = 7 and Q = 1. For Jit: results with training on 75,000 and 150,000 traces.

Dataset	Preprocessing		Z	H	Bit0	Bit4	Bit7	SumBits	SV	WSV
ASCAD$_{100}$	Temp	w	<0.01	<0.01	0.29	0.18	0.19	0.19		
		NGE$_{40}$	∞	∞	–	–	–	485	∞	1465
	Spec	w	0.02	0.22	0.39	0.31	0.32	0.31		
		NGE$_{40}$	3527	3392	–	–	–	**57**	2126	**242**
	Scat	w	0.29	0.15	0.32	0.23	0.21	0.20		
		NGE$_{40}$	**676**	**675**	–	–	–	70	**428**	423
Jit 75k	Temp	w	<0.01	0.15	0.34	0.43	0.34	0.39		
		NGE$_{40}$	∞	∞	–	–	–	∞	∞	∞
	Spec	w	0.08	0.17	0.20	0.27	0.25	0.24		
		NGE$_{40}$	∞	∞	–	–	–	∞	∞	∞
	Scat	w	0.19	0.18	0.42	0.48	0.48	0.47		
		NGE$_{40}$	9371	8851	–	–	–	1561	6102	4513
Jit 150k	Scat	w	0.11	0.12	0.41	0.41	0.48	0.45		
		NGE$_{40}$	**7837**	**8023**	–	–	–	**884**	**3770**	**2149**

izations of this score for attacks on Jit respectively in Fig. 7. Remark that these analyses can be perturbed by the subspace induced by the PCA's eigenvectors. When the SNR is high we suppose that it gives some indication about how signals are leaking information. For SumBits we summed the SNR scores.

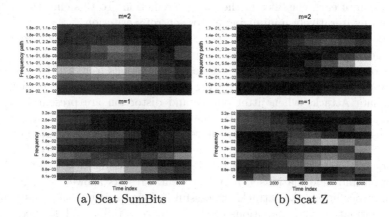

(a) Scat SumBits   (b) Scat Z

Fig. 7. Leakage visualization on Jit. On top the second level of the WST. Below the first level of the WST. We selected the top 10 frequency bands (and frequency paths for the second level) that contains the highest values of SNR. Amplitudes are scaled between 0 and 1.

On Jit Fig. 7, the SNR visualization with the scattering transform positions the leakage around time index 2,000 when considering SumBits and Z. The two-level scattering transform has proven useful, the SNR score indicates for bits that the frequency band 1.0e-01 is leaking. For Z the 1.1e0-1 frequency path gives clues about a leakage around time index 8,000, which is also shown but more discretely at the first level for z or for both level with SumBits.

6 Conclusion

Independently of choosing a classification model, we proposed two ways of injecting prior information in preprocessing and classification in order to easily increase the performance of SCA.

First, we address the problem of desynchronization and deformation generally encountered in side-channel analysis by using Wavelet Scattering Transform as a preprocessing step. This transform maps traces in a time-frequency space stable under translation and small deformation. In contrast with other time-frequency representations, such as Spectrogram and Wavelet Transform, it provides robust representations which are easily implemented and configured according to jitter effects present in traces and their spectral richness.

Secondly, based on the fact that in general the leakage model is an unknown function of the sensitive variable, we proposed a way of resolving this by considering various labelings of the sensitive variable. For that, we train classifiers on different partitions of the sensitive variable's values and combine their predictions. Our combination method involves finding a weight vector which assesses the contribution of each classifier in the global prediction. To this end, the weights are found by iteratively minimizing a cross-entropy criterion.

These two propositions have been evaluated by integrating them in a new attack method, which successfully increased the performance of Template Attacks on artificially desynchronized traces and signals from a jitter-protected implementation. The wavelet scattering transform improves the performance of Template Attacks when jitter effects and distortion are present in traces. Although, we restricted ourself to Template Attacks as classification models, this preprocessing could be particularly interesting when followed by more complex classifiers, e.g. a convolutional neural network. We argue that it could reduce the amount of data required to normally make any classifier robust under small translation and deformations. The experimental results showed that the combination procedure makes attacks successful as long as some classifiers manage to get information from partitions of the sensitive variable. While specifying a fixed leakage model constraints the classifier to a given goal, the proposed combination procedure allows an attacker to test various leakage models and quickly evaluate which ones he should focus on.

References

1. Chari, S., Rao, J.R., Rohatgi, P.: Template attacks. In: Kaliski, B.S., Koç, K., Paar, C. (eds.) CHES 2002. LNCS, vol. 2523, pp. 13–28. Springer, Heidelberg (2003). https://doi.org/10.1007/3-540-36400-5_3
2. Hastie, T., Tibshirani, R., Friedman, J.: The Elements of Statistical Learning. SSS. Springer, New York (2009). https://doi.org/10.1007/978-0-387-84858-7
3. Maghrebi, H., Portigliatti, T., Prouff, E.: Breaking cryptographic implementations using deep learning techniques. In: Carlet, C., Hasan, M.A., Saraswat, V. (eds.) SPACE 2016. LNCS, vol. 10076, pp. 3–26. Springer, Cham (2016). https://doi.org/10.1007/978-3-319-49445-6_1
4. Cagli, E., Dumas, C., Prouff, E.: Convolutional neural networks with data augmentation against jitter-based countermeasures. In: Fischer, W., Homma, N. (eds.) CHES 2017. LNCS, vol. 10529, pp. 45–68. Springer, Cham (2017). https://doi.org/10.1007/978-3-319-66787-4_3
5. Prouff, E., Strullu, R., Benadjila, R., Cagli, E., Dumas, C.: Study of deep learning techniques for side-channel analysis and introduction to ASCAD database. Cryptology ePrint Archive, Report 2018/053 (2018)
6. Yang, G., Li, H., Ming, J., Zhou, Y.: Convolutional neural network based side-channel attacks in time-frequency representations. In: Bilgin, B., Fischer, J.-B. (eds.) CARDIS 2018. LNCS, vol. 11389, pp. 1–17. Springer, Cham (2019). https://doi.org/10.1007/978-3-030-15462-2_1

7. Thiebeauld, H., Gagnerot, G., Wurcker, A., Clavier, C.: SCATTER: a new dimension in side-channel. In: Fan, J., Gierlichs, B. (eds.) COSADE 2018. LNCS, vol. 10815, pp. 135–152. Springer, Cham (2018). https://doi.org/10.1007/978-3-319-89641-0_8

8. Agrawal, D., Archambeault, B., Rao, J.R., Rohatgi, P.: The EM side—channel(s). In: Kaliski, B.S., Koç, K., Paar, C. (eds.) CHES 2002. LNCS, vol. 2523, pp. 29–45. Springer, Heidelberg (2003). https://doi.org/10.1007/3-540-36400-5_4

9. Plos, T., Hutter, M., Feldhofer, M.: Evaluation of side-channel preprocessing techniques on cryptographic-enabled HF and UHF RFID-tag prototypes. In: Workshop on RFID Security, pp. 114–127 (2008)

10. Gebotys, C.H., Ho, S., Tiu, C.C.: EM analysis of Rijndael and ECC on a wireless Java-based PDA. In: Rao, J.R., Sunar, B. (eds.) CHES 2005. LNCS, vol. 3659, pp. 250–264. Springer, Heidelberg (2005). https://doi.org/10.1007/11545262_19

11. Belgarric, P., et al.: Time-frequency analysis for second-order attacks. In: Francillon, A., Rohatgi, P. (eds.) CARDIS 2013. LNCS, vol. 8419, pp. 108–122. Springer, Cham (2014). https://doi.org/10.1007/978-3-319-08302-5_8

12. Debande, N., Souissi, Y., Aabid, M.A.E., Guilley, S., Danger, J.: Wavelet transform based pre-processing for side channel analysis. In: 2012 45th Annual IEEE/ACM International Symposium on Microarchitecture Workshops, pp. 32–38 (2012)

13. Charvet, X., Pelletier, H.: Improving the DPA attack using wavelet transform. In: NIST Physical Security Testing Workshop, vol. 46 (2005)

14. van Woudenberg, J.G.J., Witteman, M.F., Bakker, B.: Improving differential power analysis by elastic alignment. In: Kiayias, A. (ed.) CT-RSA 2011. LNCS, vol. 6558, pp. 104–119. Springer, Heidelberg (2011). https://doi.org/10.1007/978-3-642-19074-2_8

15. Muijrers, R.A., van Woudenberg, J.G.J., Batina, L.: RAM: rapid alignment method. In: Prouff, E. (ed.) CARDIS 2011. LNCS, vol. 7079, pp. 266–282. Springer, Heidelberg (2011). https://doi.org/10.1007/978-3-642-27257-8_17

16. Mallat, S.: Group invariant scattering. Commun. Pure Appl. Math. **65**(10), 1331–1398 (2012)

17. Andén, J., Mallat, S.: Deep scattering spectrum. IEEE Trans. Signal Process. **62**(16), 4114–4128 (2014)

18. Suzuki, D., Saeki, M., Ichikawa, T.: DPA leakage models for CMOS logic circuits. In: Rao, J.R., Sunar, B. (eds.) CHES 2005. LNCS, vol. 3659, pp. 366–382. Springer, Heidelberg (2005). https://doi.org/10.1007/11545262_27

19. Schindler, W., Lemke, K., Paar, C.: A stochastic model for differential side channel cryptanalysis. In: Rao, J.R., Sunar, B. (eds.) CHES 2005. LNCS, vol. 3659, pp. 30–46. Springer, Heidelberg (2005). https://doi.org/10.1007/11545262_3

20. Zhou, Z.-H.: Ensemble Methods: Foundations and Algorithms. Chapman and Hall/CRC, Boca Raton (2012)

21. Massey, J.L.: Guessing and entropy. In: Proceedings of 1994 IEEE International Symposium on Information Theory, p. 204. IEEE (1994)

22. Gabor, D.: Theory of communication. Part 1: the analysis of information. J. Inst. Electr. Eng.-Part III Radio Commun. Eng. **93**(26), 429–441 (1946)

23. Andreux, M., et al.: Kymatio: scattering transforms in Python. CoRR, abs/1812.11214 (2018)

24. Reddi, S.J., Kale, S., Kumar, S.: On the convergence of adam and beyond. In: 6th International Conference on Learning Representations, ICLR 2018, Vancouver, BC, Canada, 30 April–3 May 2018, Conference Track Proceedings (2018)

Scatter: a Missing Case?

Yuanyuan Zhou[1,2(✉)], Sébastien Duval[1], and François-Xavier Standaert[1]

[1] UCLouvain, Crypto Group, Louvain-la-Neuve, Belgium
zhou@brightsight.com
[2] Brightsight BV, Delft, The Netherlands

Abstract. Scatter is a multivariate transform proposed in combination with the Chi^2 and MIA distinguishers at COSADE 2018. Its primary motivation is to inherently deal with the misalignment and synchronization issues that may decrease the efficiency of concrete side-channel attacks. In this paper, we first show empirically that when compared to natural competitors for first-order multivariate attacks (e.g., exploiting linear regression on-the-fly), it does not bring improvements in the (simulated and actual) implementation settings studied by its authors. We then show that the same holds in the higher-order case: in most practically-relevant settings, Scatter works best when combined with a combination function mixing the leakage samples in a non-linear manner, bringing it back to a situation where it does not improve standard distinguishers.

Keywords: Side-channel analysis · Scatter Transform · Shuffling · Masking

1 Introduction

Side-channel attacks are an important threat to the security of modern embedded devices [MOP07]. Masking [CJRR99, GP99] and shuffling [HOM06, VMKS12] are among the most investigated solutions to mitigate these attacks.

Informally, masking can be viewed as a data randomization which aims at forcing the adversary to estimate higher-order statistical moments of the leakage distributions; similarly, shuffling can be viewed as a time randomization which aims at forcing the adversary to deal with information spread in multivariate distributions. As a result, evaluating a masked and/or shuffled implementation boils down to a quest for simple and efficient tools enabling the analysis of higher-order and multivariate statistical distributions. The literature typically divides such distinguishers as profiled ones, like Template Attacks (TAs) [CRR02], where the adversary can use a device he controls to build a leakage model, and non-profiled ones, like Correlation Power Analysis (CPA) [BCO04], where the adversary uses a hypothetical model based on engineering intuition.

The Scatter transform was introduced at COSADE 2018 [TGWC18]. Roughly, it is a multivariate pre-processing to use in combination with "generic-emulating" distinguishers [WOS14], such as Mutual Information Analysis

ⓒ Springer Nature Switzerland AG 2021
G. M. Bertoni and F. Regazzoni (Eds.): COSADE 2020, LNCS 12244, pp. 90–103, 2021.
https://doi.org/10.1007/978-3-030-68773-1_5

(MIA) [GBTP08] or the Chi^2 test [MRSS18]. Its main motivation comes from the observation that the efficiency of concrete side-channel attacks can be significantly reduced in case of misaligned traces, which may be due to jitter in the measurements or to dedicated countermeasures such as shuffling (or random delays [CK10]). Scatter is claimed to efficiently deal with such synchronization issues, while having potential for improving higher-order side-channel attacks (e.g., against masked implementations) [TVW19]. Preliminary experiments showed good features in these directions, but a comparison with competing distinguishers is missing.

In this paper, we complete this research in two directions.

We start by investigating the basic potential of Scatter for an efficient exploitation of first-order multivariate leakages. For this purpose, our seed observation is that the COSADE 2018 paper mostly compared Scatter with univariate CPA-based attacks. In this context, it appears natural that Scatter resists better to misaligned traces, since the misalignment will typically spread the informative samples over multiple time dimensions (i.e., a multivariate distribution). We therefore compare the efficiency of Scatter with a more natural competitor for first-order multivariate attacks, namely the on-the-fly regression-based distinguisher described in [DPRS11]. We performed experiments against a simulated shuffled implementation and a concrete jittery implementation, both similar to the settings investigated in [TGWC18]. Our results suggest that the on-the-fly regression always outperforms Scatter in these contexts.

We follow by studying the applicability of Scatter to masked implementations where computations are performed on secret-shared data.

In this respect, we first show that Scatter's basic (univariate) probabilistic transform is inherently unable to characterize the higher-order multivariate statistical leakages of a masked implementation. Hence, the only possible option to deal with such cases is (as usual) to generalize Scatter to multivariate distributions, either by estimating these distributions directly or by combining the leakage samples in a non-linear manner (see for example [PRB09,SVO+10]). Note that the latter implies that Scatter cannot avoid the combinatorial explosion of the number of samples to test in order to detect Points-of-Interest (POIs).

Our experiments next confirm the findings of Thiebeauld et al. that non-linear combination functions are beneficial for the efficiency of higher-order Scatter from a data complexity viewpoint [TVW19]. Since we are then back to a situation where on-the-fly regression is applicable, we finally compare both distinguishers and show empirically that, as in the first-order context, Scatter is outperformed by linear regression in the simulated cases we studied.

Overall, we cannot preclude another useful application of Scatter. But in the absence of theoretical or empirical arguments highlighting its interest over other established distinguishers, we conclude that it currently lacks a use case.

Note that our study is limited to the investigation of Scatter in combination with side-channel distinguishers (as it was proposed so far). One possible scope for further investigation is the study of this probabilistic transform as a preprocessing before leakage detection (e.g., with the Chi^2 test [MRSS18]).

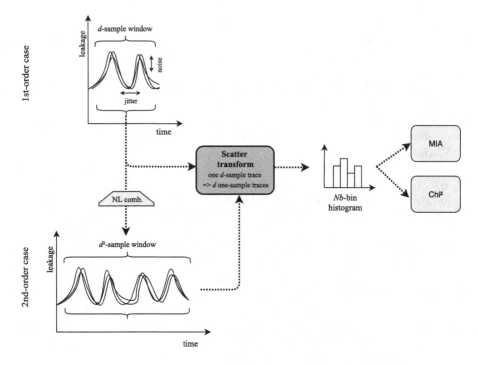

Fig. 1. Scatter transform with MIA and Chi^2 distinguishers: high-level view.

2   Background

2.1   Scatter Transform with Chi^2/MIA Distinguishers

The Scatter transform applied to first-order leakages and combined with the Chi^2 and MIA distinguishers is illustrated on the top of Figure 1. The basic idea is to consider each d-dimension trace as d (one-dimension) samples, and to estimate the distribution of these d samples thanks to histograms. The histograms are then partitioned according to the key guess and a hypothetical leakage model (e.g., the Hamming weight of an S-box output). The Chi^2 or MIA distinguishers are finally used to search for the correct key guess. More precisely:

1. We estimate histograms based on the amplitude of the sample points within a window of size d. For each measured trace, we convert the d sample points to an N_b-bin histogram. For an 8-bit oscilloscope, the max N_b is 256.
2. The "histogram traces" are then partitioned based on the key guess and hypothetical leakage model. In this work we consider the Hamming weight leakages of an AES S-box output. As a result, we obtain $N_b \times 9 \times 256$ partitioned histogram traces (i.e., 9 Hamming weights, 256 key candidates).
3. We compute the distributions $\mathsf{pdf}_{g,h}[u]$ using the partitioned histogram traces, for each key guess g and corresponding Hamming weight hypothetical leakage h, where u denotes the histogram value:

$$\text{pdf}_{g,h}[u] = \frac{\text{Acc}_{g,h}[u]}{\sum\limits_{u'=0}^{N_b-1} \text{Acc}_{g,h}[u']} , \qquad (1)$$

in which $\text{Acc}_{g,h}[u]$ is the total number of occurrences of value u for a key guess g and its corresponding Hamming weight hypothetical leakage h.

4. The correct key guess $g_{correct}$ is distinguished by applying a generic-emulating side-channel distinguisher to the estimated distributions $\text{pdf}_{g,h}[u]$.

Both the Chi^2 and MIA distinguishers can be used in combination with the Scatter transform in order to search for the correct key candidate.

The Chi^2 distinguisher is based on Pearson's $\mathcal{X}^2$-test to perform a partition-based DPA [SGV08]. When successful, the partition based on the correct key guess should lead to the highest confidence level to reject the null hypothesis. In the Scatter context, it estimates how much a distribution differs from a general distribution (e.g., in our case study, the mean distribution of all 9 Hamming weight leakage distributions for a key guess g and a value u)—the correct key guess being expected to show the most significant difference. The Chi^2 value is computed according to the following formula:

$$\mathcal{X}^2_{g,h} = \sum_{u=0}^{N_b-1} \frac{\left(\text{pdf}_{g,h}[u] - \frac{1}{9} \cdot \sum\limits_{h'=0}^{8} \text{pdf}_{g,h'}[u]\right)^2}{\frac{1}{9} \cdot \sum\limits_{h'=0}^{8} \text{pdf}_{g,h'}[u]}. \qquad (2)$$

For each key guess, there are 9 Chi^2 scores corresponding to 9 Hamming weights. The logarithm sum of all 9 scores is then used as the final score.

The MIA distinguisher was introduced by Gierlichs et al. [GBTP08]. It is based on estimating the mutual information between a hypothetical leakage model and the actual leakages. Under a correct partitioning (i.e., the correct key guess), it is expected that the largest mutual information should be observed for the correct key candidate to distinguish the correct key guess from the wrong ones. The MIA value is computed according to the following formula:

$$\text{MI}_g = \sum_{h=0}^{8} P(Y = h) \cdot (\nabla_1(g, h) - \nabla_2(h)), \qquad (3)$$

in which:

$$P(Y = h) = \frac{1}{n \cdot 9} \cdot \sum_{u=0}^{N_b-1} \text{Acc}_{g,h}[u], \qquad (4)$$

with n the number of traces collected and:

$$\nabla_1(g, h) = \sum_{u=0}^{N_b-1} \text{pdf}_{g,h}[u] \cdot (\text{pdf}_{g,h}[u]), \qquad (5)$$

$$\nabla_2(h) = \sum_{u=0}^{N_b-1} (\frac{1}{9} \cdot \sum_{h'=0}^{8} \text{pdf}_{g,h'}[u]) \cdot \log(\frac{1}{9} \cdot \sum_{h'=0}^{8} \text{pdf}_{g,h'}[u]). \qquad (6)$$

2.2 On-the-Fly Linear Regression

The use of linear regression for (profiled) side-channel attacks was introduced by Schindler et al. [SLP05]. It was then extended to non-profiled key-recovery attacks in [DPRS11]. We next denote this non-profiled extension as LRA.

Let us denote the leakage measurement as L. The target m-bit intermediate value v (e.g., the S-box output in our case) is first decomposed according to some basis. In the following, we will use the usual (linear) basis made of the 8 bits of v $(v[m-1], v[m-2], \ldots, v[0])$. LRA then simply tests the linear relation between the actual leakages and their approximation with this basis, thanks to the coefficient of determination R^2. More precisely:

1. We first compute $(v_{\hat{g}}[m-1], v_{\hat{g}}[m-2], \ldots, v_{\hat{g}}[0])$ for each key guess $\hat{g}$ and each input plaintext & measurement $L_i, i = 0, 1, \ldots, n-1$.
2. We then estimate the linear regression model between the measurement L and the following approximation:

$$L_{\text{app}} = \beta_{\hat{g},0} + \beta_{\hat{g},1} \cdot v_{\hat{g}}[0] + \ldots + \beta_{\hat{g},m} \cdot v_{\hat{g}}[m-1], \tag{7}$$

   using ordinary least square method to estimate the parameter $\beta_{\hat{g},j}$.
3. We finally compute the coefficient of determination $R_{\hat{g}}^2$ for each key guess. The correct key guess g_{correct} is supposed to show the highest R^2 value.

2.3 Selection of Parameters

The efficiency of the three aforementioned distinguishers is quite dependent on the good selection of their parameters: number of bins for the Chi^2 and MIA distingsuihers, size of the basis for LRA. As already mentioned, our experiments are based on LRA with a linear 9-element basis (the eight S-box output bits and a constant), which is a standard choice for this distinguisher [SLP05]. For the Chi^2 and MIA distinguishers, choosing the optimal number of bins is usually tricky. We selected 9 and 25 bins in our experiments: 9 since it naturally corresponds to Hamming weight leakages, 25 to assess the impact of more bins. We note that this choice is expected to be slightly detrimental to the LRA distinguisher (since under a Hamming weight assumption, a 2-element basis with the Hamming weight of the S-box output should be even faster to estimate).

3 First-Order Experiments

We first investigate a simulated shuffled implementation, since this was the case study put forward in the COSADE 2018 paper on Scatter. We continue by targeting a real device of which the measurements are affected by a strong jitter, preventing the good alignment of the traces around the leaking part.

3.1 Setting #1: A Simulated Shuffled Implementation

Shuffling is a widely-used side-channel countermeasure [HOM06, VMKS12]. Its main principle is to execute sensitive operations in a random order so that their leakages are spread over a multivariate distribution. As a result, each single point in time can correspond to the execution of various operations.

Shuffled implementations are the typical context in which Scatter's multivariate transform was claimed to be a useful tool at COSADE 2018.

Implementation Settings. The main parameter influencing the security of a shuffled implementation is the number of parallel operations which are randomized. We next consider a default size of 16 (corresponding to the AES case) and additionally experimented with a permutation of size 64, which could correspond to the execution of 48 dummy S-boxes. In our default setup, a single POI is leaking (corresponding to the target S-box execution) but we also considered a case with four POIs (which does not reflect a concrete AES implementation and was just aimed to understand the impact of a denser leakage in the Scatter window). Finally, we used a Signal-to-Noise Ratio (SNR) of 10, 1 and 0.1, reflecting low-noise, medium-noise and high-noise contexts [Man04]. The way we generated simulated traces is similar to the Scatter paper. For a window size d (i.e., the shuffling size in our experiments), we:

1. Choose the number of informative points (n_i),
2. Pick up their location in the d possible positions uniformly at random,
3. Put random leakages (of the same shape) in all the other points,
4. Add Gaussian noise to the entire trace based on the chosen SNR.

Our simulations focus on Hamming weight leakages for the first-round first S-box of an AES-128 encryption, namely $\mathsf{HW}(\mathsf{Sbox}(p[0] \oplus k[0]))$, where $p[0]$ and $k[0]$ correspond to the first bytes of the 16-byte AES input and key, respectively.

For each simulation setting, we estimated the Success Rate (SR) of the different attacks under investigation based on 100 independent experiments [SMY09].

Attack Results. The results of our experiments are in Fig. 2. We analyzed a wide range of parameters reflecting the various settings in which the Scatter transform could be exploited. As previously mentioned, we also evaluated this transform with both the Chi^2 and MIA distinguishers, using 9 and 25 bins. Those are systematically compared with the LRA distinguisher (9-element basis).

In general, these experiments carry the expected intuitions regarding the impact of our different parameters: decreasing the SNR makes the attacks more difficult (i.e., when moving from the left of the figure to the right of the figure); increasing d (i.e., the permutation size) makes the attacks more difficult (i.e., when moving from lines 1 and 2 to lines 3 and 4); increasing the number of POIs makes the attack easier (i.e., when moving from line 1 to line 2 and from line 3 to line 4). More specifically related to Scatter:

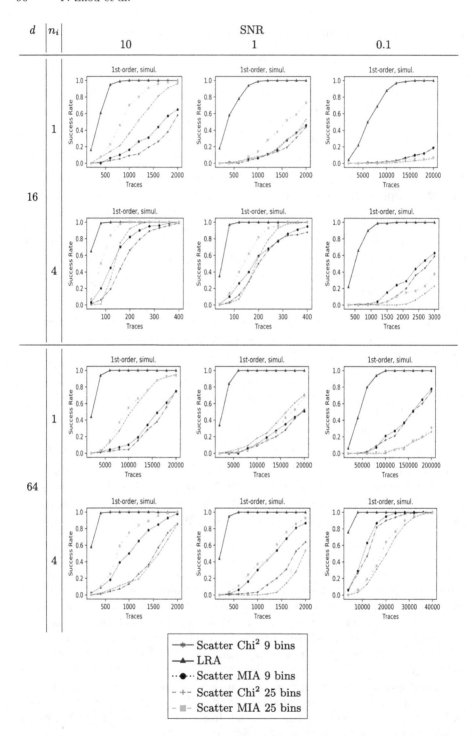

Fig. 2. Success rate on simulated shuffled implementations, with d the window size, n_i the number of POIs per window and various SNR values.

- LRA always outperforms Scatter with both the Chi^2 and MIA distinguishers, no matter the permutation size, noise level and number of POIs;
- The performance gap between LRA and Scatter is getting bigger as the attacks become more difficult (i.e., when the permutation size increases, the noise level increases and the number of POIs decreases);
- Scatter with the MIA distinguisher performs slightly better than Scatter with the Chi^2 distinguisher (which is in line with the COSADE 2018 results).
- As for the impact of the number of bins for Scatter: more bins generally show better results with lower noise and less bins generally works better with higher noise. The latter is in line with the findings of [GBTP08].

3.2   Setting #2: A Concrete Jittery Implementation

We now extend our investigations to a real device, namely a software AES implementation using a secure processor. Due to the variable internal clock, the inserted random instructions during AES calculations, and the interrupts caused by the running Android-like operating system (OS), the measured traces are very jittery and we cannot really align the traces at the leaking time interval. We study how well Scatter can handle this challenging scenario.

Implementation Settings. The target secure processor is a Cortex-M4 chip running at 50 MHz next to a Qualcomm MSM8998 general processor which is running an Android-like OS. The secure processor is used for cryptography calculations and it communicates with the MSM8998 processor via UART (Universal Asynchronous Receiver/Transmitter) interface. The AES implementation is unprotected except for the random instructions inserted during the AES execution. Interrupts are additionally caused by the running Android-like OS and make the measured traces more noisy and hard-to-align. We measured 100,000 ElectroMagnetic (EM) traces on top of the secure processor using an EM probe, with a LeCroy Waverunner 620Zi oscilloscope, at a sampling rate of 5 GHz.

During the measurements, we triggered the oscilloscope at the end of the entire AES encryption command processing. The raw EM traces are noisy and hardly show distinct patterns that can be used for alignment, as can be seen in Fig. 3(a). We therefore used a simple correlation-based pre-processing in order to better synchronize these EM traces, working as follows:

- Two intervals are chosen. First, a searching interval A that contains the operation to be synchronized is manually selected among all the traces. Next, a smaller reference interval B_q specific to each trace q is also chosen.
- For each trace, we find the portion to be synchronized by using the second window B_q to search over the whole interval A. The right portion is selected as the one having the maximum correlation with the reference interval. If the correlation is lower than a given threshold (chosen by the attacker/evaluator), the trace is assumed not good enough and discarded.

After performing such an alignment, we were able to determine where the AES computations occur by means of SEMA (Simple Electro Magnetic Analysis) and CEMA (Correlation Electro Magnetic Analysis), as shown in Fig. 3(b).

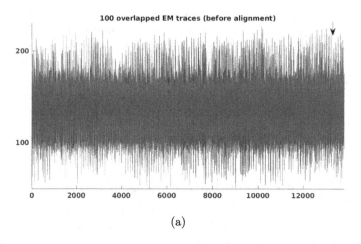

(a)

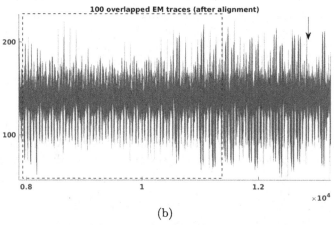

(b)

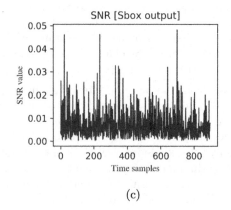

(c)

Fig. 3. 100 overlapped EM traces before alignment (a) and after alignment (b), and target S-box estimated SNR (c).

Attack Results. Our comparisons are based on 99,902 aligned EM traces focusing on the leaking part (the other traces were discarded). As a first note, none of the investigated distinguishers directly succeeded in recovering key bytes by exploiting the leakage in the time domain. We then applied a Fast Fourier Transform (FFT) in order to convert the traces into the frequency domain and to mitigate the impact of misalignment. After this pre-processing, LRA was able to recover all 16 key bytes of an AES state, but Scatter was not (neither with the Chi^2 nor with the MIA distinguishers). These results are illustrated in Fig. 4 where the success rate is estimated based on 100 independent experiments.

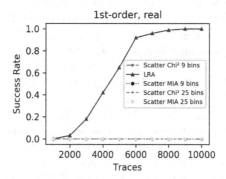

Fig. 4. Attacks against a real implementation with strong jitter.

4 Higher-Order Scatter

4.1 The Need of a Combination Function

We start with a simple negative result highlighting the need to generalize the Scatter transform before application to higher-order side-channel attacks. For this purpose, let us imagine that the two "clock cycles" represented at the top of Fig. 1 correspond to the two shares of a masked sensitive variable x. Let us further consider that this sensitive variable is one bit and can be written as $x = x_1 \oplus x_2$ with x_1 picked up uniformly at random. Let us finally assume that the adversary can obtain the leakage of the two shares x_1 and x_2, denoted as l_1 and l_2: under Hamming weight leakages, we have $l_1 = x_1$ and $l_2 = x_2$, meaning that the adversary can directly observe the shares. In this context, 1st-order probing security is guaranteed because the observation of either l_1 or l_2 does not reveal anything about x. By contrast, a second-order probing attack is trivial since $l_1 \oplus l_2 = x$. More interestingly, a second-order statistical attack is also successful since the distribution of (l_1, l_2) when $x = 0$ is $(0,0)$ with probability $\frac{1}{2}$ and $(1,1)$ with probability $\frac{1}{2}$, while this distribution becomes $(0,1)$ with probability $\frac{1}{2}$ and $(1,0)$ with probability $\frac{1}{2}$ when $x = 1$ (which has a different variance).

If we now apply the Scatter transform, each bivariate trace (l_1, l_2) is split into two univariate traces l_1 and l_2, and histograms are built from these two traces. As a result, the two traces (0,0) and (1,1) that correspond to the case $x = 0$ are turned into four traces 0, 0, 1, 1. Their histogram gives 0 with probability $\frac{1}{2}$ and 1 probability $\frac{1}{2}$. Similarly, the two traces (0,1) and (1,0) that correspond to the case $x = 1$ are turned into four traces 0, 1, 1, 0, leading to exactly the same histogram. So directly applying the first-order Scatter transform to a masked implementation cancels the differences between these distributions that can be used to mount a successful second-order attack. The same example generalizes to any number of shares and probing/statistical security order.

As usual in side-channel analysis, the solution to prevent this issue is to generalize the transform to higher-orders. There are essentially two solutions for this purpose: either one considers all the pairs (and triples, quadruples, ...) of samples and applies a multivariate (e.g., Chi^2 or MIA) distinguisher to it, or one uses a combination function (e.g., the normalized product in the context of Hamming weight leakages [PRB09,SVO+10]) and applies a (univariate in the case of LRA or multivariate in the case of Scatter) distinguisher to its output. As discussed for example in [BGP+11,MRSS18], directly considering all the pairs (and triples, quadruples, ...) of samples and applying a multivariate distinguisher is usually more expensive, due to the curse of dimensionality when estimating multivariate distributions in a non-parametric manner. Our experiments showed the same trend and so do the experiments of Thiebeauld et al. in [TVW19].

As a result, we next consider higher-order attacks based on a combination function illustrated at the bottom of Fig. 1. That is, in the second-order case we will concretely investigate, we start by extending the original d-sample window to a d^2-sample window containing all the normalized product samples and then apply the Scatter transform combined with the Chi^2 or MIA distinguishers, or LRA. Note that this solution suffers from the usual drawback that the cost of finding the POIs in the traces grows exponentially in the number of shares (and exactly the same would hold for the first aforementioned solution where a multivariate distinguisher is applied to all the tuples of samples).[1]

4.2   Second-Order Simulated Experiments

Implementation Settings. We now complete the previous first-order experiments with second-order simulations. We consider a 2-share implementation where the adversary obtains the two Hamming weights corresponding to the two shares of a target S-box's output. Based on the previous observation that Scatter tends to behave better in less challenging scenarios (and in order to limit

---

[1] In the report on the second-order application of Scatter [TVW19], an optional projection of the histogram traces is considered. In our experiments, this projection (just as the direct bivariate attacks) did not exhibit any improvement. This seems natural in a simulated setting where the normalized product combination function is known to be optimal [PRB09]. So we next ignore this optional projection.

the cost of our simulations, which increases with the security levels), we selected the following parameters: a permutation of size $d = 4$ with a single POI (i.e., $n_i = 1$) and a SNR of 10, 1 and 0.25. For completeness, we also report results with $d = 16$, 4 POIs (i.e., $n_i = 4$) and a SNR of 10 and 1. We focused on Scatter with the MIA distinguisher that was the best in class for our first-order experiments. (This is also similar to what has been done in [TVW19]).

Attack Results. The results of our second-order experiments based on a normalized product combination function are displayed in Fig. 5.

Observations are essentially similar to the first-order case: again, LRA systematically outperforms attacks based on Scatter and the more "challenging" the implementation (e.g., the lower the SNR), the bigger the gap. This can be explained by the fact that the product combining pre-processing generates traces that can be exploited in a very similar way as an unprotected implementation (up to the noise level that is amplified by the product operation).

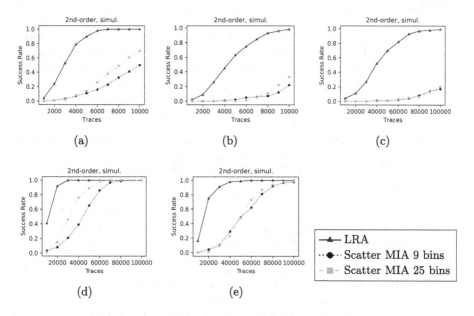

Fig. 5. Simulated shuffled & masked implementation: (a) $d = 4$, $n_i = 1$, SNR=10; (b) $d = 4$, $n_i = 1$, SNR=1; (c) $d = 4$, $n_i = 1$, SNR=0.25; (d) $d = 16$, $n_i = 4$, SNR=10; (e) $d = 16$, $n_i = 4$, SNR=1.

5 Conclusion

Exploiting the side-channel leakages of an implementation protected with jitter, shuffling and/or masking is a challenging problem. The Scatter transform was introduced at COSADE 2018 as a novel transform aimed to make such attacks more efficient. In this work, we nailed down its specificity and compare it with a natural competitor for unprofiled multivariate side-channel analysis.

It turns out a standard on-the-fly application of linear regression leads to more efficient attacks in many practically-relevant contexts, including all the ones initially put forward by the Scatter authors. It is therefore an interesting open problem to determine whether this transform can sometimes be a useful ingredient in a side-channel security evaluation. The exhibition of a simulated case where such a gain can be observed appears as a natural next to answer this question. Without such a case, evaluators are left with the conclusion that it currently does not improve over existing solutions.

Acknowledgments. François-Xavier Standaert is a senior research associate of the Belgian Fund for Scientific Research (F.R.S.-FNRS). This work has been funded in parts by the ERC project SWORD (Grant Number 724725), the H2020 project REASSURE and the UCLouvain ARC project NANOSEC.

References

BCO04.   Brier, E., Clavier, C., Olivier, F.: Correlation power analysis with a leakage model. In: Joye, M., Quisquater, J.-J. (eds.) CHES 2004. LNCS, vol. 3156, pp. 16–29. Springer, Heidelberg (2004). https://doi.org/10.1007/978-3-540-28632-5_2

BGP+11.   Batina, L., Gierlichs, B., Prouff, E., Rivain, M., Standaert, F.-X., Veyrat-Charvillon, N.: Mutual information analysis: a comprehensive study. J. Cryptol. **24**(2), 269–291 (2011)

CJRR99.   Chari, S., Jutla, C.S., Rao, J.R., Rohatgi, P.: Towards sound approaches to counteract power-analysis attacks. In: Wiener, M. (ed.) CRYPTO 1999. LNCS, vol. 1666, pp. 398–412. Springer, Heidelberg (1999). https://doi.org/10.1007/3-540-48405-1_26

CK10.   Coron, J.-S., Kizhvatov, I.: Analysis and improvement of the random delay countermeasure of CHES 2009. In: Mangard, S., Standaert, F.-X. (eds.) CHES 2010. LNCS, vol. 6225, pp. 95–109. Springer, Heidelberg (2010). https://doi.org/10.1007/978-3-642-15031-9_7

CRR02.   Chari, S., Rao, J.R., Rohatgi, P.: Template attacks. In: Kaliski, B.S., Koç, K., Paar, C. (eds.) CHES 2002. LNCS, vol. 2523, pp. 13–28. Springer, Heidelberg (2003). https://doi.org/10.1007/3-540-36400-5_3

DPRS11.   Doget, J., Prouff, E., Rivain, M., Standaert, F.-X.: Univariate side channel attacks and leakage modeling. J. Cryptogr. Eng. **1**(2), 123–144 (2011)

GBTP08.   Gierlichs, B., Batina, L., Tuyls, P., Preneel, B.: Mutual information analysis. In: Oswald, E., Rohatgi, P. (eds.) CHES 2008. LNCS, vol. 5154, pp. 426–442. Springer, Heidelberg (2008). https://doi.org/10.1007/978-3-540-85053-3_27

GP99.   Goubin, L., Patarin, J.: DES and differential power analysis the "Duplication" method. In: Koç, Ç.K., Paar, C. (eds.) CHES 1999. LNCS, vol. 1717, pp. 158–172. Springer, Heidelberg (1999). https://doi.org/10.1007/3-540-48059-5_15

HOM06. Herbst, C., Oswald, E., Mangard, S.: An AES smart card implementation resistant to power analysis attacks. In: Zhou, J., Yung, M., Bao, F. (eds.) ACNS 2006. LNCS, vol. 3989, pp. 239–252. Springer, Heidelberg (2006). https://doi.org/10.1007/11767480_16

Man04. Mangard, S.: Hardware countermeasures against DPA – a statistical analysis of their effectiveness. In: Okamoto, T. (ed.) CT-RSA 2004. LNCS, vol. 2964, pp. 222–235. Springer, Heidelberg (2004). https://doi.org/10.1007/978-3-540-24660-2_18

MOP07. Mangard, S., Oswald, E., Popp, T.: Power Analysis Attacks. Springer, Boston, MA (2007). https://doi.org/10.1007/978-0-387-38162-6

MRSS18. Moradi, A., Richter, B., Schneider, T., Standaert, F.-X.: Leakage detection with the x2-test. IACR Trans. Cryptogr. Hardware Embed. Syst. **2018**(1), 209–237 (2018)

PRB09. Prouff, E., Rivain, M., Bevan, R.: Statistical analysis of second order differential power analysis. IEEE Trans. Comput. **58**(6), 799–811 (2009)

SGV08. Standaert, F.-X., Gierlichs, B., Verbauwhede, I.: Partition *vs.* comparison side-channel distinguishers: an empirical evaluation of statistical tests for univariate side-channel attacks against two unprotected CMOS devices. In: Lee, P.J., Cheon, J.H. (eds.) ICISC 2008. LNCS, vol. 5461, pp. 253–267. Springer, Heidelberg (2009). https://doi.org/10.1007/978-3-642-00730-9_16

SLP05. Schindler, W., Lemke, K., Paar, C.: A stochastic model for differential side channel cryptanalysis. In: Rao, J.R., Sunar, B. (eds.) CHES 2005. LNCS, vol. 3659, pp. 30–46. Springer, Heidelberg (2005). https://doi.org/10.1007/11545262_3

SMY09. Standaert, F.-X., Malkin, T.G., Yung, M.: A unified framework for the analysis of side-channel key recovery attacks. In: Joux, A. (ed.) EUROCRYPT 2009. LNCS, vol. 5479, pp. 443–461. Springer, Heidelberg (2009). https://doi.org/10.1007/978-3-642-01001-9_26

SVO+10. Standaert, F.-X., Veyrat-Charvillon, N., Oswald, E., Gierlichs, B., Medwed, M., Kasper, M., Mangard, S.: The world is not enough: another look on second-order DPA. In: Abe, M. (ed.) ASIACRYPT 2010. LNCS, vol. 6477, pp. 112–129. Springer, Heidelberg (2010). https://doi.org/10.1007/978-3-642-17373-8_7

TGWC18. Thiebeauld, H., Gagnerot, G., Wurcker, A., Clavier, C.: SCATTER: a new dimension in side-channel. In: Fan, J., Gierlichs, B. (eds.) COSADE 2018. LNCS, vol. 10815, pp. 135–152. Springer, Cham (2018). https://doi.org/10.1007/978-3-319-89641-0_8

TVW19. Thiebeauld, H., Vasselle, A., Wurcker, A.: Second-order scatter attack. IACR Cryptol. ePrint Arch. **2019**, 345 (2019)

VMKS12. Veyrat-Charvillon, N., Medwed, M., Kerckhof, S., Standaert, F.-X.: Shuffling against side-channel attacks: a comprehensive study with cautionary note. In: Wang, X., Sako, K. (eds.) ASIACRYPT 2012. LNCS, vol. 7658, pp. 740–757. Springer, Heidelberg (2012). https://doi.org/10.1007/978-3-642-34961-4_44

WOS14. Whitnall, C., Oswald, E., Standaert, F.-X.: The myth of Generic DPA...and the magic of learning. In: Benaloh, J. (ed.) CT-RSA 2014. LNCS, vol. 8366, pp. 183–205. Springer, Cham (2014). https://doi.org/10.1007/978-3-319-04852-9_10

Augmenting Leakage Detection Using Bootstrapping

Yuan Yao[1]([✉]), Michael Tunstall[2], Elke De Mulder[2], Anton Kochepasov[2], and Patrick Schaumont[1]

[1] Virginia Tech, Blacksburg, VA 24060, USA
{yuan9,schaum}@vt.edu
[2] Rambus Cryptography Research, 425 Market Street, 11th Floor, San Francisco, CA 94105, USA
{michael.tunstall,elke.demulder,anton.kochepasov}@cryptography.com

Abstract. Side-channel leakage detection methods based on statistical tests, such as t-test or χ^2-test, provide a high confidence in the presence of leakage with a large number of traces. However, practical limitations on testing time and equipment may set an upper-bound on the number of traces available, turning the number of traces into a limiting factor in side-channel leakage detection. We describe a statistical technique, based on statistical bootstrapping, that significantly improves the effectiveness of leakage detection using a limited set of traces. Bootstrapping generates additional sample sets from an initial set by assuming that it is representative of the entire population. The additional sample sets are then used to conduct additional leakage detection tests, and we show how to combine the results of these tests. The proposed technique, applied to side-channel leakage detection, can significantly reduce the number of traces required to detect leakage by one, or more orders of magnitude. Furthermore, for an existing measured sample set, the method can significantly increase the confidence of existing leakage hypotheses over a traditional (non-bootstrap) leakage detection test. This paper introduces the bootstrapping technique for leakage detection, applies it to three practical cases, and describes techniques for its efficient computation.

Keywords: Side-channel analysis · Leakage detection · Bootstrapping

1 Introduction

Testing the side-channel leakage of a design is a challenging task. The test requires careful planning of an experiment to measure a side-channel, such as the power consumption, followed by analysis of the measurements. The objective of the analysis is to detect side-channel leakage within a reasonable amount of time. Traditionally, the analysis was done using a side-channel analysis attack such as Differential Power Analysis [8]. However, the number of attacks and possible attack targets in a typical cryptographic implementation can be very large.

© Springer Nature Switzerland AG 2021
G. M. Bertoni and F. Regazzoni (Eds.): COSADE 2020, LNCS 12244, pp. 104–119, 2021.
https://doi.org/10.1007/978-3-030-68773-1_6

Therefore, it becomes desirable to formulate the analysis in a generic manner independent of specific attacks for a side-channel leakage assessment. The most popular among those assessments is Test Vector Leakage Assessment (TLVA), proposed in 2011 by Goodwill et al. [6]. TVLA uses Welch's t-test, under a null hypothesis that no leakage is present, in a pointwise comparison of two sets of power consumption traces. In a non-specific TVLA test, the two sets correspond to power traces under a constant (plaintext) input on the one hand, and power traces under a random (plaintext) input on the other hand. Any t-statistic greater than 4.5σ (corresponding to a false positive rate of 1×10^{-5}) would indicate the presence of leakage. A known, but accepted, disadvantage of TVLA is that the test does not establish a relationship between leakage and exploitability. Hence, side-channel leakage confirmed by TVLA does not imply that the leakage can be efficiently exploited by a side-channel attack. An example of a difficult-to-exploit side-channel leakage would occur during the middle round of a cipher, since an efficient side-channel attack such as DPA would typically require side-channel leakage in the initial and/or final round of the cipher.

While TVLA is widely used for research and testing, it brings its own unique challenges. False negatives occur when the measurements contain side-channel information but TVLA fails to detect it. This can have several causes. First, TVLA confirms side-channel leakage by demonstrating a statistically meaningful difference-of-means between two sets of measurements. If the amount of side-channel leakage is small, that difference of means will be small as well. The number of measurements in that case may be insufficient to discern a meaningful difference. Second, the measurements could be very noisy and have a low Signal-to-Noise Ration (SNR) [9,18]) and, again, the number of measurements may be too small to detect a statistically meaningful difference.

The risk of a false negative in TVLA can be minimized by increasing the number of measurements or by enhancing the test by, for example, using multiple input vectors for the fixed set [2,15]. Another strategy is to deploy a fixed-versus-fixed TVLA test [15] (as opposed to fixed-versus-random). This will reduce the algorithmic noise but it has the added drawback that some leakage may not show up due to the choice of inputs. Ideally, the confidence in the outcome of the evaluation can be improved by repeating the TVLA test multiple times over new measurements.

Hence, all known techniques that reduce the number of false negatives for TVLA require an increase in the total number of measurements. This is problematic, since the number of measurements is typically limited in practice by the available testing time.

In this work, we seek to reduce the number of false negatives in TVLA, without the need for more physical measurements, or, looking at it from a different angle, we aim to decrease the number of measurements needed for detecting leakage. We base our work on statistical bootstrapping, a computer-based technique for statistical inference proposed by Efron [5]. Bootstrapping starts from an initial sample set, which is assumed to be representative of the population. The bootstrapping procedure infers population parameters by repeated re-sampling of the initial sample set and by analyzing the resulting re-sampled data sets. Applied to side-channel leakage detection, we aim to decide if the population, corresponding to the set of power traces, shows side-channel leakage at a given confidence level. To demonstrate this hypothesis, we make use of an initial sample of a limited set of power traces and use the bootstrapping method. Our results show that bootstrapping based leakage detection reduces the size of the sample (i.e., the number of traces required) by at least one order of magnitude while maintaining the same confidence level.

We first demonstrate the proposed methodology using simulations, where we control the amount of leakage that is present. We then further demonstrate our findings by analyzing three practical implementations, including a software AES with Boolean masking, an unprotected hardware AES and a lightly protected hardware AES. In addition to this experimental work, we also describe the limitations of the proposed bootstrap method. Finally, we discuss an optimized technique to compute leakage detection parameters using bootstrapping on an initial sample. Our proposed technique enhances earlier work that computes the test statistics using trace histograms instead of individual traces [13].

This paper is organized as follows. Section 2 introduces several preliminary concepts: the Welch's t-test, the bootstrapping mechanism, and the Kolmogorov-Smirnov test. Section 3 applies bootstrapping to the leakage detection problem. We discuss results based on simulations and a variety of software and hardware implementations. Section 4 clarifies the limitations of bootstrapping. Section 5 describes a technique for the efficient implementation of bootstrapping applied to TVLA. We then conclude the paper.

2 Preliminaries

We first provide an introduction to the methods we will use throughout the text.

2.1 Leakage Detection Using Welch's t-test

Welch's t-test is a statistical test used to compare sample means of two sets with, possibly, unequal variance but still under the assumption of normality. The output of the test provides a test statistic which can be combined with a threshold to validate the null hypothesis H_0 that both sets have equal means, or state there is no evidence supporting the null hypothesis so the alternative hypothesis H_a holds. We consider sets A, B of size n_A, n_B, with means μ_A, μ_B and standard deviation σ_A, σ_B, respectively. With these notations, the null hypothesis and the alternative hypothesis are noted as follows,

$$H_0 : \mu_A = \mu_B \quad H_a : \mu_A \neq \mu_B \tag{1}$$

and the t-statistic is calculated with the following formula:

$$\psi = \frac{\mu_A - \mu_B}{\sqrt{\frac{\sigma_A{}^2}{n_A} + \frac{\sigma_B{}^2}{n_B}}} \tag{2}$$

where $\psi \sim t(0, \nu)$ with ν degrees of freedom. In practice, we use the result that the t-distribution is asymptotically equivalent to the standard normal distribution as the degrees of freedom increase, i.e. we can assume $\psi \sim N(0, 1)$. We then transform the t-statistic into a p-value using the Cumulative Density Function (CDF) to argue about the validity of H_0.

Goodwill et al. [6] proposed to use Welch's t-test to detect leakage in implementations of cryptographic algorithms by comparing two sets of side-channel acquisitions. One set would be acquired with fixed input and the other with random input. Welch's t-test can be computed point-wise on the acquisitions. A null hypothesis is formulated at each point individually assuming independence of the points. Intuitively, one can see that if the means of those two sets (or the distributions) are not equal, the power consumption is data-dependent and could potentially leak information.

Goodwill et al. [6] proposed a Type I error, i.e. a false positive, rate of 1×10^{-5}, meaning the two-tailed p-value $p < 1 \times 10^{-5}$ would stipulate there is no evidence H_0 is true. This corresponds to an absolute value of $|\psi| > 4.5$. In practice, Welch's t-test is applied point-wise across a set of acquisitions so the probability of seeing at least one Type I error is significantly larger than 1×10^{-5}. Ding et al. [18] proposed adjusting the threshold by taking the trace length (total number of points in a measurement) into consideration. For ease of expression, we will use the threshold defined by Goodwill et al. [6], but a different threshold may be appropriate when applying our method.

2.2 The Bootstrapping Method

The bootstrapping method is a computation-based statistical tool proposed by Efron [5] to make inferences about a population parameter based on a sample set. It is typically used to estimate statistical distributions and to quantify uncertainty, under the assumption that the sample set is representative of the population.

Given a set of observations S_{obs} consisting of n samples, $\{s_1, \ldots, s_n\}$, from a given population we can apply bootstrapping by repeated sampling, with replacement, from S_{obs}. This process can be repeated b times, producing b sets $\{S'_1, \ldots, S'_b\}$, where b is chosen arbitrarily. More explicitly, we detail this process in Algorithm 1, where we define the operation $\xleftarrow{R}$ as taking a random sample from a set. Statistical tests can then be applied to each of these sets producing a set of statistics, which can allow a better analysis than just relying on the observed set S_{orig}.

Pattengale et al. [11] recommended repeating this process 100–500 times to get a robust description of the distribution of the population. In our work, we show that far fewer iterations are required for leakage detection.

Algorithm 1: Generating Bootstrapping Sets

Input: $S_{obs} = \{s_1, \ldots, s_n\}$ with $n, b \in \mathbb{Z}_{>0}$
Output: $\{S_1', \ldots, S_b'\}$

1 **for** $i = 1$ **to** b **do**
2 $\quad$ **for** $i = 1$ **to** n **do**
3 $\quad\quad$ $s_j' \xleftarrow{R} \{s_1, \ldots, s_n\}$;
4 $\quad$ **end**
5 $\quad$ $S_i' \leftarrow \{s_1', \ldots, s_n'\}$;
6 **end**

7 **return** $\{S_1', \ldots, S_b'\}$

2.3 Kolmogorov-Smirnov Test

In this paper, we also apply the one-sample Kolmogorov-Smirnov test (KS test), which is a measure of the difference between a sample distribution and a defined distribution. The null hypothesis of the test H_0 is that the samples come from the defined distribution, with the alternative hypothesis H_a that the samples have a different distribution.

Let $(s_1, s_2, \ldots, s_n)$ be the samples in a data-set. For any number x, the empirical distribution function value is the fraction of the data that is smaller than x:

$$F_n(t) = \frac{1}{n} \sum_{i=1}^{n} I_{\left\{ s_j \leq x \right\}} \tag{3}$$

Where I is the indicator function. The test statistic D exploits the maximum distance of the empirical distribution from the sampled distribution and the defined distribution:

$$D = \sup_x |F_n(x) - G(x)| \tag{4}$$

Where G computes the CDF of the defined distribution and sup is the supremum function. After getting the D statistic for the KS-test, the corresponding p-value can be calculated from the CDF of the one-sample Kolmogorov-Smirnov distribution.

3 Applying Bootstrapping to Leakage Detection

In this section, we describe how we apply bootstrapping to leakage detection. Without loss of generality, we discuss our results using Welch's t-test, since the same method could be applied to any other test that produces a p-value. That is, similar improvements would be seen if one were to use other statistical tests, such as the χ^2 test [10], Hoteling's T^2-test or Diagonal-test(D-test) [4].

Let $S_{obs} = \{s_1, \ldots, s_n\}$ be the set of n acquisitions to be used in a leakage detection test, as described in Sect. 2.1. Each s_i, for $i \in \{1, \ldots, n\}$, consists of an acquisition and the corresponding metadata indicating whether it belongs to set A or B. We apply bootstrapping, as shown in Algorithm 1, to S_{obs} to provide b sample sets $\{S'_1, \ldots, S'_b\}$, where the choice of b is arbitrary. We then conduct Welch's t-test on each set and compute the resulting p-value, giving $\{p'_1, \ldots, p'_b\}$. Each p-value represents a test with

$$H_0 : \text{no leakage} \quad H_a : \text{leakage} \tag{5}$$

and we wish to combine the p-values to test this null hypothesis. Figure 1 demonstrates the proposed methodology.

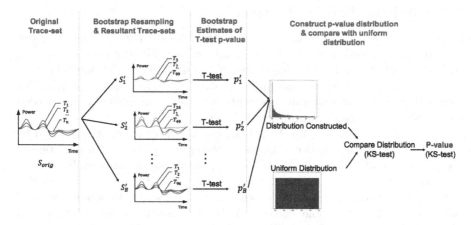

Fig. 1. Bootstrap leakage detection enhancement

In general, the p-value is a measure of evidence on whether the null hypothesis is true, where a p-value close to 0 can be taken as a lack of evidence that the null hypothesis is true, and that the alternate hypothesis may be true. By definition, if the null hypothesis is true then the p-value is uniformly distributed over the interval $[0, 1]$. It has been shown that the p-value distribution is highly skewed when the alternative hypothesis is true [7].

In this work, we use the distribution of the p-values $\{p'_1, \ldots, p'_b\}$ to evaluate whether there is evidence that the null hypotheses are true. That is, if the null hypotheses are true then

$$\{p'_1, \ldots, p'_b\} \sim U(0, 1).$$

We can test whether this is the case using the one-sample Kolmogorov-Smirnov test to compare $\{p'_1, \ldots, p'_b\}$ to a uniform distribution. In the KS-test we have the null hypothesis that the data-set is drawn from the defined distribution, and the alternate hypothesis that it is not. That is,

$$H_0 : \{p'_1, \ldots, p'_b\} \sim U(0, 1) \quad \text{and} \quad H_a : \{p'_1, \ldots, p'_b\} \nsim U(0, 1). \tag{6}$$

The resultant KS test statistic reflects the similarity of the distribution of the p-values with the uniform distribution. That is, we use the KS-test to combine $\{p'_1, \ldots, p'_b\}$ to a single p-value to test the null hypothesis:

$$H_0 : \text{no leakage} \quad H_a : \text{leakage} \qquad (7)$$

As proposed by Goodwill et al. [6], we shall assume the significance level α of 1×10^{-5}, and reject the null hypothesis if the p-value return by the KS-test gives $p < 1 \times 10^{-5}$.

3.1   Simulating Leakage Detection

To demonstrate the effectiveness of our method we simulated a single sample, i.e.a simulated acquisition with a trace length of one. We generated sets of data where the sample is the Hamming weight of an 8-bit value with added Gaussian noise to achieve a signal-to-noise ratio of 1 dB. This simulates the setup in the practical environment where the traces are noisy and multiple traces are needed for the t-test to reach the threshold used to indicate leakage.

In Fig. 2, we show how the t-statistic, converted to a p-value, produced by TVLA evolves as the number of traces increases, compared to the evolution of the p-values produced by the KS test on the p-values generated by Bootstrapping, as described above. As proposed by Moradi et al. [10], we plot the negative logarithm base 10 of the p-value in both cases. This allows for simple comparison and the 4.5σ threshold becomes 5. In our simulation, a straightforward implementation of the TVLA will show leakage after 1600 traces. If we apply bootstrapping we can see the leakage from 200 to 400 traces, depending on the number of iterations of the bootstrapping method that is applied.

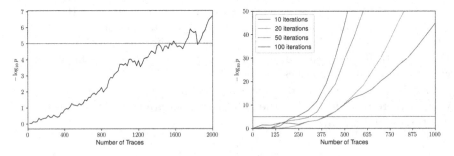

Fig. 2. The evolution of the p-value with increasing number of traces for TVLA (left) and with bootstrapping (right) using simulated traces

To demonstrate why this occurs we generated three sets of single-point traces: Trace-set-A is calculated as the fixed value 5. Trace-set-B and Trace-set-C are calculated from the Hamming weights of 8-bit random values. As above, we added Gaussian noise to achieve a signal-to-noise ratio of 1 dB. In Fig. 3, we can see two plots of frequency versus p-value, where the p-values are generated from 5000 iterations of the bootstrapping method on 1000 samples. The left plot is the result of applying bootstrapping to TVLA between Trace-set-A and Trace-set-B, and the right plot from applying bootstrap enhanced TVLA to Trace-set-B and Trace-set-C. These tests represent the fixed-versus-random case and a comparison case of random-versus-random. In each case the resulting p-values are grouped into bins defined by dividing up the interval $[0, 1]$ into 100 equally sized bins. The difference in the observed distributions is quite striking.

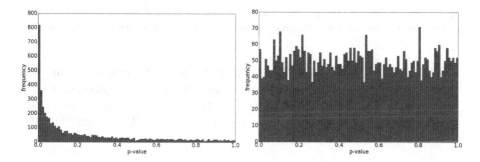

Fig. 3. The sample distribution of the p-values taken from 5000 iterations of the bootstrapping method applied to samples where a the null hypothesis is false (left) and true (right)

3.2   Experimental Results

We then performed experiments to evaluate the practical benefits of bootstrapped enhanced TVLA on a variety of implementations and platforms.

Software AES with Boolean masking. The first experiment is an application of the proposed test to a naïve implementation of a Boolean masked AES on an NXP LPC2124, a 16/32 bit ARM7TDMI-S chip. The implementation was a straightforward 8-bit implementation making use of randomized masked tables for the S-box and the xtime operations. As noted by Balash et al. [2], such implementations are unlikely to be secure. Measurements were acquired with a Langer $RF - U2, 5 - 2$ electromagnetic probe over a decoupling capacitor using a PicoScope 3206D at 400 MS/s with 200 MHz bandwidth. The results of applying bootstrapping to TVLA compared to a straightforward application of TVLA are given in Fig. 4. A straightforward implementation of TVLA shows leakage after around 800 traces. In comparison, we can detect leakage from 60 to 90 traces using Bootstrapping, depending on the number of iterations of the bootstrapping method that is applied.

Unprotected hardware AES. Our next target was a straightforward single round per clock cycle hardware implementation, i.e.all 16 S-boxes are computed in parallel, on a Xilinx Kintex-7 FPGA. We used a custom FPGA prototyping board where we measured the voltage drop across a measurement

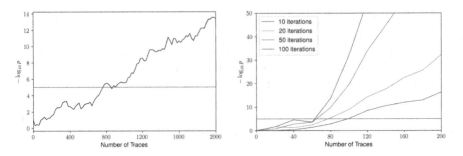

Fig. 4. The evolution of the p-value with increasing number of traces for TVLA (left) and with bootstrapping (right) applied to an implementation of AES in software

resistor using a Tektronix DPO7104C at 1 GS/s. The results of applying bootstrapping to TVLA compared to a straightforward application of TVLA are given in Fig. 5. We only need, at most, around 70 traces to detect the leakage using bootstrapping, while 1000 traces are needed for straightforward TVLA.

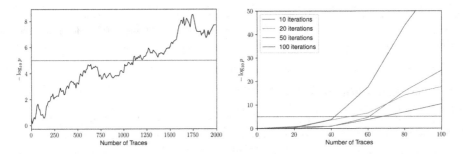

Fig. 5. The evolution of the p-value with increasing number of traces for TVLA (left) and with bootstrapping (right) applied to an unprotected implementation of AES on an FPGA

Lightly protected hardware AES. Our last target was an AES implementation protected with a dual-rail countermeasure with no regard to glitches [16] implemented on the same FPGA platform as the unprotected AES implementation, described above. As previously, we used a custom FPGA prototyping board where we measured the voltage drop across a measurement resistor using a Tektronix DPO7104C at 1 GS/s. Figure 6 shows the results of applying bootstrapping to TVLA compared to a straightforward application of TVLA. Similar to previous cases, significant acceleration of leakage detection can be observed when applying Bootstrapping.

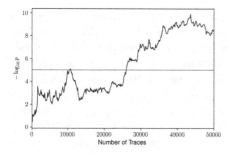 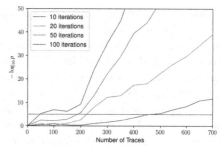

Fig. 6. The evolution of the p-value with increasing number of traces for TVLA (left) and with bootstrapping (right)

In the three experiments presented above, we can see that the bootstrapping method reduces the number of traces required to detect leakage by at least one order of magnitude in all cases. Or, were we to use all the measurements, we would get with a high certainty all the leaking points this set could uncover. For the first two targets presented there is some modest variation in the required number of traces required to see leakage as we increase the number of iterations of the bootstrapping method. However, for the third target (lightly protected hardware AES) the difference is much larger. If bootstrapping is applied 10 times we require 450 traces to detect leakage, whereas we only require 40 traces if bootstrapping is applied 100 times. Both of these numbers stand in stark contrast to the number of traces required by a straightforward TVLA, which is in the order of 1×10^4. This highlights that Bootstrapping significantly accelerates leakage detection.

4   Limitations

The idea of the bootstrap technique is to get an estimate of the deviation of a sample statistic from the true value of the statistic, and relies on the independence of the samples to do so. It does not allow one to extrapolate information from the underlying data if it is not represented in the acquired set. What it can do is give us some assurance on the test statistic and its variation to give more accurate picture. That is, if the collected data set is representative of the underlying distribution, re-sampling will help produce a more accurate statistical analysis. There exists limitations of this technique, as demonstrated in Fig. 7. The top left plot shows the result of a straightforward fixed-versus-random TVLA test, as described in Sect. 2.1, on 5×10^5 traces, where the t-test statistic is turned into a p-value under the null hypothesis that there is no leakage. From this picture, it is clear that some points are already crossing the 4.5σ line (i.e. where $-\log_{10} p = 5$), while other points are getting close to the line. As has been clear from the literature, the results of a t-test are greatly affected by the signal-to-noise ratio of the measurements, and reliably identifying false negatives and false positives is problematic. The bottom right plot shows the bootstrapping method applied $b = 5$ times to the same 5×10^5 traces (we note recommendations on b are significantly larger in literature [11]). This demonstrates that we get a lot more assurance on the points that do not provide evidence the null hypothesis is correct and all points which showed leakage in the original figure are present. The top right plot shows the result of bootstrapping a 1000 traces with $b = 20$, and the bottom left plot shows the result of a bootstrapping of 5000 traces with bootstrapping method applied $b = 5$ times. Neither of these figures are showing the peak around sample point 30 visible in the top left plot indicating that the underlying data is not sufficiently representative of the full set because we have restricted the number of traces. However, we do have peaks at other points that are not visible in the entire set, again caused by bias in the smaller number of traces. While bootstrapping can allow one to determine if leakage is visible on a smaller number of traces, it is subject to bias in the acquired traces.

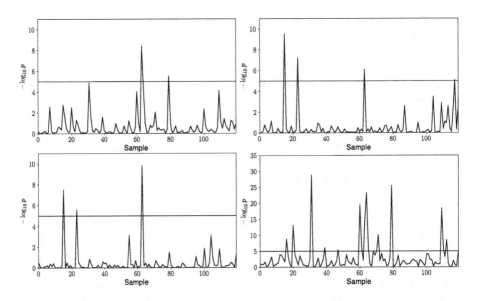

Fig. 7. The negative log of p-value returned by the TVLA test for a fixed-versus-random t-test with 50000 traces (top left), 1000 traces with 20 iterations of the bootstrapping method (top right), 5000 traces with 5 iterations of the bootstrapping method (bottom left) and 50000 traces with 5 iterations of the bootstrapping method (bottom right)

5   Implementation Details

Algorithm 2: Updating $\mathcal{H}$

Input: $\mathcal{H}$ with elements e_{ijkl} where $i \in \{1, \ldots, c\}$, $j \in \{1, \ldots, q\}$,
   $k \in \{1, \ldots, m\}$, $l \in \{1, \ldots, 2^r\}$, a set of n traces $S = \{s_1, \ldots, s_n\}$
   with $s_t = \{s_{t1}, \ldots, s_{tm}\}$ for $t \in 1, \ldots, n$ and associated classifier
   values z_{ti} for each of the classifications. For ease of notation,
   classifier values will be in $1, \ldots, q$ rather than the actual value.

Output: $\mathcal{H}$

```
1  for t = 1 to n do
2  |   for i = 1 to c do
3  |   |   for k = 1 to m do
4  |   |   |   j ← c_i ;
5  |   |   |   l ← s_{t,k} ;
6  |   |   |   e_{i,j,k,l} ← e_{i,j,k,l} + 1 ;
7  |   |   end
8  |   end
9  end
10 return H
```

Statistical processing for side-channel analysis can be computationally intensive and, since bootstrapping runs a statistical analysis multiple times, the process can be even more demanding. The most straightforward approach to computing statistical tests is to store all the acquisitions to a hard disk, read the measurements, run the data through the algorithm of interest and compute the results. Another approach is to use one-pass algorithms, which find the required statistical characteristics during acquisition. Implementations of this concept vary from having all the statistics ready and updating them on-the-fly to updating an accumulator for each new sample and computing results on demand [12–14,17].

Our bootstrapping method requires calculating different statistical tests (i.e., Welch's t-test and KS-test), which use statistical moments and observed frequencies. Hence, we chose a histogram approach, where the histogram contains all the information about the sample distribution that becomes available while acquiring traces and, therefore, describes the sample distributions. It is then possible to derive properties appropriate for both tests as required. Our statistical technique is based on the work by Reparaz et al. [13]. However, we describe in more detail how to implement it using a tensor and how to apply the technique for statistics other than the t-statistic.

We assume that the leakage assessment is performed over a set of observed samples S with n traces of m sample points with c classifications. Each sample point in the measurement has r meaningful bits, corresponding to 2^r integer values, which are used as indices of counter bins. Each classification should have q sets of histograms, where q is the number of bins required to cover each possible classifier value. This approach can be represented as a 4-dimensional set

$\mathbb{Z}_c\mathbb{Z}_q\mathbb{Z}_m\mathbb{Z}_{2^r}$. We shall denote an instance of this set as $\mathcal{H}$. An element of $\mathcal{H}$ is denoted e_{ijkl} where $i \in \{1,\ldots,c\}, j \in \{1,\ldots,q\}, k \in \{1,\ldots,m\}, l \in \{1,\ldots,2^r\}$. For example, in an evaluation of the non-specific fixed-versus-random test, we have $c = 1$ and $q = 2$. If we would wish to conduct a correlation power analysis [3] on an 8-bit intermediate state with the hamming weight model we would have a separate classifier with $c = 256$ and $q = 9$.

Before acquiring data one would set $\mathcal{H}$ to all zeros and update $\mathcal{H}$ after each acquisition of n traces with using Algorithm 2. At any given moment, the results of the statistical tests can be rapidly computed from $\mathcal{H}$.

In this approach, the first two statistical moments, μ and σ^2, with respective elements μ_{ijk} and σ^2_{ijk}, for Welch's t-test become:

$$\mu_{ijk} = \frac{1}{N_{ijk}} \sum_{l=1}^{2^r} e_{i,j,k,l}l$$

$$\sigma^2_{ijk} = \frac{1}{N_{ijk} - 1} \sum_{l=1}^{2^b} e_{i,j,k,l}(l - \mu_{ijk})^2 \tag{8}$$

where $N_{ij} = \sum_{l=1}^{2^r} e_{i,j,1,l}$.

The CDF function d, which is used to define the sampled distribution, see (3), and to compute the KS test, for each point k, classifier i and classifier value j becomes:

$$d_{ijkl} = \sum_{s=1}^{l} e_{i,j,k,s}. \tag{9}$$

Note that it is easy to compute more statistics in a straightforward way. As an example, the correlation traces ρ with elements r_{ik}, representing the k-th point in the i-th trace, are computed from $\mathcal{H}$ as shown in Eq. (10).

We define a mean and variance trace as the first two statistical moments of the trace samples, split by classifiers, with respective elements μ_{ik} and σ^2_{ik}. We define the mean and variance of the classifiers as the μ'_i and σ'^2_i. The pointwise covariance of the traces and classifiers is defined as cov_{ik} with the number of traces defined as N.

$$N = \sum_{j=1}^{q} \sum_{\ell=1}^{2^r} e_{1,j,1,l}$$

$$\mu_{ik} = \frac{1}{N} \sum_{j=1}^{q} \sum_{\ell=1}^{2^r} \ell\, e_{i,j,k,l}$$

$$\sigma_{ik}^2 = \frac{1}{N} \sum_{j=1}^{q} \sum_{\ell=1}^{2^r} H_{i,j,k,l}(\ell - \mu_{ik})^2$$

$$\mu_i' = \frac{1}{N} \sum_{j=1}^{q} \sum_{\ell=1}^{2^r} \ell\, e_{i,j,1,l} \tag{10}$$

$$\sigma_i'^2 = \frac{1}{N} \sum_{j=1}^{q} \sum_{\ell=1}^{2^r} e_{i,j,1,l}(\ell - \mu_{ij}')^2$$

$$cov_{ik} = \sum_{j=1}^{q} \sum_{\ell=1}^{2^r} \ell\, e_{i,j,k,l}$$

$$r_{ik} = \frac{(cov_{ik} - \mu_{ik}\,\mu_i')}{\sqrt{\sigma_{ik}\sigma_i'}}$$

Equations (8), (9) and (10) use the notation used in Algorithm 2, where i is a classifier index, j is a bin, k is a trace sample point, and l is a counter bin index.

This approach has been implemented as a native code python module, compiled from cython code to C code to a dynamically linked DLL. The Intel MKL library has been used to derive the required statistics. The space $\mathcal{H}$ has an element type represented by a 32-bit unsigned integer, which establishes the memory requirement for $\mathcal{H}$ as $4 \times c \times q \times m \cdot 2^r$ bytes. This would allow one to process up to 4 billion traces, which is typically more than sufficient to evaluate leakage. It is important to note that the size of $\mathcal{H}$ should be small enough to fit within CPU L3 cache, which is typically 5, 7 or 15 MB. This implementation strategy allowed us to efficiently evaluate the bootstrapping method.

The speed increase achieved by using bootstrapping is highly dependent on the collection speed. For fast implementations, analysis may take around the same amount of time as the time required to collect all the acquisitions. For some other implementations, where inputs have to be provided for each acquisition, e.g.over a serial port, the time required to collect all the acquisitions can be considerably slower than the subsequent analysis. As noted by Reparaz et al. [13], the speedup of using histograms is a factor of 500 times faster than a regular implementation of the t-statistic calculation, assuming that the acquisitions fit within CPU L3 cache. If we consider bootstrapping, one can argue that an order of magnitude fewer traces are required to get the same information, which will mean that the time required to collect all the acquisitions will decrease by same amount, at the cost of running b bootstrapped regular tests fewer traces.

Fortunately, as shown above, we do not require b to be very large to get significant results, and in general it does make sense to apply bootstrapping.

6   Conclusion

In this paper, we describe how to use bootstrapping to augment side-channel leakage detection tests by repeated sampling with replacement from an acquired set of traces and combining the results of each set. Simulations and experiments show that even a small number of iterations of the bootstrapping method present significant improvements over straightforward TVLA [6]. The bootstrapping method presented above can be applied to other statistical leakage detection methods [4,10], and we would likewise expect a similar increase in performance at the cost of extra calculation time. We also show an efficient way of computing the necessary statistics to compensate for the extra calculation time, based on methods described by Reparaz et al. [13].

Recent work by Bache et al. [1] proposed a somewhat similar approach to our work, although without the application of bootstrapping. They describe using the confidence interval, instead of a single p-value/t-statistic, to improve the assurance of the presence, or absence, of leakage. The confidence interval provides the error-probability for a false negative. However, the confidence interval makes it harder for an evaluator to make a judgment about leakage, when compared to the pass/fail criteria used in straightforward TVLA. In comparison, applying bootstrapping to TVLA, as we describe, provides a single pass/fail parameter from combining p-values, making the results easier to interpret than those provided by the method presented by Bache et al. [1]. Moreover, since applying bootstrapping extracts more information from an existing set of acquisitions, applying bootstrapping to TVLA improves the data-efficiency in leakage detection. That is, it can predict/detect leakage with fewer acquisitions. In comparison, the accuracy of the method presented by Bache et al. using the confidence interval is highly dependent on the number of acquisitions.

Acknowledgement. This research was supported in part by National Science Foundation Award 1617203. The authors would like to thank anonymous reviewers for their valuable feedback.

References

1. Bache, F., Plump, C., Güneysu, T.: Confident leakage assessment—a side-channel evaluation framework based on confidence intervals. In: DATE 2018, pp. 1117–1122. IEEE (2018)
2. Balasch, J., Gierlichs, B., Grosso, V., Reparaz, O., Standaert, F.-X.: On the cost of lazy engineering for masked software implementations. In: Joye, M., Moradi, A. (eds.) CARDIS 2014. LNCS, vol. 8968, pp. 64–81. Springer, Cham (2015). https://doi.org/10.1007/978-3-319-16763-3_5

3. Brier, E., Clavier, C., Olivier, F.: Correlation power analysis with a leakage model. In: Joye, M., Quisquater, J.-J. (eds.) CHES 2004. LNCS, vol. 3156, pp. 16–29. Springer, Heidelberg (2004). https://doi.org/10.1007/978-3-540-28632-5_2

4. Bronchain, O., Schneider, T., Standaert, F.X.: Multi-tuple leakage detection and the dependent signal issue. IACR Transactions on Cryptographic Hardware and Embedded Systems **2**, 318–345 (2019)

5. Efron, B.: Bootstrap methods: another look at the jackknife. Annl. Stat. **7**(1), 1–26 (1979)

6. Goodwill, G., Jun, B., Jaffe, J., Rohatgi, P.: A testing methodology for side-channel resistance validation. NIST non-invasive attack testing workshop. **7**, 115–136 (2011)

7. Hung, H.J., O'Neill, R.T., Bauer, P., Kohne, K.: The behavior of the p-value when the alternative hypothesis is true. Biometrics, 11–22 (1997)

8. Kocher, P., Jaffe, J., Jun, B.: Differential power analysis. In: Wiener, M. (ed.) CRYPTO 1999. LNCS, vol. 1666, pp. 388–397. Springer, Heidelberg (1999). https://doi.org/10.1007/3-540-48405-1_25

9. Mangard, S., Oswald, E., Standaert, F.X.: One for all-all for one: unifying standard differential power analysis attacks. IET Inf. Secur. **5**(2), 100–110 (2011)

10. Moradi, A., Richter, B., Schneider, T., Standaert, F.X.: Leakage detection with the χ^2-test. IACR Trans. Cryptographic Hardware and Embedded Systems **1**, 209–237 (2018)

11. Pattengale, N.D., Alipour, M., Bininda-Emonds, O.R.P., Moret, B.M.E., Stamatakis, A.: How many bootstrap replicates are necessary? J. Comput. Biol. **17**(3), 337–354 (2010)

12. Pebay, P.P.: Formulas for robust, one-pass parallel computation of covariances and arbitrary-order statistical moments. Tech. rep, Sandia National Laboratories (2008)

13. Reparaz, O., Gierlichs, B., Verbauwhede, I.: Fast leakage assessment. In: Fischer, W., Homma, N. (eds.) CHES 2017. LNCS, vol. 10529, pp. 387–399. Springer, Cham (2017). https://doi.org/10.1007/978-3-319-66787-4_19

14. Schneider, T., Moradi, A.: Leakage assessment methodology. In: Güneysu, T., Handschuh, H. (eds.) CHES 2015. LNCS, vol. 9293, pp. 495–513. Springer, Heidelberg (2015). https://doi.org/10.1007/978-3-662-48324-4_25

15. Standaert, F.-X.: How (Not) to use welch's T-test in side-channel security evaluations. In: Bilgin, B., Fischer, J.-B. (eds.) CARDIS 2018. LNCS, vol. 11389, pp. 65–79. Springer, Cham (2019). https://doi.org/10.1007/978-3-030-15462-2_5

16. Tiri, K., Verbauwhede, I.: Securing encryption algorithms against DPA at the logic level: next generation smart card technology. In: Walter, C.D., Koç, Ç.K., Paar, C. (eds.) CHES 2003. LNCS, vol. 2779, pp. 125–136. Springer, Heidelberg (2003). https://doi.org/10.1007/978-3-540-45238-6_11

17. Welford, B.: Note on a method for calculating corrected sums of squares and products. Technometrics **4**(3), 419–420 (1962)

18. Zhang, L., Ding, A.A., Durvaux, F., Standaert, F.X., Fei, Y.: Towards sound and optimal leakage detection procedure. IACR Cryptology ePrint Archive **2017**, 287 (2017)

Evaluation of Attacks and Security

Security Assessment of White-Box Design Submissions of the CHES 2017 CTF Challenge

Estuardo Alpirez Bock[1](✉) and Alexander Treff[2]

[1] Aalto University, Espoo, Finland
`estuardo.alpirezbock@aalto.fi`
[2] University of Lübeck, Lübeck, Germany
`alexander.treff@student.uni-luebeck.de`

Abstract. In 2017, the first CHES Capture the Flag Challenge was organized in an effort to promote good design candidates for white-box cryptography. In particular, the challenge assessed the security of the designs with regard to key extraction attacks. A total of 94 candidate programs were submitted, and all of them were broken eventually. Even though most candidates were broken within a few hours, some candidates remained robust against key extraction attacks for several days, and even weeks. In this paper, we perform a qualitative analysis on all candidates submitted to the CHES 2017 Capture the Flag Challenge. We test the robustness of each challenge against different types of attacks, such as automated attacks, extensions thereof and reverse engineering attacks. We are able to classify each challenge depending on their robustness against these attacks, highlighting how challenges vulnerable to automated attacks can be broken in a very short amount of time, while more robust challenges demand for big reverse engineering efforts and therefore for more time from the adversaries. Besides classifying the robustness of each challenge, we also give data regarding their size and efficiency and explain how some of the more robust challenges could actually provide acceptable levels of security for some real-life applications.

Keywords: White-box cryptography · Capture the flag · Differential computation analysis · Differential fault analysis

1 Introduction

White-box cryptography was introduced by Chow, Eisen, Johnson and van Oorschot (CEJO [16,17]) as a method for implementing cryptographic software running in insecure environments. In the white-box attack model, an adversary is assumed to be in full control of the execution environment of an implementation and to have complete access to the implementation code. White-box cryptography aims to implement cryptographic programs in such way that they remain secure in such attack scenarios.

ⓒ Springer Nature Switzerland AG 2021
G. M. Bertoni and F. Regazzoni (Eds.): COSADE 2020, LNCS 12244, pp. 123–146, 2021.
https://doi.org/10.1007/978-3-030-68773-1_7

The original use case of white-box cryptography concerned digital rights management (DRM) applications. In recent years, white-box cryptography regained popularity with the introduction of host card emulation (HCE) in Android 4.4. HCE introduces the possibility to handle near field communication (NFC) traffic via software programs, running in the CPU in a mobile phone. In this context, applications using NFC protocols can be implemented in *software only*, which provides advantages in terms of cost, efficiency and upgrading of the programs. In this line, NFC protocols running on HCE have been embraced by the payment industry and white-box cryptography has been suggested as a software countermeasure technique for protecting cryptographic keys in mobile payment applications (see e.g. [24, 43]).

In the meantime, a branch of academic research has been dedicated to constructing secure white-box implementations. Initial steps have been taken on formally defining security notions for white-box cryptography, i.e. on defining *which* security goals should be achieved by a white-box cryptographic scheme [21, 25]. An important and necessary security goal for white-box cryptography is the property of security against key extraction (or *unbreakability* as defined in [21]). Namely, given that in the white-box attack model an adversary is assumed to have complete access to an implementation code, it is important that the adversary is still unable to extract the value of the embedded secret key of that implementation. To approach this goal, many design frameworks follow the initial proposal from CEJO, where the authors suggest to implement a cipher as a network of pre calculated look-up tables. The look-up tables correspond to calculation steps of the cipher and these steps are dependent on the value of the secret key. To stop an adversary from easily deriving the value of the secret key from the look-up tables, the entries of the look-up tables are usually encoded via a combination of wide linear encodings and narrow non-linear encodings (see [36] for a detailed description of this design framework for AES implementations). Following this line, white-box constructions for DES [17, 35] and AES [5, 15, 16, 30, 45] have been proposed, but subsequently broken by [26, 29, 44] and [8, 22, 34, 37, 38], respectively. As it turns out, many proposed constructions were shown to be vulnerable against key extraction attacks, performed via algebraic or differential cryptanalysis.

In recent years, a new branch of *grey-box attacks* on white-box cryptographic implementations was introduced, putting forward the differential computation and differential fault analysis attacks [3]. The differential computation analysis (DCA) corresponds to the software counterpart of the differential power analysis (DPA) attack performed on hardware cryptographic implementations [32]. Similarly, the differential fault analysis (DFA) on white-box programs is performed in the same way as fault injection attacks are performed on hardware implementations [7, 13]. The introduction of the DCA and DFA attacks lead to a new branch of *automated* attacks on white-box implementations. The most attractive advantage of such automated attacks is that they allow an adversary to extract the secret key from numerous white-box implementations, with little to no need of reverse engineering efforts. The adversary thereby does not need to know internal details of the implementations under attack, and can simply run a script on the white-box program, collecting data which is later analysed via statistical methods and reveals key dependencies. Extensions and generalizations of the DCA attack have been presented in [3,12,40]. As these works show (and as we confirm in this paper), popular design frameworks for implementing white-box cryptography are specially vulnerable to such automated attacks.

1.1 CHES 2017 Capture the Flag Challenge

In an effort to promote good design candidates for white-box cryptography, the ECRYPT-CSA consortium organized the white-box competition CHES 2017 Capture the Flag Challenge [23], and a second edition was later organized by Cybercrypt in 2019 [20]. In the 2017 competition, designers were invited to submit white-box implementations of AES-128, which should thereby remain robust against key extraction attacks. The source code of the submitted programs should be no bigger than 50 MB in size, with the executable being no bigger than 20 MB. Finally, submitted programs should need no longer than 1 s per each execution, i.e. for performing an encryption. On the other side, attackers were invited to try to break submitted candidate implementations by extracting their embedded secret keys. Note that attackers would have access to the source code of the implementations. In this competition, a program would be ranked according to the amount of time it remained unbroken: the longest a program would remain unbroken, the higher rank it became. A total of 94 candidate programs were submitted and all candidates were broken eventually. Most candidates remained unbroken for less than a day after their submission. Interestingly however, a number of candidates remained unbroken for several days, with the winning candidate resisting key extraction attacks for a total of 28 days. It is fair to assume that candidate implementation which were broken within hours were vulnerable to automated attacks, while longer lived candidates initially provided resistance against such attacks, and demanded bigger reverse-engineering efforts from the attackers.

The table below summarizes the results obtained for the 5 highest ranked challenges, with challenge 777 being ranked the highest as it remained robust for a total of 28 days. Besides remaining robust for several days, some of these candidates also provide interesting numbers with regard to their size and efficiency. For instance the second ranked challenge, challenge 815, remained robust for 12 days and had thereby a size of 18 MB and an execution time of 0.07 s. This challenge is 10 MB smaller and notably faster than the winning challenge. Similarly, challenge 854, 5th ranked, remained robust for 8 days had a size of 11 MB and an execution time of 0.23 s.

The results shown in the white-box competition regarding the highest ranked candidates invite for some optimism in the research field of white-box cryptography.[1] While studies of white-box cryptography aim to construct programs which remain secure against a polynomial time adversary, a reasonable level of security

---

[1] In fact during the 2019 edition, a total of 3 candidates remained unbroken.

Rank	Challenge ID	Size	Speed	Days unbroken
1	777	28 MB	0.37 s	28
2	815	18 MB	0.07 s	12
3	753	23 MB	0.16 s	11
4	877	32 MB	0.004 s	10
5	845	11 MB	0.23 s	8

for some real-life applications could be achieved via white-box programs which remain robust for at least several days. Namely, since we are considering cryptographic programs implemented completely in software, one could take advantage of a *software renewal* characteristic and update the white-box programs on a regular basis. In this case, we could consider an adversary who invests several days on reverse engineering a white-box implementation running on an application. However before the adversary manages to extract the secret key from the implementation, the application could be updated with a new white-box program using a new secret key. This would cancel out the efforts performed by an attacker up to that point, and force him to start all over again. Note however that for this approach to work as expected, each updated white-box implementation needs to be compiled according to different and independent design frameworks, such that what the adversary learns while analyzing the first design does not help him in any way when analyzing future versions of the program. Moreover, white-box designs could already be updated as soon as any design mistakes or vulnerabilities are spotted, or after a security breach is discovered. In case that a breach is discovered and an attacker manages to break one implementation, we can aim to quickly update all designs with a new version of the program. Here, even if the attacker managed to break one program, he still does not gain so much from it as we manage to update and protect all other programs.

1.2   Our Contribution

In this paper, we take a closer look at each candidate implementation submitted to the CHES 2017 Capture the Flag Challenge. As all candidates were eventually broken during the competition, we know that they are not completely resistant against key extraction attacks. In this paper however, we want to understand how each challenge can be broken and we analyze each implementation by performing a selected line of attacks on them. This way we perform a study regarding the size, speed and robustness of each candidate implementation. We test their vulnerability against automated attacks such as the traditional DCA and DFA. For performing automated attacks, we use the frameworks provided by the Side-Channel Marvels[2] and Jlsca[3], which we describe as part of this work. Via our analysis, we are able to classify the challenges in the following four groups: (1)

---

[2] https://github.com/SideChannelMarvels.
[3] https://github.com/Riscure/Jlsca.

challenges which are vulnerable to DCA attacks, (2) challenges which are vulnerable to DFA attacks, (3) challenges which are vulnerable to extended versions of DCA attacks, such as *second order* DCA and finally (4) challenges which are resistant to automated attacks and demand bigger reverse engineering efforts from the adversaries. This classification gives insights on the amount of time needed for extracting the key from each implementation. Namely, running a traditional automated attack usually demands only some minutes, while extended versions of the automated attacks demand several hours and reverse engineering attacks demand for days and in some cases even multiple weeks.

We explain how some of these challenges are initially resistant to these attacks, but are then easily modified such that automated attacks against them are bearable. We also show how we extend a traditional DCA attack to a second order DCA attack in order to extract the key from a masked implementation. Finally, we give insights to the challenges that were not vulnerable to such attacks and which provided higher layers of security. Our success performing the attacks on the challenges stands in line with the robustness many challenges showed during the competition. Namely as we show, automated attacks were successful on a large group of challenges, which were the lowest ranked challenges in the competition. Similarly, the highest ranked challenges demanded bigger efforts from the adversaries and could not be simply broken via automated attacks. Finally, we give a short overview on the results of the 2019 edition of the competition. We leave a detailed analysis of the designs submitted to the 2019 edition as future work.

Successively to our survey, we describe how robust white-box implementations might be useful for some real-life applications as long as we are able to upgrade them on a regular basis. We explain how the property of *scalability* and a considerable gap between the compilation time of a program and the time an attacker needs for breaking it need to be considered.

The rest of this paper is structured as follows. In Sect. 2 we describe the tools used for performing our analyses on the design candidates. More precisely, we describe the scripts we use for running DCA, DFA and variations of those attacks. In Sect. 3 we describe the results we obtain from our security assessment, where we classify the design candidates according to the attacks they are vulnerable to and we discuss interesting aspects of the most robust candidates. We conclude the paper in Sect. 4 with a discussion on how robust white-box candidates can provide a reasonable level of security for real life applications.

2   Tooling

In this section, we describe the attack tools used for analyzing the design candidates of the competition. Each candidate was first analyzed via DCA. If no successful key recovery was performed, we would follow to attack via DFA. In case none of these two attacks was successful, we would turn back to reverse engineering part of the implementation code of the design under attack to try to adjust it such that our tooling worked on the design.

2.1 Preprocessing the Source Code

In the competition, designers were required to hand in the source code of their candidate implementations. Attackers could therefore also analyze the source code in order to perform key extraction attacks. For this reason, robust candidate implementations obfuscated not only the control flow of the cryptographic operations, but also the source code of the implementation. Some candidates managed to prevent commonly used text editors from parsing the file by using very long lines. Some candidates also included specific sequences of bytes that only a subset of editors and compilers would handle correctly. For example, relaxed_brown contains a line consisting of 31 588 characters (see Fig. 1). Moreover, the code hides a function definition between two huge arrays, presumably by using specific control characters such that the function is visible to the compiler, but is hidden when analyzed in the editor.

```
void AES_128(char*ct, char*pt)    void AES_128(char*ct, char*pt)
{                                 {
    /*
        h
        a
        c
        k                             strcpyn(ct,pt,1<<24);
        e                             memcpy(ct,pt,16);
        d
    */
    return;                           return;
}                                 }
```

Fig. 1. Fragments of the source code of relaxed_brown. The left side shows the code visible when opening it on a text editor. It looks as if the code consists only of a comment. However, the comment line containing the 'k' expands to the right and consists of 31 588 characters hiding two function calls and almost all other characters are white spaces. The right side shows the code after preprocessing it with clang-format (the function strcpyn contains the actual AES code).

A second example is the winning challenge adoring_poitras which can be successfully compiled using gcc, but cannot be compiled using clang. We use clang-format to parse source files in an automated way to generate a modified, yet functionally equivalent source file that does not contain any of these tricks and is easier to understand.

2.2 Tooling for DCA

We perform the DCA attack as described in Sect. 3 of [3]. We use a custom Intel PIN[4] plugin specifically adapted to the competition rules. That is, our plugin is

---

[4] https://software.intel.com/en-us/articles/pin-a-dynamic-binary-instrumentation-tool.

hooked to the call `AES_128_encrypt` to acquire computation traces that exactly resemble the actual encryption function. These traces are then converted to a *Riscure Inspector Trace set* files (TRS) via a python library *trsfile*[5] such that they can be analyzed using Jlsca[6]. We annotate the computation trace with both the program input and output to be able to launch the attack from either the input or output values.

Jlsca. Jlsca is an open-source side-channel toolbox written in Julia by Cees-Bart Breunesse that allows to perform highly optimized differential computation analysis on software execution traces. It supports different leakage models, e.g. the Klemsa model where we also consider 240 AES dual ciphers as described in [6]. Dual ciphers of AES use different SBoxes throughout the computation but yield the same result as a standard AES at the end of the computations. More specifically, they can be seen as isomorphisms of AES, which are not based on the Rijndael Sboxes. Instead, the dual ciphers implement alternative Sboxes and additional computations are later performed on intermediate values, such that the dual ciphers are functional equivalent to a standard AES cipher. We refer to the Diploma thesis of Jakub Klemsa [31] for a more detailed explanation and analysis of dual ciphers. Some submitted challenges were implementing dual ciphers of AES. For such implementations, the SideChannelMarvels' Daredevil does not reveal the correct key. Namely, Daredevil is configured such that it targets standard Rijndael Sboxes, so the predicted Sbox outputs do not match when attacking dual cipher implementations. Jlsca on the other hand predicts the intermediate values for all possible Sboxes and hence reveals the correct key for challenges implementing dual ciphers as well.

Jlsca also implements optimization techniques such as Duplicate Column Removal (DCR) and Conditional Sample Reduction (CSR). Such techniques enable us to check these 240 dual ciphers in the same amount of time (or even less) than Daredevil needs for running the analysis. For a more detailed discussion on the above mentioned reduction techniques, we refer to the paper by Breunesse, Kizhvatov, Muijrers and Spruyt [14].

Analyzing a Single Computation Trace. Some implementations generated very long traces, e.g. `determined_goldwasser` or `friendly_wing`. In some cases, we were still able to launch the attack after some (very) limited manual effort in locating the first (or last) round. We configured our tracing tool to allow tracing just a specific region of interest by giving lower and upper bounds of sample indices, thus speeding up the trace acquisition process. Sometimes, we were not able to launch an automated DCA attack because the traces were too long and we weren't successful in locating a usable subset of samples of manageable size. In cases this was not working, this was mostly caused by the design artificially extending the execution time, for example by using a virtualization technique

---

[5] https://github.com/Riscure/python-trsfile.
[6] https://github.com/Riscure/Jlsca.

(see [42] for insights on the virtualization technique and a generic approach on how to recover a devirtualized code from a virtualized one). Specifically Tigress[7] was used in favour of code obfuscation throughout the competition (see e.g. relaxed_allen). Our experience shows that automated DFA might be more feasible in these cases as one usually will find a fault-sensitive look-up table using the corresponding DFA scripts in a reasonable amount of time.

2.3 Tooling for DFA

We perform the DFA attack as described in Sect. 7 of [3]. We use the JeanGrey tool from the (open source) SideChannelMarvels repository. This tool induces faults by randomly flipping bits of different regions of the binary. In some cases, we perform the DFA *manually*. That is, we inspect the source code and induce faults by flipping bits in specific lines of code. As an example: state[0] ^= 1; is used to flip one bit of a byte belonging to some state array.

3 Security Assessment and Classification

We evaluate the robustness of the design candidates by testing automated attacks (DCA and DFA) on them, as well as modifications of such attacks. Our aim is to find out how many candidates can actually be broken via automated attacks and without big reverse engineering efforts. We classify the candidates in two main groups: one group for *automated vulnerable* and one group for *automated resistant*. These groups should reflect the difficulty an adversary might have when attempting to break each white-box and the time we can expect each white-box to remain unbroken. This also holds for recovery from a successful attack: if an attacker succeeds at breaking an implementation using an automated attack, a new implementation based on the same design can be broken by the same automated attack. If on the other hand reverse engineering efforts are needed, even a slightly different design already requires adaptations to the attack. In the end of this section, we focus on the automated resistant candidates and classify them according to their size and speed. Some candidates achieve robustness but demand high numbers in terms of size and execution time. Other candidates, on the other hand, reflect more useful designs as they provide a good trade-off between efficiency and security.

In the following, we describe our assessment process. Given a candidate implementation, we first assess its security via DCA. If we are able to extract the key from that implementation via DCA, we classify the given candidate under automated vulnerable, and in a subgroup thereof which we call *DCA vulnerable*. If no successful DCA attack can be performed, we run a DFA attack on the implementation and in case of success, we classify the candidate under *DFA vulnerable*. Note that in some cases, a white-box design might resist a traditional DCA attack by implementing masking countermeasures. In this case a *higher order*

DCA might be a successful way of attacking [10,12]. Therefore, if neither first order DCA or DFA succeeds, we perform a second order DCA. Note that the second order DCA can also be implemented in an automated way as we explain later in this section.

A total of 94 challenges were submitted. One of these challenges, thirsty_aryabhata, was not a valid submission as it didn't implement any AES operation. For this reason, our studies consider a total of 93 challenges.

3.1 DCA Vulnerable Designs

A total of 50 design candidates were vulnerable to a traditional DCA attack, which we could perform in a completely automated way. That is, we were able to extract the key from all 50 designs by simply running the DCA script, with no need of adapting it for any implementation. All of these designs were broken within minutes during the competition. In fact, a large number of these submissions were not even white-box designs. 37 designs were reference AES implementations (or similar) which did not implement any white-box countermeasures. 19 of these 37 designs were submitted by *chaes* and were all implemented using a total of six lookup tables each consisting of 256 entries from which the key can be retrieved directly by looking at the right offset. The remaining 13 candidates did implement white-box countermeasures, such as code obfuscation or they were table based implementations (e.g. following the approach proposed by CEJO [16]).

Table 1 lists the design candidates vulnerable to the DCA attack which showed at least minimal effort of implementing countermeasures – reference implementations were omitted to improve readability. In the table we rank the candidates according to the time they remained unbroken during the competition, where the candidate implementation on the top remained unbroken for the longest and the candidate at the bottom remained unbroken for the shortest period of time. We use the same ranking approach for the other tables shown in this paper. Note however that this ranking does not necessarily reflect the robustness of an implementation in comparison to other implementations listed in the same table. Namely in some cases, candidate designs remained unbroken for certain amounts of time due to the competition setup, and not due to the robustness of their implementations (see Sect. 3.2). In the table, the entry *size* gives the size of the source code of the implementation in megabytes. *Runtime* gives the time in milliseconds needed for one execution of the program, i.e. for performing one encryption. *Time unbroken* indicates the time (hours) the implementation remained unbroken during the competition time.

Besides the 50 candidates mentioned above, 5 further candidates could be broken via DCA after manually performing some simple modifications on the source code of the programs. These candidates implemented countermeasures against the DCA attack such as dummy operations which led to a misalignment of the software traces, or implementation of the round functions in a non constant way. That is, the sequence of the operations was performed differently depending on the input message to be encrypted. However, in most of these

Table 1. DCA vulnerable designs. ε corresponds to a runtime of less than 0.01 ms.

Rank	Name	Id	Size	Runtime	Time unbroken
1	focused_gary	20	17.044	0.24	08:01
2	cranky_mccarthy	27	17.912	5.35	05:19
3	famous_stonebraker	55	1.336	0.02	04:29
4	youthful_hawking	150	18.509	0.34	03:23
5	elastic_brahmagupta	146	12.415	0.02	00:51
6	hopeful_liskov	3	4.702	ε	00:47
7	thirsty_fermat	57	8.404	2.21	00:44
8	happy_yalow	60	5.002	0.07	00:28
9	nostalgic_noether	61	4.97	0.07	00:26
10	lucid_roentgen	24	4.777	1.17	00:22
11	modest_clarke	30	7.559	1.26	00:18
12	zealous_ardinghelli	31	7.572	1.23	00:12
13	stupefied_varahamihira	16	4.704	ε	00:11

cases, the code was not heavily obfuscated on source level, and particularly the algorithmic part was usually of magnitudes smaller than the data part of the code (tables, etc.). Therefore, it was simple to identify the specific non-constant logic or dummy operations by hand. For some challenges, the difference plots were used to estimate the position where the non-constant code is being placed (i.e., it occurs on all rounds vs. only on the last round).

We then modified the codes in a way that they would have a constant runtime, which enabled us to perform a DCA attack. As an example, we show in Fig. 2 fragments of the candidate `pensive_shaw`, which included instructions for increasing the number of operations in order to artificially enlarge trace files and slow down the attacking process.

Table 2 lists the five challenges we could attack via DCA after small modifications. Some design candidates implemented virtualization, but it was simple to de-virtualize the code and make it run without the virtualization layer.

Table 2. DCA vulnerable designs after minimal modifications

Rank	Name	Id	Size	Runtime	Time unbroken	Notes
1	dreamy_fermi	754	1.328	0.33	17:24	Dummy code removal
2	relaxed_brown	852	18.461	121.93	05:32	Devirtualization
3	reverent_beaver	48	6.187	1.12	01:51	Variable to constant rewrite
4	cool_cori	791	1.61	37.16	00:15	Dummy code removal
5	pensive_shaw	778	1.518	82.34	00:12	Dummy code removal

```
switch (*((int *)_obf_3_MOD_AES_encrypt_$pc[0])) {
case 47:
    // cT() is computationally expensive
    // but always computes the same value
    *((unsigned long *)(_obf_3_MOD_AES_encrypt_$locals + 856)) = cT();
    break;
// several more cases, all similar to the one above
}

// we replace the computation with its result
u32 cT() { return 1262335309; }
```

Fig. 2. Source code of pensive_shaw. The code contains a computationally expensive function cT(), yielding always the same result. We dump the value and replace the function by its result. This reduces runtime and trace size to a minimum, making DCA feasible again.

3.2 DFA Vulnerable Designs

DFA was only applied for analyzing candidate designs resistant against the DCA attack. Namely, some designs implemented virtualization layers, where the encryption program uses a virtual machine to execute part of the code [41]. In this context, virtualization made it difficult to implement a traditional DCA attack as it artificially blew up the number of samples per trace. Instead of a single atomic operation, a large sequence of operations emulating this atomic operation is being traced when virtualization is implemented. However in some cases, virtualization did not represent a countermeasure against DFA, since DFA works by inducing faults at the right spot of computation. Instead of inducing a fault (e.g., flipping a single bit) on the aforementioned atomic operation, the fault is induced at some point of the corresponding (large) sequence of operations. The fault is propagated throughout the computation, yielding the desired effect on the output. The following 14 designs could be broken using the Jean-Grey tool from the SideChannelMarvels repository. We could break each design by simply running the script for (at most) one hour.

Note that half of the designs in Table 3 were broken within minutes after they were submitted to the competition. Interestingly the first 3 designs remained unbroken for over three hours, with the first challenge remaining unbroken for 5:46 h. The reason why some of these challenges remained unbroken for several hours during the competition might have more to do with the setting of the competition, and less with the robustness of the challenges themselves. Namely during the competition, some attackers used automated scripts for constantly checking if new challenges were submitted. The scripts would immediately download the challenges upon their submission and attack them via DFA or DCA in an automated way. This way, some attackers were able to break many challenges within minutes. However the submission server implemented challenge-response tests such as Captchas in order to stop the scripts from working in such a fully automated way (see Philippe Teuwen's talk during the WhibOx 2019 Workshop for notes on his experience attacking the challenges during the 2017 competi-

Table 3. Automated DFA vulnerable designs

Rank	Name	Id	Size	Runtime	Time unbroken	Notes
1	compassionate_albattani	816	26.135	174.66	05:46	Virtualized
2	xenodochial_northcutt	106	21.969	5.16	04:09	
3	smart_ardinghelli	846	3.016	367.99	03:09	Virtualized
4	musing_lalande	813	2.562	147.38	02:42	Virtualized
5	frosty_hypatia	812	2.575	206.28	02:11	Virtualized
6	dazzling_panini	46	38.911	4.67	01:17	
7	angry_jones	880	2.97	337.37	00:55	Virtualized
8	determined_goldwasser	34	19.987	3.607	00:50	
9	relaxed_allen	755	13.274	16.13	00:32	Virtualized
10	smart_lamarr	749	13.159	11.79	00:22	Virtualized
11	friendly_lewin	811	2.605	0.216	00:21	Virtualized
12	friendly_edison	35	21.902	3.12	00:17	
13	quirky_mayer	142	8.305	0.87	00:16	
14	dazzling_neumann	143	8.302	0.99	00:03	

tion [39]). One might assume that the attackers were not always able to react quickly to such challenge-response tests. This could explain why some challenges in Table 3 remained unbroken for several hours, while we were able to break them within an hour during our studies. Additionally, there might have been cases where a large number of challenges were submitted at the same time, thus delaying the automated assessment of some challenges.

Manual DFA. Some submissions implemented classic DFA countermeasures, such as redundant computations (see e.g. [1,28]). Given such countermeasures, it was not possible to run the DFA script from the SideChannelMarvels repository in a fully automated way. However for some challenges, it was easy to deactivate such countermeasures manually as their implementations were not highly obfuscated. An example can be seen in Fig. 3, where we show part of the source code of silly_feynman. The program implements countermeasures checking for faulty computations, but it is easy to locate the lines of the code which implement these countermeasures. Table 4 lists 7 challenges which we successfully attacked via a *manual* DFA. For these challenges, we either removed lines of the code such that our DFA script would run successfully, or we added specific lines of code which would help us identify the correct spots for injecting faults. We explain the second approach below.

For some design candidates, running the DFA script did not work accordingly due to the static nature of how JeanGrey works. JeanGrey modifies the binary file prior to attempting to perform the DFA attack. The script XORs regions of the binary file using a type of binary search to iteratively find the correct spot

```
/* dummy round */
SubByte_aes2(dumst, AES2_Sprime[tindex], permu1, permu2);
// S-box
ShiftRows(dumst, 1);
MixColumns(dumst, aes2_mixcolprod[tindex]); /* transformed mixcolprod table */
AddRoundKey_aes2(dumst, dumclef, permu1, permu2);

/* real round */
SubByte_aes2(st, AES2_Sprime[tindex], permu1, permu2);
// S-box
ShiftRows(st, 1);
MixColumns(st, aes2_mixcolprod[tindex]); /* transformed mixcolprod table */
AddRoundKey_aes2(st, clef, permu1, permu2);

/* fault check round */
SubByte_aes2(fltst, AES2_Sprime[tindex], permu0, permu0);
// S-box
ShiftRows(fltst, 1);
MixColumns(fltst, aes2_mixcolprod[tindex]); /* transformed mixcolprod table */
AddRoundKey_aes2(fltst, clef, permu0, permu0);
```

Fig. 3. Source code of silly_feynman. The code included comments explaining the purpose of the functions defined. This made it very easy to locate functions implementing DFA countermeasures, such as redundant computation.

to induce a fault by reacting to the outcome of the modification. This approach works well when manipulating actual data such as lookup tables or when just a simple adjustment of control flow is needed to induce useful faulty outputs. However, this approach often does not yield a useful result when a more complicated control flow change is needed. To deal with these shortcomings, we opted for a slightly more complicated, yet non-automated approach for locating the correct spot for inducing faults, which we refer to as *conditional* fault injection. Conditional fault injection consisted on altering the source code in such way that we would keep track of some internal variable (e.g. a counter), and we would inject a fault only after the value of that variable would reach some threshold. The idea here is that the repeated execution of some lines of code usually corresponds to the execution of some round function and the value of the variable could help us recognize the round that is being executed. For instance, one can observe an internal loop counter which starts, say, at value 0 and reaches a value of 60 000 after all AES rounds have been computed. This internal loop counter might already belong to the implementation itself or we can add it manually. The first 45 000 iterations will most probably not yield any useful fault injection, as we usually target the eighth or ninth round for injecting faults. On the other hand, one may assume that targeting one of the remaining 15 000 iterations might yield a useful fault injection which can then be done in an automated way using the internal counter as a trigger.

We implemented the approach mentioned above by adding a few lines to the corresponding implementations, specifically crafted to the specific implementation, as outlined in Fig. 4. One important aspect to consider is that these modifications do not need to work for any specific input. It suffices to obtain correctly faulted outputs for one specific plaintext-ciphertext pair chosen beforehand to compute the last round key. In those cases, we took advantage of the fact that we had access to the corresponding source code of the design candidates. Namely in some cases a relatively simple inspection of the source code helped us locate the precise spots for injecting faults and performing a successful DFA attack.

```
void AES_128_encrypt(char* ciphertext, char* plaintext)
{
  int COUNTER = atoi(ARGV[1]); // injected code
  for (int i = 0; i < 60000; i++) {
    if (COUNTER == i) { // injected code
      continue;
    }
    func(a,b,c,d); // original WB code
  }
}
```

Fig. 4. Example for conditional fault injection. We add code to skip a specific loop iteration. The exact iteration is given as a parameter to enable automated search of useful values by repeated execution.

Table 4. Manual DFA vulnerable designs. The top challenge festive_jennings earned one strawberry point during the competition.

Rank	Name	Id	Size	Runtime	Time unbroken	Notes/
1	festive_jennings	11	23.716	0.09	24:01	Brute-forced last 4 bytes
2	eloquent_indiana	52	14.897	23.80	24:00	Attacked loop structure
3	nifty_heisenberg	48	14.650	3.48	18:23	Removed DFA protection
4	vigilant_wescoff	12	3.465	92.74	10:59	Faulted 32-byte state array
5	friendly_wing	132	22.606	18.19	02:05	Attacked loop structure
6	silly_feynman	742	0.072	0.10	01:09	Removed DFA protection
7	agitated_wilson	141	11.599	43.43	01:01	

Note that all challenges listed in Table 4 remained unbroken during the competition for at least one hour. This suggests that attackers also needed to first inspect the code and implement some changes before actually attacking them or extracting their secrets. This assumption is more evident when focusing on the top four challenges, which remained unbroken for 11 to 24 h. The top challenge festive_jennings even managed to gain one strawberry point during the competition, which was awarded if the challenge managed to remain unbroken for at least 24 h.

3.3   Second Order DCA

We were unable to recover the key of design candidate `priceless_stallman` via DCA or DFA attacks. In particular, it achieved resistance against DCA via a masking scheme, where intermediate values were masked with different shares for each input plaintext. We were able, however, to successfully attack this design candidate via second order DCA [12]. As it is known for higher-order DCA, the number of samples used for performing an analysis increases quadratically compared to a first order DCA attack. This is due to the nature that all possible combinations of samples are evaluated, which results in a total number of $n(n-1)/2$ samples for second-order analysis compared to n samples for first-order analysis. Using optimization techniques such as DCR and CSR [14], this number can be heavily reduced and higher-order attacks become feasible. Figure 5 shows a difference plot for the given challenge, showing periods of execution where the data is heavily changed. Locating such regions helped us identify the correct spot for recording software execution traces and perform a second order DCA. We ran our analysis for about 8 h in order to extract the first 8 key bytes in parallel. Afterwards, the analysis for the other 8 key bytes ran for another 8 h resulting in a total runtime of about 16 h using Jlsca. Table 5 summarizes some details of the implementation.

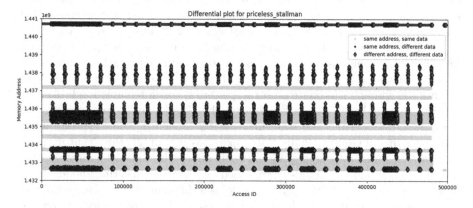

Fig. 5. Difference plot for `priceless_stallman`. Accumulation of dark spots indicates a change of data and control flow whereas green regions resemble constant parts of the implementation. We successfully recovered the key using a second-order analysis of the first quarter of the heavily changing region in the beginning (approx. 20 000 samples).

Interestingly, this challenge only remained unbroken for a bit more than one hour during the competition. We assume that a more efficient attack path can be taken to obtain the secret key, such as possibly a variation of a DFA attack. Namely, such masking countermeasures, where the shares are determined by the input message, do not imply robustness against DFA since some input plaintext

Table 5. Second order DCA vulnerable design

Rank	Name	Id	Size	Runtime	Time unbroken	Notes
1	priceless_stallman	738	5.386	0.29	01:18	Implements masking

m will always use the same masking. Thus in theory, one could perform a DFA, since one always uses the same input message and injects different faults. We refer to [10] for alternative attack strategies on masked white-box implementations.

3.4 Automated Resistant Challenges

A total of 16 challenges remained resistant to our attempts using DCA and DFA attacks. 12 of these challenges earned strawberry points during the competition time. These challenges implemented notably stronger layers of obfuscation, such that we were not able to remove the virtualization or masking techniques as described in the previous sections. Table 6 lists the candidate challenges that we were not able to break. The first part of the table shows the candidates which earned points during the competition, i.e. which remained unbroken for at least 24 h. The bottom part of the table consists of candidates which did not earn any points. Note however that the candidates in the bottom part of the table also remained unbroken for a considerable amount of time, possibly confirming that those candidates also provide some robustness against automated attacks.

Given that most of these challenges remained unbroken for a considerable time during the competition phase, it is fair to assume that attackers were forced to invest considerable reverse engineering efforts for breaking them. Consider for instance the winning candidate adoring_poitras, which remained unbroken for 28 days. This challenge was submitted by the CryptoLux[8] team consisting of Biryukov and Udovenko and was subsequently broken by the CryptoExperts[9] team consisting of Goubin, Paillier, Rivain and Wang. In [27] the CryptoExperts team provides a step-by-step guide on their approach applied for breaking the challenge. Their main techniques were based on reverse engineering and algebraic attacks. The authors explain that the code uses different obfuscation techniques such as *name* obfuscation (giving each function and variable random, unrelated names) and virtualization. Additionally, the source code consists of many functions which are never used (up to 80%). This was probably implemented with the goal of making it difficult for an attacker to deobfuscate the code. In fact, the process of deobfuscating and *cleaning* the code such that it consists only of functions which are actually used demands large efforts as it can only be done manually. Once this is done, more generalized methodologies can be followed in order to break such obscure implementations (the authors list further steps such as single static analysis, transformation of the circuit, circuit minimization, data dependency analysis, etc.).

---

[8] https://www.cryptolux.org/index.php/Home.
[9] https://www.cryptoexperts.com/technologies/white-box/.

Table 6. Unbroken candidates. The first part of the table consists of challenges which earned points during the competition phase. sad_goldstine was the smallest challenge from those which earned any points.

Rank	Name	Id	Size	Runtime	Time unbroken	Notes
1	adoring_poitras	777	27.252	379.83	685:42	Winning challenge
2	competent_agnesi	815	17.359	6.923	290:15	
3	bright_morse	753	22.649	163.14	283:50	
4	vibrant_goldberg	877	30.126	5.15	254:59	
5	hungry_clarke	845	10.925	230.76	196:44	
6	jolly_davinci	751	18.299	47.77	190:09	
7	nervous_montalcini	644	16.17	0.07	139:19	Fastest challenge
8	sad_goldstine	786	10.401	143.83	61:09	Smallest challenge*
9	mystifying_galileo	84	19.236	114.59	32:33	
10	elastic_bell	49	20.709	261.05	27:11	
11	practical_franklin	49	15.527	2.58	24:01	
12	agitated_ritchie	44	22.946	20.33	24:00	
13	clever_hoover	32	18.319	0.97	20:14	
14	gallant_ramanujan	153	0.898	0.04	15:15	
15	peaceful_williams	47	11.950	2.29	11:47	
16	eager_golick	572	38.146	83.53	06:22	

The high levels of obfuscation applied to adoring_poitras certainly implied high costs in terms of size and efficiency of the design. While adoring_poitras was the strongest design in terms of robustness, other designs presented better numbers in terms of size and efficiency, while also achieving a notable level of robustness. For instance the 7th ranked challenge nervous_montalcini was notably faster than all other designs listed in Table 6. Thereby, nervous_montalcini remained unbroken for 5 days. In terms of size, the 5th and 8th ranked challenges were notably smaller than the rest, with sizes of 10.9 and 10.4 MB respectively. Note that the 5th ranked challenge, hungry_clarke remained unbroken for more than 8 days. Figure 6 plots the top 7 ranked implementations of Table 6 according to their size and execution time. The legend displays the corresponding challenge names with the number of days they remained unbroken during the competition. These 7 challenges remained unbroken for at least 5 days, which was significantly longer than for the rest of the challenges.

As we observe in this plot, the winning challenge adoring_poitras largely demands a longer execution time than the rest. In terms of size, only vibrant_goldberg is slightly larger than adoring_poitras. Out of these 7 designs, challenge 7, nervous_montalcini is the fastest one and challenge 5, hungry_clarke, is by far the smallest one. These two challenges however

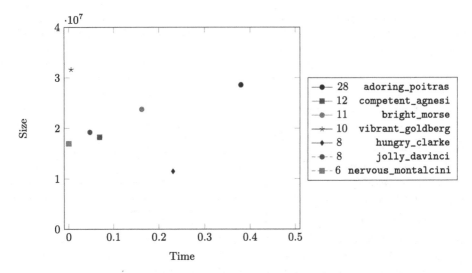

Fig. 6. Overview of the most robust candidates with regard to their size and execution time

remained unbroken for *only* 8 and 6 days respectively. On the other hand, the second ranked candidate, `competent_agnesi`, remained unbroken for up to 12 days while providing relatively good numbers in terms of size and efficiency, specially when comparing it with the winning challenge.

A design such as `competent_agnesi` provides very useful steps towards white-box implementations for real life applications due to its positive numbers in terms of size and efficiency. Namely in some scenarios, it might be useful for a white-box design to remain unbroken for 12 days, as long as one can update it regularly. As mentioned before, if one chooses this avenue for achieving security, further attention should be placed on *how* the updated versions are compiled. Namely, if the recompiled version of the white-box program is similar to the first one, an adversary might need much less time to attack the recompiled version. This is because while analyzing the first program, the adversary learns a lot about the structure, countermeasures and obfuscation techniques implemented by the program. If the recompiled program applies the same techniques, the adversary already has an advantage as he knows *how* the recompiled white-box can be analyzed. The CryptoExperts team also makes this observation when saying that breaking a re-compiled version of `adoring_poitras` (i.e. a program generated with the same compiler, but using a different key and different randomness) would certainly demand less time. The authors point out that a lot of the time needed for breaking the challenge was spent trying out different reverse-engineering techniques and attack strategies which turned out to be ineffective. Therefore when analyzing a re-compiled version of `adoring_poitras`, the authors would at least already know which attack strategies do not work for that class of implementations. Moreover, part of their analyses could even be automated, which would reduce the attacking time even more.

3.5   2019 Edition of the White-Box Competition

In 2019 Cybercrypt organized a second edition of the white-box capture the flag challenge [20]. Here, designers were again invited to submit candidate implementations and attackers were challenged with breaking them by extracting their embedded secret keys. Additionally, candidate designs were also assessed with regard to their *one-wayness* property (see [21]). That is, the white-box encryption programs should not allow one to decrypt. This property was assessed in the competition by asking the attackers to find a pre-image for certain target ciphertexts. In this competition, the efficiency of the programs was also assessed. Namely, the more efficient a program was, the most points it would obtain when remaining robust over time. Efficiency was measured with regard to the running time, code size and memory consumption of the programs.

A total of 27 challenges were submitted. 22 of these challenges resisted key extraction attacks for at least one day, where some of those challenges were submitted in the early stages of the competition. Impressively, 3 challenges submitted by the CryptoLux team remained unbroken during the competition time: `hopeful_kirch`, `goofy_lichterman` and `elegant_turing`. Later after the competition ended, all three challenges were broken by the CryptoExperts team (`hopeful_kirch`) and by the whiteCryption[10] team (`goofy_lichterman` and `elegant_turing`) [19]. However, they could only be broken 30, 50 and 51 days after their publication. In comparison to the 2017 edition, the 2019 edition of the white-box competition showed big improvements in terms of the security levels achieved by the submitted candidates.

4   Real-Life Usefulness of White-Box Cryptography

In light of the state-of-the-art of academic research on white-box cryptography for AES presented in this paper, the practical usefulness of white-box cryptography is not immediate. In this section, we explore relevant parameters for the usefulness of white-box cryptography in practice.

Mitigating Attacks. There is a substantial difference between white-box implementations that can be attacked by automated attacks and those that require substantial amounts of human reverse-engineering. As discussed in the last section, white-box designs vulnerable to automated attacks could be broken within minutes. However if one has a design paradigm that reliably generates white-box implementations that require substantial reverse-engineering, then one can achieve a meaningful level of security. Here, we can expect an adversary to need a large amount of time for breaking the white-box design, and we can opt

---

[10] https://www.intertrust.com/products/application-shielding/.

to regularly updating the design implementation. As one only needs to update software, renewability cycles can be short and thus avoid reverse-engineering attacks.

A second important consideration for attack mitigation is the scalability of an attack, as we have mentioned before. That is, reverse-engineering one instance of a white-box implementation of generation X should not allow the attacker to implement an automated attack that, with limited modifications, can attack all instances of generation X. That is, for each new instance, the attacker should again spend a considerable amount of reverse-engineering effort.

White-Box Implementations Robust Against Code-Lifting Attacks. The designs submitted to the CHES 2017 CTF Challenge aim to achieve robustness against key extraction attacks. However in practice, white-box designs also implement countermeasures against *code-lifting attacks*, where an adversary simply copies a white-box design and runs it on an device of their choice. In the literature (and in practice) properties achieved by white-box designs as means to counter code-lifting attacks include the following: (1) incompressibility [21,25], where a program is implemented such that it cannot be compressed and it only remains functional on its complete form. The idea is that if the program is implemented in a very large size, then transmitting it over the network should be difficult, making it thus difficult for an adversary to copy it and run it on a device of its choice. (2) Hardware-binding [2,4], where a program is configured such that it is only functional on a precise hardware device. And (3) application-binding [2,18], where a program should only be functional within a precise application. Here, robustness against code-lifting can be aimed if the application implements, for instance, authentication operations.

If the white-box under attack effectively implements one of these countermeasures, an adversary might need a significantly larger amount of time to attack it. Namely in many cases, an adversary executes and analyzes the white-box on a device of his choice. This is specially relevant when performing DCA or DFA attacks where the adversary collects data over several executions of the code. However the binding countermeasure would stop him from conducting such analyses so easily and would to the least force the adversary to first reverse engineer the program such that it can run on the device of the adversary.

Side-Stepping Attacks. Another way to side-step the powerful key extraction attacks on white-box implementations is to use non-standard ciphers, as an alternative to AES or DES (see e.g. [9,11,33]). We are not aware of this avenue being widely followed in practical applications.

Protection Techniques Not Specific to White-Box Cryptography. Further anti-reverse engineering techniques, such as binary packers or self-modifying code would certainly increase the robustness of a white-box program, specially regarding to its binary file. We note however that these techniques could not be considered within the white-box competition. Namely, designers were required to upload the source code of their design candidates, written in plain C without any further includes, linked libraries or application of binary packers.

Acknowledgments. The analyses presented in this work were carried out while Alexander Treff was an intern at Riscure B.V., where he was advised by Albert Spruyt and Kevin Valk, which he hereby acknowledges. The authors are grateful to Cees-Bart Breunesse and Ilya Kizhvatov, who provided additional support during the internship. The authors would like to thank Chris Brzuska and Wil Michiels for their helpful feedback during the preparation of this paper.

References

1. Aghaie, A., Moradi, A., Rasoolzadeh, S., Shahmirzadi, A.R., Schellenberg, F., Schneider, T.: Impeccable circuits. Cryptology ePrint Archive, Report 2018/203 (2018). https://eprint.iacr.org/2018/203

2. Alpirez Bock, E., Amadori, A., Brzuska, C., Michiels, W.: On the security goals of white-box cryptography. Cryptology ePrint Archive, Report 2020/104 (2020). https://eprint.iacr.org/2020/104

3. Alpirez Bock, E., et al.: White-box cryptography: don't forget about grey-box attacks. J. Cryptol. **32**(4), 1095–1143 (2019)

4. Alpirez Bock, E., Brzuska, C., Fischlin, M., Janson, C., Michiels, W.: Security reductions for white-box key-storage in mobile payments. Cryptology ePrint Archive, Report 2019/1014 (2019). https://eprint.iacr.org/2019/1014

5. Baek, C.H., Cheon, J.H., Hong, H.: White-box AES implementation revisited. J. Commun. Netw. **18**(3), 273–287 (2016)

6. Barkan, E., Biham, E.: In how many ways can you write Rijndael? In: Zheng, Y. (ed.) ASIACRYPT 2002. LNCS, vol. 2501, pp. 160–175. Springer, Heidelberg (2002). https://doi.org/10.1007/3-540-36178-2_10

7. Biham, E., Shamir, A.: Differential fault analysis of secret key cryptosystems. In: Kaliski, B.S. (ed.) CRYPTO 1997. LNCS, vol. 1294, pp. 513–525. Springer, Heidelberg (1997). https://doi.org/10.1007/BFb0052259

8. Billet, O., Gilbert, H., Ech-Chatbi, C.: Cryptanalysis of a white box AES implementation. In: Handschuh, H., Hasan, M.A. (eds.) SAC 2004. LNCS, vol. 3357, pp. 227–240. Springer, Heidelberg (2004). https://doi.org/10.1007/978-3-540-30564-4_16

9. Biryukov, A., Bouillaguet, C., Khovratovich, D.: Cryptographic schemes based on the ASASA structure: black-box, white-box, and public-key (extended abstract). In: Sarkar, P., Iwata, T. (eds.) ASIACRYPT 2014, Part I. LNCS, vol. 8873, pp. 63–84. Springer, Heidelberg (2014). https://doi.org/10.1007/978-3-662-45611-8_4

10. Biryukov, A., Udovenko, A.: Attacks and countermeasures for white-box designs. In: Peyrin, T., Galbraith, S. (eds.) ASIACRYPT 2018, Part II. LNCS, vol. 11273, pp. 373–402. Springer, Cham (2018). https://doi.org/10.1007/978-3-030-03329-3_13

11. Bogdanov, A., Isobe, T., Tischhauser, E.: Towards practical whitebox cryptography: optimizing efficiency and space hardness. In: Cheon, J.H., Takagi, T. (eds.) ASIACRYPT 2016, Part I. LNCS, vol. 10031, pp. 126–158. Springer, Heidelberg (2016). https://doi.org/10.1007/978-3-662-53887-6_5

12. Bogdanov, A., Rivain, M., Vejre, P.S., Wang, J.: Higher-order DCA against standard side-channel countermeasures. In: Polian, I., Stöttinger, M. (eds.) COSADE 2019. LNCS, vol. 11421, pp. 118–141. Springer, Cham (2019). https://doi.org/10.1007/978-3-030-16350-1_8

13. Boneh, D., DeMillo, R.A., Lipton, R.J.: On the importance of checking cryptographic protocols for faults. In: Fumy, W. (ed.) EUROCRYPT 1997. LNCS, vol. 1233, pp. 37–51. Springer, Heidelberg (1997). https://doi.org/10.1007/3-540-69053-0_4

14. Breunesse, C.-B., Kizhvatov, I., Muijrers, R., Spruyt, A.: Towards fully automated analysis of whiteboxes: Perfect dimensionality reduction for perfect leakage. Cryptology ePrint Archive, Report 2018/095 (2018). https://eprint.iacr.org/2018/095

15. Bringer, J., Chabanne, H., Dottax, E.: White box cryptography: Another attempt. Cryptology ePrint Archive, Report 2006/468 (2006). http://eprint.iacr.org/2006/468

16. Chow, S., Eisen, P., Johnson, H., Van Oorschot, P.C.: White-box cryptography and an AES implementation. In: Nyberg, K., Heys, H. (eds.) SAC 2002. LNCS, vol. 2595, pp. 250–270. Springer, Heidelberg (2003). https://doi.org/10.1007/3-540-36492-7_17

17. Chow, S., Eisen, P., Johnson, H., van Oorschot, P.C.: A white-box DES implementation for DRM applications. In: Feigenbaum, J. (ed.) DRM 2002. LNCS, vol. 2696, pp. 1–15. Springer, Heidelberg (2003). https://doi.org/10.1007/978-3-540-44993-5_1

18. Cooijmans, T., de Ruiter, J., Poll, E.: Analysis of secure key storage solutions on android. In: Proceedings of the 4th ACM Workshop on Security and Privacy in Smartphones & #38; Mobile Devices, SPSM '14, pp. 11–20. ACM (2014)

19. CryptoLux: White-box cryptography. https://www.cryptolux.org/index.php/Whitebox_cryptography

20. cybercrypt: CHES 2019 capture the flag challenge - the whibox contest - 2nd edn. (2019). https://www.cyber-crypt.com/whibox-contest/

21. Delerablée, C., Lepoint, T., Paillier, P., Rivain, M.: White-box security notions for symmetric encryption schemes. In: Lange, T., Lauter, K., Lisoněk, P. (eds.) SAC 2013. LNCS, vol. 8282, pp. 247–264. Springer, Heidelberg (2014). https://doi.org/10.1007/978-3-662-43414-7_13

22. Derbez, P., Fouque, P.-A., Lambin, B., Minaud, B.: On recovering affine encodings in white-box implementations. IACR Trans. Cryptogr. Hardw. Embed. Syst. **2018**(3), 121–149 (2018)

23. ECRYPT: CHES 2017 capture the flag challenge - the whibox contest (2017). https://whibox.cr.yp.to/

24. EMV Mobile Payment: Software-based mobile payment security requirements v1.2 (2019). https://www.emvco.com/wp-content/uploads/documents/EMVCo-SBMP-16-G01-V1.2_SBMP_Security_Requirements.pdf

25. Fouque, P.-A., Karpman, P., Kirchner, P., Minaud, B.: Efficient and provable white-box primitives. In: Cheon, J.H., Takagi, T. (eds.) ASIACRYPT 2016, Part I. LNCS, vol. 10031, pp. 159–188. Springer, Heidelberg (2016). https://doi.org/10.1007/978-3-662-53887-6_6

26. Goubin, L., Masereel, J.-M., Quisquater, M.: Cryptanalysis of white box DES implementations. In: Adams, C., Miri, A., Wiener, M. (eds.) SAC 2007. LNCS, vol. 4876, pp. 278–295. Springer, Heidelberg (2007). https://doi.org/10.1007/978-3-540-77360-3_18

27. Goubin, L., Paillier, P., Rivain, M., Wang, J.: How to reveal the secrets of an obscure white-box implementation. J. Cryptogr. Eng. **10**(1), 49–66 (2019). https://doi.org/10.1007/s13389-019-00207-5

28. Guo, X., Karri, R.: Invariance-based concurrent error detection for advanced encryption standard. In: Proceedings of the 49th Annual Design Automation Conference, DAC '12, pp. 573–578, New York, NY, USA, 2012. ACM

29. Jacob, M., Boneh, D., Felten, E.: Attacking an obfuscated cipher by injecting faults. In: Feigenbaum, J. (ed.) DRM 2002. LNCS, vol. 2696, pp. 16–31. Springer, Heidelberg (2003). https://doi.org/10.1007/978-3-540-44993-5_2

30. Karroumi, M.: Protecting white-box AES with dual ciphers. In: Rhee, K.-H., Nyang, D.H. (eds.) ICISC 2010. LNCS, vol. 6829, pp. 278–291. Springer, Heidelberg (2011). https://doi.org/10.1007/978-3-642-24209-0_19

31. Klemsa, J.: Side-channel attack analysis of AES white-box schemes. Master's thesis, Czech Technical University in Prague (2016). https://github.com/fakub/DiplomaThesis

32. Kocher, P., Jaffe, J., Jun, B.: Differential power analysis. In: Wiener, M. (ed.) CRYPTO 1999. LNCS, vol. 1666, pp. 388–397. Springer, Heidelberg (1999). https://doi.org/10.1007/3-540-48405-1_25

33. Kwon, J., Lee, B., Lee, J., Moon, D.: FPL: white-box secure block cipher using parallel table look-ups. In: Jarecki, S. (ed.) CT-RSA 2020. LNCS, vol. 12006, pp. 106–128. Springer, Cham (2020). https://doi.org/10.1007/978-3-030-40186-3_6

34. Lepoint, T., Rivain, M., De Mulder, Y., Roelse, P., Preneel, B.: Two attacks on a white-box AES implementation. In: Lange, T., Lauter, K., Lisoněk, P. (eds.) SAC 2013. LNCS, vol. 8282, pp. 265–285. Springer, Heidelberg (2014). https://doi.org/10.1007/978-3-662-43414-7_14

35. Link, H.E., Neumann, W.D.: Clarifying obfuscation: Improving the security of white-box encoding. Cryptology ePrint Archive, Report 2004/025 (2004). http://eprint.iacr.org/2004/025

36. Muir, J.A.: A tutorial on white-box AES. Cryptology ePrint Archive, Report 2013/104 (2013). http://eprint.iacr.org/2013/104

37. De Mulder, Y., Roelse, P., Preneel, B.: Cryptanalysis of the Xiao – Lai white-box AES implementation. In: Knudsen, L.R., Wu, H. (eds.) SAC 2012. LNCS, vol. 7707, pp. 34–49. Springer, Heidelberg (2013). https://doi.org/10.1007/978-3-642-35999-6_3

38. De Mulder, Y., Wyseur, B., Preneel, B.: Cryptanalysis of a perturbated white-box AES implementation. In: Gong, G., Gupta, K.C. (eds.) INDOCRYPT 2010. LNCS, vol. 6498, pp. 292–310. Springer, Heidelberg (2010). https://doi.org/10.1007/978-3-642-17401-8_21

39. Teuwen, P.: Grey-box attacks, four years later. 2019 WhibOx Workshop, Darmstadt, Germany. https://www.cryptoexperts.com/whibox2019/slides-whibox2019/Philippe_Teuwen.pdf

40. Rivain, M., Wang, J.: Analysis and improvement of differential computation attacks against internally-encoded white-box implementations. IACR Trans. Cryptogr. Hardw. Embed. Syst. **2019**(2), 225–255 (2019)

41. Rolles, R.: Unpacking virtualization obfuscators. In: Proceedings of the 3rd USENIX Conference on Offensive Technologies, WOOT'09, p. 1, Berkeley, CA, USA, 2009. USENIX Association

42. Salwan, J., Bardin, S., Potet, M.-L.: Symbolic deobfuscation: from virtualized code back to the original. In: Giuffrida, C., Bardin, S., Blanc, G. (eds.) DIMVA 2018. LNCS, vol. 10885, pp. 372–392. Springer, Cham (2018). https://doi.org/10.1007/978-3-319-93411-2_17

43. Smart Card Alliance Mobile and NFC Council. Host card emulation 101. white paper (2014). https://www.securetechalliance.org/wp-content/uploads/HCE-101-WP-FINAL-081114-clean.pdf
44. Wyseur, B., Michiels, W., Gorissen, P., Preneel, B.: Cryptanalysis of white-box DES implementations with arbitrary external encodings. In: Adams, C., Miri, A., Wiener, M. (eds.) SAC 2007. LNCS, vol. 4876, pp. 264–277. Springer, Heidelberg (2007). https://doi.org/10.1007/978-3-540-77360-3_17
45. Xiao, Y., Lai, X.: A secure implementation of white-box AES. In: 2009 2nd International Conference on Computer Science and Its Applications, pp. 1–6. IEEE Computer Society (2009)

On the Implementation Efficiency of Linear Regression-Based Side-Channel Attacks

Maamar Ouladj[1]([✉]), Sylvain Guilley[2,3], and Emmanuel Prouff[4,5]

[1] LAGA, UMR 7539, CNRS, Université de Paris VIII,
2 Rue de la liberté, 93200 Saint Denis, France
`maamar.ouladj@etud.univ-paris8.fr`
[2] TELECOM-ParisTech, Crypto Group, Paris Cedex 13, France Secure-IC S.A.S.,
Rennes, France
[3] Secure-IC S.A.S., Think Ahead Business Line, Paris, France
[4] Sorbonne Universités, UPMC Univ Paris 06, POLSYS, UMR 7606, LIP6, F-75005
Paris, France
[5] ANSSI, Paris, France
`emmanuel.prouff@ssi.gouv.fr`

Abstract. Cryptographic protocol implementations in both software and hardware leak sensitive information during their execution. Side-channel attacks (SCA) consist in analyzing this information in order to reveal the secret parameters of the protocols. Among the different SCA introduced in the literature, the Linear Regression Analysis (LRA) has been argued to be particularly interesting when few information is available on the hardware architecture of the device executing the protocol (e.g. if the so called Hamming weight model does not hold).

However, the computing complexity of the existing LRA implementation is high, which explains why other techniques like e.g. the Correlation Power Analysis (CPA) is often preferred in practice.

This paper aims improving the LRA implementation complexity (in memory space and computation) against both unprotected and protected implementations in uni- and multi-variate contexts. In addition we exhibit the relationship between the LRA and the Numerical Normal Form (NNF), which has been originally introduced in the field of Boolean functions. Thanks to this relationship, we deduce the polynomial degree of the *normalized product* combination of the arithmetic masking. Our improvements have been assessed using simulated leakage of a running AES.

Keywords: Side-channel analysis · Linear Regression Analysis · Stochastic model · Modular addition masking · Spectral approach

1 Introduction

1.1 Context: Side-Channel Analysis

Since the seminal paper on side-channel attacks (SCA) by Kocher *et al.* [16], several improvements have been published. The most efficient SCA to date is

© Springer Nature Switzerland AG 2021
G. M. Bertoni and F. Regazzoni (Eds.): COSADE 2020, LNCS 12244, pp. 147–172, 2021.
https://doi.org/10.1007/978-3-030-68773-1_8

the Template Attack (TA) [6]. This method is split into two phases, that is a profiling and a matching stage. An important weakness of this attack is the large number of measurements required during the profiling stage. This requirement is due to the need of an accurate estimation of the probability densities of different instances of leakage [30]. Another limitation of TA is that it requires the access to an open copy of the target device to conduct the profiling phase with known secret parameters. To overcome this inconvenience, Schindler introduced a new stochastic approach, that consists in approximating probability densities [29]. In fact, even if the stochastic approach is less efficient than the Template Attack (TA), it has the advantage that it requires less traces in the profiling stage than TA [30] and that it can be turned into non-profiled attacks [9]. Since the publication of [29], several researches studied the stochastic approach as an SCA [3,28].

1.2   State-of-the-Art's Review

In the original paper published by Schindler et al. [29], the LRA is presented with a profiling step, as an alternative to the Template Attack [6,11]. In [11], the authors state the ability of the stochastic attack to "learn" quickly from a smaller number of samples than the Template Attack. A profiling attack using multivariate regression analysis, followed by a Pearson correlation coefficient processing, is presented in [35]. The authors of this paper have shown empirically that this approach is more efficient than the conventional stochastic model attack.

In [9], it has been shown that the LRA can be carried out without a profiling stage. In this paper, authors argued that the LRA can be conducted in the uni-variate context like the Correlation Power Analysis (CPA) [2]. The advantage of this suggestion is that the LRA needs less assumptions than CPA. The relationship between the CPA and the stochastic approach is studied in [27].

Recently, LRA applied to XOR operations has been studied using the Hamming weight and the distance models by the authors of [10]. They found that in many common scenarios, LRA is a more efficient tool than CPA.

Subsequently, extensions of LRA to protected implementations are studied in [8,19,30]. Using the later paper, authors of [21] address the question of the LRA efficiency processing. Our paper provides a near exponential improvement of the LRA computing time and an exponential improvement of memory space compared with [21]. Our improvements apply to the LRA either with or without a profiling phase, knowing the subkey during the profiling phase or not.

Recently, the authors of [12] suggested to use the Walsh-Hadamard orthogonal basis to characterize the leakage. The authors of this paper improve the processing time on this particular basis. Our improvements are held independently from the basis.

1.3   Contributions

Let us assume that N observations $(\vec{l_i})_{0 \leq i \leq N-1}$ (d-dimensional traces) have been measured during the processing of an operation $F(x_i, k)$ where F and the x_i are assumed to be known and where k is a target secret assumed to be constant.

Moreover, let $\mathcal{L}$ denote the $N \times d$-matrix whose rows are the $\vec{l_i}$'s. The stochastic approach essentially consists in modeling, for each key candidate $\hat{k}$, the leakage $\mathcal{L}$ according to a basis parametrized by $\hat{k}$. The core idea is that a good choice of the basis should imply that the modeling achieves best accuracy when the key guess $\hat{k}$ is correct.

Let us denote by $\mathcal{M}_{\hat{k}}$ the $N \times s$-matrix whose rows correspond to the evaluation of the s basis functions in the values $F(x_i, \hat{k})$. All of the previously published papers suggest to compute the matrix $\mathcal{P}_{\hat{k}} \doteq \left(\mathcal{M}_{\hat{k}}{}^{\mathsf{T}} \mathcal{M}_{\hat{k}} \right)^{-1} \mathcal{M}_{\hat{k}}{}^{\mathsf{T}}$ in order to carry out the coefficients of the leakage on the chosen basis. Then $\mathcal{M}_{\hat{k}} \mathcal{P}_{\hat{k}} \mathcal{L}$ is computed as an estimator of the leakage (or directly $(\mathcal{M}_{\hat{k}} \mathcal{P}_{\hat{k}}) \mathcal{L}$) as shown in Algorithm 1. This processing is the bottleneck of the LRA processing, because it is repeated for all guessed subkeys $\hat{k}$.

Let us denote by n the bit-length of $\hat{k}$ and x_i. Even though the authors of [8] and [21] give some computation improvements, the complexity of their algorithm is $\mathcal{O}(2^{3n})$ in the space memory and $\mathcal{O}(2^{3n} \times d)$ in the processing time. Our paper provides further significant improvements in both of them; the required memory space becomes $\mathcal{O}(s \times 2^n)$ and the processing time reduced to $\mathcal{O}(sn2^n d)$. In what follows, we summarize our contributions.

First, an invariant computation of matrices is exhibited (the matrix $\left(\mathcal{M}_{\hat{k}}{}^{\mathsf{T}} \mathcal{M}_{\hat{k}} \right)^{-1}$ is independent from the guessed subkey $\hat{k}$), thereby avoiding $2^n - 1$ repeated computations. In particular, only one matrix inversion is required during the whole attack, which leads to a significant reduction in the processing time.

Second, a relationship between stochastic model expressions for the guessed subkey 0 and an arbitrary guessed subkey $\hat{k}$ is exhibited (namely, between $\mathcal{M}_0 \mathcal{P}_0$ and $\mathcal{M}_{\hat{k}} \mathcal{P}_{\hat{k}}$). This relationship allows for drastic improvements both in the preprocessing time and in the memory space required to carry out an LRA. Thanks to this relation, only one product matrix is needed for all possible subkeys k.

Third, we exhibit a spectral approach to further accelerate LRA computations (Algorithm 4 instead of Algorithm 1). This allows for a near exponential computational improvement (a time attack factor is reduced from 2^n to n). For reference, the use of the spectral approach in SCAs was introduced in [13]. In what follows, we provide a further improvement of ratio $2^n/s$ both in the space memory and the processing time (Algorithm 2 instead of Algorithm 4).

Fourth, we extend those improvements in the higher-order masking context (Sect. 4). For our experimental validation, two masking methods are challenged, namely the Boolean masking and the 2^n-modular additive masking [18].

Finally, we exhibit, for the first time the relationship between the LRA and the Numerical Normal Form (NNF) [5] of the leakage function. In fact, in order to carry out a higher order (H-O) SCA, an optimal combination between the shares leakages must be found (see [20] for more details). If the noise variance is high, the optimal combination is the *normalized product*, independently from the masking technique [4]. Thanks to the relation between the NNF and the LRA, we show that it is possible to exhibit the polynomial expression of this combination against the first-order additive masking. In fact, knowing such a polynomial expression is useful for the H-O CPA. Also, knowing the degree of the polynomial is useful for the adversary to choose the basis used in the LRA.

1.4   Outline

In Sect. 2, a mathematical modelization of the problem is presented. In Sect. 3, we develop our contributions in a monovariate context (where the sensitive variable is not shared). In Sect. 4, we extend them to multivariate contexts (i.e. when masking countermeasure is applied). In Sect. 5, we verify our contributions on simulated AES traces. Finally, we conclude our study in Sect. 6.

2   Mathematical Modelization

2.1   Notations

Throughout this work we use the same notations of the related paper [21]. Random variables are denoted by large letters. A realization of a random variable (*ex.* X) is denoted by the corresponding lowercase letter (*ex.* x). A *sample* of several observations of X is denoted by $(x_i)_i$. Sometimes it is viewed as a vector. The notation $(x_i)_i \hookleftarrow X$ means the initialization of the set $(x_i)_i$ from X. $E[X]$ and $\sigma[X]$ denote respectively the mean and the standard deviation of X.

The notation $\vec{X}$ denotes column vectors and $\vec{X}[u]$ denotes its uth coordinate. Calligraphic letters will be used to denote matrices, such that the elements of a matrix $\mathcal{M}$ will be denoted by $\mathcal{M}[i][j]$. Furthermore its uth column is denoted by $\vec{\mathcal{M}}[u]$ and its ith line denoted by $\vec{\mathcal{M}^\mathsf{T}}[i]$. The symbols $\cdot^2$ and $\sqrt{\cdot}$, applied to vectors and matrices, denote respectively the square and the square root off all the vector/matrix coordinates.

During the attack, we consider that the adversary targets the manipulation of a single sensitive variable Z. Our results can be directly extended to the general case, where several variables are targeted in parallel. The sensitive variable Z depends on a public variable X (typically a plaintext or ciphertext) and on a secret subkey k such that $Z = F(X, k)$ where $F : \mathbb{F}_2^n \times \mathbb{F}_2^n \longrightarrow \mathbb{F}_2^m$. The bit-lengths n and m depend on the cryptographic algorithm and the device architecture. Typically $Z = sbox(X \oplus k)$, such that $sbox$ denotes a substitution box and $\oplus$ denotes the bitwise addition.

The attack is carried out with N traces $\vec{l}_0, \ldots, \vec{l}_{N-1}$. Each $\vec{l}_i \hookleftarrow \vec{L}$ corresponds to the processing of $z_i = F(x_i, k)$, such that $x_i \hookleftarrow X$ and $z_i \hookleftarrow Z$. The number of samples per traces (instantaneous leakage points) is denoted by d.

2.2   Description of Stochastic Attacks

LRA consists first in choosing a basis of s functions $(m_p)_{0 \le p \le s-1}$, such that m_0 is a constant function (typically equal to 1). For each subkey guess $\hat{k}$, the adversary constructs an $(N \times s)-prediction\ matrix$ $\left(\mathcal{M}_{\hat{k}}[i][p] \doteq m_p(\hat{z}_i)\right)_{i,p}$, such that $\hat{z}_i = F(x_i, \hat{k})$ is the guessed value of the sensitive variable corresponding to the plaintext x_i. For example, if one aims at regressing the leakage as a linear combination of the bits of the $\hat{z}_i$'s, then for this basis one has $s = 9$, $m_0(z) = 1$ and $m_p(z)$ returning the pth bit of z.

The comparison of this matrix with the set of d-dimensional leakage traces $(\vec{l}_i)_i \hookleftarrow \vec{L}$ is carried out by linear regression of each coordinate of $(\vec{l}_i)$ in the basis formed by the rows of $\mathcal{M}_{\hat{k}}$. Namely, a real-valued $(s \times d)$-matrix $\beta_{\hat{k}}$ with column vectors $\vec{\beta}_{\hat{k}}[1], \ldots, \vec{\beta}_{\hat{k}}[d]$ are estimated in order to minimize the error when approximating $\vec{\mathcal{L}}[u]$ by $(\mathcal{M}_{\hat{k}} \times \beta_{\hat{k}})[u]$. The vector $\vec{\beta}_{\hat{k}}[u]$ is defined, for each time sample u and each guess $\hat{k}$, such that [31, Theo. 3]:

$$\vec{\beta}_{\hat{k}}[u] = (\mathcal{M}_{\hat{k}}{}^\mathsf{T} \mathcal{M}_{\hat{k}})^{-1} \mathcal{M}_{\hat{k}}{}^\mathsf{T} \vec{\mathcal{L}}[u], \tag{1}$$

where $\mathcal{L}$ is a $(N \times d)$−matrix, whose rows are the $\vec{l_i}{}^\mathsf{T}$ vectors, and where $\vec{\mathcal{L}}[u]$ denotes the uth column of the matrix $\mathcal{L}$.

As defined in [21], to quantify the estimation error, the *goodness of fit model* is used and the *correlation coefficient of determination* R is computed for each u. R is defined by $R \doteq 1 - SSR/\overrightarrow{SST}$, where $\overrightarrow{SST}$ denotes the leakage *Total Sum of Squares* and SSR denotes the leakage *Residual Sum of Squares* [21].

Let us remind that the dimension of $\mathcal{M}_{\hat{k}}$ is $N \times s$. So carrying out LRA naively on the real traces is difficult and even impossible in presence of countermeasures (a large number N of measurements is required) with high dimension d. One can show that the attack efficiency is unchanged if it is performed over the averaged leakages per class (the averaged leakage equals ($\frac{1}{\#i:x_i=x} \sum_{i:x_i=x} \vec{l}_i)_{x \in \mathbb{F}_2^n}$, if ($\#i : x_i = x) \neq 0$, and it equals 0 else) instead of over rough traces [8]. Thanks to this improvement, the size of $\mathcal{M}_{\hat{k}}$ is reduced from $\mathcal{O}(N \times s)$ to $\mathcal{O}(2^n \times s)$. We recall that N (which is the number of traces involved in the attack, e.g. $N = 10^6$) is often much greater than 2^n (the number of possible subkeys, e.g. $2^n = 256$).

Algorithm 1 shows the LRA processing on the averaged leakages per sensitive variable value, as suggested in the literature ([8] and [31]). As we can see from this algorithm, for each guessed subkey $\hat{k}$, the attack can be conducted by pre-processing $\mathcal{P}_{\hat{k}} = (\mathcal{M}_{\hat{k}}{}^\mathsf{T} \mathcal{M}_{\hat{k}})^{-1} \mathcal{M}_{\hat{k}}{}^\mathsf{T}$ once, then by computing the weights of linear regression $\vec{\beta}_{\hat{k}}[u] = \mathcal{P}_{\hat{k}} \times \vec{\mathcal{L}}[u]$ for each u, and eventually by computing the leakage estimation $\vec{\mathcal{E}}_{\hat{k}}[u] = \mathcal{M}_{\hat{k}} \mathcal{P}_{\hat{k}} \times \vec{\mathcal{L}}[u]$. Remember that the overall complexity of the inversion is about $\mathcal{O}(s^{2.373})$ using Optimized Coppersmith–Winograd-like algorithm [37]. So, the time complexity of the pre-processing of the 2^n matrices $\mathcal{P}_{\hat{k}}$ is about $\mathcal{O}(2^n \times (s^{2.373} + 2^n \times s^2))$ and that of the vectors $\vec{\beta}_{\hat{k}}[u]$ is about $\mathcal{O}(2^{2n} \times s \times d)$ multiplications.

Since the adversary does not need the coefficients of $\vec{\beta}_{\hat{k}}[u]$ explicitly, during a non-profiled attack, one can pre-process $\mathcal{G}_{\hat{k}} = \mathcal{M}_{\hat{k}} \mathcal{P}_{\hat{k}}$ once, then straightforwardly compute the leakage estimation $\vec{\mathcal{E}}_{\hat{k}}[u] = \mathcal{G}_{\hat{k}} \times \vec{\mathcal{L}}[u]$, for each u. So, we can save one matrix product per $(\hat{k}, u)$ [21]. Whether using this optimization or not, the LRA is still difficult (even impossible against higher-order masking). In fact, one must pre-compute and save 2^n matrices $\mathcal{G}_{\hat{k}}$ and compute one matrices'

Input :
- a set of d-dimensional leakage $(\vec{l}_i)_{1 \leq i \leq N}$ and the corresponding plaintexts $(x_i)_{1 \leq i \leq N}$,
- a set of model functions $(m_p)_{p \leq s}$.

Output : The candidate subkey $\hat{k}$

1 **for** $i \leftarrow 0$ **to** $N-1$ **do**   // Processing of the leakage Total Sum of Squares ($\overrightarrow{SST}$)
2      $\mu_{\vec{\mathcal{L}}} \leftarrow \mu_{\vec{\mathcal{L}}} + \vec{l}_i$
3      $\nu_{\vec{\mathcal{L}}} \leftarrow \nu_{\vec{\mathcal{L}}} + \vec{l}_i^{\,2}$
4 $\overrightarrow{SST} \leftarrow \nu_{\vec{\mathcal{L}}} - \frac{1}{N}\mu_{\vec{\mathcal{L}}}^2$
5 **for** $\hat{k} \leftarrow 0$ **to** $2^n - 1$ **do**   // Pre-processing of the 2^n prediction matrices $\mathcal{M}_{\hat{k}}$ and $\mathcal{P}_{\hat{k}}$
6   **for** $p \leftarrow 0$ **to** s **do**
7   **for** $x \leftarrow 0$ **to** $2^n - 1$ **do**
8          $\mathcal{M}_{\hat{k}}[x][p] \leftarrow m_p[F(x,\hat{k})]$
9      $\mathcal{P}_{\hat{k}} \leftarrow (\mathcal{M}_{\hat{k}}^{\mathsf{T}} \times \mathcal{M}_{\hat{k}})^{-1} \times \mathcal{M}_{\hat{k}}^{\mathsf{T}}$
10 **for** $i \leftarrow 0$ **to** $N-1$ **do**   // Computation of the coalesced matrix $\mathcal{L}$
11      $\vec{\mathcal{L}}^{\mathsf{T}}[x_i] = \vec{\mathcal{L}}^{\mathsf{T}}[x_i] + l_i$
12   count$[x_i]$=count$[x_i]$+1
13 **for** $x \leftarrow 0$ **to** $2^n - 1$ **do**
14   **if** $count[x]$ **then**
15        $\vec{\mathcal{L}}^{\mathsf{T}}[x] = \vec{\mathcal{L}}^{\mathsf{T}}[x]/\text{count}[x]$
16 **for** $\hat{k} \leftarrow 0$ **to** $2^n - 1$ **do**   // Test hyp. $\hat{k}$ for all leakage coordinates
17   **for** $u \leftarrow 0$ **to** $d-1$ **do**   // Instantaneous attack (at time u)
18        $\vec{\beta} \leftarrow \mathcal{P}_{\hat{k}} \times \vec{\mathcal{L}}[u]$
19        $\vec{\mathcal{E}}[u] \leftarrow \mathcal{M}_{\hat{k}} \times \vec{\beta}$ // $\vec{\mathcal{E}}[u] = \mathcal{M}_{\hat{k}} \times (\mathcal{M}_{\hat{k}}^{\mathsf{T}} \times \mathcal{M}_{\hat{k}})^{-1} \times \mathcal{M}_{\hat{k}}^{\mathsf{T}} \times \vec{\mathcal{L}}[u]$: Estimator of $\vec{\mathcal{L}}[u]$
20        $SSR \leftarrow 0$
21   **for** $x \leftarrow 0$ **to** $2^n - 1$ **do**   // Computation of the Residual Sum of Squares (SSR)
22          $SSR \leftarrow SSR + (\mathcal{E}[x][u] - \mathcal{L}[x][u])^2$
23        $R[\hat{k}][u] \leftarrow 1 - \frac{SSR}{\overrightarrow{SST}[u]}$ // coefficient of determination [8]
24 **return** $\text{argmax}_{\hat{k}}\left(max_u R[\hat{k}][u]\right)$

Algorithm 1: Linear Regression Analysis with coalescence (without using the Proposition 3 and 4).

product $\vec{\mathcal{E}}_{\hat{k}}[u] = \mathcal{G}_{\hat{k}} \times \vec{\mathcal{L}}[u]$ for each pair $(\hat{k}, u)$. So, the pre-processing time complexity of the 2^n matrices $\mathcal{G}_{\hat{k}}$ is about $\mathcal{O}(s^{2.373} \times 2^n + 2^{2n} \times s^2 + 2^{3n} \times s)$ and that of the estimators $\vec{\mathcal{E}}_{\hat{k}}[u]$ is about $\mathcal{O}(2^{3n} \times d)$ multiplications.

To circumvent these bottlenecks, an LRA study with some important improvements in term of memory space and processing time will be provided in the following sections. These improvements concern both scenarios with and without processing of the regression weights $\vec{\beta}_{\hat{k}}[u]$.

3   LRA Study and Improvements of Its Implementation

As previously recalled, in practice the LRA is carried out over the leakages averaged according to the value of the corresponding sensitive variable (or equivalently according to the value of the corresponding message). This approach was first put forward by [8,31] and [21] and is called 'coalesced' in [34]. One of the advantages of averaging the leakage is that, as long as $N \geq 2^n$, it leads to less memory space and more processing time efficiency.

In fact, as studied in the followed Subsect. 3.1, carrying out an SCA with or without averaging traces are asymptotically equivalent.

3.1   Difference Between SCAs with and Without Coalescence

Let us first study the difference between the distribution of rough traces and that of the averaged ones per class (a so called coalescence approach). From Cochran's Theorem [7] one has the following proposition:

Proposition 1 (simplified   version   of   Cochran's   Theorem).   *Let* $(l_i)_{0 \leq i \leq N-1}$ *be N univariate observations of a random variable L that follows a normal distribution $\mathcal{N}(\mu, \sigma)$. Let $\hat{\mu}$ and $\hat{\sigma}^2$ be respectively the estimators of μ and σ^2 defined by $\hat{\mu} = \frac{1}{N} \sum_{i=0}^{N-1} l_i$, and $\hat{\sigma}^2 = \frac{1}{N} \sum_{i=0}^{N-1} (l_i - E[L])^2$. Then, one has:*

- *$\hat{\mu}$ and $\hat{\sigma}^2$ are independents random variables,*
- *$\hat{\mu} \sim \mathcal{N}(\mu, \sigma/\sqrt{N})$ and $\frac{n\hat{\sigma}}{\sigma^2} \sim \chi^2(N-1)$.*

Proposition 2.   *Under the additive independent noise assumption, carrying out an SCA with or without coalescence are asymptotically equivalent.*

To compare the efficiency of an SCA with and without coalescence, let us consider that, under the additive independent noise assumption, the adversary knows the leakage model. In this situation both CPA and covariance distinguishers are the optimal distinguishers [14]. To prove Proposition 2, we limit ourselves to these two optimal distinguishers.

Proof. See the Appendix A (that uses Cochran's Theorem).   ◇

Due to this asymptotic equivalence between SCAs with and without coalescence, LRA (introduced first with coalescence) tends toward LRA without coalescence, as it will be also shown experimentally in Sect. 5.

In the rest of this paper we study the LRA with coalescence, hence assuming that the adversary does not directly attack using the N traces $\vec{l}_i$ but using their averaged (*coalesced*) version (let define $n_j \doteq \#\{x_i = j;\ 0 \leq i \leq N - 1\}$, the averaged trace equals $\frac{1}{n_j} \sum_{x_i=j}^{N} \vec{l_i}$, if $n_j \neq 0$, and it equals 0 else). To simplify the notations, the 2^n averaged traces are still denoted by $\vec{l_i}$ and the dimension N in the definition of the matrices $\mathcal{M}_{\hat{k}}$, $\mathcal{P}_{\hat{k}}$, $\mathcal{G}_{\hat{k}}$ and $\mathcal{L}$ is replaced by 2^n. Namely, the matrix $\mathcal{M}_{\hat{k}}$ dimension becomes $2^n \times s$ instead of $N \times s$ and the matrix $\mathcal{L}$ dimension becomes $2^n \times d$ instead of $N \times d$ and similarly for all the derived matrices and vectors. Those new matrices shall be called *coalesced* in the sequel.

3.2   LRA with Assumption of Equal Images Under Different Subkeys

An important property, that holds true for the most key mixing based cryptographic functions, is introduced in [31].

Definition 1. (Equal Images under different Subkeys (EIS) [31, **Def. 2]).** *Let V denotes an arbitrary set and let ϕ:$\{0,1\}^n \times \{0,1\}^{n'} \to V$ be a function, such that for every subkey k all $\phi(\{0,1\}^n \times \{k\}) \subseteq V$ are equal. We say that the function F has the "Equal Images under different Subkeys (EIS)" property if a function $\overline{F}$: $V \to \mathbb{R}$ exists such that $F = \overline{F} \circ \phi$.*

A more specific case is when $F(x,k)$ depends only on $x \oplus k$ as in common block ciphers (*i.e.* on ciphers as DES [22] and AES [23]). Other cases are the 2^n-modular addition ($\mod (2^n)$), and the $2^{2^m} + 1$-modular multiplication of non-zero numbers, such that m = 1,2,3,4 ($2^{2^m} + 1$ are the Fermat numbers).

The first important contribution of our paper is the following proposition.

Proposition 3. *Using the coalescence, let $\mathcal{H} \doteq \mathcal{M}_{\hat{k}}^{\mathsf{T}}\mathcal{M}_{\hat{k}}$, $\mathcal{P}_{\hat{k}} \doteq (\mathcal{M}_{\hat{k}}^{\mathsf{T}}\mathcal{M}_{\hat{k}})^{-1}\mathcal{M}_{\hat{k}}^{\mathsf{T}}$ and $\mathcal{G}_{\hat{k}} \doteq \mathcal{M}_{\hat{k}}\mathcal{P}_{\hat{k}}$, such that $\mathcal{M}_{\hat{k}}$ is as defined above. Under the EIS assumption:*

1. *$\mathcal{H}$ is independent from the guessed subkey $\hat{k}$.*
2. *If the leakage function depends only on $x \oplus \hat{k}$, then for every $(j, \hat{k})$ we have:*

$$\mathcal{M}_{\hat{k}}[j][.] = \mathcal{M}_0[j \oplus \hat{k}][.]$$

and,

(a) $\mathcal{P}_{\hat{k}}[i][j] = \mathcal{P}_0[i][j \oplus \hat{k}]$
(b) $\mathcal{G}_{\hat{k}}[i][j] = \mathcal{G}_0[i \oplus \hat{k}][j \oplus \hat{k}]$

Proof. 1. From the EIS assumption,

$$\mathcal{H}_{\hat{k}}[i][j] = \sum_{x=0}^{2^n-1} \mathcal{M}_{\hat{k}}^{\mathsf{T}}[i][x]\mathcal{M}_{\hat{k}}[x][j] = \sum_{x=0}^{2^n-1} m_i[F(x,\hat{k})]m_j[F(x,\hat{k})]$$

$$= \sum_{y=0}^{2^n-1} m_i[F(y,\hat{0})]m_j[F(y,\hat{0})] = \mathcal{H}_0[i][j]$$

If the leakage only depends on $x \oplus k$, then

$$\mathcal{H}_{\hat{k}}[i][j] = \sum_{x=0}^{2^n-1} \mathcal{M}_{\hat{k}}^{\mathsf{T}}[i][x]\mathcal{M}_{\hat{k}}[x][j] = \sum_{x=0}^{2^n-1} \mathcal{M}_0^{\mathsf{T}}[i][x \oplus \hat{k}]\mathcal{M}_0[x \oplus \hat{k}][j]$$

$$= \sum_{y=0}^{2^n-1} \mathcal{M}_0^{\mathsf{T}}[i][y]\mathcal{M}_0[y][j] = \mathcal{H}_0[i][j] \quad ; \text{such that } y = x \oplus \hat{k}.$$

2. (a)

$$\mathcal{P}_{\hat{k}}[i][j] = (\mathcal{H}^{-1} \times \mathcal{M}_{\hat{k}}^{\mathsf{T}})[i][j] = \sum_{p=0}^{s-1} \mathcal{H}^{-1}[i][p]\mathcal{M}_{\hat{k}}^{\mathsf{T}}[p][j]$$

$$= \sum_{p=0}^{s-1} \mathcal{H}^{-1}[i][p]\mathcal{M}_0^{\mathsf{T}}[p][j \oplus \hat{k}] = \mathcal{P}_0[i][j \oplus \hat{k}].$$

2. (b)

$$\mathcal{G}_{\hat{k}}[i][j] = (\mathcal{M}_{\hat{k}} \times \mathcal{P}_{\hat{k}})[i][j] = \sum_{p=0}^{s-1} \mathcal{M}_{\hat{k}}[i][p]\mathcal{P}_{\hat{k}}[p][j]$$

$$= \sum_{p=0}^{s-1} \mathcal{M}_0[i \oplus \hat{k}][p]\mathcal{P}_0[p][j \oplus \hat{k}] = \mathcal{G}_0[i \oplus \hat{k}][j \oplus \hat{k}].$$

◇

Proposition 3 implies a significant time and memory gain. First, only one matrix $\mathcal{H}_0$ has to be computed and inverted instead of 2^n.

Second, for each time simple u, if we need the weight $\vec{\beta}_{\hat{k}}[u]$ returned by the linear regression, then we just need to first pre-process the single matrix $\mathcal{P}_0$. All the other $2^n - 1$ matrices $\mathcal{P}_{\hat{k}}$ can be directly deduced using Proposition 3 instead of pre-processing and saving 2^n matrices products. Afterwards, for every guessed subkey $\hat{k}$ and for each time sample u, one matrices' product needs to be carried out to get the coefficients $\vec{\beta}_{\hat{k}}[u] = \mathcal{P}_{\hat{k}}\vec{\mathcal{L}}[u]$.

Third, similarly to above, to conduct LRA without computing $\vec{\beta}_{\hat{k}}[u]$ vectors, the adversary needs first to pre-process a single matrix $\mathcal{G}_0$. All the other 2^n matrices $\mathcal{G}_{\hat{k}}$ can be directly deduced using Proposition 3 instead of 2^n matrices products pre-processings and savings, as suggested in [21]. Then for every guessed subkey $\hat{k}$ and for each time sample u, one matrix product has to be carried out to compute $\vec{\mathcal{E}}_{\hat{k}}[u] = \mathcal{G}_{\hat{k}}\vec{\mathcal{L}}[u]$. In fact, whether this improvement is used or not, the estimator's computing is still difficult.

3.3   Spectral Approach Computation to Speed up LRA (with EIS)

In this section, we will show that the LRA processing can still be improved. Indeed, instead of computing coefficients $\vec{\beta}_{\hat{k}}[u]$ (resp. vectors $\vec{\mathcal{E}}_{\hat{k}}[u]$) for each subkey $\hat{k}$, only one computation is sufficient, as shown in the sequel.

Let us first recall the definition of a convolution product that we need.

Definition 2. *Let $(\mathbb{S}, \oplus)$ be a group of size 2^n. Let g, h be two functions from $\mathbb{S}$ to $\mathbb{R}$. A convolution product between g and h is a function denoted by $g \otimes h$ and defined from $\mathbb{S}$ to $\mathbb{R}$ such that for every $k \in \mathbb{S}$, $(g \otimes h)(k) = \sum_{j \in \mathbb{S}} g(j)h(j \oplus k)$.*

To naively evaluate the convolution product for all possible values of k, one needs $\mathcal{O}(2^{2n})$ multiplications. Let us also denote a so-called *functions' product* by $g \bullet h$ such that $g \bullet h(j) = g(j)h(j)$. It is nothing but a coordinate-wise product. Furthermore, we denote by WHT the Walsh-Hadamard Transform, which is nothing but the Fourier Transform over the group $(\mathbb{S}, \oplus)$. A flowgraph for computing WHT for $n = 3$ is added in Appendix C. It is noteworthy that WHT is the inverse of itself. An important property of the convolution product is that, for every $k \in \mathbb{S}$, we have:

$$g \otimes h(k) = WHT^{-1}\left(WHT(g) \bullet WHT(h)\right)(k). \tag{2}$$

Thanks to this property, one can evaluate the convolution product in all possible values k in once, with an overall complexity of $\mathcal{O}(n2^n)$ instead of $\mathcal{O}(2^{2n})$.

Proposition 4. *With the same previous notations, if $F(x, k) = F(x \oplus k)$ for every possible values of x and k, then we have:*

1. $\beta_{\hat{k}}[i][u] = WHT^{-1}\left(WHT(\mathcal{P}_0[i][.]) \bullet WHT(\vec{\mathcal{L}}[u])\right)(\hat{k})$

2. $\mathcal{E}_{\hat{k}}[i][u] = WHT^{-1}\left(WHT(\mathcal{G}_0[i \oplus \hat{k}][.]) \bullet WHT(\vec{\mathcal{L}}[u])\right)(\hat{k})$,

where:

- *$\mathcal{P}_0[i][.]$ denotes the ith line of the matrix $\mathcal{P}_0$,*
- *$\vec{\mathcal{L}}[u]$ denotes the uth column of the matrix $\mathcal{L}$,*

Proof. 1.

$$\beta_{\hat{k}}[i][u] = (\mathcal{P}_{\hat{k}}\mathcal{L}[u])[i] = \sum_{j=0}^{2^n} \mathcal{P}_{\hat{k}}[i][j]\mathcal{L}[j][u] = \sum_{j=0}^{2^n} \mathcal{P}_0[i][j \oplus \hat{k}]\mathcal{L}[j][u]$$

$$= \mathcal{P}_0[i][.] \otimes \vec{\mathcal{L}}[u](\hat{k}) = WHT^{-1}\left(WHT(\mathcal{P}_0[i][.]) \bullet WHT(\vec{\mathcal{L}}[u])\right)(\hat{k}),$$

by seeing the line $\mathcal{P}_0[i][.]$ and the vector $\vec{\mathcal{L}}[u]$) as function evaluation tables.
2. Similarly,

$$\mathcal{E}_{\hat{k}}[i][u] = (\mathcal{G}_{\hat{k}}\vec{\mathcal{L}}[u])[i] = \sum_{j=0}^{2^n-1} \mathcal{G}_0[i \oplus \hat{k}][j \oplus \hat{k}]\mathcal{L}[j][u] = \mathcal{G}_0[i \oplus \hat{k}][.] \otimes \vec{\mathcal{L}}[u](\hat{k})$$

$$= WHT^{-1}\left(WHT(\mathcal{G}_0[i \oplus \hat{k}][.]) \bullet WHT(\vec{\mathcal{L}}[u])\right)(\hat{k}).$$

$\diamond$

So, Proposition 4 allows us to further save time. Indeed if we need the $\vec{\beta}_{\hat{k}}[u]$ coefficients, we first need to pre-process only one matrix $\mathcal{P}_0$. Then we compute $WHT(\mathcal{P}_0[i][.])$ for each line $0 \leq i \leq s - 1$, only once. Then we also compute

$WHT(\vec{\mathcal{L}}[u])$ only once. Then for each line $0 \leq i \leq s-1$, we compute the vector $WHT^{-1}\left(WHT(\mathcal{P}_0[i][.]) \bullet WHT(\vec{\mathcal{L}}[u])\right)$. In fact, according to Proposition 4, for each $\hat{k}$ the coefficient $\vec{\beta}_{\hat{k}}[i][u]$ is the $\hat{k}^{th}$ scalar of the last vector. So, no matrix product should be done to compute the coefficient $\vec{\beta}_{\hat{k}}[i][u]$. The overall time complexity of the pre-processing is about $\mathcal{O}(s^{2.373} + 2^n \times s^2 + s \times n2^n)$ and that of vectors $\vec{\beta}_{\hat{k}}[u]$ computation is about $\mathcal{O}((n+1)2^n \times s \times d)$. So, the vectors' $\vec{\beta}_{\hat{k}}[u]$ computation has an overall complexity of $\mathcal{O}((n+1)2^n \times s \times d)$ instead of $\mathcal{O}(2^{2n} \times s \times d)$.

Similarly, to conduct LRA without computing the $\vec{\beta}_{\hat{k}}[u]$ vectors, the adversary needs first to pre-process only one matrix $\mathcal{G}_0$. Then she pre-processes a WHT for each line $0 \leq i \leq 2^n - 1$ of $\mathcal{G}_0$. Then she modifies the leakage vector $\vec{\mathcal{L}}[u]$ by $WHT(\vec{\mathcal{L}}[u])$. Then she modifies each line $0 \leq i \leq 2^n - 1$ of $\mathcal{G}_0$ by the vector $WHT^{-1}(WHT(\mathcal{G}_0[i][.]) \bullet WHT(\vec{\mathcal{L}}[u]))$ (only a coordinate-wise product and a processing of WHT^{-1} to do per line). Finally, for each guessed subkey k and each plaintext $0 \leq i \leq 2^n - 1$, the estimated leakage $\mathcal{E}_{\hat{k}}[i][u]$ is just a scalar of the updated matrix $\mathcal{G}_0$. Namely it is the current value of $\mathcal{G}_0[i \oplus \hat{k}][\hat{k}]$. So, no matrix product must be done during the estimated leakage matrix $\mathcal{E}_{\hat{k}}$ computation. The overall time complexity of the pre-processing is about $\mathcal{O}(s^{2.373} + 2^{n+1} \times s^2 + n2^{2n})$ and that of the estimated leakage matrix $\mathcal{E}_{\hat{k}}$ computation is about $\mathcal{O}((n2^n + (n+1)2^{2n})d)$. So, the estimated leakage matrix's $\mathcal{E}_{\hat{k}}$ computation has an overall complexity of $\mathcal{O}((n+1)2^{2n} \times d)$ instead of $\mathcal{O}(2^{3n} \times d)$. Algorithm 4 in Appendix B shows LRA processing with this spectral approach.

3.4 Further Improvement

The new bottleneck of the last algorithm (Algorithm 4) is the lines 19–20. To avoid computing 2^n Walsh-Hadamard Transform inverse WHT^{-1}, one can see that lines from 19 to 24 aim to compute the error square quadratic norm $\left\|\vec{\mathcal{L}}[u] - \vec{\mathcal{E}}_{\hat{k}}[u]\right\|^2$. In fact, the LRA aims to minimize this error. One can minimize it otherwise:

$$\left\|\vec{\mathcal{L}}[u] - \vec{\mathcal{E}}_{\hat{k}}[u]\right\|^2 = \sum_{i=0}^{2^n-1} (\mathcal{L}[i][u] - \mathcal{E}_{\hat{k}}[i][u])^2$$

$$= \sum_{i=0}^{2^n-1} \mathcal{L}[i][u]^2 + \sum_{i=0}^{2^n-1} \mathcal{E}_{\hat{k}}[i][u]^2 - 2\sum_{i=0}^{2^n-1} \mathcal{L}[i][u]\mathcal{E}_{\hat{k}}[i][u]$$

First, $\sum_{i=0}^{2^n-1} \mathcal{L}[i][u]^2$ is clearly independent from $\hat{k}$.

Second, since the symmetric matrix $\mathcal{G}_{\hat{k}}$ is idempotent (i.e. $\mathcal{G}_{\hat{k}}^\top \mathcal{G}_{\hat{k}} = \mathcal{G}_{\hat{k}}$), so

$$\sum_{i=0}^{2^n-1} \mathcal{E}_{\hat{k}}[i][u]^2 = \sum_{i=0}^{2^n-1} (\mathcal{G}_{\hat{k}}\vec{\mathcal{L}}[u])[i]^2 = \sum_{i=0}^{2^n-1} ((\mathcal{G}_{\hat{k}}\vec{\mathcal{L}}[u])^{\mathsf{T}}[i]) \times ((\mathcal{G}_{\hat{k}}\vec{\mathcal{L}}[u])[i])$$

$$= (\mathcal{G}_{\hat{k}}\vec{\mathcal{L}}[u])^{\mathsf{T}} \times ((\mathcal{G}_{\hat{k}}\vec{\mathcal{L}}[u])) = \vec{\mathcal{L}}[u]^{\mathsf{T}} \mathcal{G}_{\hat{k}}^{\mathsf{T}} \mathcal{G}_{\hat{k}} \vec{\mathcal{L}}[u] = \vec{\mathcal{L}}[u]^{\mathsf{T}} \mathcal{G}_{\hat{k}} \vec{\mathcal{L}}[u]$$

$$= \sum_{i=0}^{2^n-1} \mathcal{L}[i][u]\mathcal{E}_{\hat{k}}[i][u]$$

Finally, we have $\left\| \vec{\mathcal{L}}[u] - \vec{\mathcal{E}}_{\hat{k}}[u] \right\|^2 = \sum_{i=0}^{2^n-1} \mathcal{L}[i][u]^2 - \sum_{i=0}^{2^n-1} \mathcal{L}[i][u]\mathcal{E}_{\hat{k}}$ $[i][u]$. So, minimizing the estimation error is equivalent to maximizing $\sum_{i=0}^{2^n-1} \mathcal{L}[i][u]\mathcal{E}_{\hat{k}}[i][u]$.

Recall that $\mathcal{G}_{\hat{k}} = \mathcal{M}_{\hat{k}}(\mathcal{M}_{\hat{k}}^{\mathsf{T}}\mathcal{M}_{\hat{k}})^{-1}\mathcal{M}_{\hat{k}}^{\mathsf{T}}$. Since $(\mathcal{M}_{\hat{k}}^{\mathsf{T}}\mathcal{M}_{\hat{k}})$ is a positive defined matrix, one can factorize it by Cholesky's decomposition into a matrix product $\mathcal{T}^{\mathsf{T}}\mathcal{T}$, such that $\mathcal{T}$ is an $s \times s$ upper triangular matrix [17]. So, let us define by $\mathcal{U}_{\hat{k}}$ the matrix $\mathcal{T}^{\mathsf{T}^{-1}}\mathcal{M}_{\hat{k}}^{\mathsf{T}}$. Then, we have $\mathcal{G}_{\hat{k}} = \mathcal{U}_{\hat{k}}^{\mathsf{T}}\mathcal{U}_{\hat{k}}$ and,

$$\sum_{i=0}^{2^n-1} \mathcal{L}[i][u]\mathcal{E}_{\hat{k}}[i][u] = \vec{\mathcal{L}}[u]^{\mathsf{T}}\mathcal{G}_{\hat{k}}\vec{\mathcal{L}}[u] = (\mathcal{U}_{\hat{k}}\vec{\mathcal{L}}[u])^{\mathsf{T}}(\mathcal{U}_{\hat{k}}\vec{\mathcal{L}}) = \left\| \mathcal{U}_{\hat{k}}\vec{\mathcal{L}}[u] \right\|^2.$$

So, minimizing the error square quadratic norm is equivalent to maximizing $\left\| \mathcal{U}_{\hat{k}}\vec{\mathcal{L}}[u] \right\|^2$. Moreover, one can show that $\mathcal{U}_{\hat{k}}[.][j] = \mathcal{U}_0[.][j \oplus \hat{k}]$. Hence, we have:

$$\left\| \mathcal{U}_{\hat{k}}\vec{\mathcal{L}}[u] \right\|^2 = \sum_{p=0}^{s-1} \left((\mathcal{U}_{\hat{k}}\vec{\mathcal{L}}[u])[p] \right)^2 = \sum_{p=0}^{s-1} \left(\sum_{j=0}^{2^n-1} \mathcal{U}_0[p][j \oplus \hat{k}]\mathcal{L}[j][u] \right)^2$$

$$= \sum_{p=0}^{s-1} \left(\mathcal{U}_0[p][.] \otimes \vec{\mathcal{L}}[u](\hat{k}) \right)^2$$

$$= \sum_{p=0}^{s-1} \left(WHT^{-1} \left(WHT\left(\mathcal{U}_0[p][.]\right) \bullet WHT(\vec{\mathcal{L}}[u]) \right)(\hat{k}) \right)^2$$

So, $\left\| \mathcal{U}_{\hat{k}}\vec{\mathcal{L}}[u] \right\|^2 = \left\| WHT^{-1} \left(WHT\left(\mathcal{U}_0[.][.]\right) \bullet WHT(\vec{\mathcal{L}}[u]) \right)(\hat{k}) \right\|^2,$ (3)

such that $WHT(\mathcal{U}_0[.][.])$ denotes WHT for each line of the matrix $\mathcal{U}_0$.

Finally, one can carry out the LRA by saving only one matrix $\mathcal{U}_0$ of dimension $s \times 2^n$, then computing $WHT(\mathcal{U}_0[.][.])$, and processing for each u the convolution of each line with the leakage vector according to Eq. (3). The obtained key by the LRA is the column index that has the highest norm in the result matrix. One can easily sow that the *correlation coefficient of determination* $R \doteq 1 - \overrightarrow{SSR/SST}$ it nothing but $\left\| \mathcal{U}_{\hat{k}}\vec{\mathcal{L}}[u] \right\|^2 / SST[u]$.

Algorithm 2 shows the most efficient LRA processing that we have obtained, thanks to (1) the coalescence, (2) the last transformation using $\mathcal{U}_{\hat{k}}$, and (3) the spectral approach. In fact Algorithm 2 is $2^n/s$ times more efficient than Algorithm 4 both in space memory and processing time. Tables 1 and 2 summarize the LRA best complexities, with and without computing $\vec{\beta}_{\hat{k}}[u]$ vectors, respectively. The third lines give our improvement in the AES case of study ($n = 8$) for basis size $s = 9$.

It is noteworthy that all our results that assume the group operation $\oplus$ over the set $\{0,1\}^n$ (i.e. $F(x,k) = F(x \oplus k)$) hold true for any other group operation $\odot$ as long as Walsh-Hadamard Transform is replaced by Fourier Transform (FFT) on this group ($\{0,1\}^n, \odot$). For example, if the operation is $+(\mod (2^n))$, then Cyclical Fourier Transform must replace Walsh-Hadamard Transform (WHT).

It is also noteworthy that to increase the numerical stability of the least square estimation, authors of [12,30] advise to select an orthogonal basis. Another advantage of our improvements is that is independent from the chosen basis.

Furthermore, our improvements relate to the LRA either with or without a profiling phase, either knowing the subkey during the profiling phase or not.

3.5   Incremental Implementation of LRA

Incremental implementation of LRA means the carrying out of an LRA using some set of traces, then update its computation when a new trace is added, and so on. From Algorithm 4 one can see that the instructions 5–10 should be carried out only once. All the other instructions can easily be implemented incrementally according to the new added leakage traces. It is useful to note that the instructions 18–20 can also be implemented incrementally, due to the linearity of WHT and the bi-linearity of the coordinate-wise product ($\bullet$).

4   Extension of the Improvements to the Protected Implementations by Masking

Let us consider a leaking cryptographic device protected by *masking*. Let t denotes a strictly positive integer. The protection by a masking of order t consists in dividing each sensitive variable Z into $t + 1$ shares $Z_0,..., Z_t$. In practice at least two different kinds of masking can be used; the Boolean masking and the arithmetic masking [18]. While the Boolean masking is compatible with linear Boolean functions, the arithmetic masking is compatible with arithmetic operations such as the modular addition in IDEA and TEA Algorithms [36]. Without loss of generality, we assume that the u-th sample in the measured leakage $\vec{L}$ corresponds to the u-th share of the sensitive variable Z, such that $0 \leq u \leq t$. Let the deterministic part of the leakage $\vec{L}$ (namely $E[\vec{L}|(Z_u)_u]$) be denoted by $\vec{Y}$. In order to recover information on Z, an adversary must combine the leakages on all the $t + 1$ shares in a so-called $(t + 1)$-th higher-order SCA.

In order to conduct a higher-order attack, many combination functions (which aim at combining the leakages of the different shares to form a new exploitable signal) were proposed in the literature [15,24,32]. According to [4,25],

Input :

- a set of d-dimensional leakage $(\vec{l_i})_{0 \le i \le N-1}$ and the corresponding plaintexts $(x_i)_{0 \le i \le N-1}$,
- a set of model functions $(m_p)_{p \le s}$.

Output : The candidate subkey $\hat{k}$

1 **for** $i \leftarrow 0$ **to** $N-1$ **do**   // Processing of the leakage Total Sum of Squares ($\overrightarrow{SST}$)
2      $\mu_{\vec{\mathcal{L}}} \leftarrow \mu_{\vec{\mathcal{L}}} + \vec{l_i}$
3      $\nu_{\vec{\mathcal{L}}} \leftarrow \nu_{\vec{\mathcal{L}}} + \vec{l_i}^{\,2}$
4 $\overrightarrow{SST} \leftarrow \nu_{\vec{\mathcal{L}}} - \frac{1}{N}\mu_{\vec{\mathcal{L}}}^2$
5 **for** $p \leftarrow 0$ **to** s **do**   // Pre-processing of the unique prediction matrix $\mathcal{M}_0$
6   **for** $x \leftarrow 0$ **to** $2^n - 1$ **do**
7          $\mathcal{M}_0[x][p] \leftarrow m_p[F(x,\hat{0})]$

8 $\mathcal{U}_0 \leftarrow \mathcal{T}^{\mathsf{T}^{-1}} \mathcal{M}_0^{\mathsf{T}}$ // $\mathcal{T} \doteq \left(Cholesky \left(\mathcal{M}_0^{\mathsf{T}} \times \mathcal{M}_0 \right) \right)^{-1}$
9 **for** $p \leftarrow 0$ **to** s **do**   // Pre-processing WHT of the lines of matrix $\mathcal{U}_0$
10     $\mathcal{U}_0[p][.] \leftarrow WHT(\mathcal{U}_0[p][.])$

11 **for** $i \leftarrow 0$ **to** $N-1$ **do**   // Computation of the coalesced matrix $\vec{\mathcal{L}}$
12     $\vec{\mathcal{L}}^{\mathsf{T}}[x_i] = \vec{\mathcal{L}}^{\mathsf{T}}[x_i] + l_i$
13   count$[x_i]$=count$[x_i]$+1
14 **for** $x \leftarrow 0$ **to** $2^n - 1$ **do**
15   **if** $count[x]$ **then**
16         $\vec{\mathcal{L}}^{\mathsf{T}}[x] = \vec{\mathcal{L}}^{\mathsf{T}}[x]/\text{count}[x]$

17 **for** $u \leftarrow 0$ **to** $d-1$ **do**   // Instantaneous attack (at time u)
18     $\vec{W}_L[u] \leftarrow WHT(\vec{\mathcal{L}}[u])$
19   **for** $p \leftarrow 0$ **to** $s-1$ **do**   // Computation of the error according to Eq. (3)
20         $\mathcal{U}_0[p][.] \leftarrow WHT^{-1}\left(\mathcal{U}_0[p][.] \bullet \vec{W}_L[u]\right)$

21   **for** $\hat{k} \leftarrow 0$ **to** $2^n - 1$ **do**   // Test hyp. $\hat{k}$ for all leakage coordinates
22         $SSR \leftarrow 0$
23   **for** $p \leftarrow 0$ **to** $s-1$ **do**   // Computation of the Residual Sum of Squares (SSR)
24             $SSR \leftarrow SSR + \left(\mathcal{U}_0[p][\hat{k}]\right)^2$
25         $R[\hat{k}][u] \leftarrow \frac{SSR}{\overrightarrow{SST}[u]}$ // coefficient of determination [8]

26 **return** $\text{argmax}_{\hat{k}} \left(max_u R[\hat{k}][u] \right)$

Algorithm 2: The most efficient LRA thanks to the spectral approach.

Table 1. Space memory and executing time complexities with computing $\vec{\beta}$.

	Memory	$\mathcal{P}$ pre-processing	$\vec{\beta}$ processing
Old implementations	$s \times 2^{2n}$	$s^{2.373} \times 2^n + 2^{2n} \times s^2$	$2^{2n} \times s \times d$
Our implementation	$s \times 2^n$	$s^{2.373} + 2^n \times s^2 + s \times n2^n$	$(n+1)2^n \times s \times d$
AES ($n = 8$) with $s = 9$	256 times	136 times	28 times

Table 2. Space memory and executing time complexities without computing $\vec{\beta}$.

	Memory	Pre-processing	$\vec{\mathcal{E}}$ processing
Old implementations	2^{3n}	$s^{2.373} \times 2^n + 2^{2n} \times s^2 + 2^{3n} \times s$	$2^{3n} \times d$
Our implementation	$s \times 2^n$	$s^{2.373} + 2^{n-1} \times s^2 + s \times n2^n$	$(n + s(n+1))2^n d$
AES ($n = 8$) with $s = 9$	7282 times	5426 times	736 times

for a high noise, the optimal combination technique against masking is the *normalized* product (for a first-order masking: $(\vec{\mathcal{L}}[0] - E[\vec{\mathcal{L}}[0]])(\vec{\mathcal{L}}[1] - E[\vec{\mathcal{L}}[1]])$), and this combination function should be accompanied by an optimal model (for a first-order masking: $E[(\vec{Y}_{\hat{k}}[0] - E[\vec{Y}[0]])(\vec{Y}_{\hat{k}}[1] - E[\vec{Y}[1]]) \mid Z]$). While the LRA is carried out on the combination leakage, as suggested in [8], all the ideas developed in the previous sections to improve the LRA efficiency can straightforwardly be applied on the protected implementations. In Subsect. 5.3, we experimentally show through several examples that the effectiveness of LRA against masked implementations stays unchanged when applying our improvements (the timing and the memory complexities are significantly improved).

4.1   Normalized Product Combination Against Arithmetic Masking

Since the construction of a proper SCA leakage model is at least as important as the selection of a good distinguisher [9], in this subsection we assess the optimal leakage model of the multiplication combination against arithmetic masking.

Recall that in practice the n-variables polynomials' basis is the most used basis in the LRA-based SCAs. In such a case, LRA consists in projecting the leakage function $\vec{\mathcal{L}^{\mathsf{T}}}[.]$ on the polynomials' basis. Our core idea is that for any function f defined from $\{0, \ldots 2^n - 1\}$ to $\mathbb{R}$ such that for each $Z \in \{0, \ldots 2^n - 1\}$ the value $f(Z)$ is known, the Numerical Normal Form (NNF) [5] consists to project f also on this polynomials' basis. So, in H-O attacks knowing the polynomial projection of the model (or at least knowing its degree), the (normalized) multiplication combination allows the adversary to choose the optimal polynomials' basis for LRA. In fact, if one uses the polynomials' basis, which is the most used in LRA, the expected coefficients $\vec{\beta}_{\hat{k}}[u]$ are non other then the coefficients of the Numerical Normal Form (NNF) [5] of $\vec{\mathcal{E}}[u]$. That means LRA does nothing but regresses the NNF of the Leakage function when a polynomials' basis is used.

Thanks to [26, Lemma 1], one knows that if the leakage follows the Hamming weight model, then the combination against the tth-order Boolean masking is a degree 1 polynomial. Namely it equals $(-\frac{1}{2})^t \left(\sum_i z_i - \frac{n}{2} \right)$, such that $(z_i)_{i=0...7}$ denotes the bits of the sensitive value Z. This important result holds for the Boolean masking but it does not hold for the arithmetic masking.

For the modular addition masking, let the combination function $f \doteq E[(\mathrm{hw}(Z+R) - E[\mathrm{hw}(Z+R)])(\mathrm{hw}(R) - E[\mathrm{hw}(R)]) \mod 256 | Z]$. In fact thanks to the Numerical Normal Form of the function f denoted $\widetilde{f}$, one can show that it is a degree 2 polynomial of Z's bits. Namely $\widetilde{f} = 4608 + \sum_i (2^i - 256)z_i + \sum_{i,j;i<j} (2^{8+i-j} z_i z_j)$. Similarly, if the leakage follows the Hamming weight model, the optimal combination of t shares $(t < 9)$ for such masking is a tth-degree polynomial. To exhibit this result, one should compute $f(Z)$ for each possible value Z, then carry out the NNF of f using Algorithm 3 obtained from [5].

Input   : f, n.
Output : f as its $\widetilde{f}$

1
2 **for** $i \leftarrow 0$ **to** $n-1$ **do**
3 | $b \leftarrow 0$
4 | **repeat**
5 | | **for** $x \leftarrow b$ **to** $b + 2^i - 1$ **do**
6 | | | $f[x + 2^i] \leftarrow f[x + 2^i] - f[x]$
7 | | $b \leftarrow b + 2^{i+1}$
8 | **until** $b = 2^n$

Algorithm 3: Numerical Normal Form [5].

5   Experiments

During our experiments two simulated leakage models are studied by:

1. The Hamming weight model: $\sum_{z_i=0}^{7} z_i$,
2. A degree 2 polynomial model: $\sum_{z_i=0}^{7} z_i + \frac{1}{2} \sum_{z_i=0}^{6} \sum_{z_j=z_i+1}^{7} z_i z_j$.

In both of them we added a zero-mean additive Gaussian noise, with different standard deviation values σ. In this work we compare CPA with coalescence, CPA, LRA with coalescence and LRA as long as its carrying out is possible. All these attacks are targeting the *sbox* output of the first AES round.

We assess different attacks both against unprotected implementations and against implementations protected by the Boolean masking or arithmetic masking. In the different scenarios, we assume that, with the exception of the additive independent noise, the CPA's adversary knows the leakage model. The effectiveness of our attacks is assessed by processing success rates (SR) according to the numbers of traces (#measurements) [33].

5.1   LRA with and Without Spectral Approach

First, we assess the efficiency of LRA with and without the spectral approach. Figure 1 shows that there is no difference between them in term of success rate, in all scenarios (protected/unprotected implementations with 1 or 2 degree polynomial leakage model). So, thanks to our improvements, one can conduct LRA without loss in the effectiveness, while it is significantly faster, with less memory space (as shown theoretically in Tables 1, 2 and experimentally in Tables 3, 4).

Table 3. Space memory & executing time of LRA with computing $\vec{\beta}$; AES use case.

	Memory	$\mathcal{P}$ pre-processing	$\vec{\beta}$ processing
Old implementations	589824 floats	58×10^{-3} s	8.297×10^{-3} s
Our implementation	2304 floats	$0,445 \times 10^{-3}$ s	0.332×10^{-3} s
AES $(n = 8)$ with $s = 9$	256 times	130 times	25 times

Table 4. Space memory & executing time of LRA without computing $\vec{\beta}$; AES use case.

	Memory	Pre-processing	$\vec{\mathcal{E}}$ processing
Old implementations	16777216 floats	1.63 s	0.236 s
Our implementation	2304 floats	0.329×10^{-3} s	0.333×10^{-3} s
AES $(n = 8)$ with $s = 9$	7282 times	4954 times	709 times

5.2   SCAs with and Without Coalescence

The coalescence approach leads to more efficient attacks in term of computing time. Figure 1 shows that there is a big difference between attacks with and without coalescence, in term of success rate. In fact, as shown in Subsect. 3.1 and explained in Appendix A, the coalescence approach requires to have asymptotically the same number n_i of messages x_i per class. This assumption does not hold if the attack requires few leakages/messages, that is the case for these figures ($\sigma = 0$).

In order to show the asymptotic equivalence between the SCAs with and without coalescence, one can study their success rates for high covariance noise. Figure 2 and 3, show this asymptotic equivalence when the noise is high.

5.3   LRA Against Higher-Order Masking

To study the efficiency of the SCA attacks against masking (especially LRA with our computing improvements), comparisons between the first order Boolean and the arithmetic masking (more precisely the addition modulo 2^8) are carried out

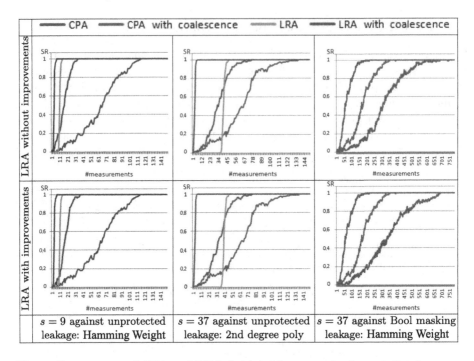

Fig. 1. Success rate of CPA and LRA (with/without our implementation improvements) according to the number of measurements, such that $\sigma = 0$.

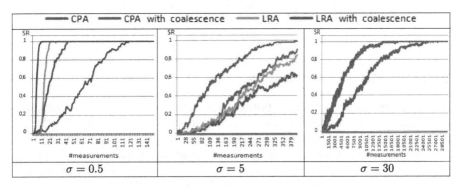

Fig. 2. Success rate of CPA and LRA (with/without coalescence) with basis size 9, against unprotected implementation, according to the number of measurements, such that the leakage is simulated to the Hamming weight model.

on the AES Sbox. Even if the modular addition masking is not useful for AES Sbox, we study its efficiency over it in order to compare both masking techniques against same attacks on the same Sbox. In these attacks we use the normalized multiplicative combination.

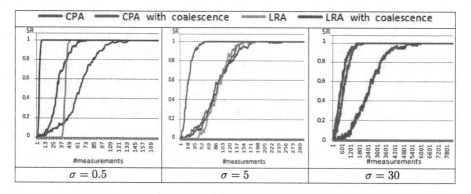

Fig. 3. Success rate of CPA and LRA (with our implementation improvements) with basis size 37, against unprotected implementation, according to the number of measurements, such that the leakage is simulated to degree 2 polynomial model.

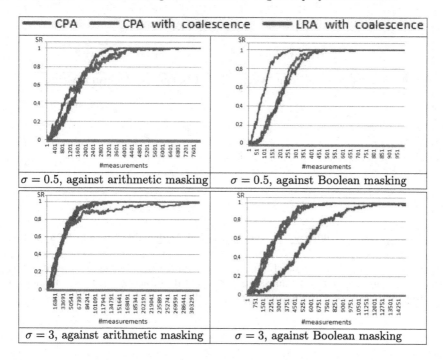

Fig. 4. Success rate of CPA and LRA (with our implementation improvements) with basis size 9, against 1st order masking implementation, according to the number of measurements, such that the leakage is simulated to the Hamming weight model.

As shown in Fig. 4 and 5, and as explained in Subsect. 4.1, the 9-size basis is suitable for the multiplication combination against Boolean masking. One can see that, against Boolean masking, the LRA is more efficient if the 9-size basis is used (right of Fig. 4) than that if the 37-size basis is used (right of Fig. 5).

In contrast, for the modular addition arithmetic masking, the suitable basis is a 37-size basis, which corresponds to degree 2 polynomial leakage function. One can see that, against arithmetic masking, LRA is less efficient if the 9-size basis is used (left of Fig. 4) than that if the 37-size basis is used (left of Fig. 5). Furthermore, Fig. 5 shows that the optimal leakage model of the normalized multiplicative combination is $4608 + \sum_i (2^i - 256)z_i + \sum_{i,j;i<j} (2^{8+i-j} z_i z_j)$ as exhibited in Sect. 4.1, thanks to the NNF. It labeled by *optimal CPA* in Fig. 5.

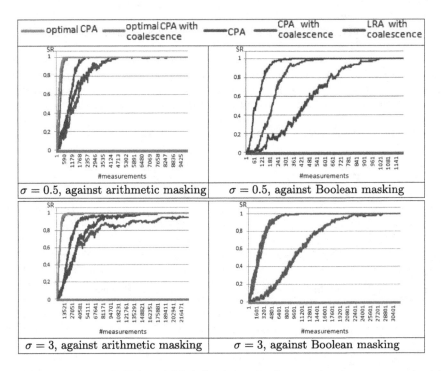

Fig. 5. Success rate of CPA and LRA (with our implementation improvements) with basis size 37, against 1st order masking implementation, according to the number of measurements, such that the leakage is simulated to the Hamming weight model.

6   Conclusion and Perspectives

In this paper we studied the use of coalescence both in LRA, in CPA and in covariance distinguishers. We also show that coalescence can accelerate the computation of LRA distinguisher, even in presence of masking countermeasure. Our study provides breakthrough improvements both in memory space and in running time required to carry out the LRA. Furthermore we exhibit the polynomial form of the normalized product combination which is useful in SCA against masking, especially for LRA. It is the first time when LRA is related to the Numerical Normal Form (NNF).

We believe that this work democratize the use of LRA and that it leads to further research results in the field of parametric side-channel attacks.

A   Proof of Proposition 2

Proof. Under the additive independent noise assumption, the leakage $\vec{l_i}$ is divided into two independent parts, such that $\vec{l_i} = E[\vec{L}|x_i] + b_i$, where $E[\vec{L}|x_i]$ is the determinist part and b_i is the noise. Let us denote the leakage model used in the attack by $g_k(x_i)$ (that corresponds to the sensitive variable $Z = x_i \oplus k$, for example). So, the covariance distinguisher is:

$$\frac{1}{N} \sum_{i=0}^{N-1} g_k(x_i) \cdot \vec{l_i} = \frac{1}{N} \sum_{i=0}^{N-1} g_k(x_i) \cdot \left(E[\vec{L}|x_i] + b_i \right)$$

$$= \frac{1}{N} \sum_{i=0}^{N-1} g_k(x_i) \cdot E[\vec{L}|x_i] + \frac{1}{N} \sum_{i=0}^{N-1} g_k(x_i) \cdot b_i$$

$$= \frac{1}{N} \sum_{j=0}^{2^n-1} n_j \cdot g_k(j) \cdot E[\vec{L}|j] + \frac{1}{N} \sum_{j=0}^{2^n-1} g_k(j) \cdot (\sum_{x_i=j} b_i),$$

Such that $n_j = \#\{x_i; \ x_i = j\}$.

By regrouping b_i in the classes (j), one can note $\sum_{x_i=j} b_i$ by $\sum_{c=1}^{n_j} b_{j,c}$. So, the covariance distinguisher becomes:

$$\frac{1}{N} \sum_{i=0}^{N-1} g_k(x_i) \cdot \vec{l_i} = \frac{1}{N} \sum_{j=0}^{2^n-1} n_j \cdot g_k(j) \cdot E[\vec{L}|j] + \frac{1}{N} \sum_{j=0}^{2^n-1} g_k(j) \cdot (\sum_{c=1}^{n_j} b_{j,c})$$

$$= \frac{1}{2^n} \sum_{j=0}^{2^n-1} \frac{n_j 2^n}{N} \cdot g_k(j) \cdot \left(E[\vec{L}|j] + \frac{\sum_{c=1}^{n_j} b_{j,c}}{n_j} \right),$$

such that the coalesced traces of the jth class is: $\frac{1}{n_j} \sum_{x_i=j} \vec{l_i} = E[\vec{L}|j] + \frac{\sum_{c=1}^{n_j} b_{j,c}}{n_j}$ if $n_j \neq 0$ (the coalesced traces equals 0 if $n_j = 0$). So, up to a weight factor per class $(\frac{n_j 2^n}{N})$, the traces being coalesced or not, we have the same distinguisher with a different noise variance $\left(\frac{\sum_{c=1}^{n_j} b_{j,c}}{n_j} \text{instead of } b_j \right)$.

In fact, studying the rough traces distribution means studying a random variable with a fix standard deviation σ and an arbitrary number N of traces. If the required number of traces N is large, one has to consider all of them, which is difficult (even impossible in high noise variance and countermeasures). By the Law of Large Numbers (LLN), doing the coalescence, with equal probabilities of each possible message $p = \frac{1}{2^n}$, gives $\frac{n_j 2^n}{N}$ tending towards 1. Furthermore, in such a case the number of the artificial traces (grouped by class) is at most 2^n, and according to Cochran Theorem 1, the noise standard deviation becomes $\sqrt{\frac{\sigma}{n_j}}$. That leads to a possible (even a fast) attack processing. Finally we conclude that carrying out the attack with averaging traces means reducing the standard deviation of the artificial random variable (by averaging traces per j values) instead of increasing the number of rough traces.

Furthermore, since the Cochran theorem holds for the Gaussian random vectors, the averaging traces by class principle can be applied in the multidimensional analysis, as in [34].

The asymptotic equivalence between SCA with and without coalesced traces holds also for CPA. This comes as a consequence of the following important property of Pearson's correlation coefficient:

Proposition 5. ([25, **Prop. 5**]). *Let $\vec{L}$ and X be two random variables. Then, for every function g_k defined over $\mathbb{Z}$, we have*

$$\rho(g_k(X), \vec{L}) = \rho\left(g_k(X), E\left[\vec{L}|X\right]\right) \times \rho\left(E\left[\vec{L}|X\right], \vec{L}\right) \tag{4}$$

So, an adversary that carrying out a CPA on leakage traces $\vec{l_i} \hookleftarrow \vec{L}$ with a leakage model function $g_k(x_i)$, such that $x_i \hookleftarrow X$, will estimate $\rho(g_k(X), \vec{L}) = \rho\left(g_k(X), E\left[\vec{L}|X\right]\right) \times \rho\left(E\left[\vec{L}|X\right], \vec{L}\right)$. Since $\rho\left(E\left[\vec{L}|X\right], \vec{L}\right)$ is independent from k, she can carry out a CPA by only estimating $\rho\left(g_k(X), E\left[\vec{L}|X\right]\right)$. This approach holds if and only if the adversary has a good estimator of $E\left[\vec{L}|X\right]$. This estimator can be obtained by simply averaging the traces per x_i values. In other terms, the adversary can carry out a CPA over the coalesced measurements by processing $\rho\left(g_k(X), E\left[\vec{L}|X\right]\right)$ instead of carrying it out with the rough traces by processing $\rho(g_k(X), \vec{L})$. So one can conclude the asymptotic equivalence between SCA with and without coalescence. $\diamond$

B   LRA Algorithm 4

```
Input   :
   – a set of d-dimensional leakage (l⃗ᵢ)₀≤ᵢ≤N−1 and the corresponding plaintexts
     (xᵢ)₀≤ᵢ≤N−1,
   – a set of model functions (mₚ)ₚ≤ₛ.

Output : The candidate subkey k̂
```

$$
\begin{array}{ll}
1 \;\; \textbf{for } i \leftarrow 0 \textbf{ to } N-1 \textbf{ do} & \text{// Processing of the leakage Total Sum of Squares } (\overrightarrow{SST}) \\
2 \quad\quad \mu_{\vec{\mathcal{L}}} \leftarrow \mu_{\vec{\mathcal{L}}} + \vec{l}_i & \\
3 \quad\quad \nu_{\vec{\mathcal{L}}} \leftarrow \nu_{\vec{\mathcal{L}}} + \vec{l}_i^{\,2} & \\
4 \;\; \overrightarrow{SST} \leftarrow \nu_{\vec{\mathcal{L}}} - \frac{1}{N}\mu_{\vec{\mathcal{L}}}^2 & \\
5 \;\; \textbf{for } p \leftarrow 0 \textbf{ to } s \textbf{ do} & \text{// Pre-processing of the unique prediction matrix } \mathcal{M}_0 \\
6 \quad\quad \textbf{for } x \leftarrow 0 \textbf{ to } 2^n-1 \textbf{ do} & \\
7 \quad\quad\quad \mathcal{M}_0[x][p] \leftarrow m_p[F(x,\hat{0})] & \\
8 \;\; \mathcal{G}_0 \leftarrow \mathcal{M}_0 \times (\mathcal{M}_0^\mathsf{T} \times \mathcal{M}_0)^{-1} \times \mathcal{M}_0^\mathsf{T} & \\
9 \;\; \textbf{for } i \leftarrow 0 \textbf{ to } 2^n-1 \textbf{ do} & \text{// Pre-processing WHT of the lines of matrix } \mathcal{G}_0 \\
10 \quad\quad \mathcal{G}_0[i][.] \leftarrow WHT(\mathcal{G}_0[i][.]) & \\
11 \;\; \textbf{for } i \leftarrow 0 \textbf{ to } N-1 \textbf{ do} & \text{// Computation of the coalesced matrix } \vec{\mathcal{L}} \\
12 \quad\quad \vec{\mathcal{L}}^\mathsf{T}[x_i] = \vec{\mathcal{L}}^\mathsf{T}[x_i] + l_i & \\
13 \quad\quad \text{count}[x_i] = \text{count}[x_i] + 1 & \\
14 \;\; \textbf{for } x \leftarrow 0 \textbf{ to } 2^n-1 \textbf{ do} & \\
15 \quad\quad \textbf{if } count[x] \textbf{ then} & \\
16 \quad\quad\quad \vec{\mathcal{L}}^\mathsf{T}[x] = \vec{\mathcal{L}}^\mathsf{T}[x]/\text{count}[x] & \\
17 \;\; \textbf{for } u \leftarrow 0 \textbf{ to } d-1 \textbf{ do} & \text{// Instantaneous attack (at time } u) \\
18 \quad\quad \overrightarrow{W}_L[u] \leftarrow WHT(\vec{\mathcal{L}}[u]) & \\
19 \quad\quad \textbf{for } x \leftarrow 0 \textbf{ to } 2^n-1 \textbf{ do} & \text{// Computation of the estimator } \vec{\mathcal{E}}[u] \text{ according to Proposition 4} \\
20 \quad\quad\quad \mathcal{E}[x][.] \leftarrow WHT^{-1}\left(\mathcal{G}_0[x][.] \bullet \overrightarrow{W}_L[u]\right) & \\
21 \quad\quad \textbf{for } \hat{k} \leftarrow 0 \textbf{ to } 2^n-1 \textbf{ do} & \text{// Test hyp. } \hat{k} \text{ for all leakage coordinates} \\
22 \quad\quad\quad SSR \leftarrow 0 & \\
23 \quad\quad\quad \textbf{for } x \leftarrow 0 \textbf{ to } 2^n-1 \textbf{ do} & \text{// Computation of the Residual Sum of Squares (SSR)} \\
24 \quad\quad\quad\quad SSR \leftarrow SSR + \left(\mathcal{E}[x\oplus\hat{k}][\hat{k}] - \mathcal{L}[x][u]\right)^2 & \\
25 \quad\quad\quad R[\hat{k}][u] \leftarrow 1 - \frac{SSR}{SST[u]} & \text{// coefficient of determination [8]} \\
26 \;\; \textbf{return } \operatorname{argmax}_{\hat{k}}\left(max_u R[\hat{k}][u]\right) &
\end{array}
$$

Algorithm 4: Linear Regression Analysis with coalescence and the spectral approach.

C WHT Algorithm

Up to a coefficient $\frac{1}{\sqrt{2^n}}$, an example of WHT processing for $n = 3$ is illustrated in Fig. 6.

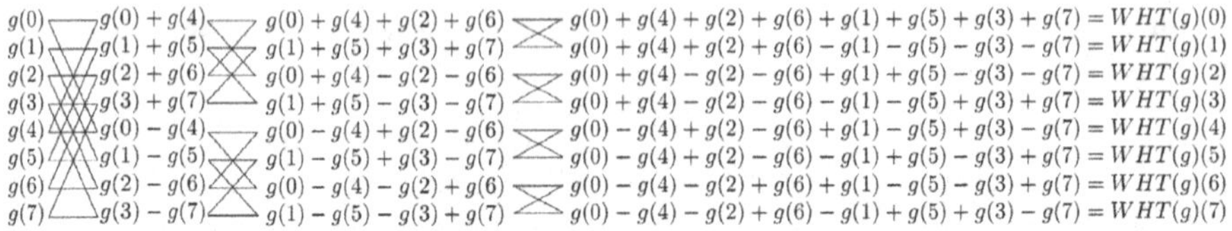

$$
\begin{aligned}
g(0) &\quad g(0)+g(4) &\quad g(0)+g(4)+g(2)+g(6) &\quad g(0)+g(4)+g(2)+g(6)+g(1)+g(5)+g(3)+g(7) = WHT(g)(0)\\
g(1) &\quad g(1)+g(5) &\quad g(1)+g(5)+g(3)+g(7) &\quad g(0)+g(4)+g(2)+g(6)-g(1)-g(5)-g(3)-g(7) = WHT(g)(1)\\
g(2) &\quad g(2)+g(6) &\quad g(0)+g(4)-g(2)-g(6) &\quad g(0)+g(4)-g(2)-g(6)+g(1)+g(5)-g(3)-g(7) = WHT(g)(2)\\
g(3) &\quad g(3)+g(7) &\quad g(1)+g(5)-g(3)-g(7) &\quad g(0)+g(4)-g(2)-g(6)-g(1)-g(5)+g(3)+g(7) = WHT(g)(3)\\
g(4) &\quad g(0)-g(4) &\quad g(0)-g(4)+g(2)-g(6) &\quad g(0)-g(4)+g(2)-g(6)+g(1)-g(5)+g(3)-g(7) = WHT(g)(4)\\
g(5) &\quad g(1)-g(5) &\quad g(1)-g(5)+g(3)-g(7) &\quad g(0)-g(4)+g(2)-g(6)-g(1)+g(5)-g(3)+g(7) = WHT(g)(5)\\
g(6) &\quad g(2)-g(6) &\quad g(0)-g(4)-g(2)+g(6) &\quad g(0)-g(4)-g(2)+g(6)+g(1)-g(5)-g(3)+g(7) = WHT(g)(6)\\
g(7) &\quad g(3)-g(7) &\quad g(1)-g(5)-g(3)+g(7) &\quad g(0)-g(4)-g(2)+g(6)-g(1)+g(5)+g(3)-g(7) = WHT(g)(7)
\end{aligned}
$$

Fig. 6. Flowgraph for computing WHT for $n = 3$.

References

1. Batina, L., Robshaw, M. (eds.): CHES 2014. LNCS, vol. 8731. Springer, Heidelberg (2014). https://doi.org/10.1007/978-3-662-44709-3
2. Brier, E., Clavier, C., Olivier, F.: Correlation power analysis with a leakage model. In: Joye, M., Quisquater, J.-J. (eds.) CHES 2004. LNCS, vol. 3156, pp. 16–29. Springer, Heidelberg (2004). https://doi.org/10.1007/978-3-540-28632-5_2
3. Bruneau, N., Carlet, C., Guilley, S., Heuser, A., Prouff, E., Rioul, O.: Stochastic collision attack. IEEE Trans. Inf. Forensics Secur. **12**(9), 2090–2104 (2017)
4. Bruneau, N., Guilley, S., Heuser, A., Rioul, O.: *Masks will fall off*. In: Sarkar, P., Iwata, T. (eds.) ASIACRYPT 2014. LNCS, vol. 8874, pp. 344–365. Springer, Heidelberg (2014). https://doi.org/10.1007/978-3-662-45608-8_19
5. Carlet, C., Guillot, P.: A new representation of Boolean functions. In: Fossorier, M., Imai, H., Lin, S., Poli, A. (eds.) AAECC 1999. LNCS, vol. 1719, pp. 94–103. Springer, Heidelberg (1999). https://doi.org/10.1007/3-540-46796-3_10
6. Chari, S., Rao, J.R., Rohatgi, P.: Template attacks. In: Kaliski, B.S., Koç, K., Paar, C. (eds.) CHES 2002. LNCS, vol. 2523, pp. 13–28. Springer, Heidelberg (2003). https://doi.org/10.1007/3-540-36400-5_3
7. Cochran, W.G.: The distribution of quadratic forms in a normal system, with application to the analysis of covariance. In: Mathematical Proceedings of the Cambridge Philosophical Society, vol. 30, pp. 178–191 (1934)
8. Dabosville, G., Doget, J., Prouff, E.: A new second-order side channel attack based on linear regression. IEEE Trans. Comput. **62**(8), 1629–1640 (2013)
9. Doget, J., Prouff, E., Rivain, M., Standaert, F.-X.: Univariate side channel attacks and leakage modeling. J. Cryptograph. Eng. **1**(2), 123–144 (2011). https://doi.org/10.1007/s13389-011-0010-2
10. Shan, F., Wang, Z., Wei, F., Guoai, X., Wang, A.: Linear regression side channel attack applied on constant XOR. IACR Cryptology ePrint Archive 2017:1217 (2017)
11. Gierlichs, B., Lemke-Rust, K., Paar, C.: Templates vs. stochastic methods. In: Goubin, L., Matsui, M. (eds.) CHES 2006. LNCS, vol. 4249, pp. 15–29. Springer, Heidelberg (2006). https://doi.org/10.1007/11894063_2

12. Guilley, S., Heuser, A., Ming, T., Rioul, O.: Stochastic side-channel leakage analysis *via* orthonormal decomposition. In: Farshim, P., Simion, E. (eds.) SecITC 2017. LNCS, vol. 10543, pp. 12–27. Springer, Cham (2017). https://doi.org/10.1007/978-3-319-69284-5_2

13. Guillot, P., Millérioux, G., Dravie, B., El Mrabet, N.: Spectral approach for correlation power analysis. In: El Hajji, S., Nitaj, A., Souidi, E.M. (eds.) C2SI 2017. LNCS, vol. 10194, pp. 238–253. Springer, Cham (2017). https://doi.org/10.1007/978-3-319-55589-8_16

14. Heuser, A., Rioul, O., Guilley, S.: Good is not good enough - deriving optimal distinguishers from communication theory. In: Batina and Robshaw [1], pp. 55–74

15. Joye, M., Paillier, P., Schoenmakers, B.: On second-order differential power analysis. In: Rao, J.R., Sunar, B. (eds.) CHES 2005. LNCS, vol. 3659, pp. 293–308. Springer, Heidelberg (2005). https://doi.org/10.1007/11545262_22

16. Kocher, P., Jaffe, J., Jun, B.: Differential power analysis. In: Wiener, M. (ed.) CRYPTO 1999. LNCS, vol. 1666, pp. 388–397. Springer, Heidelberg (1999). https://doi.org/10.1007/3-540-48405-1_25

17. Krishnamoorthy, A., Menon, D.: Matrix inversion using Cholesky decomposition. In: 2013 Signal Processing: Algorithms, Architectures, Arrangements, and Applications (SPA), pp. 70–72, September 2013. ISBN 978-83-62065-17-2, INSPEC Accession Number: 14041759, Electronic ISSN 2326-0319, Print ISSN 2326-0262

18. Lemke, K., Schramm, K., Paar, C.: DPA on n-bit sized boolean and arithmetic operations and its application to IDEA, RC6, and the HMAC-Construction. In: Joye, M., Quisquater, J.-J. (eds.) CHES 2004. LNCS, vol. 3156, pp. 205–219. Springer, Heidelberg (2004). https://doi.org/10.1007/978-3-540-28632-5_15

19. Lemke-Rust, K., Paar, C.: Analyzing side channel leakage of masked implementations with stochastic methods. In: Biskup, J., López, J. (eds.) ESORICS 2007. LNCS, vol. 4734, pp. 454–468. Springer, Heidelberg (2007). https://doi.org/10.1007/978-3-540-74835-9_30

20. Lomné, V., Prouff, E., Rivain, M., Roche, T., Thillard, A.: How to estimate the success rate of higher-order side-channel attacks. In: Batina and Robshaw [1], pp. 35–54

21. Lomné, V., Prouff, E., Roche, T.: Behind the scene of side channel attacks. In: Sako, K., Sarkar, P. (eds.) ASIACRYPT 2013. LNCS, vol. 8269, pp. 506–525. Springer, Heidelberg (2013). https://doi.org/10.1007/978-3-642-42033-7_26

22. NIST/ITL/CSD. Data Encryption Standard. FIPS PUB 46–3, October 1999. http://csrc.nist.gov/publications/fips/fips46-3/fips46-3.pdf

23. NIST/ITL/CSD. Advanced Encryption Standard (AES). FIPS PUB 197, November 2001. http://nvlpubs.nist.gov/nistpubs/FIPS/NIST.FIPS.197.pdf (also ISO/IEC 18033–3:2010)

24. Oswald, E., Mangard, S.: Template attacks on masking—resistance is futile. In: Abe, M. (ed.) CT-RSA 2007. LNCS, vol. 4377, pp. 243–256. Springer, Heidelberg (2006). https://doi.org/10.1007/11967668_16

25. Prouff, E., Rivain, M., Bevan, R.: Statistical analysis of second order differential power analysis. IEEE Trans. Comput. **58**(6), 799–811 (2009)

26. Rivain, M., Prouff, E., Doget, J.: Higher-order masking and shuffling for software implementations of block ciphers. In: Clavier, C., Gaj, K. (eds.) CHES 2009. LNCS, vol. 5747, pp. 171–188. Springer, Heidelberg (2009). https://doi.org/10.1007/978-3-642-04138-9_13

27. De Santis, F., Kasper, M., Mangard, S., Sigl, G., Stein, O., Stöttinger, M.: On the relationship between correlation power analysis and the stochastic approach: an ASIC designer perspective. In: Paul, G., Vaudenay, S. (eds.) INDOCRYPT 2013. LNCS, vol. 8250, pp. 215–226. Springer, Cham (2013). https://doi.org/10.1007/978-3-319-03515-4_14

28. Schaub, A., et al.: Attacking suggest boxes in web applications over HTTPS using side-channel stochastic algorithms. In: Lopez, J., Ray, I., Crispo, B. (eds.) CRiSIS 2014. LNCS, vol. 8924, pp. 116–130. Springer, Cham (2015). https://doi.org/10.1007/978-3-319-17127-2_8

29. Schindler, W.: On the optimization of side-channel attacks by advanced stochastic methods. In: Vaudenay, S. (ed.) PKC 2005. LNCS, vol. 3386, pp. 85–103. Springer, Heidelberg (2005). https://doi.org/10.1007/978-3-540-30580-4_7

30. Schindler, W.: Advanced stochastic methods in side channel analysis on block ciphers in the presence of masking. J. Math. Cryptol. 2(3), 291–310. (2008). https://doi.org/10.1515/JMC.2008.013, ISSN (Online) 1862-2984. ISSN (Print) 1862-2976

31. Schindler, W., Lemke, K., Paar, C.: A stochastic model for differential side channel cryptanalysis. In: Rao, J.R., Sunar, B. (eds.) CHES 2005. LNCS, vol. 3659, pp. 30–46. Springer, Heidelberg (2005). https://doi.org/10.1007/11545262_3

32. Schramm, K., Paar, C.: Higher order masking of the AES. In: Pointcheval, D. (ed.) CT-RSA 2006. LNCS, vol. 3860, pp. 208–225. Springer, Heidelberg (2006). https://doi.org/10.1007/11605805_14

33. Standaert, F.-X., Malkin, T.G., Yung, M.: A unified framework for the analysis of side-channel key recovery attacks. In: Joux, A. (ed.) EUROCRYPT 2009. LNCS, vol. 5479, pp. 443–461. Springer, Heidelberg (2009). https://doi.org/10.1007/978-3-642-01001-9_26

34. Under submission. On the power of template attacks in highly multivariate context

35. Sugawara, T., Homma, N., Aoki, T., Satoh, A.: Profiling attack using multivariate regression analysis. IEICE Electron. Express 7(15), 1139–1144 (2010)

36. Wheeler, D.J., Needham, R.M.: TEA, a tiny encryption algorithm. In: Preneel, B. (ed.) FSE 1994. LNCS, vol. 1008, pp. 363–366. Springer, Heidelberg (1995). https://doi.org/10.1007/3-540-60590-8_29

37. Williams, V.V.: Multiplying matrices faster than coppersmith-winograd. In: STOC 2012 Proceedings of the Forty-Fourth Annual ACM Symposium on Theory of Computing, New York, USA, 19–22 May 2012, pp. 887–898, May 2012

Side-Channel Attacks and Deep Learning

Kilroy Was Here: The First Step Towards Explainability of Neural Networks in Profiled Side-Channel Analysis

Daan van der Valk[1], Stjepan Picek[1(✉)], and Shivam Bhasin[2]

[1] Delft University of Technology, Delft, The Netherlands
daan@dvandervalk.nl, s.picek@tudelft.nl
[2] Physical Analysis and Cryptographic Engineering,
Temasek Laboratories at Nanyang Technological University, Singapore, Singapore
sbhasin@ntu.edu.sg

Abstract. While several works have explored the application of deep learning for efficient profiled side-channel analysis, explainability, or, in other words, what neural networks learn remains a rather untouched topic. As a first step, this paper explores the Singular Vector Canonical Correlation Analysis (SVCCA) tool to interpret what neural networks learn while training on different side-channel datasets, by concentrating on deep layers of the network. Information from SVCCA can help, to an extent, with several practical problems in a profiled side-channel analysis like portability issue and criteria to choose a number of layers/neurons to fight portability, provide insight on the correct size of training dataset and detect deceptive conditions like over-specialization of networks.

Keywords: Side-channel analysis · Deep learning · Neural networks · Representation learning

1 Introduction

Profiled side-channel analysis (SCA) represents the worst-case security analysis by considering the most powerful side-channel attacker with access to an open (since the keys are chosen/known by the attacker) clone device. In recent years, machine learning techniques, and especially deep learning techniques, became a standard choice for profiled attacks as they allow very good performance where even targets protected with countermeasures can be broken [2,8]. As such, the progress from the first paper considering convolutional neural networks in 2016 [10] is tremendous. Besides "only" improving the performance of our attacks, we should also aim to understand and explain the machine learning process and models it produces. This problem is commonly known as the *explainability* problem in machine learning.

Unfortunately, explainability is a difficult problem. It is a central problem in a large part of machine learning research, and yet, it is far from solved [5].

G. M. Bertoni and F. Regazzoni (Eds.): COSADE 2020, LNCS 12244, pp. 175–199, 2021.
https://doi.org/10.1007/978-3-030-68773-1_9

One aspect of explainability is the representation learning where one tries to understand why a certain representation of a problem (i.e., how the problem is represented in the layers of a deep learning algorithm) is better than some other representation. By understanding this, we can select a good representation that makes the subsequent learning problem easier. More precisely, the supervised learning with feed-forward neural networks performs a type of representation learning [5]. The last layer gives information about the classes, while every hidden layer should ideally find a representation that will make the classification process easier.

While this problem is interesting, it is also very difficult to define the representation of a neuron. Naively, one could define a table of all possible input/output mappings for a neuron (and then do this for the whole network). The problem is then that such tables would be huge and impractical to make conclusions. Consequently, we must consider techniques that allow us to capture relevant information while not requiring too much information. There are only a handful of works that are (relatively) successful in devising tools for investigating the internal representations, as discussed in Sect. 2.3. *To the best of our knowledge, there are no results in representation learning for the domain of side-channel analysis.* In the side-channel domain, we have distinctive challenges due to countermeasures and portability (settings where an attacker has no access to measurements from the device under attack to conduct a training but only to measurements from a similar or clone device). Therefore, it is important to consider different kinds of data, e.g., protected vs. unprotected implementations, or device A vs. device B. So, instead of just focusing on explaining the classifiers' predictions, it is also useful to compare the representations learned by different profiling models.

In this paper, we use the Singular Vector Canonical Correlation Analysis (SVCCA) [22] technique to inspect internal representations learned by two popular types of neural networks: multilayer perceptron and convolutional neural networks. While usually research works concentrate on what can be done with the information at the input (such as feature selection, see, e.g., [18]) or the information at the output of a neural network (accuracy, success rate, guessing entropy [23]), we take a different path and ask what useful information can be obtained from the middle (hidden layers) in the neural network. We analyze several SCA datasets, and we show that, indeed, different datasets have different internal representations. We see that changing the leakage model or adding/removing countermeasures can result in significantly different internal representations. Additionally, with such a tool, we can better understand the learning process dynamics, which can help design more appropriate architectures. We then concentrate on the portability where we compare internal representations when the clone and attack devices are different and have different keys. Our results show we can gain insights about the internal representations of different SCA datasets. Such knowledge can then be used to design better neural network architectures, e.g., how to select the number of neurons in a layer, the number of layers, and the training dataset size. Finally, we show the hidden layers learn about labels despite never being explicitly provided with that information.

2   Background

2.1   Multilayer Perceptron and Convolutional Neural Networks

The multilayer perceptron (MLP) algorithm is a feed-forward neural network that maps sets of inputs onto sets of appropriate outputs. An MLP consists of multiple layers (one input layer, one output layer, and at least one hidden layer) of nodes in a directed graph, where each layer is fully connected to the next one, and training of the network is done with the backpropagation algorithm.

CNNs are similar to ordinary neural networks (e.g., feed-forward networks like multilayer perceptron): they consist of several layers, and each layer is made up of neurons. CNNs use three main types of layers: convolutional layers, pooling layers, and fully-connected layers.

2.2   Comparison of Neural Networks and SVCCA Methodology

Raghu et al. proposed Singular Vector Canonical Correlation Analysis to compare two layers in a network, based on the neurons' activation outputs [22]. By doing so, they were able to compare the learned representations from two neural networks in a way that is invariant to affine transformation (thus, allowing comparison between different layers and networks) and fast to compute.

SVCCA uses the following definitions:

Definition 1. *A **neuron** i is defined by the output it generates over a dataset $X = x_1, \ldots, x_N$. The ith neuron of layer l is represented by $\mathbf{z}_i^l = (z_i^l(x_1), \ldots, z_i^l(x_N))$. Here, $z_i^l(x_j)$ indicates the output (a single number) of the neuron for data sample x_j. Thus, a neuron is a vector in $\mathbb{R}^N$.*

Such an output is also called an activation vector: it stores the neuron's outcome after the activation function is applied, for all N data samples that are fed as inputs to the neural network. For convolutional layers, we treat every output of the as a separate neuron. This means c_j, the number of outputs in a layer, is defined as

$$c_j = \text{input size} \cdot \text{kernel width} \cdot \text{number of channels}, \tag{1}$$

for a convolutional layer j. For a fully-connected layer, c_j is simply the number of neurons in that layer.

Definition 2. *A **layer** j is defined as the subspace spanned by its neurons, i.e., a subspace in $\mathbb{R}^N \times \mathbb{R}^{c_j}$. It is constructed as a $N \times c_j$ matrix, where c_j is the number of outputs in layer j where layer j is $l_j = \mathbf{z}_1^{l_j}, \ldots, \mathbf{z}_{c_j}^{l_j}$.*

Based on this definition, the SVCCA algorithm compares two layers l_1 and l_2. It operates on two matrices, each having an entry per neuron per data sample (trace). The layers can have a different number of neurons, but there should be an equal number of samples N used to compare the layers. After the layers have been trained, and their outputs have been stored as l_1 and l_2, the SVCCA procedure for layer comparison works as follows:

1. Singular Value (SV) decomposition of both layers separately. For both layers l_1 and l_2, their singular value (SV) decompositions are computed and outputted as $l_1' \subset l_1$ and $l_2' \subset l_2$. This transformation represents the same data in another form: matrices l_1' and l_2' will still have N rows (one row per data sample), but contain $L_1' \leq c_1$ and $L_2' \leq c_2$ columns, respectively. With this transformation, a preset percentage of the variance is explained. After this step, two reduced subspaces $l_1' \subset l_1$ and $l_2' \subset l_2$ are used as inputs for the next step.

2. Canonical Correlation Analysis (CCA) computes the linear transformations on l_1', l_2' to maximize correlation, which results in an ordered set of SVCCA components. These operations can be defined as matrices W_X and W_Y to operate on l_1' and l_2', respectively. The outputted subspaces $\tilde{l}_1 = W_X l_1'$ and $\tilde{l}_2 = W_Y l_2'$ are maximally correlated. Consequently, the algorithm returns the following outputs:

   – CCA components: the number of components is $min(L_1', L_2')$, the smallest dimension of the SVD-reduced layers. For each component, there is:
      • The value of the CCA component for both of the networks, for each trace in the comparison dataset. $o_m^i(x_j)$ denotes the value of the ith component for profiling model m for data sample x_j;
      • the correlations $corrs = \rho_1, \ldots, \rho_{min(L_1', L_2')}$, which indicate how well each component correlates between both layers.
   – To express the output of SVCCA in a single metric, the SVCCA similarity $\bar{\rho}$ represents how well the representations of two layers are aligned with each other:

$$\bar{\rho} = \frac{1}{min(m_1, m_2)} \sum_i \rho_i. \tag{2}$$

Note that the first step of the algorithm, Singular Value Decomposition, is the backbone of Principal Component Analysis (PCA), which is commonly used in machine learning for data reduction but also in profiled side-channel analysis. The SVCCA steps are depicted in Fig. 1. The produced correlations $corrs$ and the average correlation $\bar{\rho}$ will be used as a metric to evaluate common knowledge. *Common knowledge describes the similarity between the layers' representations. If two layers have common knowledge, that means their layer representations are similar and vice versa.* SVCCA can be used on any layer regardless of its position in the neural network architecture. Still, it does not make sense to consider the input layer (as there is nothing done yet) and the output layer (as this is what is commonly evaluated through various metrics).

2.3 Related Work

Templates [3] were proposed as the first profiled side-channel analysis and widely used over the years. It is shown that templates are optimal from the information-theoretic point of view if the assumed leakage model is correct, and the adversary has access to a sufficient number of traces [3]. In practical settings with limited profiling traces and added noise, machine learning algorithms can perform better

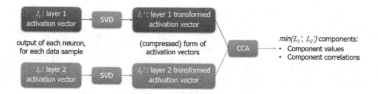

Fig. 1. Overview of the operations in SVCCA. As input, it takes the activation vectors from both layers, containing each neuron's output for all samples in the dataset. The singular vector decomposition (SVD) is applied to both layers individually, resulting in a (reduced) matrix per layer. These matrices are compared using Canonical Correlation Analysis (CCA), which is a linear transformation that maximizes the correlation between both layers. Both the correlations (from high to low correlation) and the values of the components, per sample in the dataset, are outputted.

than templates [20]. Maghrebi et al. [10] first started with a comparison of deep neural networks (DNN) with classical machine learning and templates and its application to break masking countermeasure using convolution neural networks. DNN was further shown to break jitter based countermeasures [2]. Later, Kim et al. [8] used Gaussian noise-based regularization to break protected implementation in as low as three traces.

Some works have also explored other aspects of DNN for side-channel analysis rather than just attack performance. The conflict of the standard metrics used in side-channel (success rate, guessing entropy) and machine learning (loss, accuracy) is studied in [19]. Picek et al. considered limiting the number of traces for the profiling phase to better evaluate the attack performance [17]. Deep learning model generalization and understanding exploiting the class probabilities provided by the output layer was proposed in [14]. Several works have looked into the interpretation of the profiling model learned by a DNN after training to extract the interesting features by evaluation of input activation gradient [11], occlusion techniques [7], layer-wise backpropagation [15], and sensitivity analysis [25] as a metric. These techniques consider every feature's contribution to the output of the last layer, i.e., to the prediction. These techniques are not aimed at comparing different layers in a neural network. The performance of machine learning techniques can also be cast as the robustness problem where one explores how different perturbations influence their performance [16]. *Despite these attempts, there is still little known about the inner working of neural networks in the domain of side-channel analysis.*

Considering general research in the deep learning domain, certain efforts have been made to explain predictions of black-box techniques better, typically focusing on insight in prediction decisions. This includes rule extraction, visual representations, feature importance, sensitivity analysis, and activation maximization [6]. Note, some of these techniques are used in profiling SCA, as discussed in the paragraph above. In 2017, Raghu et al. proposed Singular Vector Canonical Correlation Analysis to compare two layers in a network [22]. The authors used this technique to measure the intrinsic dimensionality of layers, to explore learning dynamics throughout training, to show where class-specific information in networks is formed, and to suggest new training regimes. In the follow-up research, Morcos et al. further developed and tested the SVCCA methodology [13]. There, the authors use projection weighted CCA to understand neural networks and their internal representations. This technique is based on SVCCA but enables further differentiation between signal and noise.

3   Establishing a Baseline

3.1   DPAcontest V4 Dataset

DPAcontest v4 (DPAv4) provides measurements of a masked AES software implementation [24]. As the masking is found to leak first-order information [12], the mask can be considered as known and dataset as unprotected one. The leakage model equals:

$$Y(k^*) = \text{Sbox}[P_i \oplus k^*] \oplus \underbrace{M}_{\text{known mask}}, \tag{3}$$

where P_i is a plaintext byte where we choose to attack the first byte, i.e., $i = 1$. The measurements consist of 3 000 features around the S-box part of the algorithm execution, and in total, there is 100 000 traces available. This dataset is available at http://www.dpacontest.org/v4/. We denote this dataset as "DPAv4 (unmasked)". Additionally, we can also ignore the information about the mask and consider the dataset as being protected. Then, Eq. (3) changes to:

$$Y(k^*) = \text{Sbox}[PT_1 \oplus k^*]. \tag{4}$$

Here, we simply classify by considering the output of the first S-box. In the rest of this paper, we denote this setting as "DPAv4 (ignoring masks)".

3.2   Comparison Datasets

To get a better picture of what SVCCA outcomes mean, we compare profiling models for DPAv4 with several other datasets. These include a dataset from another field, a set of generated "side-channel" measurements, and random data.

CIFAR-10 Dataset. We use the CIFAR-10 dataset as a reference problem from the computer vision domain [9]. It consists of 50 000 training and 10 000 test images. Each image consists of 32×32 pixels in 3 channels (colors); for this comparison, we "flatten" those to obtain 3 076 features. CIFAR-10 is an interesting dataset for our comparison, as 1) it is from a completely different domain, so no patterns are expected to overlap between DPAv4 and CIFAR-10, 2) a neural network can be built with a very similar architecture: it has 3 076 features and ten classes (quite close to the 3 000 features around the S-box computation of DPAv4, where we can select nine classes (HW leakage model)), and 3) it was also used in the SVCCA paper [22] as a baseline.

Generated Traces. To further compare with similar data, we generated a random dataset similar to the DPAv4 dataset and has common assumptions about side-channel measurements: 1) there are 3 000 features: 2 900 are drawn completely random from the standard normal distribution. The other 100 are semi-random (for all classes, a class mean is computed for each of the 100 semi-random features. For these 100 features, for some sample i, feature j is drawn: $x_{i,j} = 0.5 \cdot N(0,1) + 0.5 \cdot \mu_{k,j}$ where k is the class of sample i and $\mu_{k,j}$ indicates this class k's mean for feature j), and 2) the columns are shuffled randomly. Note, although artificial, this dataset follows the Gaussian noise distribution.

Random "Outputs" Dataset. Finally, instead of computing activation vectors from some neural network layer, a matrix of the same size is randomly generated. As this has no relation with deep learning representations, we expect to see no common knowledge with other datasets. All entries are randomly drawn from the standard normal distribution ($\sim N(0,1)$).

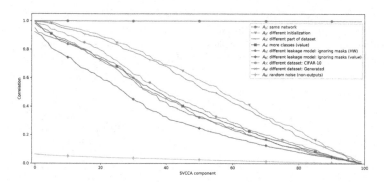

Fig. 2. Results for baseline experiment A, the SVCCA comparison between a profiling model trained on DPAv4 (HW) and several other profiling models. A detailed description of these settings is listed in Table 1.

3.3 Experimental Setup

To test the SVCCA methodology, we compare small MLP instances with (nearly) the same architecture.

We consider only a very simple MLP with a single hidden layer, consisting of 100 neurons with the ReLU activation function. The next layer is the output layer, having either 9 (DPAv4 HW, Generated), 10 (CIFAR-10), or 256 (DPAv4 intermediate value) classes/neurons. The output layer uses the Softmax activation function. The profiling models are trained to minimize the categorical cross-entropy loss, using the Adam optimizer, and the training runs for 50 epochs. All profiling models are trained on 25 000 measurements.

Note that all networks have 3 000 inputs, except for those trained on CIFAR-10, which have 3 076. The comparison data is either padded with zeros at the end (when there are not enough features) or cropped at the end (when there are too many features) to adjust for this feature number mismatch. The profiling models generally performed well after training, with close to 100% accuracy for the DPAv4 and Generated dataset and roughly 50% accuracy for the CIFAR-10 dataset. The comparison given here is conducted between the only hidden layer of each profiling model. For each of the scenarios, an MLP is randomly initialized and trained. We list all considered settings in Table 1. It compares a profiling model trained on the first 25 000 DPAv4 traces, with labels as described by the unmasked leakage model (Eq. (3), in the HW leakage model) with itself and several other profiling models.

Table 1. Baseline experiment A: a single network trained on the DPAv4 dataset in the HW leakage model compared with itself and several other profiling models. The comparisons are based on the networks' hidden layer outputs, using all 100 000 traces in the DPAv4 dataset. Random "activation vectors" are not network outputs, but are randomly drawn from the standard normal distribution.

Network 1	Network 2			Scenario	
	Dataset	Indexes	Leakage model		
DPAv4 (unmasked), HW leakage model, trained on indexes 0–25 000	DPAv4 (unmasked)	0–25 000	HW	A_1	Same network
		0–25 000	HW	A_2	Different initialization
		25 000–50 000	HW	A_3	Different part of dataset
		0–25 000	Value	A_4	More classes (value leakage model)
	DPAv4 (ignoring masks)	0–25 000	HW	A_5	Different leakage model: ignoring masks
		0–25 000	Value	A_6	Different leakage model: ignoring masks
	CIFAR-10	0–25 000	–	A_7	Different dataset: CIFAR-10
	Generated	0–25 000	–	A_8	Different dataset: generated traces
	Random "activation vectors"			A_9	Comparison with random data

The resulting SVCCA correlations are shown in Fig. 2. For each comparison, the entire DPAv4 dataset is used to generate the profiling models' activation vectors. The blue line indicates the comparison with the same network's outputs (A_1). As expected, it shows a perfect correlation ($\rho_i = 1$ for all i).

We give a comparison with an MLP trained on the same data, but with a different random initialization of the profiling model's weights before training (A_2, orange line, $\overline{\rho} = 0.5646$). The green line (A_3) compares with another network, trained on the different 25 000 traces from DPAv4, showing a slightly lower correlation ($\overline{\rho} = 0.5404$). A slight modification of the original network's problem is the change from the HW leakage model to the intermediate value leakage model (A_4, $\overline{\rho} = 0.4162$). Based on the same data, a network can also learn the original S-box output (i.e., Eq. (4)) in the HW (A_5, $\overline{\rho} = 0.3992$) or the intermediate value leakage model (A_6, $\overline{\rho} = 0.3287$). A_5 and A_6 are interesting datasets as they depict the significant impact of adding a masking countermeasure on common knowledge (and internal representation of models). Although these DPAv4-related profiling models still show some similarities with the original profiling model, we observe a stronger similarity between the original profiling model and some unrelated profiling models. In particular, we see a slightly higher correlation with the CIFAR-10 profiling model (A_7, $\overline{\rho} = 0.4429$) when compared to the profiling models with/without masking. Roughly on the same levels as the others, we see a similarity with the profiling model trained on generated data (A_8, $\overline{\rho} = 0.4031$). As expected, we see almost no correlation with a completely random vector drawn from the standard normal distribution (A_9, $\overline{\rho} = 0.0271$). Here we do not give guessing entropy results, as for the datasets outside SCA, it does not make sense to consider the key ranking (as there is no key).

Label-Based Inspection. To further investigate SVCCA, Fig. 3 shows the values of the first component for each of the scenarios in Fig. 2 – except the first one, as identical profiling models result in identical outcomes. While the profiling model 1 remains fixed in Fig. 3, the blue lines indicate profiling model 1's SVCCA-transformed output, which depends on the profiling model to which it is compared. As SVCCA finds the best linear mapping to align the two profiling models' outputs, each graph shows different values for profiling model 1. Along the x-axis, 100 samples are randomly selected for all nine classes in the HW leakage model. The y-axis shows the first SVCCA component value per data sample. Notice that SVCCA is purely based on the activation vectors, in this case, of the hidden layer. SVCCA is not based on class labels, but interestingly enough, we can see a relationship between the class labels and the first component value for some scenarios. Besides considering the first component, one can also use other SVCCA components, but the most correlated information is contained in the first one. Next, we require a definition for the relation between an SVCCA component and the class label. For this, the following correlation metric suffices:

Definition 3. *The class-correlation of some experiment E for two profiling models ($m \in [1, 2]$) for an ordered list of class labels Y is $\rho_{Y, m}^E$ equals the Pearson correlation between the first SVCCA component, based on experiment E, and the class labels Y, for one of the two compared profiling models m.*

Here, Y represents the labels of DPAv4 where the known mask is removed (Eq. (3)) in the HW leakage model. We observe that when different MLPs are trained on exactly the same data, there is a very high correlation with the class label for both networks (Fig. 3a, $\rho_{Y, 1}^{A_2} = -0.9824$, $\rho_{Y, 2}^{A_2} = -0.9827$). This means that the strongest pattern (i.e., the first component) that SVCCA finds among the hidden layer's outputs, are highly correlated with the class labels learned by the networks. When training on similar, but not identical data, we see a comparable situation (Fig. 3b, $\rho_{Y, 1}^{A_3} = -0.9826$, $\rho_{Y, 2}^{A_3} = -0.9820$). In the next scenario, we compare with a profiling model trained with identical data, but taking intermediate values, instead of HW as labels. Notice that these 256 classes are "encapsulated" in the nine HW classes. For example, value "42"

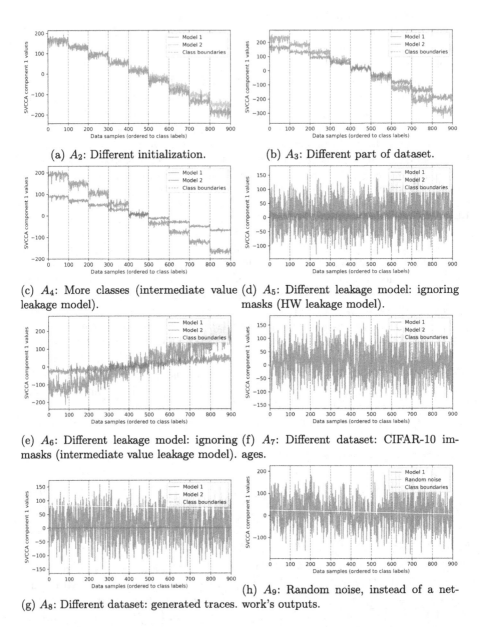

(a) A_2: Different initialization.

(b) A_3: Different part of dataset.

(c) A_4: More classes (intermediate value leakage model).

(d) A_5: Different leakage model: ignoring masks (HW leakage model).

(e) A_6: Different leakage model: ignoring masks (intermediate value leakage model).

(f) A_7: Different dataset: CIFAR-10 images.

(g) A_8: Different dataset: generated traces.

(h) A_9: Random noise, instead of a network's outputs.

Fig. 3. First SVCCA component for comparisons as described in Table 1 and shown in Fig. 2. Along the x-axis, data samples are sorted according to class label; for each class, 100 samples are randomly selected. The y-axis indicates the value of the first SVCCA component for these samples. When training in the same leakage model (regardless of being HW or intermediate value), a strong correlation between the class label and SVCCA component is observed.

always maps to the Hamming weight "3". Figure 3c shows the result: again, we see a high correlation between the first component values for both profiling models, and the HW class label $\rho_{Y,1}^{A_4} = -0.9895$, $\rho_{Y,2}^{A_4} = -0.9885$. In other scenarios, we see lower correlations between the first SVCCA component and labels. When comparing with a profiling model trained for DPAv4 HW labels, while ignoring the mask (Eq. (4)), we see no significant relation between the component values and the class labels (Fig. 3d, $\rho_{Y,1}^{A_5} = 0.0371$, $\rho_{Y,2}^{A_5} = 0.0356$). Clearly, the most similar patterns in these layers say nothing meaningful about the samples' classes. Similar lack of correlation is observed in Figs. 3d until 3h. We see that internal representation is extremely similar for profiling models trained on similar data and the same leakage model. This does not depend on the choice of the leakage model. Although SVCCA is not provided with class labels, the underlying patterns it finds show that the MLPs have an extremely similar internal representation, aiming for large class separability. Based on the obtained results, we observe the following:

- Changing the parts of the dataset used in training has a similar effect as changing the initialization values. Both changes have little impact on internal representation, which indicates one should not be too worried about such changes (compared to some other possible changes).
- When comparing networks trained with the HW leakage model to those on the intermediate value leakage model, the inner representation can be similar.
- The effect of having or not having a masking countermeasure influences the internal representation of a profiling model significantly.
- Certain correlation is to be expected even when comparing very different datasets (as seen for DPAv4 and CIFAR-10).
- Simply looking at the correlation values can be misleading as the datasets that are closer from the domain perspective (DPAv4 with and without masks) can differ more than datasets that are completely non-related (DPAv4 and CIFAR-10).
- Although SVCCA is independent of class labels, its components can be highly correlated with the labels.
- It is difficult to know if the common knowledge is high because the small networks have less knowledge (expressiveness) in general, or because there is indeed information they share.
- To conclude, we can use SVCCA to compare internal representations of different profiling models. Unfortunately, SVCCA is not a reliable measure for comparing arbitrary datasets as we can see correlation differences, but we cannot estimate how significant is that difference in practice.

4   Portability

In the previous section, we concluded that SVCCA is not suitable for comparing neural networks trained on entirely different datasets. In realistic scenarios in SCA, we use two different devices for profiling and attacking (commonly known as portability), where those devices are similar, which means that the acquired datasets should be similar. Several works have explored the portability issue for deep learning attacks and concluded it represents a problem for their performance [1, 4].

4.1   Datasets and Experimental Setup

We use data from several devices running AES-128 in software. The target device is an 8-bit AVR microcontroller running at $16MHz$. The devices are not protected with any countermeasures, and we attack the first S-box of the first round. For each copy of the device, there are 50 000 traces where each trace has 600 features. We use three datasets with the following relationship among them:

- Datasets 1 and 2 are taken from different devices but have the same key.
- Datasets 1 and 3 are taken from different devices and use different keys.
- Datasets 2 and 3 are taken from the same device but have different keys.

To allow a meaningful comparison, we use the neural network architectures as proposed in [1]:

- MLP: a small multilayer perceptron with three hidden layers, having 50, 25, and 50 neurons. The input layer consists of 50 features, which are selected based on the Pearson correlation.
- MLP2: a multilayer perceptron with four hidden layers, having 500 neurons each. For this architecture, all 600 features are used.
- CNN: a convolutional neural network with one convolutional block and two fully-connected layers. The convolutional layer has a filter size of 64 and kernel 11. We use the average pooling layer with pooling size two and stride two. The fully-connected layers have 128 neurons each. Again, we use all 600 features.

All algorithms aim to optimize the categorical cross-entropy, with a batch size of 256, and $RMSProp$ optimizer. For multilayer perceptron, we train for 50 epochs and use a learning rate of 0.001, while for CNN, we train for 125 epochs and use a learning rate of 0.0001. These hyperparameter values are based on [21]. Following the scenarios from [1], we train those networks with either 10 000, or 40 000 training examples. Due to the lack of space, some of the figures are given in Appendix A, and when presenting guessing entropy results, we show only the 10 000 or 40 000 training traces scenario. The guessing entropy (GE) metric is the average number of successive guesses required to determine the true value of a secret key, where one ranks all possible key values from the most likely one to the least likely one. Then, low GE means low entropy and, thus, a successful attack. Note that with GE, we give comparisons for each combination of the train/test dataset.

4.2   Results

Figure 4 shows a comparison of several MLP profiling models in the intermediate value leakage model for different hidden layers. Comparing networks trained on

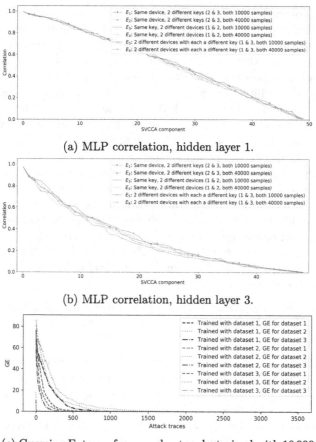

(a) MLP correlation, hidden layer 1.

(b) MLP correlation, hidden layer 3.

(c) Guessing Entropy for neural networks trained with 10 000 traces.

Fig. 4. Correlation results for MLP in the intermediate value leakage model for hidden layers 1 and 3. Other hidden layers are given in Fig. 9. GE results for 10 000 traces.

different datasets (1 vs. 2, 1 vs. 3, and 2 vs. 3) seems to result in a homogeneous amount of common knowledge (i.e., the internal representation is very similar despite changing the devices/keys). Also, the training set size seems not to influence the correlation between networks. MLP's small architecture may explain this: the networks roughly learn the same function, which approximates the training data but do not overfit. Finally, we see that all neurons are involved in every layer, which indicates those neurons indeed carry the information relevant for the internal representation. There is a faster drop in the correlation value for the hidden layer three, which indicates one could use fewer neurons in that layer without limiting the internal representation. We omitted the results for the HW leakage model as they produce very similar results. When considering the GE results, we show comparisons for every combination of the datasets with 10 000 traces. We can observe that the results are similar, indicating that small differences in the hidden layers' correlation values also result in the small differences in the attack performance as one would expect. If each hidden layer learns a similar representation, then the whole profiling model should perform similarly from the GE perspective. For 40 000 traces, we observed similar behavior.

For the MLP2 architecture, we show results for the HW leakage model in Fig. 5 and for the intermediate value leakage model in Fig. 6. When considering the HW leakage model, in the first layer, we see that the correlation is much lower when using a larger training set size. This could indicate that with a larger network like MLP2, the neurons fit much more precisely around the training data. Although [1] reports better performance for larger neural networks, specialization leads there to a divergence from profiling models learning other (large) datasets. This also suggests that one could benefit from using smaller training set sizes when in portability settings, as those will result in less specialization. This is also following observations made by Bhasin et al. [1]. *Here, by specialization, we consider the phenomenon where a part of the network learns the feature representation for a specific dataset.* We formalize the notion of over-specialization in the context of portability.

Definition 4. *Over-specialization is an effect where a neural network (or a part of it) learns to generalize only for a specific dataset and cannot generalize for other datasets, as seen in portability.*

If a neural network overfits, it also over-specializes, but the converse is not necessarily true. Indeed, one can easily have a neural network that generalizes well for the unseen data from the same dataset (device/key), but will not generalize to another device/key setting.

The results for hidden layers 2 and 3 indicate that the learned representations can differ significantly, signifying that portability can represent a problem for deep learning. Interestingly, we also see that the number of SVCCA components is much lower than the number of neurons, which means we do not require so many neurons in these layers to capture data's internal representation. For hidden layer 3, there is an even larger influence of over-specialization if we use more training examples. The fourth hidden layer also requires a much smaller number of neurons as this is the last layer before the output layer, where there are nine classes (thus, having a smaller number of neurons also makes sense). Finally, we see the largest part of the specialization is happening in the middle layers. As at the last hidden layer, correlations are similar, we can expect also similar results for GE, which is confirmed in Figs. 5c and 5d.

When considering the intermediate value leakage model (Fig. 6), we see the findings are somewhat similar to those for the HW leakage model. In the first hidden layer, the internal representations are very similar and using all neurons. This indicates that the first hidden layer's internal representation still did not manage to pinpoint on finer differences in the datasets. Already in the second hidden layer, there is a significant drop in correlation for datasets using 40 000 in the training phase. This confirms that having more measurements could lead to over-specialization, resulting in worse performance in portability settings.

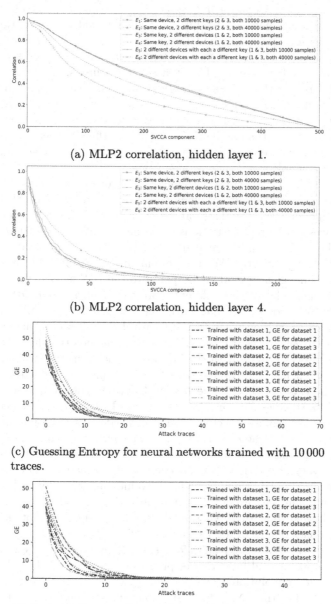

(a) MLP2 correlation, hidden layer 1.

(b) MLP2 correlation, hidden layer 4.

(c) Guessing Entropy for neural networks trained with 10 000 traces.

(d) Guessing Entropy for neural networks trained with 40 000 traces.

Fig. 5. Correlation results for MLP2 in the Hamming weight leakage model for hidden layers 1 and 4. Other hidden layers are given in Fig. 10. GE results for 10 000 and 40 000 traces.

The last hidden layer shows a relatively stable behavior but with quite a fast drop in the correlation. Consequently, some of the settings with a bad correlation in the previous layer managed to improve their internal representation, but it is still quite low for most of the SVCCA components, which indicates potential problems for the classification process. Interestingly, we see several scenarios for hidden layers 2 to 4, where we do not need 500 neurons. We do not observe significant differences (for certain scenarios) between layers 2, 3, and 4, which means there is no added benefit of having those layers. Consequently, it could be beneficial to explore smaller architectures here. Finally, we remark that the specialization occurs in the middle layers, similar to the HW scenario. Naturally, the effect is smaller here as we use more classes, and to specialize, we also need more training examples.

From the GE graphs, we observe similar behavior over datasets. Still, we do see larger performance differences when compared to the MLP or MLP2 in the HW leakage model scenarios. This can be explained by the fact that there are more differences among representations in the middle layers. Nevertheless, as the last hidden layer gives similar correlation levels, it is expected that GE results should not differ significantly. We observe that the GE result differs more for the intermediate value leakage model (compared to the HW leakage model), which is expected as more classes and different representations of the middle layers are more difficult to be completely aligned in the last hidden layer only. Notice the effect of over-specialization when training with dataset 1 and attacking dataset 3. Indeed, for 10 000 traces, we see GE is lower. On the other hand, for 40 000 traces, GE improves rapidly with the increase in the number of attack traces.

In Fig. 7, we depict the results for MLP2 first and last hidden layer, when correlating the class labels and the first SVCCA component. As before, along the x-axis, data samples are sorted according to the class label. For each class, 100 samples are randomly selected. The y-axis indicates the value of the first SVCCA component for these samples. Since we consider the intermediate value leakage model, 256 classes are encapsulated in the Hamming weight classes. We can see the values of the first SVCCA component to increase as going toward deeper hidden layers. Additionally, while the values are generally well correlated, we see certain differences, especially apparent in the last hidden layer. So, while the layers managed to learn about the labels, one could expect potential attack performance issues due to over-specialization with training sets.

Finally, we investigate the results for the CNN architecture. We remark that we omit the convolutional layer due to practical limitations. While the number of parameters in convolutional layers is low, they produce massive activation vectors. For example, the CNNs' first layers outputs are roughly 750 times larger than those of the MLP, taking more than 28 GB to store a single convolution activation vector. In Fig. 8, we depict results for the second fully-connected layers for both the HW and intermediate value leakage models. When considering the HW leakage model, we see that the internal representations are similar, and we require fewer neurons than used. This means that the portability setting does not produce many issues in the HW leakage model and that one fully-connected

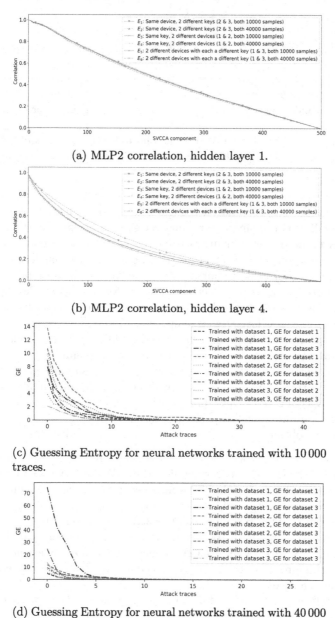

(a) MLP2 correlation, hidden layer 1.

(b) MLP2 correlation, hidden layer 4.

(c) Guessing Entropy for neural networks trained with 10 000 traces.

(d) Guessing Entropy for neural networks trained with 40 000 traces.

Fig. 6. Correlation results for MLP2 in the intermediate value leakage model for hidden layers 1 and 4. Other hidden layers are given in Fig. 11. GE results for 10 000 and 40 000 traces.

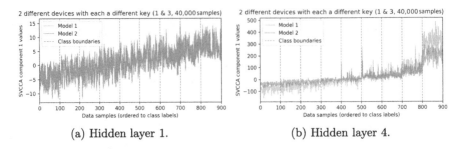

Fig. 7. Label-based inspection for MLP2 when both devices and keys differ, intermediate value leakage model for hidden layers 1 and 4. Other hidden layers are given in Fig. 12.

layer could suffice. The correlation is higher for the intermediate value leakage model, especially for the smaller training set size. Additionally, the first fully-connected layer needs fewer neurons than the second one. Again, we observe the problem reported by Bhasin et al. [1] that having too much training data can cause over-specialization in portability scenarios. As the correlation behaves similarly in both layers (while decreasing faster for the second layer), we can assume that only a single hidden layer would be sufficient. Finally, we notice that the first fully-connected layer tends to specialize more. This is aligned with the MLP2 scenario results, where we also noticed middle layers to specialize more. For CNNs and the HW leakage model, the behavior is similar to the previous cases: small differences in the fully-connected layers result in small differences in GE. On the other hand, for the intermediate value leakage model, we notice that both fully-connected layers differ in the level of common knowledge, and this also results in different GE performance.

Based on the obtained results, we make the following observations:

- There is some common knowledge (shared inner representation) across networks that were trained on very similar data. We observe a similar level of common knowledge across the portability scenarios; it does not matter much whether the device, key, or both, are changed.
- When looking from a portability perspective, one should be careful not to train neural networks with too much data (leading to over-specialization of certain hidden layers). The SVCCA correlations decrease when networks are trained with more data, thus allowing to conclude about the needed number of training examples.
- SVCCA indicates that the middle layers (e.g., hidden layers two and three in MLP2) specialize more than the first and last hidden layers.
- SVCCA can indicate the required number of layers and neurons.
- SVCCA components can be highly correlated with the class labels in the portability setting.
- Similar common knowledge in all hidden layers leads to a similar GE.
- Differences in the middle hidden layers can be reduced by the last hidden layer, resulting in only smaller differences in GE.

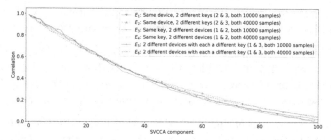

(a) CNN correlation in the Hamming weight leakage model, the second fully-connected layer.

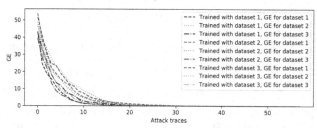

(b) Guessing Entropy for neural networks trained with 10 000 traces

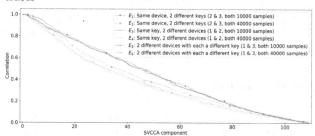

(c) CNN correlation in the intermediate value leakage model, the second fully-connected layer.

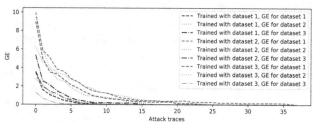

(d) Guessing Entropy for neural networks trained with 10 000 traces

Fig. 8. Correlation results for CNN for the second fully-connected layer. Other hidden layer is given in Fig. 13. GE results for 10 000 traces.

- More complex leakage models (i.e., with more classes) result in larger GE differences if there are differences among the representations of hidden layers.
- SVCCA differences in the last hidden layer also result in different GE.

Finally, our results indicate certain advantages and disadvantages of SVCCA. Most importantly, it is not possible to use SVCCA (as a sole tool) to design a neural network for profiled SCA, but rather it can be used to give insights into the neural network's behavior. The main advantages of SVCCA are:

- The method allows comparing similarity across layers, independently of output shape and context (i.e., type of data processed by the neural network).
- It shows the largest possible correlation when the inputs are linearly transformed.
- It is invariant to affine transformations: no re-scaling or ordering the most important neurons is required.
- The method enables dissecting the similarity for particular samples or classes.

On the downside, SVCCA has the following shortcomings:

- Its results are difficult to interpret: there is no formal relationship with the networks' performance, only the similarity is measured. Also, some context of other SVCCA outcomes (i.e., Fig. 2) is required to understand whether the correlation is meaningful.
- The method does not find non-linear relations: when changing the learned function (e.g., adding a mask), no significant correlation is found.
- SVCCA is computationally intensive when comparing convolutional layers, as the outputs have large dimensions.

5   Conclusions and Future Work

This paper uses the SVCCA tool and shows that there is common knowledge between various datasets. While this tool is far from perfect, it still provides a great deal of useful information. As an example, there seems to be more common knowledge between the HW or intermediate value leakage models than when considering datasets with and without countermeasures. This indicates that while we can hope to use the same neural networks for the HW/intermediate value leakage models, the same networks for both protected and unprotected scenarios will have a much more challenging task. Next, we observe how information about the class labels is captured by SVCC, but also how the information about the correlation for SVCCA components can help us in the design of the attacks by selecting the more appropriate number of hidden layers and the number of neurons, as well as the training set size. In future work, we will concentrate on SVCCA for convolutional layers as this information should further help in understanding the dynamics of internal representation within the profiling model.

Acknowledgment. The authors acknowledge the support from the 'National Integrated Centre of Evaluation' (NICE); a facility of Cyber Security Agency, Singapore (CSA).

A   Additional Figures

In this section, we depict the results for hidden layers we omitted from the paper's main body due to their similar behavior as those already presented. In Fig. 9, we depict the correlation results for the second hidden layer of an MLP in the intermediate value leakage model. Similarly, Fig. 10 shows results for the MLP2 architecture, the Hamming weight leakage model for hidden layers 2 and 3.

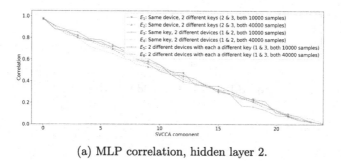

(a) MLP correlation, hidden layer 2.

Fig. 9. Correlation results for MLP in the intermediate value leakage model for the second hidden layer.

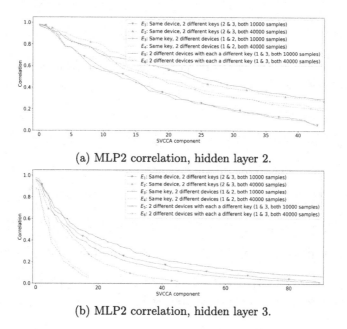

(a) MLP2 correlation, hidden layer 2.

(b) MLP2 correlation, hidden layer 3.

Fig. 10. Correlation results for MLP2 in the Hamming weight leakage model for hidden layers 2 and 3.

In Fig. 12, we show the results for the label-based inspection approach for the MLP2 architecture. We consider a scenario where both device and keys differ for the intermediate value leakage model for hidden layers 2 and 3.

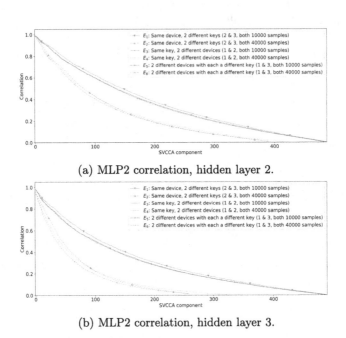

(a) MLP2 correlation, hidden layer 2.

(b) MLP2 correlation, hidden layer 3.

Fig. 11. Correlation results for MLP2 in the intermediate value leakage model for hidden layers 2 and 3.

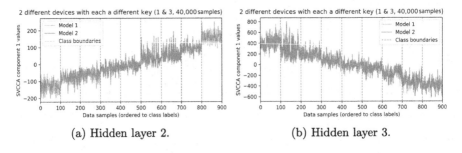

(a) Hidden layer 2.   (b) Hidden layer 3.

Fig. 12. Label-based inspection for MLP2 when both devices and keys differ, intermediate value leakage model for hidden layers 2 and 3.

Figure 13 gives correlation results for CNN for the first fully-connected layers for both the Hamming weight and intermediate value leakage models.

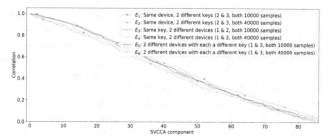

(a) CNN correlation in the Hamming weight leakage model, the first fully-connected layer.

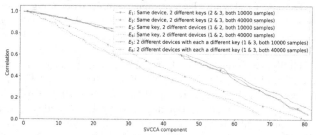

(b) CNN correlation in the intermediate value leakage model, the first fully-connected layer.

Fig. 13. Correlation results for CNN for the first fully-connected layer.

References

1. Bhasin, S., Jap, D., Chattopadhyay, A., Picek, S., Heuser, A., Ranjan Shrivastwa, R.: Mind the portability: a warriors guide through realistic profiled side-channel analysis. Cryptology ePrint Archive, Report 2019/661 (2019). https://eprint.iacr.org/2019/661
2. Cagli, E., Dumas, C., Prouff, E.: Convolutional neural networks with data augmentation against Jitter-based countermeasures. In: Fischer, W., Homma, N. (eds.) CHES 2017. LNCS, vol. 10529, pp. 45–68. Springer, Cham (2017). https://doi.org/10.1007/978-3-319-66787-4_3
3. Chari, S., Rao, J.R., Rohatgi, P.: Template attacks. In: Kaliski, B.S., Koç, K., Paar, C. (eds.) CHES 2002. LNCS, vol. 2523, pp. 13–28. Springer, Heidelberg (2003). https://doi.org/10.1007/3-540-36400-5_3
4. Das, D., Golder, A., Danial, J., Ghosh, S., Raychowdhury, A., Sen, S.: X-DeepSCA: cross-device deep learning side channel attack. In: Proceedings of the 56th Annual Design Automation Conference 2019 on - DAC 2019, vol. 1, pp. 1–6. ACM Press, New York (2019)
5. Goodfellow, I., Bengio, Y., Courville, A.: Deep Learning. MIT Press, Cambridge (2016)
6. Guidotti, R., Monreale, A., Ruggieri, S., Turini, F., Giannotti, F., Pedreschi, D.: A survey of methods for explaining black box models. ACM Comput. Surv. **51**(5) (2018). https://doi.org/10.1145/3236009

7. Hettwer, B., Gehrer, S., Tim, G.: Deep neural network attribution methods for leakage analysis and symmetric key recovery. CoRR, pp. 1–17 (2019)
8. Kim, J., Picek, S., Heuser, A., Bhasin, S., Hanjalic, A.: Make some noise. Unleashing the power of convolutional neural networks for profiled side-channel analysis. IACR Trans. Cryptograph. Hardw. Embedded Syst. **2019**(3), 148–179 (2019)
9. Krizhevsky, A., Nair, V., Hinton, G.: CIFAR-10 (Canadian Institute for Advanced Research) (2009). http://www.cs.toronto.edu/~kriz/cifar.html
10. Maghrebi, H., Portigliatti, T., Prouff, E.: Breaking cryptographic implementations using deep learning techniques. In: Carlet, C., Hasan, M.A., Saraswat, V. (eds.) SPACE 2016. LNCS, vol. 10076, pp. 3–26. Springer, Cham (2016). https://doi.org/10.1007/978-3-319-49445-6_1
11. Masure, L., Dumas, C., Prouff, E.: Gradient visualization for general characterization in profiling attacks. In: Polian, I., Stöttinger, M. (eds.) COSADE 2019. LNCS, vol. 11421, pp. 145–167. Springer, Cham (2019). https://doi.org/10.1007/978-3-030-16350-1_9
12. Moradi, A., Guilley, S., Heuser, A.: Detecting hidden leakages. In: Boureanu, I., Owesarski, P., Vaudenay, S. (eds.) ACNS 2014. LNCS, vol. 8479, pp. 324–342. Springer, Cham (2014). https://doi.org/10.1007/978-3-319-07536-5_20
13. Morcos, A., Raghu, M., Bengio, S.: Insights on representational similarity in neural networks with canonical correlation. In: Bengio, S., Wallach, H., Larochelle, H., Grauman, K., Cesa-Bianchi, N., Garnett, R. (eds.) Advances in Neural Information Processing Systems 31, pp. 5727–5736. Curran Associates, Inc. (2018)
14. Perin, G.: Deep learning model generalization in side-channel analysis. Cryptology ePrint Archive, Report 2019/978 (2019). https://eprint.iacr.org/2019/978
15. Perin, G., Ege, B., Chmielewski, L.: Neural network model assessment for side-channel analysis. Cryptology ePrint Archive, Report 2019/722 (2019). https://eprint.iacr.org/2019/722
16. Picek, S., Heuser, A., Alippi, C., Regazzoni, F.: When theory meets practice: a framework for robust profiled side-channel analysis. Cryptology ePrint Archive, Report 2018/1123 (2018). https://eprint.iacr.org/2018/1123
17. Picek, S., Heuser, A., Guilley, S.: Profiling side-channel analysis in the restricted attacker framework. Cryptology ePrint Archive, Report 2019/168 (2019). https://eprint.iacr.org/2019/168
18. Picek, S., Heuser, A., Jovic, A., Batina, L.: A systematic evaluation of profiling through focused feature selection. IEEE Trans. Very Large Scale Integr. (VLSI) Syst. 1–14 (2019). https://doi.org/10.1109/TVLSI.2019.2937365
19. Picek, S., Heuser, A., Jovic, A., Bhasin, S., Regazzoni, F.: The curse of class imbalance and conflicting metrics with machine learning for side-channel evaluations. IACR Trans. Cryptograph. Hardw. Embedded Syst. **2019**(1), 209–237 (2018). https://tches.iacr.org/index.php/TCHES/article/view/7339
20. Picek, S., et al.: Side-channel analysis and machine learning: a practical perspective. In: 2017 International Joint Conference on Neural Networks (IJCNN), pp. 4095–4102. IEEE (2017)
21. Prouff, E., Strullu, R., Benadjila, R., Cagli, E., Dumas, C.: Study of deep learning techniques for side-channel analysis and introduction to ascad database. Cryptology ePrint Archive, Report 2018/053 (2018). https://eprint.iacr.org/2018/053
22. Raghu, M., Gilmer, J., Yosinski, J., Sohl-Dickstein, J.: SVCCA: singular vector canonical correlation analysis for deep learning dynamics and interpretability. In: Guyon, I., et al. (eds.) Advances in Neural Information Processing Systems 30, pp. 6076–6085. Curran Associates, Inc. (2017)

23. Standaert, F.-X., Malkin, T.G., Yung, M.: A unified framework for the analysis of side-channel key recovery attacks. In: Joux, A. (ed.) EUROCRYPT 2009. LNCS, vol. 5479, pp. 443–461. Springer, Heidelberg (2009). https://doi.org/10.1007/978-3-642-01001-9_26
24. TELECOM ParisTech SEN research group: DPA Contest (4th edition) (2011). http://www.dpacontest.org/v4/index.php
25. Timon, B.: Non-profiled deep learning-based side-channel attacks with sensitivity analysis. IACR Trans. Cryptograph. Hardw. Embedded Syst. **2019**(2), 107–131 (2019). https://tches.iacr.org/index.php/TCHES/article/view/7387

Online Performance Evaluation of Deep Learning Networks for Profiled Side-Channel Analysis

Damien Robissout[1]([✉]), Gabriel Zaid[1,2], Brice Colombier[1], Lilian Bossuet[1], and Amaury Habrard[1]

[1] University of Lyon, UJM-Saint-Etienne, CNRS Laboratoire Hubert Curien UMR
5516 F-42023, Saint-Etienne, France
{damien.robissout,gabriel.zaid,brice.colombier,
lilian.bossuet,amaury.habrard}@univ-st-etienne.fr
[2] Thales ITSEF, Toulouse, France
gabriel.zaid@thalesgroup.com

Abstract. Deep learning based side-channel analysis has seen a rise in popularity over the last few years. A lot of work is done to understand the inner workings of the neural networks used to perform the attacks and a lot is still left to do. However, finding a metric suitable for evaluating the capacity of the neural networks is an open problem that is discussed in many articles. We propose an answer to this problem by introducing an online evaluation metric dedicated to the context of side-channel analysis and use it to perform early stopping on existing convolutional neural networks found in the literature. This metric compares the performance of a network on the training set and on the validation set to detect underfitting and overfitting. Consequently, we improve the performance of the networks by finding their best training epoch and thus reduce the number of traces used by 30%. The training time is also reduced for most of the networks considered.

Keywords: Side-channel attacks · Metrics · Deep learning · Underfitting · Overfitting

1 Introduction

Side-channel attacks are a class of cryptographic attacks in which an adversary exploit vulnerabilities of a system by analyzing its physical properties, such as the power consumption [8] or electromagnetic emanations [1], to reveal secret information. The implementation of a cryptographic algorithm involves the manipulation of sensitive variables which depend on the secret. This is the base concept behind side-channel attacks, among which we find *profiling attacks*. In this scenario, an adversary has access to a test device on which he can choose the plaintext and the secret key. With that information, he is able to estimate the conditional distribution associated with the sensitive variable of interest. On

G. M. Bertoni and F. Regazzoni (Eds.): COSADE 2020, LNCS 12244, pp. 200–218, 2021.
https://doi.org/10.1007/978-3-030-68773-1_10

a target device containing a secret to retrieve, the adversary can then predict the actual sensitive value and reveal the secret. In 2002, the first profiling attacks, named *template attacks*, were introduced by Chari *et al.* [4] but their proposal was limited by its computational complexity.

Very similar to profiling attacks, deep learning algorithms were inevitably applied in the side-channel context. Indeed, some articles have shown the robustness of convolutional neural networks (CNNs) to the most common countermeasures, namely *masking* [10,11] and *desynchronization* [3,16]. One of their main advantages is that they do not require pre-processing of the traces. The training process, through which the network learns to solve one specific problem, consists in two phases [5]: the forward propagation and the backward propagation. Given an input, the aim of the forward propagation is to feed training examples to the network in the forward direction by processing successive linear and nonlinear transformations in order to predict a value related to the input. Once this is done, the backward propagation measures the error between the predictions and the correct output and tries to reduce it by updating the parameters that compose the network.

To evaluate the training process and its performance, classical deep learning metrics can be used. One of the most popular is the accuracy. Unfortunately, as Picek *et al.* have shown [12], this metric is poorly suited in the context of side-channel analysis. Using the accuracy tends to favor the class with the highest output probability. This solution cannot be considered, in side-channel analysis, because the classifiers are often only loosely correlated with the true classification because of the very small leakage information present in the traces used for learning. Then, to perform a successful attack, the adversary must combine the classification results obtained for multiple traces to extract the estimate of the true class.

Contributions. In this article, we evaluate the ability of a network to generalize the knowledge found in the learning samples. By comparing the performance on the training set, containing the examples used by the network to learn, and the validation set, containing examples the network has never seen before, we get an insight into how well the network performs on new examples. Our proposed metric, called $\Delta_{train,val}^d$, is derived from the success rate [14], commonly used in side-channel analysis. Defined as the number of successful attacks over 100 realizations, the success rate is a suitable metric to evaluate the performance of attacks compared to the accuracy, which corresponds to taking into account only one trace to perform only one attack. By measuring the number of traces that are needed to get a successful d^{th} order success rate on the training and the validation sets, we can accurately evaluate the ability of the network to generalize its knowledge. We confirm the relevance of our metric by applying it on the ASCAD public dataset [13]. Using $\Delta_{train,val}^d$ has two benefits: during training, this metric can be used to detect the internal state of the network (underfitting/overfitting) and to find the best number of epochs to perform early stopping [5]. Furthermore, $\Delta_{train,val}^d$ helps to compare the performance between the networks once they are trained. Therefore, it allows us to optimize the performance of a network used for side-channel analysis.

Article Organization. The article is organized as follows. Section 2 is dedicated to the neural networks and evaluation metrics used in the article. After defining the machine learning approach for evaluating the generalization capacity of a network, Sect. 3 defines a new evaluation metric, called $\Delta_{train,val}^{d}$, which measures this generalization in the context of side-channel analysis. This new metric is applied on the public dataset ASCAD [13] and its main CNN architecture in Sect. 4 and then compared against the only comparable existing metric, the guessing entropy bias variance decomposition [15]. Finally in Sect. 5, we discuss some future works that could be investigated and conclude on the results presented in the article.

2   Preliminaries

2.1   Notations

Let calligraphic letters $\mathcal{X}$ denote sets, the corresponding capital letters X (resp. bold capital letters) denote random variables (resp. random vectors $\mathbf{T}$) and the lowercase x (resp. $\mathbf{t}$) denote their realizations. The i-th entry of a vector $\mathbf{t}$ is written as $\mathbf{t}[i]$.

A side-channel trace is a random vector $\mathbf{T} \in \mathbb{R}^{D}$ where D defines the dimension of the trace. The targeted sensitive variable is $Z = f(P, K)$ where f denotes a cryptographic primitive, P ($\in \mathcal{P}$) denotes a public variable (*e.g.*. plaintext or ciphertext) and K ($\in \mathcal{K}$) denotes a part of the key (*e.g.*. byte) that an adversary tries to retrieve. Z takes values in $\mathcal{Z} = \{s_1, ..., s_{|\mathcal{Z}|}\}$. Let us denotes $\mathbf{k}^{*}$ the secret key used by the cryptographic algorithm.

2.2   Profiling Attacks

A profiling attack is performed in two stages: a profiling phase and a matching phase. During the profiling phase, an adversary has access to a test device on which he can control the input and the secret key of the cryptographic algorithm. He uses this knowledge to find the relevant leakages depending on the sensitive variable Z. The adversary builds a model $F : \mathbb{R}^{D} \rightarrow \mathbb{R}^{|\mathcal{Z}|}$ that estimates the probability $Pr[\mathbf{T}|Z = z]$ from a profiling set $\mathcal{T} = \{(\mathbf{t}_0, z_0), ..., (\mathbf{t}_{N_p-1}, z_{N_p-1})\}$ of size N_p.

Once the model F is built, in the matching phase, the adversary estimates which intermediate value is processed. By predicting this sensitive variable and knowing the public variable used during the encryption, the adversary can compute a score vector, based on $F(\mathbf{t}_i), i \in [\![0, N_a - 1]\!]$, for each trace included in a dataset of N_a attack traces. The key candidate with the highest values will be defined as the recovered key.

To evaluate the performance related to the estimations, we can classify all the key candidates into a vector of size $|\mathcal{K}|$, denoted $\mathbf{g} = (g_1, g_2, ..., g_{|\mathcal{K}|})$, following their resulting probability. We consider g_1 as the most likely candidate and $g_{|\mathcal{K}|}$ as the least likely one. Let us denote $\mathbf{g}(\mathbf{k}^*[b])$ the actual position of the bth byte of the secret key in $\mathbf{g}$. This position is called *rank*. In side-channel analysis, a common metric, called guessing entropy (GE) [14], defines the average rank of a byte b of $\mathbf{k}^*$, denoted $\mathbf{k}^*[b]$, among all key hypotheses. We consider an attack as successful, using N_a traces, when the guessing entropy is equal to 1.

The rank of the correct key gives us an insight into how well our model performs. A related metric is the success rate, the probability that an attack succeeds in recovering $\mathbf{k}^*[b]$ among all the hypotheses. A success rate of p means that p attacks, over 100 realizations, succeed to retrieve $\mathbf{k}^*[b]$. In [14], Standaert *et al.* propose to extend the notion of success rate to an arbitrary order d. Let $A_{E_k,L}$ be an adversary trying to attack a cryptographic computation E_k using to a leakage model L. The adversary has to conduct some experiments $Exp^d_{A_{E_k,L}}$ in order to exploit the relevant information that leaks. The output of the attack is a guessing vector $\mathbf{g}$ of length d that is composed of the key candidates sorted according to the attack result. If $\mathbf{k}^*[b] \in \mathbf{g}$, then we consider the attack as a success and $Exp^d_{A_{E_k,L}} = 1$. Thus, the dth order success rate can be defined as:

$$SR^d_{A_{E_k,L}} = Pr[Exp^d_{A_{E_k,L}} = 1].$$

In other words, the dth order success rate is defined as the probability that the target secret $\mathbf{k}^*[b]$ is ranked among the d first key guesses in the score vector. In the rest of the article, the dth order success rate is denoted SR^d.

2.3   Neural Networks

Neural networks have risen in popularity over the past ten years due to the increase in computing power and the democratization of GPUs. They proved to be very efficient at solving a large variety of problems like classification or feature extraction. It is for these reasons that the application of machine learning techniques was eventually explored in side-channel analysis [2,6,9] and soon after followed the application of deep learning and the use of neural networks [3,10]. For a classification task, a neural network aims at constructing a function $F : \mathbb{R}^D \to \mathbb{R}^{|\mathcal{Z}|}$ that computes an output called a *prediction* represented as a vector of size $|\mathcal{Z}|$, the number of possible classes. To solve a classification problem, the function F has to find the right prediction y associated with the input $\mathbf{t}$ with high confidence. To approximate the optimal solution, a neural network must be trained given a profiling set of N_p pairs $(\mathbf{t}_i, y_i)$ where $\mathbf{t}$ is the i-th profiling input and y_i is the label associated with the i-th input. To construct F, neural networks are built from several layers composed of unit blocks called neurons. These neurons perform operations to select the relevant features that allow for an efficient classification of $\mathbf{t}$.

One special kind of network is the convolutional neural network. The particularity of CNNs is the use of filters for improving the pattern recognition. The main advantage of the filters and convolutional layers is their time-invariance property that allows the network to be robust against desynchronization (*e.g.*. shifting, jitter) [3, 16]. Therefore, the resynchronization pre-processing is not necessary anymore. However, Zhou and Standaert [17] have shown that resynchronization still helps the network during the learning phase and improves the network performance.

Once the architecture of the network is fixed, the training can begin but we need to be able to evaluate *how well* a network is learning. In order to do so, some evaluation metrics have been developed.

2.4   Evaluation Metrics

In machine learning, to accurately evaluate the networks, it is common to look at the progression of different metrics that can be decomposed into two categories:

- **The learning metrics**, such as the *empirical risk*, which is the average of a *loss function*, over all the examples of the training set, estimating the classification error. They help the network to update its trainable parameters (*i.e.* weights) in order to optimize F.

The classification error is defined by a comparison between a label y_i and the related predicted value $\hat{y}_i$. The function measuring this error is the loss function. The goal of the training is to minimize the loss in order to reduce the errors made by the network on the training examples. The most commonly used loss is the *categorical cross-entropy* [5]. Minimizing the categorical cross-entropy reduces the dissimilarity between the correct distributions and the predicted distributions for a set of inputs. Thus, the evaluation of this learning metric helps to interpret the training error of a model. It can be visualized after the training to better understand how well the network learned.

- **The performance metrics**, such as the *accuracy*, that define the performance of a network for a given input. This metric computes the number of good predictions for a set of traces. In side-channel analysis, it corresponds to a first order success rate using only one trace [12].

The performance metrics are exploited in order to evaluate the internal state of a network [5] and used to detect both *underfitting* and *overfitting*.

Underfitting typically describes the moment of the learning phase where the network has not seen enough training examples to extract relevant information from them. It is therefore not able to make correct predictions. It can also be a sign that the architecture of the network is not complex enough to properly estimate the underlying function. To prevent underfitting, it is possible to increase the number of training examples, the number of epochs and the complexity of the network [5].

Overfitting happens when the network is starting to learn features from the training examples that are not relevant for generalization. Thus it is loosing its generalization power which means it is better at predicting training examples but performs poorly on the validation set. The consequence is that the network learns the training examples by heart, learning features that are not useful for classification purposes. For example, in side-channel analysis, we can assume that the network learns noise patterns from the training set, where the noise is considered to be independent from the intermediate value Z. Since those patterns are random, they will most likely negatively influence the prediction of new examples. Another factor can be an overly complex architecture. As a consequence, the network is able to estimate functions F much more complex than the optimal one. To reduce the impact of overfitting, some techniques can be used such as data augmentation [3], noise addition [7], regularization or a more fitting architecture [16].

As mentioned before, the accuracy is not a suitable metric for evaluating the network performance for side-channel attacks. It differs from the paradigm of the side-channel attacks where one considers and uses a set of traces to accumulate information about the secret key. According to Picek et al. [12], it is more relevant to use the success rate when a side-channel developer wants to evaluate the performance related to his network. Indeed, contrary to the accuracy, the success rate is based on the accumulation of information over several traces.

2.5   Related Work on Metrics for Side-Channel Analysis

The guessing entropy is a suitable metric to evaluate the performance of a network. However, this tool does not give an insight about the internal state of the network. Indeed, the guessing entropy evaluates the performance associated with a set of traces but does not compare the performance between the training dataset and the validation one. Then, it is difficult for an evaluator to identify the appropriate moment where the model starts overfitting. Detection of overfitting is an important problem to consider since it lowers the performance of the network. Moreover, an early detection of the overfitting can bring a substantial gain in terms of training time by reducing the number of epochs the network has to train for. Therefore, to solve this problem, van der Valk and Picek [15] introduced the guessing entropy bias variance decomposition (GEBVD). By doing so, they are able to separately study the evolution of the bias and the variance of the guessing entropy and draw conclusions on the influence of some hyperparameters on the performance of the network. A high bias may indicate that the network is underfitting and a high variance that it is overfitting.

Our approach is different in the sense that we evaluate the generalization capability of a given architecture by studying its performance at training and validation. If the network can be improved, *e.g..* when having much better performance on training than on validation, then regularization can be applied to improve the training of the network and reach better performance. We also study the link between good performance at training and good performance at validation.

In order to do that, we propose a new metric called $\Delta^d_{train,val}$. The aim of this new metric is to characterize the generalization power of a network dedicated to side-channel analysis.

3 $\Delta^d_{train,val}$: A Deep Learning Evaluation Metric for Side-Channel Analysis

$\Delta^d_{train,val}$ uses a common side-channel metric, namely the success rate, to evaluate the performances of a network both on the training set and on the validation set. Therefore, $\Delta^d_{train,val}$ allows the attacker to draw conclusions on the internal state of the network, namely underfitting or overfitting.

3.1 $\Delta^d_{train,val}$: Internal State Detection

Let a *model* be the result function F of the training of an architecture for a given amount of epochs. We define $N^d_{train}(model)$ and $N^d_{val}(model)$ as the minimal number of traces that a model needs in order to reach an dth-order success rate:

$$N^d_{train}(model) = min\{n_{train} \mid \forall n \geq n_{train},\ SR^d_{train}(model(n)) = 90\%\}$$

and,

$$N^d_{val}(model) = min\{n_{val} \mid \forall n \geq n_{val},\ SR^d_{val}(model(n)) = 90\%\}.$$

An dth order success rate means that the attacker has at most d key guesses to test after the attack in order to recover the correct one.

By comparing the performances of the attacks on training and on validation, we obtain information on how well the network is able to generalize its knowledge. The choice of the euclidean norm seemed the most natural to compare two number of traces. Therefore, $\Delta^d_{train,val}$ is computed as follow:

$$\Delta^d_{train,val} = |N^d_{val} - N^d_{train}|.$$

The computation of N^d_{train} and N^d_{val} is based on the existing side-channel metrics that are known to exploit the full information available. By comparing them, we combine the machine learning and the side-channel approaches to evaluate any network.

Our proposal has the advantage that it is possible to evaluate the internal state of the network during the training and afterwards by visualizing this new metric. Indeed, we are able to efficiently visualize when our network is in an underfitting, good or overfitting state. The choice of a success rate of 90% was made, instead of 100%, to bring more stability to the values of N^d_{train} and N^d_{val}.

3.2   Detection of Overfitting/underfitting

The evolution of $\Delta_{train,val}^d$ and the internal state of a model are illustrated with three areas in Fig. 1, showing an example of the evolution of $\Delta_{train,val}^1$ during the training of a network:

- **Underfitting**: as mentioned in Sect. 2.4, underfitting occurs when the network has not learned enough information from the training set. Thus, the attack cannot be performed. The values related to N_{train}^d and N_{val}^d are often not defined or are both very high. In other words, when the number of training epochs is low, $\Delta_{train,val}^d$ is also not defined or its value is very high (area on the left of Fig. 1). Such cases call for an augmentation of the number of epochs or the amount of training data to reach a success rate of 90%.
- **Good trade-off**: when the network is able to learn enough relevant information from the training set, the value of $\Delta_{train,val}^d$ converges towards $N_{bias}(\mathcal{T}_{train})$, which represent the minimal difference between N_{train}^d and N_{val}^d given a training set $\mathcal{T}_{train}$. Let us denote e the number of epochs needed to reach a good trade-off, we have:

$$\Delta_{train,val}^d \xrightarrow[epoch \to e]{} N_{bias}(\mathcal{T}_{train}). \tag{1}$$

A good trade-off occurs at the number of epochs for which $\Delta_{train,val}^d$ is close to $N_{bias}(\mathcal{T}_{train})$. The network generalizes the relevant information for performing as well on the training set as on the validation set (area in the middle of Fig. 1). This metric gives information on the ability of the network to generalize well. In the following, we use best trade-off to describe the best network we were able to train without guaranteeing that it is optimal.

- **Overfitting**: as mentioned in Sect. 2.4, overfitting occurs when the network is starting to learn the training features by heart. As a consequence, the network looses its generalization power on the validation set to obtain better performance on the training set. The value of N_{train}^d approaches 1 and more generally converges to a very small value. At the same time, N_{val}^d increases towards a value $N_{max}(\mathcal{T}_{train})$, *i.e.*:

$$\Delta_{train,val}^d \xrightarrow[epoch \to \infty]{} N_{max}(\mathcal{T}_{train}). \tag{2}$$

This value represents the maximal number of traces needed by the network to reach a success rate of 90% once the training has stabilized, *i.e.* the network cannot improve its performance on the training set anymore. Thus, the update of its weights does not change the prediction made on the validation set and the performance of the overfitted model stays low (area on the right of Fig. 1).

With that knowledge, we can optimize the training of the network by performing early stopping.

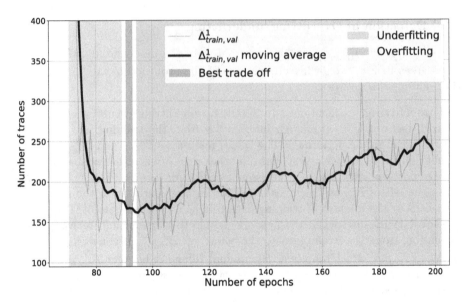

Fig. 1. Evolution of $\Delta^1_{train,val}$ for different number of epochs. The plot of $\Delta^1_{train,val}$ is done using a moving average of size 10.

3.3 $\Delta^d_{train,val}$: A Suitable Metric for Early Stopping

Early stopping consists in monitoring the learning of the network and stopping the training when the learning metrics, usually the accuracy and the loss, are optimal, *i.e.* just before the network starts to overfit. As mentioned in [5], early stopping has other effects on the network. It is a mean of applying regularization without having to penalize weights and therefore can be used in parallel without other methods of regularization. It can also be considered as an additional hyperparameter, the number of training steps or number of epochs, that is tuned during the training of the network using the computation of its associated metrics. All in all, it is recommended to perform early stopping as long as there is an appropriate metric to use in combination. The learning metrics are computed both on the training set and on a validation set to be able to properly tell whether or not the network performs well. The comparison between performance at training and on validation yields important information about the network. In our case, $\Delta^d_{train,val}$ gives us the information needed to identify when to stop the training (see Fig. 1). If our metric does not grow for a given number of epochs then we can assume the optimal state is reached and stop the training.

The computation of $\Delta^d_{train,val}$ can be done in parallel to the training of the next epoch. As illustrated on Fig. 2, as long as the training time of an epoch is superior to the time it takes to compute $\Delta^d_{train,val}$, there is no time overhead. In the cases where it takes longer than an epoch, for example when the training set is small, the computation of $\Delta^d_{train,val}$ can be done once every few epochs to prevent time overhead as shown in Fig. 3.

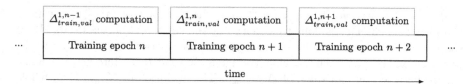

Fig. 2. Computation of $\Delta^1_{train,val}$ for different consecutive epochs when the computation is shorter than the training of one epoch

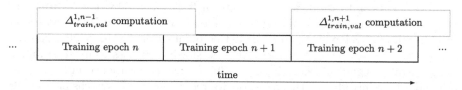

Fig. 3. Computation of $\Delta^1_{train,val}$ for different consecutive epochs when the computation is longer than the training of one epoch

4 Experimental Results

For all the experiments presented in this section we computed $\Delta^1_{train,val}$ on neural networks during their training phase to evaluate their best capacity. The networks are trained using the ASCAD[1] database, introduced in [13] to be a common database for researchers. The device used to acquire the electromagnetic measurements is an 8-bit AVR ATMega8515 running an AES implementation secured against first order side-channel attacks. The dataset is composed of a training set of 50000 traces and a test set of 10000 traces both coming from the same device. From the raw traces, 700 points are selected which contain leakage of the mask and the masked value of the third key byte in the first round. The leakage model associated with the traces is:

$$Y(\mathbf{k}^*) = Sbox(\mathbf{p}[3] \oplus \mathbf{k}^*[3]),$$

where $\mathbf{p}$ is the plaintext and $\mathbf{k}^*$ the correct key.

The main advantage of using this database is to compare our results to the ones presented in the ASCAD reference article.

4.1 Early Stopping on the ASCAD Database

To perform early stopping during the training, we computed $\Delta^1_{train,val}$ at the end of each epoch. We started by applying this method to the architecture CNN_{best} presented in Appendix A, Table 2. This is the best performing CNN architecture presented in [13]. It uses the categorical cross-entropy (CCE) loss, the RMSprop optimizer with a learning rate of 10^{-5} and a base number of epochs for training of 75.

---

[1] https://github.com/ANSSI-FR/ASCAD.

For readability, we show, in Fig. 4, a moving average of $\Delta^1_{train,val}$ using a window of size 3. This is done to smooth out the curve and better see its global shape and explains why the minimal value of the metric is not always at the minimum of the curve. The moving average is thus not taken into account while computing the minimal value of $\Delta^1_{train,val}$. The evolution of N_{train} for a whole training is also shown and the attacks are performed on a set of synchronized traces, called $Desync_0$. The addition of the performance at training helps to understand the state of the network. At around 30 epochs, the training of the network allows it to reach a success rate of 90% using 4900 traces from the validation set. From that point on, the value of $\Delta^1_{train,val}$ quickly decreases to reach a minimal value at 47 epochs. At this point, it is able to reach a success rate of 90% with around 800 traces. It then slowly increases again to stabilize in an unstable regime at $N_{max}(\mathcal{T}_{train}) \approx 3000$ traces as mentioned in Eq. 2. The original article introducing this network [13] recommended 75 epochs of training to reach the best performances but here we find that, after 75 epochs of training, the success rate of 90% is reached with around 1150 traces. Performing early stopping using $\Delta^1_{train,val}$ allowed for an improvement of 30% of the performances of the network. The time it takes to train the network also went down from 1 h to 40 min which is a 33% decrease in computation time compared to [13]. We can clearly identify the learning phase where the network is underfitting that lasts until epoch 47. At this point the network is at its best capacity given its hyperparameters and training set. Due to its great complexity, the network starts to overfit after the next epoch. Therefore, $\Delta^1_{train,val}$ shows us that there is no benefit in continuing the training after epoch 47. It can also be seen that the value of N_{train} decreases much faster than $\Delta^1_{train,val}$ and its value is very low even at the best capacity of the network. This is a sign of overfitting even though it does not yet impact negatively the performances on validation. Possible solutions to fix this problem would be to change the complexity of the network or to add regularization [5].

4.2   Comparison Between GEBVD and $\Delta^1_{train,val}$

In this section, we take a look at the guessing entropy bias variance decomposition as introduced in [15]. The goal of this decomposition is to separate the bias from the variance in the performance of a network. This allows to evaluate the state of the network because a high bias is typically linked to underfitting while a high variance implies some overfitting. GEBVD therefore aims at separating the bias and the variance of the guessing entropy. Van der Valk *et al.* manage to do so by estimating the bias by the mean of the guessing entropy and the variance to be its variance. We try to compare both $\Delta^d_{train,val}$ and the GEBVD regarding the information they offer on the state of a CNN.

For that, we use CNN_{BV} presented in [15] for the tests. A description of the architecture of the network can be find in Appendix A, Table 3. This network uses the mean squared error (MSE) as a loss function, the Adam optimizer with a learning rate of 10^{-4} and the base number of epochs for training is 50. As described in the original article, it has a varying complexity depending on the

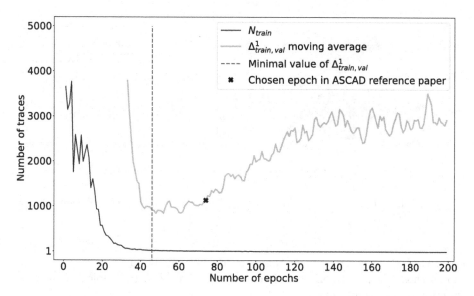

Fig. 4. Evolution of $\Delta^1_{train,val}$ for different number of epochs for CNN_{best} on $Desync_0$, the training set with no desynchronization of the ASCAD database [13], and comparison with their choice of number of epochs

number of convolutional layers used. The networks used to obtain the following results have zero (0CONV) or one (1CONV) convolutional layers. Finally, the leakage model used is the following:

$$Y(\mathbf{k}^*) = HW(Sbox(\mathbf{p}[3] \oplus \mathbf{k}^*[3])),$$

where $\mathbf{p}$ and $\mathbf{k}^*$ are the same as before. This reduces the number of output classes to 9 instead of the previous 256.

Figure 5 shows a comparison of the two metrics on CNN_{BV} with no convolution. On the left, Fig. 5a shows the evolution of the guessing entropy at each epoch of the training for different numbers of attack traces while Fig. 5b shows the evolution of $\Delta^1_{train,val}$ and N_{train}. From Fig. 5a, we see that around epoch 25, the networks is able to consistently reach a success rate of 90% with around 3800 traces which seems to indicate that is it well suited for the problem at hand. On the second picture though, it appears that the learning period lasts until epoch 40. Between epoch 25 and epoch 100, the network is in an unstable regime, meaning there are a lot of unpredictable variations from one epoch to the next, both for N_{train} and N_{val}. This directly impacts the evolution of $\Delta^1_{train,val}$ making it harder to locate the best capacity of the network. Indeed, the best-performing network requires 109 epochs of training and only takes around 2100 traces to reach a success rate of 90%. This is roughly 50% better than the network after 25 epochs and 25% better than the network after 50 epochs, which is the number of epochs recommended in [15], that needs around 3000 traces to obtain the same success rate. This behavior can be attributed to underfitting

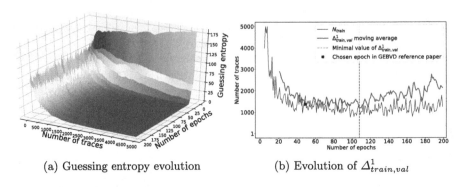

(a) Guessing entropy evolution   (b) Evolution of $\Delta^1_{train,val}$

Fig. 5. Evolution of metrics during training for CNN_{BV} with 0 convolutional block using the MSE loss

due to a lack of complexity of the network and can be an indicator that the model chosen will not converge. It can also be linked to the choice of the loss function and learning rate.

To test this last hypothesis, we trained the same network using the categorical cross-entropy instead of the mean squared error. Figure 6 shows the result of this training. We can see an overall increase in the performance of the network on the validation set as well as a smaller variance in the value of N_{train} for a large number of epochs. With $\Delta^1_{train,val}$, we reach the best capacity for the network at the epoch 37 where the network needs around 1300 traces to reach a success rate of 90%. Then, the value of $\Delta^1_{train,val}$ keeps on increasing until the end of the training. This early stopping brings significant improvements compared to the network trained for 50 epochs, used in [15], that needed around 1800 traces to reach a success rate of 90%. It is also better in terms of training time since we go from 800 s for 50 epoch to 618 s for 37 epochs. The increase of $\Delta^1_{train,val}$ after the epoch 37 is linked to a stabilization of the performance on validation while the performance of the attacks on training continues to improve. It seems that the low complexity of the CNN reduces the impact of overfitting on the performance on validation. This is further confirmed in Fig. 7 representing the evolution of the guessing entropy in Fig. 7a and of $\Delta^1_{train,val}$ in Fig. 7b for the same architecture but with one layer of convolution. We can see that it tends to overfit much faster by the shape of N_{train} and this tendency has a great impact on the performance on validation which are much worse. The best capacity, given by the minimum value of $\Delta^1_{train,val}$, is reached at the epoch 42 with around 1650 traces needed to reach a success rate of 90%. It is still an improvement compared to the epoch 25 and the epoch 50, used in [15], which require respectively 2700 and 2150 traces. The same metrics were computed for this network using the MSE loss but the architecture in combination with this loss could not consistently reach a success rate of 90% within 5000 traces throughout the training.

On the one hand, low complexity slows down the overfitting but it does not necessarily means the network will perform better in the end. On the other hand,

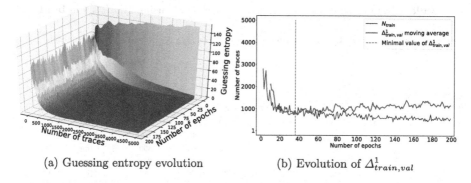

(a) Guessing entropy evolution   (b) Evolution of $\Delta^1_{train,val}$

Fig. 6. Evolution of metrics during training for CNN_{BV} with 0 convolutional block using the CCE loss

higher complexity allows the network to find more links between the input and output which leads to overfitting if not regulated. This is why regularization techniques are applied to neural networks to prevent this phenomenon from happening.

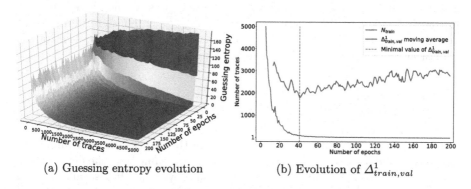

(a) Guessing entropy evolution   (b) Evolution of $\Delta^1_{train,val}$

Fig. 7. Evolution of metrics during training for CNN_{BV} with 1 convolutional block using the CCE loss

All those conclusions can be deduced using $\Delta^1_{train,val}$ and are harder to see with the GEBVD because once the guessing entropy reaches 1, the variance reaches 0, therefore no information can be extracted from it. When comparing the Figs. 6a and 7a, there is hardly any difference between the evolution of the guessing entropies. This contrasts with the evolution of $\Delta^1_{train,val}$ between the Figs. 6b and 7b in which we can see a difference in the quality of the training as well as the performance of the networks. For the network without convolutional layers, the value of N_{train} and N_{val} are much closer which leads to a lower value of $\Delta^1_{train,val}$ and indicates a better learning phase with less overfitting. In addition, since $\Delta^1_{train,val}$ is based on the number of traces needed to reach

Table 1. Summary of the results with choices made using $\Delta^1_{train,val}$ in **bold**

Networks	Nb of CONV layers	LOSS	Reference	Nb epochs	N_{val}	$\Delta^1_{train,val}$	Time to train (seconds)	Difference in time and performance in comparison to the reference
CNN best	5	CCE	[13]	75	1151	1145	3600	Time: −33.3%
			This article	**47**	**802**	**779**	**2400**	N_{val}: −30.3%
CNN BV	0	MSE	[15]	50	2960	1449	970	Time: +98.5%
			This article	**109**	**2093**	**954**	**1926**	N_{val}: −29.3%
		CCE	[15]	50	1849	915	800	Time: −22.7%
			This article	**37**	**1331**	**413**	**618**	N_{val}: −28.6%
	1	CCE	[15]	50	2177	2136	956	Time: −20.4%
			This article	**42**	**1659**	**1575**	**761**	N_{val}: −23.7%

a SR^1 of 90%, we are still able to evaluate and compare networks when all the attacks are successful, *i.e.* when the SR^1 reaches 100%. Indeed, GEBVD cannot be used when the variance is null because it gives no information on the state of the network. With $\Delta^1_{train,val}$, we consistently find the best training epoch and therefore perform early stopping which improves the capacity and the training time of the network. The results detailed in this section are summarized in Table 1, giving a comparison between the networks as mentioned in their respective article and the choices made using $\Delta^1_{train,val}$. Those results seem to confirm, as argued in [11] by Masure *et al.*, that the categorical cross-entropy is an appropriate loss to use in deep learning for side-channel analysis.

5   Conclusion

In this article, we introduced a new metric dedicated to deep learning for side-channel analysis. By comparing the efficiency of the attacks on the training set and on the validation set, this metric evaluates at the same time the performance of a given architecture and its potential for improvement. It also allows for a characterization of the state of the network and therefore for the detection of overfitting. This property makes it possible to use this metric during the training of a network to perform early stopping.

Consequently, we used $\Delta^d_{train,val}$ to evaluate the best CNN of the ASCAD public database. We found out by applying $\Delta^1_{train,val}$ for early stopping that it reaches its best performance around 47 epochs which is less than the 75 epochs mentioned in [13]. This early stopping of the training allowed for a reduction of 31% of the number of traces needed to reach a success rate of 90% and reduced the training time by 30%. The measurement of $\Delta^1_{train,val}$ showed that it was heavily overfitting the training data. To limit this overfitting, we suggest the use of normalization and regularization. We then compared $\Delta^1_{train,val}$ to the GEBVD as introduced in [15] by evaluating an architecture presented in the article. It showed that $\Delta^1_{train,val}$ gives a better insight on how well the network is performing as well as how much it is overfitting the training data, especially when the attacks are successful. We managed to improve the performance of the network by 20 to 30% while the training time was reduce by more or less the same percentage. This shows the importance of choosing the right number of epochs.

For future work, we plan to use $\Delta^d_{train,val}$ to evaluate the improvements that can bring normalization and regularization techniques. Finally, it can be interesting to adapt this metric (or a derivative) as a loss function in order to optimize the network in the side-channel context.

A   Networks

Table 2. Network hyperparameters for CNN_{best} [13]

Layer type	Hyperparameters
Trace input	700
Convolution 1D	Filter = 64, Filter length = 11, Activation = ReLU
Average pooling	Pool length = 2
Convolution 1D	Filter = 128, Filter length = 11, Activation = ReLU
Average pooling	Pool length = 2
Convolution 1D	Filter = 256, Filter length = 11, Activation = ReLU
Average pooling	Pool length = 2
Convolution 1D	Filter = 512, Filter length = 11, Activation = ReLU
Average pooling	Pool length = 2
Convolution 1D	Filter = 512, Filter length = 11, Activation = ReLU
Average pooling	Pool length = 2
Flatten	–
Fully-connected	Neurons = 4096
Fully-connected	Neurons = 4096
Output	Softmax: 256 classes

Table 3. Network hyperparameters for CNN_{BV} [15]

Layer type	Hyperparameters
Trace input	700
Convolution 1D (Optional)	Filter = 8, Filter length = 3, Activation = ReLU
Batch normalization	–
Max pooling	Pool length = 2
Convolution 1D (Optional)	Filter = 16, Filter length = 3, Activation = ReLU
Batch normalization	–
Max pooling	Pool length = 2
Convolution 1D (Optional)	Filter = 32, Filter length = 3, Activation = ReLU
Batch normalization	–
Max pooling	Pool length = 2
Convolution 1D (Optional)	Filter = 64, Filter length = 3, Activation = ReLU
Batch normalization	–
Max pooling	Pool length = 2
Convolution 1D (Optional)	Filter = 64, Filter length = 3, Activation = ReLU
Batch normalization	–
Max pooling	Pool length = 2
Flatten	–
Dropout	Coefficient = 0.5
Fully-connected	Neurons = 512
Dropout	Coefficient = 0.5
Output	Softmax: 9 or 256 classes

References

1. Agrawal, D., Archambeault, B., Rao, J.R., Rohatgi, P.: The EM side—channel(s). In: Kaliski, B.S., Koç, K., Paar, C. (eds.) CHES 2002. LNCS, vol. 2523, pp. 29–45. Springer, Heidelberg (2003). https://doi.org/10.1007/3-540-36400-5_4

2. Bartkewitz, T., Lemke-Rust, K.: Efficient template attacks based on probabilistic multi-class support vector machines. In: Mangard, S. (ed.) CARDIS 2012. LNCS, vol. 7771, pp. 263–276. Springer, Heidelberg (2013). https://doi.org/10.1007/978-3-642-37288-9_18

3. Cagli, E., Dumas, C., Prouff, E.: Convolutional neural networks with data augmentation against jitter-based countermeasures. In: Fischer, W., Homma, N. (eds.) CHES 2017. LNCS, vol. 10529, pp. 45–68. Springer, Cham (2017). https://doi.org/10.1007/978-3-319-66787-4_3

4. Chari, S., Rao, J.R., Rohatgi, P.: Template attacks. In: Kaliski, B.S., Koç, K., Paar, C. (eds.) CHES 2002. LNCS, vol. 2523, pp. 13–28. Springer, Heidelberg (2003). https://doi.org/10.1007/3-540-36400-5_3. http://dl.acm.org/citation.cfm?id=648255.752740

5. Goodfellow, I.J., Bengio, Y., Courville, A.C.: Deep Learning. Adaptive Computation and Machine Learning. MIT Press, Cambridge (2016). http://www.deeplearningbook.org/

6. Hospodar, G., Gierlichs, B., Mulder, E.D., Verbauwhede, I., Vandewalle, J.: Machine learning in side-channel analysis: a first study. J. Cryptogr. Eng. 1(4), 293–302 (2011). https://doi.org/10.1007/s13389-011-0023-x

7. Kim, J., Picek, S., Heuser, A., Bhasin, S., Hanjalic, A.: Make some noise. Unleashing the power of convolutional neural networks for profiled side-channel analysis. IACR Trans. Cryptogr. Hardw. Embed. Syst. 2019(3), 148–179 (2019). https://doi.org/10.13154/tches.v2019.i3.148-179

8. Kocher, P., Jaffe, J., Jun, B.: Differential power analysis. In: Wiener, M. (ed.) CRYPTO 1999. LNCS, vol. 1666, pp. 388–397. Springer, Heidelberg (1999). https://doi.org/10.1007/3-540-48405-1_25

9. Lerman, L., Poussier, R., Markowitch, O., Standaert, F.: Template attacks versus machine learning revisited and the curse of dimensionality in side-channel analysis: extended version. J. Cryptogr. Eng. 8(4), 301–313 (2018). https://doi.org/10.1007/s13389-017-0162-9

10. Maghrebi, H., Portigliatti, T., Prouff, E.: Breaking cryptographic implementations using deep learning techniques. In: Carlet, C., Hasan, M.A., Saraswat, V. (eds.) SPACE 2016. LNCS, vol. 10076, pp. 3–26. Springer, Cham (2016). https://doi.org/10.1007/978-3-319-49445-6_1

11. Masure, L., Dumas, C., Prouff, E.: A comprehensive study of deep learning for side-channel analysis. IACR Trans. Cryptogr. Hardw. Embed. Syst. 2020(1), 348–375 (2019). https://doi.org/10.13154/tches.v2020.i1.348-375

12. Picek, S., Heuser, A., Jovic, A., Bhasin, S., Regazzoni, F.: The curse of class imbalance and conflicting metrics with machine learning for side-channel evaluations. IACR Trans. Cryptogr. Hardw. Embed. Syst. 2019(1), 209–237 (2018). https://doi.org/10.13154/tches.v2019.i1.209-237

13. Prouff, E., Strullu, R., Benadjila, R., Cagli, E., Dumas, C.: Study of deep learning techniques for side-channel analysis and introduction to ASCAD database. IACR Cryptology ePrint Archive 2018/53 (2018). http://eprint.iacr.org/2018/053

14. Standaert, F.-X., Malkin, T.G., Yung, M.: A unified framework for the analysis of side-channel key recovery attacks. In: Joux, A. (ed.) EUROCRYPT 2009. LNCS, vol. 5479, pp. 443–461. Springer, Heidelberg (2009). https://doi.org/10.1007/978-3-642-01001-9_26

15. van der Valk, D., Picek, S.: Bias-variance decomposition in machine learning-based side-channel analysis. Cryptology ePrint Archive, Report 2019/570 (2019). https://eprint.iacr.org/2019/570

16. Zaid, G., Bossuet, L., Habrard, A., Venelli, A.: Methodology for efficient CNN architectures in profiling attacks. IACR Trans. Cryptogr. Hardw. Embed. Syst. **2020**(1), 1–36 (2019). https://doi.org/10.13154/tches.v2020.i1.1-36
17. Zhou, Y., Standaert, F.-X.: Deep learning mitigates but does not annihilate the need of aligned traces and a generalized ResNet model for side-channel attacks. J. Cryptogr. En. **10**(1), 85–95 (2019). https://doi.org/10.1007/s13389-019-00209-3

Primitives and Tools for Physical
Attacks Resistance

Custom Instruction Support for Modular Defense Against Side-Channel and Fault Attacks

Pantea Kiaei[1]([✉]), Darius Mercadier[2], Pierre-Evariste Dagand[2], Karine Heydemann[2], and Patrick Schaumont[3]

[1] Virginia Tech, Blacksburg, VA 24061, USA
pantea95@vt.edu
[2] LIP6, Paris, France
darius.mercadier@gmail.com,
{pierre-evariste.dagand,karine.heydemann}@lip6.fr
[3] Worcester Polytechnic Institute, Worcester, MA 01609, USA
pschaumont@wpi.edu

Abstract. The design of software countermeasures against active and passive adversaries is a challenging problem that has been addressed by many authors in recent years. The proposed solutions adopt a theoretical foundation (such as a leakage model) but often do not offer concrete reference implementations to validate the foundation. Contributing to the experimental dimension of this body of work, we propose a customized processor called SKIVA that supports experiments with the design of countermeasures against a broad range of implementation attacks. Based on bitslice programming and recent advances in the literature, SKIVA offers a flexible and modular combination of countermeasures against power-based and timing-based side-channel leakage and fault injection. Multiple configurations of side-channel protection and fault protection enable the programmer to select the desired number of shares and the desired redundancy level for each slice. Recurring and security-sensitive operations are supported in hardware through custom instruction-set extensions. The new instructions support bitslicing, secret-share generation, redundant logic computation, and fault detection. We demonstrate and analyze multiple versions of AES from a side-channel analysis and a fault-injection perspective, in addition to providing a detailed performance evaluation of the protected designs. To our knowledge, this is the first validated end-to-end implementation of a modular bitslice-oriented countermeasure.

Keywords: Side-channel leakage · Fault injection · Bitslice programming

1 Introduction

Side-channel analysis and fault attacks have plagued cryptographic software on embedded processors for many years. The threat of power-based and timing-based

© Springer Nature Switzerland AG 2021
G. M. Bertoni and F. Regazzoni (Eds.): COSADE 2020, LNCS 12244, pp. 221–253, 2021.
https://doi.org/10.1007/978-3-030-68773-1_11

side-channel leakage is well understood and countermeasures such as masking and constant-time programming figure prominently in the cryptographer's toolbox [5, 43]. In parallel, the research community has gained more insight into the fault behavior of hardware and software, thus greatly increasing the potency of fault attacks [46,52]. The impact of fault attacks is minimized with fault detection and temporal or spatial redundancy of the software execution [3,33].

Although there exists an extensive array of specific, dedicated countermeasures, there is surprisingly few work available [44,48,49] offering protection against both side-channel analysis *and* fault injection. This is especially true for software. The programmer is left selecting candidate solutions, figuring out if and how they can safely be assembled. This is not an easy task because countermeasures may interact in non-trivial (and unsafe) manners.

Recent related work on side-channel countermeasures has proposed partial implementations of behavior called *gadgets*. The integration of these gadgets into an overall secure implementation is a challenge that has triggered multiple revisions of the attacker model. For example, Ishai *et al.* [27], Belaïd *et al.* [8], Battistello *et al.* [6], Barthe *et al.* [5] and Cassiers *et al.* [14] present the masked implementation of a multiplication operation, each protected against attackers of a different level of sophistication. Given this broad variation in proposals, we believe there is a need for their practical evaluation in a common setting. It is not our intention to compare these proposals as in [21]. Instead, we highlight the role of custom instruction-set extensions as a tool for countermeasure implementation.

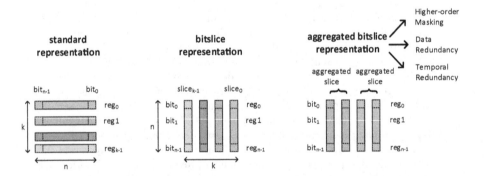

Fig. 1. In a standard representation, processor registers are allocated per data word. In a bitsliced representation, processor registers are allocated per bit-weight of a block of data words. In an aggregated bitslice representation, multiple bitslices are allocated per data bit. Aggregated bitslices can be shares of a masked design, redundant data of a fault-protected design, or a combination of those.

In this paper, we introduce SKIVA, a processor that enables a modular approach to countermeasure design, giving programmers the flexibility to protect their ciphers against timing-based side-channel analysis, power-based side-channel analysis and/or fault injection at various levels of security. We leverage existing techniques in higher-order masking, in spatial and in temporal redundancy. Modularity is achieved through bitslicing, each countermeasure being expressed as a transformation from a bitsliced design into another bitsliced design. The capabilities of SKIVA are demonstrated on the Advanced Encryption Standard, but the proposed techniques can be applied to other ciphers as well.

Countermeasure Design Through Bitslice Aggregation. SKIVA exploits the redundancy that is provided by a bitsliced execution model. The n-bit datapath of the processor is seen as n 1-bit processors operating in parallel. The symmetry of bitslices in a processor word is the basis for the modular protection schemes enabled by SKIVA. Figure 1 demonstrates three different organizations of a register file in a processor. We obtain the bitslice representation through a matrix transposition of the input data so that one processor register contains all bits of a given weight. The key idea of bitslice aggregation is to allocate multiple slices to the representation of each data-bit. We will demonstrate how bitslice aggregation enables higher-order masking (to protect against power side-channels), data redundancy (to protect against data faults), and temporal redundancy (to protect against control faults).

Contributions. SKIVA is a processor with built-in support for modular countermeasures against side-channel analysis and fault analysis. We open-source our codes to make it possible for the community to evaluate our implementation [1]. We make the following contributions.

1. We propose a flexible and modular methodology for designing countermeasures. It enables the combination of higher-order masking with spatial fault-redundancy and with temporal fault-redundancy. The number of shares and fault-redundancy levels is statically determined by the programmer (single, double, quadruple shares and single, double, quadruple fault-redundancy).
2. We describe hardware support for the proposed methodology in SKIVA, a processor with instruction set extensions specialized for bitsliced transposition, bitsliced masked operation, bitsliced fault detection, redundant bitsliced expansion, and Boolean operations on complementary data.
3. We analyze the performance and code size of the Advanced Encryption Standard on SKIVA, under multiple levels of side-channel and fault-resistance.
4. We evaluate the side-channel leakage characteristics of SKIVA implemented as a soft-core processor on a SAKURA-G FPGA board. We perform theoretical as well as empirical analysis of fault detection coverage.

Outline. In Sect. 2, we review the related work, covering the design of bitsliced software and countermeasures based on such software. In Sect. 3, we introduce several modular countermeasure schemes. Starting with bitslicing, we describe a systematic treatment of higher-order masking, intra-instruction redundancy, and temporal redundancy. In Sect. 4, we dive into the implementation aspects

---

[1] Cfr. https://github.com/Secure-Embedded-Systems/Skiva.

and propose a custom instruction-set extension to support various aspects of the bitslice-oriented countermeasures. In Sect. 5, we present the measurement results of our prototype, including performance, side-channel leakage evaluation, and fault detection/correction coverage. In Sect. 6, we conclude the paper.

2   Preliminaries

Bitslicing is an implementation technique to produce high-throughput, constant-time software implementations of cryptographic primitives [10,29]. A cipher is expressed as a Boolean circuit. The circuit is compiled into a straight-line program by leveling the circuit and translating each Boolean operation to a corresponding bitwise CPU instruction. Since the CPU manipulates registers of 32 bits, running the resulting program amounts to running 32 parallel instances of the original Boolean circuit.

Bitslicing Versus Wordslicing. In a block cipher, the state variables are k-bit wide. The bitsliced version of the cipher will store these k bits in a transposed manner, such that register i will contain the i-th bit of the state. This approach has been used for DES [10] as well as for AES [41]. However, one can also adopt wordslicing, which stores groups of b bits out of a k-bit state per register. A wordsliced design requires k/b registers, as opposed to k registers for a bitsliced design. Wordsliced design has been demonstrated for AES [29,31]. The choice between bitslicing and wordslicing has a significant impact on the efficiency of the resulting design. The resulting code also changes significantly with the slicing strategy. The bitsliced implementation of AES has to juggle with 128 machine words while being restricted to straightforward logical instructions. The wordsliced implementation of AES fits within eight registers, at the expense of complex permutations within individual words. On an embedded RISC-like CPU, our experiments have shown that the bitsliced implementation yields a higher throughput than the wordsliced one (Sect. 5.1). Conversely, on a high-end SIMD CPU, earlier work has shown that wordslicing is key to reach speed records in software encryption [29]. The lack of SIMD instructions and the lesser register pressure for RISC CPUs thus favors bitsliced implementations, hence our focus on bitslicing in the present work.

Countermeasures for Bitsliced Designs. Many hardware-oriented countermeasures can be applied as transformations on the Boolean programs of bitsliced designs. An early effort to address power-based side-channel leakage is the duplication method [17]. More recently, several masking-oriented techniques have been proposed [5,13,23,28]. Bitslicing is also a systematic countermeasure against timing attacks. By construction, a Boolean program runs in constant (or repeatable) time. Conditionals in a Boolean program are implemented through data-multiplexing: both results are sequentially computed and the relevant output is obtained by demultiplexing these intermediary results based on the conditional. Finally, the massively parallel nature of a bitsliced implementation can be exploited to provide intra-instruction redundancy (encrypting the same data in redundant slices) as well as various forms of temporal redundancy (processing data at distinct rounds in distinct, randomly-chosen slices) [32,37]. In a bitsliced setting, these techniques translate into end-to-end protection, protecting a cipher from the moment the plaintext is introduced to the moment the ciphertext is produced.

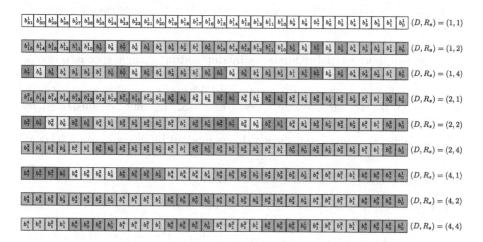

Fig. 2. Bitslice aggregations on a 32 bit register, depending on (D,R_s).

3 Modular Design of Countermeasures

In this section, we present the four protection mechanisms that can be combined in a modular manner, including (a) bitslicing to protect against timing attacks; (b) higher-order masking to protect against power side-channel leakage; (c) intra-instruction redundancy to protect against data faults and (d) temporal redundancy to protect against control faults. We demonstrate our protection on the AES cipher running on SKIVA. However, the techniques are equally applicable to other bitsliced ciphers. However, the panel of techniques is not restricted to this cipher nor this processor: they naturally generalize – in a systematic manner – to any cipher admitting a bitsliced implementation, for processors of arbitrary bitwidth as well as design (RISC as well as CISC, SIMD or not). We leave it to future work to evaluate their effectiveness on a broader range of cryptographic primitives and hardware platforms.

Our implementation of AES is fully bitsliced: the 128-bit input of the cipher is represented with 128 variables. Since each variable stores 32 bits on SKIVA, a single run of our primitive computes 32 parallel instances of AES. The protection mechanisms presented in the following assume the availability of a bitsliced design while themselves producing a bitsliced design (of lesser parallelism) in return. The modularity of our approach lies in this simple observation: as long as there is enough parallelism to compute at least one run of the algorithm, we can chain these program transformations.

Figure 2 shows the bitslice organization for masked and intra-instruction-redundant design. We support masking with 1, 2, and 4 shares leading to respectively unmasked, 1st-order, and 3rd-order masked implementations. By convention, we use the letter D to denote the number of shares ($D \in \{1, 2, 4\}$) of a given implementation. Within a machine word, the D shares encoding the ith bit are grouped together, as illustrated by the contiguously colored bits $b_i^{j \in [1,D]}$ in Fig. 2.

We also support spatial redundancy by duplicating a single slice into two or four slices. By convention, we use the letter R_s to denote the spatial redundancy ($R_s \in \{1, 2, 4\}$) of a given implementation. Within a machine word, the R_s duplicates of the ith bit are interspersed every $32/R_s$ bits, as illustrated by the alternation of colored words $b_{i \in [1,R_S]}^j$ in Fig. 2. The following subsections elaborate on doing computations using this redundant bitslice allocation scheme.

3.1   Higher-Order Masked Computation

Recent masking schemes, including those for bitsliced designs [5,6,8,14,18], have relied on the definition of *gadgets*, elementary masked logic operations that can be securely composed together. A complete cipher is then expressed as a combination of gadgets that are wired together. The most important gadgets include the multiplication gadget (as the canonical non-linear operation) and the mask refresh gadget. We will demonstrate our design based on the secure duplicated multiplication gadget by Dhooghe and Nikova [18]. For a 4-share implementation, we base our cross-product calculations on the parallel masked multiplication algorithm defined by Barthe *et al.* [5, Algorithm 3]. For 2-share masking, we use the following multiplication gadget [21]. If $\mathbf{x}$ and $\mathbf{y}$ are two-share inputs and $\mathbf{r}$ is a two-share random vector, then the two-share output is obtained by the following expression.

$$\mathbf{z} = (((\mathbf{x}.\mathbf{y} \oplus \mathbf{r}) \oplus \mathbf{x}.rot(\mathbf{y}, 1)) \oplus rot(\mathbf{r}, 1))$$

Optimizing this masked design by reducing the amount of randomness [4,9] is orthogonal to the present work. The objective of SKIVA is to define a common platform to evaluate such proposals.

3.2   Data-Redundant Computation

We protect our implementation against data faults using intra-instruction redundancy (IIR) [15,32,37]. We support either a *direct* redundant implementation, in which the duplicated slices contain the same value, or a *complementary* redundant implementation, in which the duplicated slices are complemented pairwise. For example, with $R_s = 4$, we can have four exact copies (direct redundancy) or two exact copies and two complementary copies (complementary redundancy).

In practice, we will favor complementary redundancy over direct redundancy. First, it is less likely for complemented bits to flip to consistent values due to single fault injection. For instance, timing faults during state transition [53] or memory accesses [2] follow a random word corruption or a stuck-at-0 model. Second, complementary slices ensure a constant Hamming weight for a slice throughout the computation of a cipher. Our results show that complementary redundancy results in reduced power leakage when compared to direct redundancy [11].

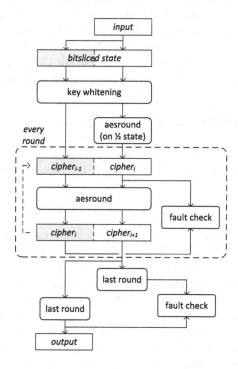

Fig. 3. Time-redundant computation of a bitsliced AES.

3.3   Time-Redundant Computation

Data-redundant computation does not protect against control faults such as instruction skip. We, therefore, use a different strategy: we protect our implementation against control faults using temporal redundancy (TR) across rounds [37]. We pipeline the execution of 2 consecutive rounds in 2 aggregated slices. By convention, we use the letter R_t to distinguish implementations with temporal redundancy ($R_t = 2$) from implementations without ($R_t = 1$). For $R_t = 2$, half of the slices compute round i while the other half compute round $i - 1$. Figure 3 illustrates the principle of time-redundant bitslicing as applied to AES computation. The operation starts the pipeline by filling half of the slices with the output of the first round of AES, and the other half with the output of the initial key whitening. At the end of round $i+1$, we have re-computed the output of round i (at a later time): we can, therefore, compare the two results and detect control faults based on the different results they may have produced. In contrast to typical temporal-redundancy countermeasures such as instruction duplication [40], this technique does not increase code size: the same instructions compute both rounds at the same time. Only the last AES round, which is different from regular rounds, must be computed twice in a non-pipelined fashion.

Whereas pipelining protects the inner round function, faults remain possible on the control path of the loop itself. We protect against these threats through standard loop hardening techniques, namely redundant loop counters – packing multiple copies of a counter in a single machine word – and duplication of the loop control structure [25] – producing multiple copies of conditional jumps so as to lower the odds of all of them being skipped through an injected fault.

4   SKIVA Implementation

In this section, we present the SKIVA hardware, a custom instruction-set extension (ISE) tailored to support efficient and safe implementation of these schemes.

4.1   Custom Instruction-Set Extensions in SKIVA

We added new instructions to SKIVA to support computing on aggregated bit-slices in three different areas. First, they help with the conversion from normal representation to bitsliced form and back. Second, they handle subword-operations for the computation of non-linear operations on two or four shares ($D \in \{2, 4\}$). Third, they handle subword-operations for spatially redundant computations and fault checking ($R_s \in \{2, 4\}$). The new instructions are summarized in Table 1 and will be described in detail in further subsections. Appendix 6 provides their functional specification. These new instructions are orthogonal; they can be used in a mix-and-match fashion to obtain the desired level of sharing and redundancy. We integrated the new instructions on the SPARC V8 instruction set of the open-source LEON3 processor and software toolchain [45].

Hardware Integration. Figure 4 illustrates the integration of the custom data-path into the seven-stage RISC pipeline. The instructions follow a two-input, one-output or two-input, two-output format, encoded as two source registers, a destination register, and an immediate field (INS rs1, rs2, rd, imm). The upper 32-bit output of the custom instruction is transferred to the Y-register, a register which is used for SPARC V8 instructions with 64-bit output, such as the regular data multiplication. Instructions with longer than 32-bit outputs can be integrated into instruction sets without this special register by duplicating the instruction for calculating the lower half of the output and the upper half of it separately (similar to MUL and SMMUL in ARM and Thumb instruction set). The integration of custom-hardware deep into the pipeline necessitates the

Table 1. Proposed ISE. These instructions are added to the standard SPARC-V instruction set, occupying unused opcodes. Symbols in the instruction format - `rs1`, `rs2`, `rd` are registers. `imm` is an immediate operand. The "Type" column shows what opcode group was used for each instruction. Appendix 6 lists the functional specification for each instruction.

Semantics	Instruction format	Immediate	Type
Normal → Bitslice	TR2 rs1, rs2, rd		logic
Bitslice → Normal	INVTR2 rs1, rs2, rd		ld/st
Slice Rotation	SUBROT rs, imm, rd	D	logic
Redundancy Generation	RED rs, imm, rd	R_s	logic
Redundancy Checking	FTCHK rs, imm, rd	R_s	logic
Redundant AND ($R_s = 2$)	ANDC16 rs1, rs2, rd		logic
Redundant XOR ($R_s = 2$)	XORC16 rs1, rs2, rd		logic
Redundant XNOR ($R_s = 2$)	XNORC16 rs1, rs2, rd		ld/st
Redundant AND ($R_s = 4$)	ANDC8 rs1, rs2, rd		logic
Redundant XOR ($R_s = 4$)	XORC8 rs1, rs2, rd		logic
Redundant XNOR ($R_s = 4$)	XNORC8 rs1, rs2, rd		ld/st

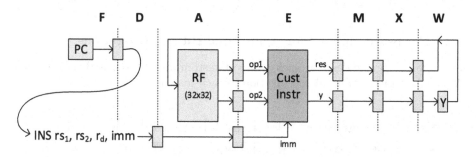

Fig. 4. Integrated in the regular 7-stage pipeline as a new execution stage.

use of simple and fast datapath hardware. However, these instructions benefit from the same performance advantages as regular instructions, including a typical throughput of one instruction per cycle and minimal stall effect thanks to forwarding [38].

The new instructions are mapped into unused opcodes of the SPARC V8 instruction set [50]. Since we did not replace any existing SPARC instruction, SKIVA is backward binary-compatible with existing LEON applications. The new instructions add minimal overhead to the design. In terms of 180nm standard cell ASIC technology, we added 1250 gate-equivalent to the design, which amounts to 3% of the area of the integer unit of SKIVA.

Software Integration. We integrated the new instructions into the software toolchain of SKIVA by extending the assembler. The new mnemonics were then integrated into the application in C through inline assembly coding. Because the custom instruction format is compatible with that of existing, standard SPARC V8 instructions, they benefit from off-the-shelf compiler optimizations.

Related Work. Earlier efforts of hardware-specific side-channel countermeasures based on custom instructions include mask generation [51] and hiding [42]. CRISP explores the use of custom instructions for bitslicing in a processor design [22]. CRISP defines three new instructions, based on two programmable lookup tables. These instructions deal with bitslicing, but they do not offer redundancy nor support for countermeasures. With the advent of open platforms such as RISC-V, instruction set extensions are now a viable mechanism for platform customization. XCrypto [34] defined instruction extensions for RISC-V while Galois has proposed a formally validated one [30]. XCrypto supports special registers for cryptographic algorithms as well as custom instructions to improve the performance of such applications. XCrypto is designed for efficient cryptographic workload processing with support for random number generation and dedicated arithmetic. The SKIVA custom instructions are instead designed as flexible countermeasures. The SKIVA programmer decides on the level of security and then applies SKIVA instructions commensurate with the selected level.

4.2   Hardware Support for Aggregated Bitslice Operations

In the following, we describe each group of custom instructions and their usage. Appendix 6 gives a formal specification of each instruction.

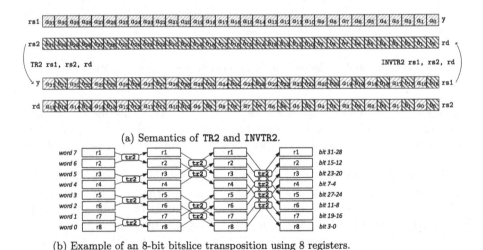

(a) Semantics of **TR2** and **INVTR2**.

(b) Example of an 8-bit bitslice transposition using 8 registers.

Fig. 5. Transposition and its inverse

Instructions for Bitslicing. We introduce two instructions to transpose data into their bitsliced representation (Fig. 5a). The first instruction, TR2 rs1, rs2, rd, performs an interleaving of the bits of two source registers into two output registers. This interleaving can be thought of as a 2-bit transposition, as it places bits within the same column of register rs1 and rs2 in adjacent positions of the output registers rd and y. The second instruction, INVTR2 rs1, rs2, rd, performs the inverse operation. Bitslice transposition for an arbitrary number of bits is achieved through repeated application of TR2. Figure 5b shows an 8-bit transposition achieved using twelve applications of TR2. In general, for a 2^n-bit transition, $n.2^{n-1}$ applications of TR2 are needed. To create aggregated bitslices ($R_s > 1$ or $D > 1$), we pre-process the source registers (in non-bitsliced form) by duplicating them first and then transposing them to bitsliced form. The side-channel protection and fault-detection of SKIVA are not active during bitslice conversion, but we check their consistency after transposition and before encryption.

Instructions for Higher-Order Masking. SKIVA supports two-share and four-share implementations of bitsliced algorithms, which provide first-order and third-order masked side-channel resistance. The shares are located in adjacent bits of a processor register. We use Boolean masking so that the XOR of all shares yields the unmasked value. Linear operations on an ensemble of shares are computed as the linear operation on each individual share. Linear operations are done using bitwise operations on the two-share and four-share representation. Computing a secure multiplication over multiple shares requires the computation of the partial share-products. For example, the secure multiplication of the two-share slices (a_1, a_0) with the two-share slices (b_1, b_0) requires the partial products $a_1.b_1$, $a_1.b_0$, $a_0.b_1$, and $a_0.b_0$. To align the slices for the cross-products, we implement a slice rotation instruction SUBROT rs, imm, rd. This instruction transforms the two-share slices (a_1, a_0) into (a_0, a_1). The same instruction SUBROT can also handle a four-share design, which transforms (a_3, a_2, a_1, a_0) into (a_2, a_1, a_0, a_3).

Instructions for Fault Redundancy Checking. SKIVA supports fault redundancy countermeasures using instructions for the generation and checking of fault-redundant slices. The redundant bits with respect to fault injection are stored in adjacent bytes of a halfword. Figure 6(a) shows the example of a halfword operation to generate redundant data, while Fig. 6(b) shows the example of a halfword operation to verify redundant data.

The RED rs1, imm, rd instruction generates redundant data. The redundant copy is stored in the upper halfword ($R_s = 2$) or in the three upper bytes ($R_s = 4$). The redundant portion can be either a direct or else a complement of the original data. There are six variants of RED rs1, imm, rd. Two of them support dual redundancy ($R_s = 2$), they duplicate the lower and upper halfword, in direct or complementary form. Four additional variants support quadruple redundancy ($R_s = 4$), and they quadruple the lower two bytes or the upper two bytes, each in direct or complementary form.

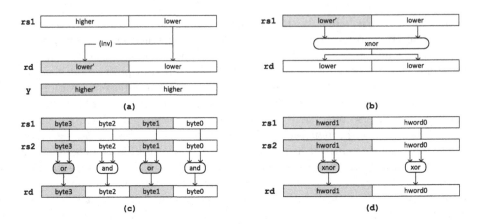

Fig. 6. (a) Example of RED on half-word (top, left). (b) Example of FTCHK on half-word (top, right). (c) Example of ANDC8 (bottom, left). (d) Example of XORC16 (bottom, right).

The FTCHK rs1, imm, rd instruction verifies the consistency of the redundant data. This instruction generates a fault-flag in the redundant form (over R_s bits, Appendix 6), which can be used to drive a fault condition test. Figure 6(b) illustrates the case of a dual-redundancy check on complementary redundant data. The fault-check is evaluated in a redundant manner so that the fault-check itself can detect fault injection on its own check. The expected faultless result of the instruction example in Fig. 6(b) is 0x00000000. There are four variants of this instruction, for either dual ($R_s = 2$) or quadruple redundancy ($R_s = 4$), and direct or complementary redundancy.

Instructions for Fault-Redundant Computations. Computations on direct-redundant bitslices can be done using standard bitwise operations. For complementary-redundant bitslices, the bitwise operations have to be adjusted to complement-operations. The complement-redundant data format can be introduced at the halfword boundary ($R_s = 2$) or the byte boundary ($R_s = 4$). We opted to provide support for bitwise AND, XOR, and XNOR on these complement-redundant data formats. Figure 6(c-d) illustrates the case of ANDC8 and XORC16.

Putting it All Together. We demonstrate how the proposed instructions can be combined by building an implementation for a recently proposed gadget that offers protection against combined attacks (side-channel attacks and faults) using the non-interference and non-accumulation (NINA) property [18]. Figure 7 shows a two-share NINA multiplication. Appendix C lists a four-share NINA multiplication. The multiplication takes four steps. First, we check the fault flags and conditionally clear an input. This diverts attacks where an adversary uses faults to influence side-channel leakage. Second, the parallel multiplication algorithm evaluates the product [5]. Third, the output is refreshed using parallel mask

```
# two-share NINA Secure Multiplication
# input:   %i2 (a),
#          %i3 (b),
#          %i4 (random),
#          %i5 (fault flags)
# output:  %o0 (a & b)
#          %i5 (accumulated fault)
# step 1: clear input in case of a fault
NOT     %i5, %o4       #
AND     %i2, %o4, %o6  #
# step 2: calculate AND result
AND     %i3, %o6, %o5  # partial product 1
SUBROT  %o6,   2, %10  # share-rotate
AND     %i3, %10, %o3  # partial product 2
XOR     %10, %10, %10  # clear SUBROT output
XOR     %o5, %i4, %o2  # random + parprod 1
XOR     %o2, %o3, %o1  #         + parprod 2
# step 3: refresh the output
SUBROT  %i4,   2, %11  # parallel refresh
XOR     %o1, %11, %o0  #           output
# step 4: update fault flags
FTCHK   %o0, imm, %g5  # imm depends on Rs and Rt
OR      %g5, %i5, %i5  #
```

Fig. 7. Two-share NINA multiplication gadget using SKIVA instructions

refreshing (required for the four-share multiplication [5]). Finally, the fault flags are updated to reflect the computation status of the result. In terms of NINA property, these gadgets are (D,R_s)-SNINA. The proposed gadget in Fig. 7 is of the fault-detecting type and does not protect against statistical ineffective fault attacks (SIFA). To overcome this vulnerability, we need fault-correction instead of detection. Fault-correction based on majority voting fits well into SKIVA scheme where $R_s = 4$ by extending the FTCHK instruction to check the redundant copies of the input and put the most agreeable copy on the output. Majority voting needs at least $2k + 1$ copies to resolve k faults; therefore, when $R_s = 4$, it can resolve one fault.

In practice, the custom instruction-set extensions of SKIVA have to be judiciously applied to prevent accidental side-channel leakage. One area of attention is the allocation of masked variables in registers. For non-bitsliced designs, accidental unmasking has been demonstrated when a mask m overwrites a masked variable $m \oplus v$ [1, 36] For bitsliced designs, the risk is lower because each share resides at a different bit-index. Still, bitslices may interfere with each other in unexpected manners [19]. In SKIVA, the SUBROT instruction shifts shares over bit-positions using a dedicated data-path. After the result of SUBROT is consumed, that register is cleared to eliminate lingering shares. In addition, we control register allocation for secure gadgets manually. For example, we ensure that SUBROT never overwrites its own input. We also maintain a strict separation between registers used for the masked algorithm (i.e. AES), and registers used for mask generation and mask distribution. This ensures that registers containing masked data cannot be overwritten by registers directly related to random masks.

5   Results

This section evaluates the performance and side-channel security of AES on SKIVA. The implementation under test is in bitsliced format and uses the secure multiplication gadgets introduced in Sect. 4.2. Next, we analyze the fault coverage of applications on SKIVA under the assumed fault model.

We used the Usuba [35] compiler to generate the 18 different implementations of AES (all combinations of $D \in \{1, 2, 4\}$, $R_s \in \{1, 2, 4\}$ and $R_t \in \{1, 2\}$). Usuba takes as input a high-level dataflow description of a cipher, which it bitslices and optimizes before generating C code. We added a new backend to Usuba to make it use our protection schemes and custom instructions in the C codes it produces. We also patched Leon Bare-C Cross Compilation System's (BCC) assembler to support SKIVA's custom instructions in order to be able to compile the C codes produced by Usuba.

5.1   Performance Evaluation

Our experimental evaluation has been carried on a prototype of SKIVA deployed on the main FPGA (Cyclone IV EP4CE115) of an Altera DE2-115 board. The processor is clocked at 50 MHz and has access to 128 kB of RAM. Our performance results are obtained by running the desired programs on bare metal. We assume that we have access to a TRNG that frequently fills a register with a fresh 32-bit random string. We use a software pseudo-random number generator (32-bit xorshift) to emulate a TRNG refreshed at a rate of our choosing. We checked that our experiments did not overflow the period of the RNG.

Several implementations of AES are available on our 32-bit, SPARC-derivative processor, with varying degrees of performance. The constant-time, byte-sliced implementation (using only 8 variables to represent 128 bits of data) of BearSSL [39] performs at 48 C/B. Our bitsliced implementation (using 128 variables to represent 128 bits of data) performs favorably at 44 C/B while weighing 8060B: despite a significant register pressure (128 live variables for 32 machine registers), the rotations of MixColumn and the ShiftRows operations are compiled away. This bitsliced implementation serves as our baseline in the following.

Throughput (AES). We report on the impact of our hardware and software design on the performance of our bitsliced implementation of AES (Sect. 3). To do so, we evaluate the performance of our 18 variants of AES, for each value of $(D \in \{1, 2, 4\}, R_s \in \{1, 2, 4\}, R_t \in \{1, 2\})$. To remove the influence of the TRNG's throughput from the performance evaluation, we assume that its refill frequency is strictly higher than the rate at which our implementation consumes

Table 2. Exhaustive evaluation of the AES design space

$R_t = 1$		D			$R_t = 2$		D		
		1	2	4			1	2	4
	1	44 C/B	176 C/B	579 C/B		1	131 C/B	465 C/B	1433 C/B
R_s	2	89 C/B	413 C/B	1298 C/B	R_s	2	269 C/B	1065 C/B	3170 C/B
	4	169 C/B	819 C/B	2593 C/B		4	529 C/B	2122 C/B	6327 C/B

(a) Reciprocal throughput ($R_t = 1$)   (b) Reciprocal throughput ($R_t = 2$)

random bits. In practice, a refill rate of 10 cycles for 32 bits is enough to meet this requirement.

We report our performance results in Table 2. For D and R_t fixed, the throughput decreases linearly with R_s. At fixed D, the variant $(D, R_s = 1, R_t = 2)$ (temporal redundancy by a factor 2) exhibits similar performances as $(D, R_s = 2, R_t = 1)$ (spatial redundancy by a factor 2). However, both implementation are *not* equivalent from a security standpoint. The former offers weaker security guarantees than the latter. Similarly, at fixed D and R_s, we may be tempted to run twice the implementation $(D, R_s, R_t = 1)$ rather than running once the implementation $(D, R_s, R_t = 2)$: once again, the security of the former is reduced compared to the latter since temporal redundancy ($R_t = 2$) couples the computation of 2 rounds within each instruction, whereas pure instruction redundancy ($R_t = 1$) does not.

Code Size (AES). We measure the impact of our hardware and software design on code size, using our bitsliced implementation of AES as a baseline. Our hardware design provides us with native support for spatial, complementary redundancy (ANDC, XORC, and XNORC). Performing these operations through software emulation would result in a ×1.3 (for $D = 2$) to ×1.4 (for $D = 4$) increase in code size. One must nonetheless bear in mind that the security provided by emulation is *not* equivalent to the one provided by native support. The temporal redundancy ($R_t = 2$) mechanism comes at the expense of a small increase (less than ×1.06) in code size, due to the loop hardening protections as well as the checks validating results across successive rounds. The higher-order masking comes at a reasonable expense in code size: going from 1 to 2 shares increases code size by ×1.5 whereas going from 1 to 4 shares corresponds to a ×1.6 increase. A fully protected implementation ($D = 4, R_s = 4, R_t = 2$) thus weighs 13148 bytes.

5.2   Side-Channel Analysis

We conduct an experiment to demonstrate how the proposed custom instructions can help decrease the power leakage. We implement SKIVA on the main FPGA of SAKURA-G board running at 9.8 MHz and powered at 5 V by an external power generator. We use a LeCroy WaveRunner 610Zi oscilloscope, sampling

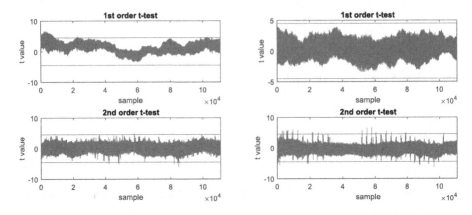

Fig. 8. 1st and 2nd order t-tests of 1st order masked implementation. Left column: 40K fixed *vs.* 40K random traces with PRNG off. Right column: 500K fixed *vs.* 500K random traces with PRNG on.

250 M samples/sec. To limit the noise level, we use a low-pass filter with a cutoff frequency of 81 MHz on the power probe.

Correlation Power Analysis. To evaluate our design, we conduct 1st order correlation power analysis (CPA) [12] on power consumption traces of the SubBytes stage of the first round of AES. We use the Hamming weight of the SubBytes output as the power model. To speed up our attack, we use a sampling rate of 50 M samples/sec. In this test case, we attack a single bitslice out of 32 parallel bitslices; the unused bitslices perform constant encryption of an all-zero plaintext with an all-zero key. Our CPA attack analyzes 50K traces and confirms that 1st order CPA on the unmasked scheme can reveal half of the key with 12K traces while it reveals all the secret key bytes with 24K traces. When masking is enabled, no key byte is revealed under any configuration at the maximum number of traces we considered (50K).

Test Vector Leakage Assessment. To test the correctness of our secure implementations with the proposed instructions, we use the TVLA methodology [7,20] and conduct the 1st and 2nd order t-tests on our 1st order masked implementation and the 1st to 4th order t-tests on our 3rd order masked encryption in two settings with and without the custom instructions. We set the trigger on one S-box in the fourth round of AES based per TVLA methodology [7].

For our experiments, we conduct the univariate non-specific fixed-*vs.*-random t-test in which a set of random inputs and a set of fixed inputs are interspersed in a random order and sent to the device. The fixed plaintext is selected such that the output of the SubBytes stage in the 4th round of AES is zero. Furthermore, for higher-order t-tests, we post-process the traces to calculate the t-scores of the target order [47]. Figure 8 and Fig. 9 show the results of the t-test on our masked implementations. The right column in Fig. 8 (resp. Fig. 9) indicates that our first

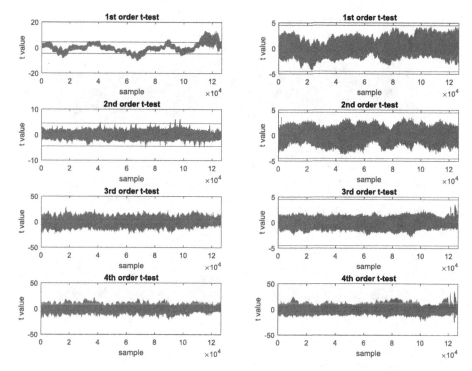

Fig. 9. 1st to 4th order t-tests of 3rd order masked implementation. Left column: 35K fixed *vs.* 35K random traces with PRNG off. Right column: 500K fixed *vs.* 500K random traces with PRNG on.

(resp. third) order masked scheme shows no leakage of first (resp. first, second, or third) order on 500K fixed *vs.* 500K random traces while showing second (resp. fourth) order leakage as expected. The left columns show how turning the PRNG off causes the implementations to have leakage of all orders.

This experiment shows that the secure implementations are sound for analysis up to 500K traces. We do not conclude that the security claim underpinning the gadgets is valid; while an experimental observation can validate a security claim, the experiment cannot be used as its proof of correctness.

Power Leakage of Direct and Complementary Redundancy. To compare the effect of the direct and complementary redundancy schemes on side-channel leakage, we run the following test. We make two different versions of our AES C code: (1) 16 parallel aggregated bitslices of the direct ($D = 2, R_s = 1, R_t = 1$) scheme as the input to the first S-box in the fourth round of AES; and (2) 8 parallel aggregated bitslices of the complementary ($D = 2, R_s = 2, R_t = 1$) scheme as the input to the first S-box in the fourth round of AES. We then measure 5K traces for fixed input and 5K traces for random input and apply a second-order t-test on the measured traces. To speed up our measurements, the traces were collected at 50MS/s. As expected, Figs. 10c and 10d show second-order leakage

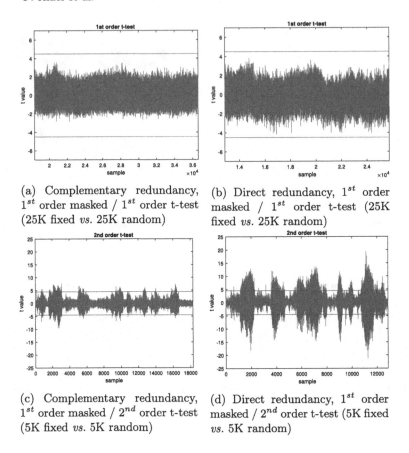

(a) Complementary redundancy, 1st order masked / 1st order t-test (25K fixed *vs.* 25K random)

(b) Direct redundancy, 1st order masked / 1st order t-test (25K fixed *vs.* 25K random)

(c) Complementary redundancy, 1st order masked / 2nd order t-test (5K fixed *vs.* 5K random)

(d) Direct redundancy, 1st order masked / 2nd order t-test (5K fixed *vs.* 5K random)

Fig. 10. Effect of type of redundancy on the power side-channel leakage.

for both schemes. However, the direct redundancy results in much higher t-values indicating a higher probability of leakage than complementary redundancy. We also confirmed that a first-order t-test on both implementations shows no leakage for a non-specific test of 25K fixed *vs.* 25K random traces even when sampled at a higher rate of 100MS/s (Figs. 10a and 10b). Appendix 6 includes additional observations.

5.3 Security Analysis of Data Faults

In the following, we analyze the fault sensitivity of our protected implementations. Our data protection scheme relies on spatial redundancy ($R_s \in \{2, 4\}$). Faults that cannot be detected are those that affect redundant copies within a single register *in a consistent manner*, which implies either identical values in case of direct redundancy or negated values in case of complemented redundancy. Note that this analysis is independent of whether sharing (D) is used or not. From the standpoint of redundancy, each share is independently protected: for example, if two shares of the same data are subjected to a bit flip, our redundancy mechanism will report an error, even though the underlying data remains unchanged ($x_1 \oplus x_2 = \overline{x_1} \oplus \overline{x_2}$).

There are different ways to achieve undetected faults, *i.e.* generate a consistent value: one may skip an instruction whose destination register already holds a consistent value; one may replace an instruction with another (*e.g.*, substitute an ANDC by an XORC); or directly perform a data fault.

If P is the probability for a data fault to result in a consistent value, then the detection rate is $1 - P$. Such a probability depends on the injection technique, its parameters, the target architecture, as well as the physical properties of the device. In the following, we develop a theoretical analysis based on the assumption that data faults follow a stuck-at 0 or stuck-at 1 model, or uniformly distributed random byte, half-word, and word model. We then complement this analysis by an empirical evaluation of the impact of instruction skip.

Theoretical Analysis of Spatial Redundancy. In this analysis, we use the fault coverage (FC) metric [24] $FC = 1 - F_{\text{undetected}}/F_{\text{total}}$ where F_{total} is the total number of faults covered by the fault model and $F_{\text{undetected}}$ is the number of faults that affect the execution while escaping detection by the countermeasure.

By construction, data fault effects such as single bit set, single reset, single bit flip, byte or half-word zeroing, faulty random byte or faulty random half-word are all detected ($FC = 100\%$). Word zeroing or stuck-at 1 on complementary redundant data are also all detected ($FC = 100\%$) but direct redundancy will never detect it ($FC = 0\%$).

If the attacker injects random data faults following a uniform distribution, it means that there are $F_{\text{total}} = 2^{32}$ fault injection possibilities. For $R_s = 2$ and independently of the redundancy (direct or complementary), 2^{16} of those values are consistent, including the expected output. Hence $F_{\text{undetected}} = 2^{16} - 1$ and $FC = 99.99\%$. For $R_s = 4$, there are $F_{\text{undetected}} = 2^8 - 1$ faults that are left undetected, thus $FC = 99.99\%$.

For illustrative purposes, we now consider a slightly stronger attacker who may flip p randomly chosen data bits. In practice, such analysis ought to be tailored to account for the specific distribution of faults of a given injection technique on a given platform. Under this attacker model, there are $F_{\text{total}} = \binom{32}{p}$ fault injection possibilities leading to a p-bit flip (with p an even number). For $R_s = 2$, there are $F_{\text{undetected}} = \binom{16}{\frac{p}{2}}$ faults corresponding to a p-bit flip that are left undetected. The lower-bound for FC is reached for $p = 2$ and $p = 30$, where $FC = 96.77\%$. For $R_s = 4$, there are $F_{\text{undetected}} = \binom{8}{\frac{p}{4}}$ faults corresponding to a p-bit flip that are left undetected. The lower-bound for FC is reached for $p = 4$ and $p = 28$, where $FC = 99.97\%$. A p-bit set or reset fault model leads to a 100% detection rate if complementary redundancy is used. If direct redundancy is used, then this amounts to the p-bit flip model. Either way the detection rate is very high.

Experimental Evaluation of Temporal Redundancy. We have simulated the
impact of faults on our implementation of AES. We focus our attention exclu-
sively on control faults (instruction skips) since our above analytical model
already predicts the outcome of data faults. To this end, we use a fault injection simulator based on gdb running through the JTAG interface of the FPGA
board. We execute our implementation up to a chosen breakpoint, after which
we instruct the processor to jump to a given address, hence simulating the effect
of an instruction skip. In particular, we have exhaustively targeted every instruction of the first and last round as well as the AES_secure routine (for $R_t = 2$)
and its counterpart for $R_t = 1$. Since rounds 2 to 9 use the same code as the first
round, the absence of vulnerabilities against instruction skips within the latter
means that the former is secure against instruction skip as well. This exposes a
total of 1248 injection points for $R_t = 2$ and 1093 injection points for $R_t = 1$.
For each such injection point, we perform an instruction skip from 512 random
combinations of key and plaintext for $R_t = 2$ and 352 random combinations for
$R_t = 1$.

The results are summarized in Table 3. Injecting a fault had one of five effects.
A fault may yield an incorrect ciphertext with (1) or without (2) being detected.
A fault may yield a correct ciphertext, with (3) or without (4) being detected.
Finally, a fault may cause the program or the board to crash (5). According to
our attacker model, only outcome (2) witnesses a vulnerability. In every other
outcome, the fault either does not produce a faulty ciphertext or is detected
within two rounds. For $R_t = 2$, we verify that every instruction skip was either
detected (outcome 1 or 3) or had no effect on the output of the corresponding
round (outcome 4) or lead to a crash (outcome 5). Comparatively, with $R_t = 1$,
nearly 95% of the instruction skips lead to an undetected fault impacting the
ciphertext. In 0.19% of the cases, the fault actually impacts the fault-detection
mechanism itself, thus triggering a false positive.

Table 3. Experimental results of simulated instruction skips

	With impact		Without impact			
	Detected (1)	Not detected (2)	Detected (3)	Not detected (4)	Crash (5)	# of faults
$R_t = 1$	0.19%	92.34%	0.00%	4.31%	3.15%	12840
$R_t = 2$	78.19%	0.00%	5.22%	12.18%	4.40%	21160

6   Conclusion

We have presented SKIVA, a general-purpose 32-bit processor supporting high-
throughput, secure block ciphers on embedded devices. Our objective in extending the SPARC instruction set was to provide cryptographers with a manageable
programming model for implementing secure ciphers on a general-purpose CPU.

On the software side, we advocate an approach centered around bitslicing, where cryptographic primitives are treated as combinational circuits. By design, bitslicing protects an implementation against timing-based side-channel attacks. However, it also provides a sound basis for modular protections against fault and/or power-based side-channel attacks, thus paving the way for a pay-as-you-go security approach. In essence, SKIVA can be understood as a Turing machine for efficiently and securely executing combinational circuits in software.

These design choices translate into protection mechanisms that can naturally and systematically be integrated together. To protect against faults, we have shown that intra-instruction redundancy enables purely analytic security analysis, guaranteeing significant coverage, while we experimentally showed that temporal redundancy protects against instruction skips. To protect against side-channel, we crucially rely on the physical isolation of slices, thus significantly reducing the risk of involuntary interference due to architectural details invisible to the programmer.

We have demonstrated the benefits of our approach with a bitsliced implementation of AES with 1, 2, and 4 shares, a temporal redundancy of 1 and 2, as well as a spatial redundancy of 1, 2, and 4. In terms of code size, we have shown that all security levels can be implemented in less than 13148B. In terms of performance, we have seen that it scales well with protection levels, dividing the throughput by 161 with all protections enabled at their maximum $(D = 4, R_s = 4, R_t = 2)$.

Acknowledgements. This project was supported in part by NSF Grant 1617203, NSF Grant 1931639, NIST Grant 70NANB17H280, the Émergence(s) program of the City of Paris and the EDITE doctoral school.

Custom instructions details

TR2 instruction

```
TR2 rs1, rs2, rd

    reg_rd[31:0] := CONCAT( ...
        reg_rs1[15],reg_rs2[15],reg_rs1[14],reg_rs2[14], ...
        reg_rs1[13],reg_rs2[13],reg_rs1[12],reg_rs2[12], ...
        reg_rs1[11],reg_rs2[11],reg_rs1[10],reg_rs2[10], ...
        reg_rs1[9],reg_rs2[9],reg_rs1[8],reg_rs2[8], ...
        reg_rs1[7],reg_rs2[7],reg_rs1[6],reg_rs2[6], ...
        reg_rs1[5],reg_rs2[5],reg_rs1[4],reg_rs2[4], ...
        reg_rs1[3],reg_rs2[3],reg_rs1[2],reg_rs2[2], ...
        reg_rs1[1],reg_rs2[1],reg_rs1[0],reg_rs2[0])
    y[31:0] := CONCAT( ...
        reg_rs1[31],reg_rs2[31],reg_rs1[30],reg_rs2[30], ...
        reg_rs1[29],reg_rs2[29],reg_rs1[28],reg_rs2[28], ...
        reg_rs1[27],reg_rs2[27],reg_rs1[26],reg_rs2[26], ...
```

```
      reg_rs1[25],reg_rs2[25],reg_rs1[24],reg_rs2[24], ...
      reg_rs1[23],reg_rs2[23],reg_rs1[22],reg_rs2[22], ...
      reg_rs1[21],reg_rs2[21],reg_rs1[20],reg_rs2[20], ...
      reg_rs1[19],reg_rs2[19],reg_rs1[18],reg_rs2[18], ...
      reg_rs1[17],reg_rs2[17],reg_rs1[16],reg_rs2[16])
```

INVTR2 instruction

```
INVTR2 rs1, rs2, rd

   reg_rd[31:0] := CONCAT( ...
       reg_rs1[30],reg_rs1[28],reg_rs1[26],reg_rs1[24], ...
       reg_rs1[22],reg_rs1[20],reg_rs1[18],reg_rs1[16], ...
       reg_rs1[14],reg_rs1[12],reg_rs1[10],reg_rs1[8], ...
       reg_rs1[6],reg_rs1[4],reg_rs1[2],reg_rs1[0], ...
       reg_rs2[30],reg_rs2[28],reg_rs2[26],reg_rs2[24], ...
       reg_rs2[22],reg_rs2[20],reg_rs2[18],reg_rs2[16], ...
       reg_rs2[14],reg_rs2[12],reg_rs2[10],reg_rs2[8], ...
       reg_rs2[6],reg_rs2[4],reg_rs2[2],reg_rs2[0])
   y[31:0] := CONCAT( ...
       reg_rs1[31],reg_rs1[29],reg_rs1[27],reg_rs1[25], ...
       reg_rs1[23],reg_rs1[21],reg_rs1[19],reg_rs1[17], ...
       reg_rs1[15],reg_rs1[13],reg_rs1[11],reg_rs1[9], ...
       reg_rs1[7],reg_rs1[5],reg_rs1[3],reg_rs1[1], ...
       reg_rs2[31],reg_rs2[29],reg_rs2[27],reg_rs2[25], ...
       reg_rs2[23],reg_rs2[21],reg_rs2[19],reg_rs2[17], ...
       reg_rs2[15],reg_rs2[13],reg_rs2[11],reg_rs2[9], ...
       reg_rs2[7],reg_rs2[5],reg_rs2[3],reg_rs2[1])
```

SUBROT instruction

```
SUBROT rs, imm, rd

   IF imm[2:0] = 010
      FOR i:=0:15
          j := 2*i
          reg_rd[j+1:j] := reg_rs[j:j+1]
      ENDFOR
   ELIF imm[2:0] = 100
      FOR i:=0:7
          j := 4*i
          reg_rd[j+3:j] := CONCAT(reg_rs[j+2:j],reg_rs[j+3])
      ENDFOR
   FI
```

RED instruction

```
RED rs, imm, rd

    IF imm[2:0] = 010
        reg_rd[15:0]  := reg_rs[15:0]
        reg_rd[31:16] := reg_rs[15:0]
        y[15:0]  := reg_rs[31:16]
        y[31:16] := reg_rs[31:16]
    ELIF imm[2:0] = 011
        reg_rd[15:0]  := reg_rs[15:0]
        reg_rd[31:16] := (NOT reg_rs[15:0])
        y[15:0]  := rreg_rss[31:16]
        y[31:16] := (NOT reg_rs[31:16])
    ELIF imm[2:0] = 100
        reg_rd[7:0]   := reg_rs[7:0]
        reg_rd[15:8]  := reg_rs[7:0]
        reg_rd[23:16] := reg_rs[7:0]
        reg_rd[31:24] := reg_rs[7:0]
        y[7:0]   := reg_rs[15:8]
        y[15:8]  := reg_rs[15:8]
        y[23:16] := reg_rs[15:8]
        y[31:24] := reg_rs[15:8]
    ELIF imm[2:0] = 101
        reg_rd[7:0]   := reg_rs[7:0]
        reg_rd[15:8]  := (NOT reg_rs[7:0])
        reg_rd[23:16] := reg_rs[7:0]
        reg_rd[31:24] := (NOT reg_rs[7:0])
        y[7:0]   := rs[15:8]
        y[15:8]  := (NOT reg_rs[15:8])
        y[23:16] := rs[15:8]
        y[31:24] := (NOT reg_rs[15:8])
    ELIF imm[2:0] = 110
        reg_rd[7:0]   := reg_rs[23:16]
        reg_rd[15:8]  := reg_rs[23:16]
        reg_rd[23:16] := reg_rs[23:16]
        reg_rd[31:24] := reg_rs[23:16]
        y[7:0]   := reg_rs[31:24]
        y[15:8]  := reg_rs[31:24]
        y[23:16] := reg_rs[31:24]
        y[31:24] := reg_rs[31:24]
    ELIF imm[2:0] = 111
        reg_rd[7:0]   := reg_rs[23:16]
        reg_rd[15:8]  := (NOT reg_rs[23:16])
        reg_rd[23:16] := reg_rs[23:16]
        reg_rd[31:24] := (NOT reg_rs[23:16])
```

```
        y[7:0]  := reg_rs[31:24]
        y[15:8]  := (NOT reg_rs[31:24])
        y[23:16]  := reg_rs[31:24]
        y[31:24]  := (NOT reg_rs[31:24])
    FI
```

ANDC16 instruction

```
ANDC16 rs1, rs2, rd

        reg_rd[15:0]  := (reg_rs1[15:0] AND reg_rs2[15:0])
        reg_rd[31:16]  := (reg_rs1[31:16] OR reg_rs2[31:16])
```

XORC16 instruction

```
XORC16 rs1, rs2, rd

        reg_rd[15:0]  := (reg_rs1[15:0] XOR reg_rs2[15:0])
        reg_rd[31:16]  := (reg_rs1[31:16] XNOR reg_rs2[31:16])
```

XNORC16 instruction

```
XNORC16 rs1, rs2, rd

        reg_rd[15:0]  := (reg_rs1[15:0] XNOR reg_rs2[15:0])
        reg_rd[31:16]  := (reg_rs1[31:16] XOR reg_rs2[31:16])
```

ANDC8 instruction

```
ANDC8 rs1, rs2, rd

        reg_rd[7:0]  := (reg_rs1[7:0] AND reg_rs2[7:0])
        reg_rd[15:8]  := (reg_rs1[15:8] OR reg_rs2[15:8])
        reg_rd[23:16]  := (reg_rs1[23:16] AND reg_rs2[23:16])
        reg_rd[31:24]  := (reg_rs1[31:24] OR reg_rs2[31:24])
```

XORC8 instruction

```
XORC8 rs1, rs2, rd

        reg_rd[7:0]   := (reg_rs1[7:0] XOR reg_rs2[7:0])
        reg_rd[15:8]  := (reg_rs1[15:8] XNOR reg_rs2[15:8])
        reg_rd[23:16] := (reg_rs1[23:16] XOR reg_rs2[23:16])
        reg_rd[31:24] := (reg_rs1[31:24] XNOR reg_rs2[31:24])
```

XNORC8 instruction

```
XNORC8 rs1, rs2, rd

        reg_rd[7:0]   := (reg_rs1[7:0] XNOR reg_rs2[7:0])
        reg_rd[15:8]  := (reg_rs1[15:8] XOR reg_rs2[15:8])
        reg_rd[23:16] := (reg_rs1[23:16] XNOR reg_rs2[23:16])
        reg_rd[31:24] := (reg_rs1[31:24] XOR reg_rs2[31:24])
```

FTCHK instruction

```
FTCHK rs, imm, rd

    IF imm[2:0] = 010
        FOR i:=0:15
            reg_rd[i]    := (reg_rs[i+16] XOR reg_rs[i])
            reg_rd[i+16] :=  (reg_rs[i+16] XOR reg_rs[i])
        ENDFOR
    ELIF imm[2:0] = 011
        FOR i:=0:15
            reg_rd[i]    := (reg_rs[i+16] XNOR reg_rs[i])
            reg_rd[i+16] :=  (reg_rs[i+16] XNOR reg_rs[i])
        ENDFOR
    ELIF imm[2:0] = 100
        FOR i:=0:7
            reg_rd[i]    := ((reg_rs[i+8] XOR reg_rs[i]) OR ...
                            (reg_rs[i+16] XOR reg_rs[i]) OR ...
                            (reg_rs[i+24] XOR reg_rs[i]))
            reg_rd[i+8]  := ((reg_rs[i+8] XOR reg_rs[i]) OR ...
                            (reg_rs[i+16] XOR reg_rs[i]) OR ...
                            (reg_rs[i+24] XOR reg_rs[i]))
            reg_rd[i+16] := ((reg_rs[i+8] XOR reg_rs[i]) OR ...
                            (reg_rs[i+16] XOR reg_rs[i]) OR ...
                            (reg_rs[i+24] XOR reg_rs[i]))
            reg_rd[i+24] := ((reg_rs[i+8] XOR reg_rs[i]) OR ...
                            (reg_rs[i+16] XOR reg_rs[i]) OR ...
```

```
                        (reg_rs[i+24] XOR reg_rs[i]))
      ENDFOR
  ELIF imm[2:0] = 101
     FOR i:=0:7
        reg_rd[i]    := ((reg_rs[i+8]  XNOR reg_rs[i]) OR ...
                         (reg_rs[i+16] XOR  reg_rs[i]) OR ...
                         (reg_rs[i+24] XNOR reg_rs[i]))
        reg_rd[i+8]  := ((reg_rs[i+8]  XNOR reg_rs[i]) OR ...
                         (reg_rs[i+16] XOR  reg_rs[i]) OR ...
                         (reg_rs[i+24] XNOR reg_rs[i]))
        reg_rd[i+16] := ((reg_rs[i+8]  XNOR reg_rs[i]) OR ...
                         (reg_rs[i+16] XOR  reg_rs[i]) OR ...
                         (reg_rs[i+24] XNOR reg_rs[i]))
        reg_rd[i+24] := ((reg_rs[i+8]  XNOR reg_rs[i]) OR ...
                         (reg_rs[i+16] XOR  reg_rs[i]) OR ...
                         (reg_rs[i+24] XNOR reg_rs[i]))
     ENDFOR
  FI
```

Efficient C emulation of the custom instructions

The following C code shows how to emulate selected custom instructions.

```
#define ANDC8(r,a,b)   r = (((a) | (b)) & 0xFF00FF00) | \
                           (((a) & (b)) & 0x00FF00FF)
#define XORC8(r,a,b)   r = (a) ^ (b) ^ 0xFF00FF00
#define XNORC8(r,a,b)  r = (a) ^ (b) ^ 0x00FF00FF
#define ANDC16(r,a,b)  r = (((a) | (b)) & 0xFFFF0000) | \
                           (((a) & (b)) & 0x0000FFFF)
#define XORC16(r,a,b)  r = (a) ^ (b) ^ 0xFFFF0000
#define XNORC16(r,a,b) r = (a) ^ (b) ^ 0x0000FFFF
```

Sample multiplication gadgets

```
# input: %i2 (a), %i3 (b), %i4 (random), %i5 (fault flags)
# output: %o0 (a & b), %i5 (updated fault flags)
### clear input in case of a fault:
NOT     %i5, %o4      #
AND     %i2, %o4, %o6 #
### calculate AND result:
AND     %i3, %o6, %o5 # partial product 1
SUBROT  %o6,   2, %10 # share-rotate
AND     %i3, %10, %o3 # partial product 2
XOR     %10, %10, %10 # clear SUBROT output
XOR     %o5, %i4, %o2 # random + parprod 1
XOR     %o2, %o3, %o1 #         + parprod 2
SUBROT  %i4,   2, %11 # parallel refresh
XOR     %o1, %11, %o0 #            output
### update fault flags:
FTCHK   %o0, imm, %g5 # imm depends on Rs and Rt
OR      %g5, %i5, %i5 #
```

(a) First-order secure multiplication

```
# input: %17 (a), %g1 (b), %g4 (random), %g2 (random), %i6 (fault flags)
# output: %i1 (a & b), %i6 (updated fault flags)
### clear input in case of a fault:
NOT     %i6, %g6      #
AND     %17, %g6, %o6 #
### calculate AND result:
AND     %o6, %g1, %i3 # partial product 1
SUBROT  %o6, 4, %o1   # share-rotate
AND     %g1, %o1, %i2 # partial product 2
SUBROT  %g1, 4, %o0   # share-rotate
AND     %o0, %o6, %i0 # partial product 3
SUBROT  %o1, 4, %10   # share-rotate
AND     %g1, %10, %o7 # partial product 4
XOR     %o1, %o1, %o1 # clear SUBROT output
XOR     %o0, %o0, %o0 # clear SUBROT output
XOR     %10, %10, %10 # clear SUBROT output
XOR     %i3, %g4, %o5 # random + parprod 1
XOR     %o5, %i2, %o4 #         + parprod 2
XOR     %o4, %10, %o3 #         + parprod 3
SUBROT  %g4, 4, %11   #
XOR     %o3, %11, %o2 #         + rot(random)
XOR     %o2, %o7, %g3 #         + parprod 4
XOR     %g2, %g3, %i5 # output refresh
SUBROT  %g2, 4, %12   #
XOR     %12, %i5, %i1 #
### update fault flags:
FTCHK   %i1, imm, %g5 # imm depends on Rs and Rt
OR      %g5, %i6, %i6 #
```

(b) Third-order secure multiplication

Fig. 11. Secure multiplication using SUBROT and FTCHK

Side-channel analysis results

Table 4. Detailed report of 1st order CPA results on unmasked SubBytes of 1st round AES

# of traces	# of key bytes revealed
3K	1
4K	3
9K	5
10K	6
11K	7
12K	8 (half key)
14K	10
18K	11
19K	12
21K	13
22K	14
23K	15
24K	16 (full key)

Effect of Different Redundancy Schemes on Power Leakage

Figure 12 shows the evolution of t-values for the 2nd order t-test with respect to the number of traces for both redundancy schemes. We observe that the direct redundancy shows leakage with as few as about 200 traces, while the complementary redundancy shows leakage only after around 2500 traces. We conclude that complementary redundancy is better than its direct counterpart in hiding secret data from the power leakage. We believe that this result is consistent with earlier work that investigated the impact of complementary representation on software [16, 26].

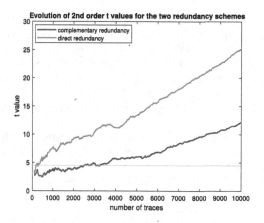

Fig. 12. Evolution of t values for 2nd order t-test on 1st order masked implementation with direct and complementary redundancy.

References

1. Balasch, J., Gierlichs, B., Grosso, V., Reparaz, O., Standaert, F.-X.: On the cost of lazy engineering for masked software implementations. In: Joye, M., Moradi, A. (eds.) CARDIS 2014. LNCS, vol. 8968, pp. 64–81. Springer, Cham (2015). https://doi.org/10.1007/978-3-319-16763-3_5
2. Balasch, J., Gierlichs, B., Verbauwhede, I.: An in-depth and black-box characterization of the effects of clock glitches on 8-bit MCUs. In 2011 Workshop on Fault Diagnosis and Tolerance in Cryptography, FDTC 2011, Tokyo, Japan, 29 September 2011, pp. 105–114 (2011). https://doi.org/10.1109/FDTC.2011.9
3. Barry, T., Couroussé, D., Robisson, B.: Compilation of a countermeasure against instruction-skip fault attacks. In: Proceedings of the Third Workshop on Cryptography and Security in Computing Systems, CS2@HiPEAC, Prague, Czech Republic, 20 January 2016, pp. 1–6 (2016). https://doi.org/10.1145/2858930.2858931
4. Barthe, G., et al.: Strong non-interference and type-directed higher-order masking. In: Proceedings of the 2016 ACM SIGSAC Conference on Computer and Communications Security, Vienna, Austria, 24–28 October 2016, pp. 116–129 (2016). https://doi.org/10.1145/2976749.2978427
5. Barthe, G., Dupressoir, F., Faust, S., Grégoire, B., Standaert, F.-X., Strub, P.-Y.: Parallel implementations of masking schemes and the bounded moment leakage model. In: Coron, J.-S., Nielsen, J.B. (eds.) EUROCRYPT 2017. LNCS, vol. 10210, pp. 535–566. Springer, Cham (2017). https://doi.org/10.1007/978-3-319-56620-7_19
6. Battistello, A., Coron, J.-S., Prouff, E., Zeitoun, R.: Horizontal side-channel attacks and countermeasures on the ISW masking scheme. In: Gierlichs, B., Poschmann, A.Y. (eds.) CHES 2016. LNCS, vol. 9813, pp. 23–39. Springer, Heidelberg (2016). https://doi.org/10.1007/978-3-662-53140-2_2
7. G. Becker, et al.: Test vector leakage assessment (TVLA) methodology in practice (2013)

8. Belaïd, S., Benhamouda, F., Passelègue, A., Prouff, E., Thillard, A., Vergnaud, D.: Randomness complexity of private circuits for multiplication. In: Fischlin, M., Coron, J.-S. (eds.) EUROCRYPT 2016. LNCS, vol. 9666, pp. 616–648. Springer, Heidelberg (2016). https://doi.org/10.1007/978-3-662-49896-5_22

9. Belaïd, S., Goudarzi, D., Rivain, M.: Tight private circuits: achieving probing security with the least refreshing. In: Peyrin, T., Galbraith, S. (eds.) ASIACRYPT 2018. LNCS, vol. 11273, pp. 343–372. Springer, Cham (2018). https://doi.org/10.1007/978-3-030-03329-3_12

10. Biham, E.: A fast new DES implementation in software. In: Biham, E. (ed.) FSE 1997. LNCS, vol. 1267, pp. 260–272. Springer, Heidelberg (1997). https://doi.org/10.1007/BFb0052352

11. Breier, J., Jap, D., Hou, X., Bhasin, S.: On side-channel vulnerabilities of bit permutations: Key recovery and reverse engineering. IACR Cryptol. ePrint Arch. **2018**, 219 (2018). http://eprint.iacr.org/2018/219

12. Brier, E., Clavier, C., Olivier, F.: Correlation power analysis with a leakage model. In: Joye, M., Quisquater, J.-J. (eds.) CHES 2004. LNCS, vol. 3156, pp. 16–29. Springer, Heidelberg (2004). https://doi.org/10.1007/978-3-540-28632-5_2

13. Cassiers, G., Standaert, F.-X.: Improved bitslice masking: from optimized non-interference to probe isolation. IACR Cryptol. ePrint Arch. **2018**, 438 (2018). URL https://eprint.iacr.org/2018/438

14. Cassiers, G., Standaert, F.-X.: Towards globally optimized masking: from low randomness to low noise rate or probe isolating multiplications with reduced randomness and security against horizontal attacks. IACR Trans. Cryptogr. Hardw. Embed. Syst. **2019**(2), 162–198 (2019). https://doi.org/10.13154/tches.v2019.i2.162-198

15. Chen, Z., Shen, J., Nicolau, A., Veidenbaum, A.V., Ghalaty, N.F., Cammarota, R.: CAMFAS: a compiler approach to mitigate fault attacks via enhanced SIMDization. In: 2017 Workshop on Fault Diagnosis and Tolerance in Cryptography, FDTC 2017, Taipei, Taiwan, 25 September 2017, pp. 57–64 (2017). https://doi.org/10.1109/FDTC.2017.10

16. Chen, Z., Sinha, A., Schaumont, P.: Using virtual secure circuit to protect embedded software from side-channel attacks. IEEE Trans. Comput. **62**(1), 124–136 (2013). https://doi.org/10.1109/TC.2011.225

17. Daemen, J., Peeters, M., Van Assche, G.: Bitslice ciphers and power analysis attacks. In: Goos, G., Hartmanis, J., van Leeuwen, J., Schneier, B. (eds.) FSE 2000. LNCS, vol. 1978, pp. 134–149. Springer, Heidelberg (2001). https://doi.org/10.1007/3-540-44706-7_10

18. Dhooghe, S., Nikova, S.: My gadget just cares for me - how NINA can prove security against combined attacks. IACR Cryptol. ePrint Arch. **2019**, 615 (2019). https://eprint.iacr.org/2019/615

19. Gao, S., Marshall, B., Page, D., Oswald, E.: Share-slicing: friend or foe? IACR Trans. Cryptogr. Hardw. Embed. Syst. **2020**(1), 152–174 (2020). https://doi.org/10.13154/tches.v2020.i1.152-174

20. Goodwill, G., Jun, B., Jaffe, J., Rohatgi, P.: A testing methodology for side channel resistance (2011). https://csrc.nist.gov/csrc/media/events/non-invasive-attack-testing-workshop/documents/08_goodwill.pdf

21. Goudarzi, D., Journault, A., Rivain, M., Standaert, F.-X.: Secure multiplication for bitslice higher-order masking: optimisation and comparison. In: Fan, J., Gierlichs, B. (eds.) COSADE 2018. LNCS, vol. 10815, pp. 3–22. Springer, Cham (2018). https://doi.org/10.1007/978-3-319-89641-0_1

22. Grabher, P., Großschädl, J., Page, D.: Light-weight instruction set extensions for bit-sliced cryptography. In: Oswald, E., Rohatgi, P. (eds.) CHES 2008. LNCS, vol. 5154, pp. 331–345. Springer, Heidelberg (2008). https://doi.org/10.1007/978-3-540-85053-3_21

23. Grégoire, B., Papagiannopoulos, K., Schwabe, P., Stoffelen, K.: Vectorizing higher-order masking. In: Fan, J., Gierlichs, B. (eds.) COSADE 2018. LNCS, vol. 10815, pp. 23–43. Springer, Cham (2018). https://doi.org/10.1007/978-3-319-89641-0_2

24. Guo, X., Mukhopadhyay, D., Karri, R.: Provably secure concurrent error detection against differential fault analysis. IACR Cryptol. ePrint Arch. **2012**, 552 (2012). http://eprint.iacr.org/2012/552

25. Heydemann, K.: Sécurité et performance des applications: analyses et optimisations multi-niveaux. LIP6, Habilitation (2017)

26. Hoogvorst, P., Duc, G., Danger, J.-L.: Software implementation of dual-rail representation. In: Schindler, W., Huss, S.A. (eds.) Constructive Side-Channel Analysis and Secure Design - Second International Workshop, COSADE (2011)

27. Ishai, Y., Sahai, A., Wagner, D.: Private circuits: securing hardware against probing attacks. In: Boneh, D. (ed.) CRYPTO 2003. LNCS, vol. 2729, pp. 463–481. Springer, Heidelberg (2003). https://doi.org/10.1007/978-3-540-45146-4_27

28. Journault, A., Standaert, F.-X.: Very high order masking: efficient implementation and security evaluation. In: Fischer, W., Homma, N. (eds.) CHES 2017. LNCS, vol. 10529, pp. 623–643. Springer, Cham (2017). https://doi.org/10.1007/978-3-319-66787-4_30

29. Käsper, E., Schwabe, P.: Faster and timing-attack resistant AES-GCM. In: Clavier, C., Gaj, K. (eds.) CHES 2009. LNCS, vol. 5747, pp. 1–17. Springer, Heidelberg (2009). https://doi.org/10.1007/978-3-642-04138-9_1

30. Kiniry, J.R., Zimmerman, D.M., Dockins, R., Nikhil, R.: A formally verified cryptographic extension to a RISC-V processor. In: Second Workshop on Computer Architecture Research with RISC-V (CARRV 2018), p. 5. ACM, New York (2018)

31. Könighofer, R.: A fast and cache-timing resistant implementation of the AES. In: Malkin, T. (ed.) CT-RSA 2008. LNCS, vol. 4964, pp. 187–202. Springer, Heidelberg (2008). https://doi.org/10.1007/978-3-540-79263-5_12

32. Lac, B., Canteaut, A., Fournier, J.J.A., Sirdey, R.: Thwarting fault attacks against lightweight cryptography using SIMD instructions. In: IEEE International Symposium on Circuits and Systems, ISCAS 2018, 27–30 May 2018, Florence, Italy, pp. 1–5 (2018). https://doi.org/10.1109/ISCAS.2018.8351693

33. Lalande, J.-F., Heydemann, K., Berthomé, P.: Software countermeasures for control flow integrity of smart card C codes. In: Kutyłowski, M., Vaidya, J. (eds.) ESORICS 2014. LNCS, vol. 8713, pp. 200–218. Springer, Cham (2014). https://doi.org/10.1007/978-3-319-11212-1_12

34. Marshall, B., Page, D., Pham, T.: XCrypto: a cryptographic ISE for RISC-V (2019). https://github.com/scarv/xcrypto

35. Mercadier, D., Dagand, P.-É.: Usuba: high-throughput and constant-time ciphers, by construction. In: Proceedings of the 40th ACM SIGPLAN Conference on Programming Language Design and Implementation, PLDI 2019, Phoenix, AZ, USA, 22–26 June 2019, pp. 157–173 (2019). https://doi.org/10.1145/3314221.3314636

36. Papagiannopoulos, K., Veshchikov, N.: Mind the gap: towards secure 1st-order masking in software. In: Guilley, S. (ed.) COSADE 2017. LNCS, vol. 10348, pp. 282–297. Springer, Cham (2017). https://doi.org/10.1007/978-3-319-64647-3_17
37. Patrick, C., Yuce, B., Ghalaty, N.F., Schaumont, P.: Lightweight fault attack resistance in software using intra-instruction redundancy. In: Avanzi, R., Heys, H. (eds.) SAC 2016. LNCS, vol. 10532, pp. 231–244. Springer, Cham (2017). https://doi.org/10.1007/978-3-319-69453-5_13
38. Patterson, D.A., Hennessy, J.L.: Computer Organization and Design - The Hardware / Software Interface (Revised 4th Edn.). The Morgan Kaufmann Series in Computer Architecture and Design. Academic Press (2012)
39. Pornin, T.: BearSSL, a smaller SSL/TLS library. https://bearssl.org. Accessed 08 Jan 2019
40. Proy, J., Heydemann, K., Berzati, A., Cohen, A.: Compiler-assisted loop hardening against fault attacks. TACO **14**(4), 36:1–36:25 (2017.) https://doi.org/10.1145/3141234
41. Rebeiro, C., Selvakumar, D., Devi, A.S.L.: Bitslice implementation of AES. In: Pointcheval, D., Mu, Y., Chen, K. (eds.) CANS 2006. LNCS, vol. 4301, pp. 203–212. Springer, Heidelberg (2006). https://doi.org/10.1007/11935070_14
42. Regazzoni, F., et al.: A design flow and evaluation framework for DPA-resistant instruction set extensions. In: Clavier, C., Gaj, K. (eds.) CHES 2009. LNCS, vol. 5747, pp. 205–219. Springer, Heidelberg (2009). https://doi.org/10.1007/978-3-642-04138-9_15
43. Reparaz, O., Balasch, J., Verbauwhede, I.: Dude, is my code constant time? In: Design, Automation & Test in Europe Conference & Exhibition, DATE 2017, Lausanne, Switzerland, 27–31 March 2017, pp. 1697–1702 (2017.) https://doi.org/10.23919/DATE.2017.7927267
44. Reparaz, O., et al.: CAPA: the spirit of beaver against physical attacks. In: Shacham, H., Boldyreva, A. (eds.) CRYPTO 2018. LNCS, vol. 10991, pp. 121–151. Springer, Cham (2018). https://doi.org/10.1007/978-3-319-96884-1_5
45. Cobham Gaisler Research. Leon-3 processor (2018). https://www.gaisler.com/index.php/products/processors/leon3
46. Rivière, L., Najm, Z., Rauzy, P., Danger, J.-L., Bringer, J., Sauvage, L.: High precision fault injections on the instruction cache of armv7-m architectures. In: IEEE International Symposium on Hardware Oriented Security and Trust, HOST 2015, Washington, DC, USA, 5–7 May 2015, pp. 62–67. IEEE Computer Society (2015). https://doi.org/10.1109/HST.2015.7140238
47. Schneider, T., Moradi, A.: Leakage assessment methodology. In: Güneysu, T., Handschuh, H. (eds.) CHES 2015. LNCS, vol. 9293, pp. 495–513. Springer, Heidelberg (2015). https://doi.org/10.1007/978-3-662-48324-4_25
48. Schneider, T., Moradi, A., Güneysu, T.: ParTI: towards combined hardware countermeasures against side-channel and fault-injection attacks. In: Proceedings of the ACM Workshop on Theory of Implementation Security, TIS@CCS 2016 Vienna, Austria, October 2016, pp. 39 (2016). https://doi.org/10.1145/2996366.2996427
49. Simon, T., et al.: Towards lightweight cryptographic primitives with built-in fault-detection. IACR Cryptol. ePrint Arch. **2018**, 729 (2018)
50. CORPORATE SPARC International, Inc., The SPARC Architecture Manual: Version 8. Prentice-Hall Inc, Upper Saddle River (1992). ISBN 0-13-825001-4
51. Tillich, S., Großschädl, J.: Power analysis resistant AES implementation with instruction set extensions. In: Paillier, P., Verbauwhede, I. (eds.) CHES 2007. LNCS, vol. 4727, pp. 303–319. Springer, Heidelberg (2007). https://doi.org/10.1007/978-3-540-74735-2_21

52. Yuce, B., Schaumont, P., Witteman, M.: Fault attacks on secure embedded software: threats, design, and evaluation. J. Hardw. Syst. Secur. **2**(2), 111–130 (2018). https://doi.org/10.1007/s41635-018-0038-1
53. Zussa, L., Dutertre, J.-M., Clédière, J., Tria, A.: Power supply glitch induced faults on FPGA: an in-depth analysis of the injection mechanism. In: 2013 IEEE 19th International On-Line Testing Symposium (IOLTS), Chania, Crete, Greece, 8–10 July 2013, pp. 110–115 (2013). https://doi.org/10.1109/IOLTS.2013.6604060

Processor Anchor to Increase the Robustness Against Fault Injection and Cyber Attacks

Jean-Luc Danger[1,2], Adrien Facon[1,3], Sylvain Guilley[1,2,3], Karine Heydemann[4], Ulrich Kühne[2], Abdelmalek Si Merabet[2], Michaël Timbert[1,2(✉)], and Baptiste Pecatte[1,5]

[1] Secure-IC S.A.S., Tour Montparnasse, 27th Floor, 75015 Paris, France
michael.timbert@secure-ic.com
[2] Télécom Paris, LTCI, 19 place Marguerite Perey, 91120 Palaiseau, France
[3] École Normale Supérieure, CNRS, PSL Research University, 75005 Paris, France
[4] LIP6, Sorbonne Université, 4 Place Jussieu, 75005 Paris, France
[5] DGA, 60 Boulevard du Général Martial Valin, 75015 Paris, France

Abstract. One major advance in software security would be to use robust processors which could assist the code developer to thwart both cyber and physical attacks. This paper presents a hardware-based solution which increases the security by checking the integrity of executed code on any microcontroller. Unlike other Control Flow Integrity (CFI) protections, this solution does not require modifications of the CPU pipeline, but relies on monitoring the interface between the processor and its instruction cache. The integrity of the execution flow and the instruction sequences (called Basic Blocks) is checked by hardware with precomputed metadata. Another module is dedicated to speed up the access to these metadata. This paper shows the effectiveness of the solution as the impact is as much as 21% in average on the execution time at the price of using memory space to store metadata along with the code.

Keywords: Control Flow Integrity · Fault injection · Control Flow Graph · Hardware protection · Cyber Escort Unit (CEU)

1 Introduction

Software implementations are prone to many kinds of attacks belonging to two main classes: cyber-attacks (or software) and physical attacks. The physical attacks on microcontrollers can be either passive (by observing leakages via side-channels analysis) or active (by fault injection). This paper addresses both fault injection attacks and software attacks. Protection against fault injection attacks is quite challenging to protect efficiently by software. Indeed, the classical manner to detect a fault is to run twice the function to check the integrity, hence decreasing the performance level by a factor of two.

© Springer Nature Switzerland AG 2021
G. M. Bertoni and F. Regazzoni (Eds.): COSADE 2020, LNCS 12244, pp. 254–274, 2021.
https://doi.org/10.1007/978-3-030-68773-1_12

The software attacks exploit bugs or wrong configurations in order to hijack the control flow. In practice, such cyber-attacks mainly operate in two distinct manners. Attacks such as Return-Oriented-Programming (ROP) consist in corrupting the stack such that it calls carefully picked pieces of code called gadgets, which altogether form the attack payload. ROP attacks are thus "code-based". The second type of cyber-attacks exploit contamination of data to force pointers to different locations. Such "data-based" attacks exploit improperly checked user-inputs, which can lead to control-flow contamination. In this article, we focus on "code-based" attacks, including their protection.

Control-flow integrity (CFI) refers to protections against control-flow hijacking and was introduced in Abadi's seminal paper [1]. The idea is to verify at run-time by a monitor process or by dedicated hardware that the correct control flow is respected. A common specification of the control flow is given by the static *control flow graph* (CFG) of the application, which can be determined at compile-time.

Since [1] was published many CFI implementation was proposed. There is two main approach to implement the CFI, software or hardware. Software CFI solutions are convenient mainly because they can be deployed on existing equipment. These solutions rely on instrumenting the software to add self verification or by using an external monitor to check the behavior of the monitored thread. The flexibility of the software solution is at the cost of performance slow down or to only ensure coarse grained CFI, like [2]. On the another hand, hardware solutions are generally proposed in academic papers and rely on hardware monitor to follow the execution of the processor. Or by using cryptographic primitive with core modification to ensure CFI and more. These hardware solution have generally less impact on processor performance but need modification of the internal of the processor, which is a very high price to pay in the industrial world, like SOFIA implementation [3].

In the recent years, many CFI approaches have been proposed. Software-only approaches that offer full CFI protection suffer from a high performance overhead [2]. Some software implementations focus only on specific protections in order to reduce this overhead.

Hardware-based solutions range from lightweight solutions – ensuring only some types of control transfer (such as a so-called *shadow stack*) or reducing the amount of reusable code by marking valid call/jump destinations – to solutions covering all control transfers that can be determined statically at compile-time, at link-time, or at load-time of the application [3,4]. Unfortunately, such approaches either offer coarse-grained protection or does not allow indirect jump or they require a significant modification of the CPU, which prevents them from being deployed in practice due to either the huge amount of work required for validating a modified processor or the use of off-the-shelf processor cores. This is why we target a *non-intrusive* solution that does not modify the CPU core.

Most CFI approaches assume that the code cannot be modified, due to the presence of widely used *data execution prevention* (DEP) protections. Such a protection is commonly present on high performance processors but rarely deployed on embedded platforms or micro-controllers. Furthermore, different threats may invalidate this assumption: There exist physical attacks able to perform fault injections that result in a modification of the executed code [5,6]. Since the discovery of the *RowHammer* attack [7], it is known that changes in write protected DRAM can even be induced by software. Hence, *code integrity* (CI) is also to be targeted in order to protect systems against a large body of attacks that disrupt the execution.

Another technical point generally not addressed by CFI implementation is how to handle interruptions. Interruption can happen at any time, and can be seen as a violation of the CFG from an external point of view. It is also necessary that the hardware implementation of CFI addresses the speculative execution or branch prediction. This adds another complexity level to the CFG verification as unused predicted instruction should not be checked by CFI.

In this paper, we present a hardware-based solution that combines CFI with CI, while being non-intrusive to the processor. The *code and control-flow integrity* (CCFI) checks are performed at runtime by a dedicated hardware module outside the processor core. The control flow information – referred to as *metadata* – is stored in a dedicated section in memory and is aligned with the instructions. This metadata is fetched by a cache named *CCFI-cache*. Whenever a new instruction is requested by the processor, the corresponding metadata is fetched transparently and in parallel, so as not to disrupt or slow down the execution flow. The *CCFI-checker* verifies the integrity of execution flow changes by checking the effective target addresses. Function calls and returns are protected by an integrated shadow stack. Additionally, we ensure code and metadata integrity by computing a signature based on the executed instructions and metadata fetched by validating it against a precomputed signature contained in the metadata.

The proposed CCFI-cache architecture has been implemented on a RISC-V [8] platform, without modifying the processor core. Our experiments show that the run-time overhead is acceptable for different benchmarks. The price to pay for this very flexible solution is a two-fold increase in instruction memory.

In summary, the contribution of this work is a novel hardware-based CFI scheme that:

- is non-intrusive, since the CPU core remains untouched,
- combines intra-procedural and inter-procedural CFI with CI,
- has low run-time overhead, and
- only requires very minor code modifications of the application code.

The rest of the paper is organized as follows: Sect. 2 presents the Control Flow Graph principle and present the concept of Control Flow Integrity. Sect. 3 lists the state of the art of hardware protection near CFI. Section 4 presents the hardware and the software part of our solution. Section 5 and 6 explain the adjustments set to the solution to work with processor using speculative execution and how metadata is modified to be able to protect interruption. Section 7 presents security guaranties achieved by the solution. Section 8 and 9 present detail of the implementation and the performance measurements.

2 Background

In this section, we introduce the basic notions and security guarantees in the context of Control-Flow integrity.

2.1 Control Flow Graph

At the level of the machine code, a program is composed of multiple functions which in turn can be decomposed into basic blocks. A *basic block* (BB) is a straight-line sequence of instructions with a unique entry point and a unique exit point, i.e. if the control flow enters a BB, it will execute all of its instructions in sequence until leaving the BB at the exit point. A control flow transfer can only take place at the last instruction. Each function can be represented as a *control-flow graph* (CFG), where each node corresponds to a BB, and edges represent the control transfers between the BBs. A whole program is composed of the CFG of each function linked by edges representing function calls and returns. It is common in compilation world to consider that a BB can contain a call to an function. In our case a call automatically set the end of the BB.

2.2 Control Flow Hijacking

There are multiple ways in which an attacker can take over the control of a machine. In many cases, buffer overflows – due to bad programming – offer an entry point for an attacker. They can be exploited to inject code and/or to compromise return addresses stored on the stack to divert the execution flow.

Executing injected code can be mitigated by Data Execution Prevention (DEP)/W^X which prevents written data to be executed. This protection can be circumvented by *code reuse attacks* that rely on (stubs of) existing functions in libraries, so-called *gadgets*. Known variants of this type of attacks are *return-oriented programming* (ROP), *jump-oriented programming* (JOP) or *call-oriented programming* (COP) [9]. As shown in [10], all such attacks rely on code pointer corruption. In this way, only legitimate code of the application is executed, but the CFG of the program is not respected anymore.

Another threat – invalidating DEP protections – are fault attacks, where memory contents are altered by physical means [5,6]. Using the *RowHammer* attack [7], a dynamic RAM cell can be changed by rapidly reading neighboring cells before a refresh. Its stealthiness makes this threat extremely dangerous: Even trusted firmware code with a digital signature can be corrupted when residing in RAM. Some examples of attacks enabled by such modifications are Shamir's bug attack [11] (e.g., on RSA) or Sbox tampering attacks [12] (e.g., on AES). Fault attacks are difficult to master, but can be used to change instructions, to manipulate access rights, to skip an instruction, or to directly change the current program counter, in some cases without violating the CFG.

2.3 Control Flow Integrity

To prevent control flow hijacking and fault attacks, it is necessary to ensure that control transfer instructions execute as expected, i.e. any control transfer originates from an address that corresponds to a control transfer instruction and targets a valid destination address for this specific instruction.

For direct jumps and conditional branches, the valid destinations can be determined at compile-time. Verifying the integrity of these control transfers boils down to checking that for each executed jump or branch, there is a corresponding edge in the function's CFG. We refer to this check as *intra-procedural CFI*.

A different treatment is needed for function calls and returns. Since common functions – such as `printf` – are called from many sites, just checking that the function returns to one of these call sites does not provide a reasonable protection against ROP attacks. Instead, the correct pairing of call and return addresses needs to be ensured. We refer to this as *inter-procedural CFI*.

It should be noted that indirect jumps and calls pose a special problem for CFI as the set of destination addresses can be significant. However, in many cases – such as a `switch` statement which has been compiled to an indirect jump – the set of target addresses is usually small and can often be determined at compile-time.

Otherwise, either manual code changes are necessary or these specific instructions must remain unprotected.

While these checks only consider control transfer instructions, it is necessary to ensure that *inside a BB*, all instructions are executed in-order, thereby preventing instruction skips. This verification, which is hard to implement in software, is called *intra-BB CFI*. Finally, *Code integrity* (CI) refers to verifying that all instructions have been executed *unaltered*.

In summary, a combined CFI and CI protection must ensure basic block integrity and verify both intra-procedural and inter-procedural control transfers.

3 Related Work

3.1 Threat Model

The threat model is as follow: we assume that the code is not executed as intended owing to the processor stepping on some bug or owing to physical alteration of code at rest or in memory.

3.2 Protection State of the Art

There exists a large body of research on protections against hardware and software attacks. Due to page limitation, we only present the most closely related work. For an overview on existing techniques, we refer the reader to the survey [10]. Table 1 summarizes the protection levels of related techniques, which will be briefly discussed in the following.

Table 1. Comparison of some of the most prominent protections

Protection	W⊕X	SOFIA [3]	Intel CET [13]	ARM PA	PICON [2]	HCODE [4]	PathArmor [14]	HCFI [15]	Our solution
a) Inter Procedural	✗	✓	✓	✓	✓	✗	✓	✓	✓
b) Intra Procedural	✗	✓	(✓)	✗	✓	✓	✗	✗	✓
c) Intra BB	✗	✓	✗	✗	✗	✓	✗	✗	✓
d) Code Integrity	✓	✓	✗	✗	✗	✓	✗	✗	✓
e) Non-intrusive	✗	✗	✗	✗	✓	✓	✓	✗	✓
f) Speculative Exec.	✓	(✓)	✓	✓	✓	✗	?	✓	✓
g) Interruption	✓	✗	✓	✓	✓	✗	?	(✓)	✓

A simple and effective protection against code injection is DEP, which is implemented in all modern general purpose CPU architectures. It allows to prevent the execution of memory segments that contain only data (such as the stack), making code injection difficult. It does however not protect against ROP and related attacks nor against hardware attacks.

In [3], de Clercq et al. present SOFIA, an architecture supporting software and control-flow integrity. The architecture has a two stage protection: Firstly, instructions are encrypted with a block cipher in a way that depends on the correct control flow, such that deviating from the CFG results in wrongly decrypted instructions. Secondly, groups of instructions are protected with a *Message Authentication Code* (MAC) to ensure code integrity and confidentiality. The proposed architecture achieves a protection level similar to our technique, while changes in the internal pipeline and the encryption and MAC computation make it both more intrusive and costly.

Intel's *Control-flow Enforcement Technology* (CET) [13] introduces a shadow stack, which stores return-addresses in addition to the normal stack. When a return instruction is encountered, the two addresses are compared and a security exception is raised in case of a mismatch.

While the shadow stack is a powerful solution for inter-procedural CFI, it does not provide any other guarantees. The second feature of CET, *Indirect Branch Tracking* provides new instructions to mark valid branch targets, which provides a rudimentary protection against ROP-style attacks. In [15], the authors present HCFI (*Hardware-enforced CFI*), which is a modified SPARC architecture. It combines a shadow stack with a CFI-dedicated extension of the SPARC instruction set. While the solution concentrates only on call/return instructions, it achieves an impressively low run-time overhead of only 1%.

ARM's *Pointer Authentication* is a very efficient way to enforce the validity of indirect branches. Using three new instructions, it can compute and verify a Pointer Authentication Code (PAC), which guarantees that the pointer can not be changed to malicious value while residing in memory. One can use it not only to secure return addresses but arbitrary function or data pointers too. The PAC is stored in the higher unused bits of the pointer's value, eliminating the need for additional memory and bus resources. The PAC is computed using the QARMA primitive which is lightweight and has a very low latency, typically inducing only a 0.5% to 1% run-time overhead.

PICON [2] is a purely software based solution, which is integrated into the LLVM compiler framework. The control flow policy is represented by a pushdown automaton, which is then used at runtime by a monitoring process to match the actual execution. PICON provides a robust and portable protection against ROP-style attacks, while it does not protect against hardware attacks and compromised binaries. A similar approach has been presented in [14]. Their solution – called PathArmor – consists in a kernel module that monitors the execution paths of user processes. Its goal is a strong but practical protection of inter-procedural control transfers. By analyzing paths (rather than just single edges) in the CFG, they achieve a context-sensitive CFI without resorting to a shadow stack. These purely software-based solutions can be considered complementary to our approach.

Overall, the originality of our approach (of brandname "Cyber Escort Unit") is a combined protection against cyber and hardware attacks, while being non-intrusive in contrast to other hardware-based solutions.

3.3   Limitation of Our Approach

Compared to state-of-the-art solutions, we have shown that our solution has the largest coverage against SOTA solution. But we do not detect:

- **Change on non-control-data:** In this scenario, the attacker changes non-control-data using software bug or using physical attack targeting memory or the processor. This class of attack is undetected because the data value are altered while respecting the CFG.
- **Correlated alteration on code and metadata:** In this sophisticated attack, the attacker is able to modify the code and at the same time modify metadata accordingly to respect rules of *CCFI-checker*.

4   Solution

In this section we present the architecture of our solution. The solution is divided in two part: hardware and software. First we present the hardware part by presenting the integration of the CCFI with an processor then detail the internal architecture of CCFI parts. In a second section we present the software part, we introduce metadata structure and toolchain modification to generate them. Section 5 present specificity needed in the architecture to be to protect processor with speculative execution. Section 6 present the modification introduced in the *CCFI-checker* and metadata to handle and protect interruptions.

Our goal is to provide a solution able to protect the CFG at the lowest level which is at the assembler instruction level. To do so our solution verify the CFG at three different level.

Inter Procedural: each call and return of function is verified.
Inter BB: the value of the PC is verified after each BB end. If the BB end with a jump instruction we check if the destination is on the CFG of the program.
Intra BB: In each BB, the continuity of PC values is guaranteed as well as the integrity of instruction executed.

Unlike the common definition of basic block in compilation where basic block can may contain call instruction to other function, in our definition of basic block, call instruction end a basic block like conditional jump.

4.1 Hardware

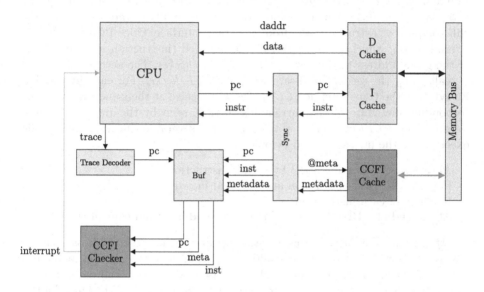

Fig. 1. Overview of the proposed architecture (Color figure online)

The platform architecture of the solution is shown in Fig. 1. We consider a simple platform based on a CPU core with separate instruction and data cache. CCFI is divided in five different module, two ensuring the CFI and CI: *CCFI-Checker* and *CCFI-Cache* (in red in Fig. 1). The other three are adaptation module which allow to adapt the solution to many different core.

The *CCFI-cache* fetches metadata which has been computed at compile-time, containing all control-flow related information. This information is used at runtime by the second module, the *CCFI-checker*. The *CCFI-cache* has the same characteristics (bit width, size, associativity, replacement policy, ...) as the instruction cache. For each basic block in the executed program, there is a corresponding block of metadata. Each block of metadata is perfectly aligned in memory to its corresponding Basic Block of code, with a constant offset. For each access to the instruction cache, a parallel access to the *CCFI-cache* will be issued. In this way, complex address calculations are avoided. Furthermore, the instruction cache and the CCFI-cache will always be consistent, i.e. either both a BB and its metadata are cached or none of them. *Sync* module on the Fig. 1 emit the correct @meta given pc from CPU. It also act as barrier to synchronise the response of the instruction cache and the *CCFI-Cache*. When instruction and metadata are ready it sends both plus the actual PC of the request into *Buf* module which is implemented as a circular buffer. The purpose of *Buf* is explained in details in Sect. 5 *Trace Decoder* module connected to the trace interface of the processor. It extract the PC of the current instruction executed. The need of this module come from the fact that trace interface is not standardized. Some processor give all information such as address of the instruction and instruction itself. Other give less information like if a conditional jump is taken or not. This is why for some processor we need the *Trace Decoder* which will compute or extract the PC from the trace interface. Once PC extracted, it is send to *Buf* which given PC return data stored (instruction and metadata) of the given address to the next module, *CCFI-checker*. The actual verification is realized by the second hardware module *CCFI-checker*. For each instruction issued from the trace interface *CCFI-Checker* receive at the same time the corresponding metadata of the current instruction, send by the *Buf*. With these informations *CCFI-checker* is able to perform several verification during the execution of the program listed below:

- Always start executing a BB by is first instruction
- Inside a BB, each instruction are executed in order.
- Integrity of each instruction
- At the end of a BB, the next address executed is a valid edge of the CFG.

At the end of each BB, it checks the validity of the target address by comparing it with the precomputed valid destination contained in the metadata, thereby ensuring intra-procedural CFI. In case of a function call or return, an integrated shadow stack is used to verify inter-procedural CFI. This shadow stack in embedded inside de CCFI-Checker and is not accessible from the main processor. Intra-BB consistency is ensured by a watch-dog counter that controls the number of executed instructions before a control transfer. Finally, code and metadata integrity is ensured by a precomputed signature that is compared to a hash value over the executed instructions computed at run-time. In case of any violation, an interrupt is raised. Internal details of the *CCFI-checker* are presented in Sect. 4.1.

CCFI Checker. This section present details of implementation of the CCFI-Checker module, describing internal register, state machine and behavior.

The CCFI-checker is composed of the following principal components:

- A set of registers to store the valid destination addresses,
- A shadow stack to store function return addresses,
- An instruction counter, and
- A signature register to compute a hash value of the executed instructions.

Table 2. Code and metadata correspondence

Instruction address	Instruction	Metadata address	Metadata	Metadata description
0x00000A88	lbu a5,0(s1)	0x40000A88	0xA0000004	StartBB | VD=1 | EndType=Branch | NInstr=4
0x00000A8C	nop	0x40000A8C	0x4000029A	ValidDest | Addr=0xA68
0x00000A90	nop	0x40000A90	0x400002A6	ValidDest | Addr=0xA98
0x00000A94	bnez a5,0xA68	0x40000A94	0xFC035B60	EndBB | Hash=0xFC035B60
0x00000A98	lw a5,-68(s0)	0x40000A98	0xA0000004	StartBB | VD=1 | EndType=Branch | NInstr=4
0x00000A9C	addi a5,a5,1	0x40000A9C	0x40000118	ValidDest | Addr=0x460
0x00000AA0	sw a5,-68(s0)	0x40000AA0	0x0	Empty
0x00000AA4	j 0x460	0x40000AA4	0xDAF87E5C	EndBB | Hash=0xDAF87E5C

A simplified view of the control state machine of the checker is shown in Fig. 2. The state machine basically follows the structure of the metadata record (cf Fig. 3). At the beginning of a BB (state **Start BB** in Fig. 2), it sets the instruction counter to the number of instructions in the BB ($count \leftarrow$ NInstr) and initializes the signature register ($sig \leftarrow H(0, instr, md)$). It also checks that the beginning of the BB is correctly labeled with StartBB metadata. The valid destination addresses are collected while traversing the BB (state **Store Dest**) and stored in the internal register bank[1]. If there are Empty entries in the metadata record, the state machine loops in the **Inside BB** state until the end of the BB. During the traversal, the signature register is updated after each instruction. For this purpose, a suitable hash digest function H needs to be chosen.

The actual verification takes place in the **End BB** state. There must be two conditions to triggers the transition into this state: an EndBB label is found and the instruction counter reaches zero. This ensures that both too long and too short BBs will be detected immediately. Normally, the end of the BB should coincide with the instruction counter reaching zero, which is verified in the **End BB** state. It is also checked if the hash value extracted from the EndBB entry equals the signature register. Depending of **EndType** at the start of the BB, In case of Call the return address is store in an internal shadow stack. In this case the destination of the call is validate against Valid Destination. In case of Return, the jump destination is validated using address stored in the shadow stack.

If there have been any valid address entries in the metadata, these are used to verify the effective target address. Note that this applies either for calls or local branches and jumps. The implementation of the internal register bank must ensure that the address comparison can be performed in parallel for all valid entries in one clock cycle, before the state machine continues to process the next BB.

In case any of the checks fails, an interrupt will be triggered, allowing the CPU to react to the attack immediately. Note that for simplicity reasons, Fig. 2 does not show the state transitions in the case of a security violation.

---

[1] Note that the size $k \geq 2$ of this register bank is an implementation parameter that can be chosen freely. Any BB with more than k valid targets can be split recursively until each BB has at most k valid successors.

4.2   Software

Metadata. Metadata contains informations depicting the Control Flow Graph of the program. These are organised in individual blocks of metadata each depicting the behavior of the execution of one Basic Block. Figure 3 show which

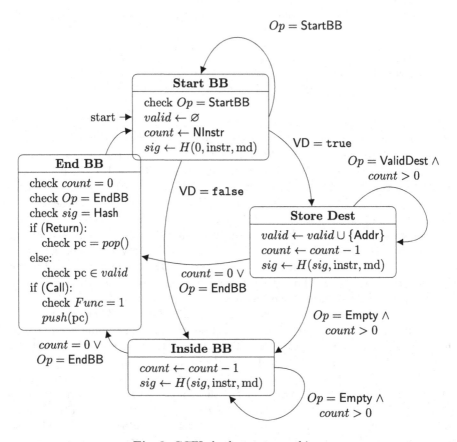

Fig. 2. CCFI-checker state machine

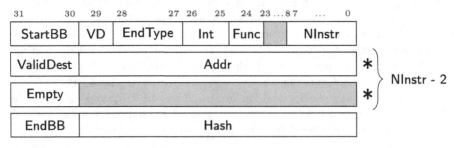

EndType ::= None | Call | Return
Int ::= Start Interruption | End Interruption

Fig. 3. Metadata format description

informations are stored in these block of metadata and how it is formatted in memory for a 32bits architecture.

These metadata contain for each basic block the list of valid destination accessible at the end of the BB. It also contains a signature of the basic block computed from its instructions as well as the number of instruction present in the BB and other informations depicted in this section.

Each block of metadata contains several entries. As show in Fig. 3, each entry type is identified by the two MSB, it can be one of the four following type: StartBB, ValidDest, Empty or EndBB.

StartBB entry is an header which describe the type and the content of the current BB. Func bit is use to mark the entry BB of functions.

NInstr field store the number of instruction of the BB. The two bits Int flag are present to mark the beginning or the end of interrupt routine, its usefulness is explain in Sect. 6. EndType flag is coded on two bits, it represent the type of control transfer at the end of the BB. There can be three type of end: None, Call or Return. None marks either a BB that will always be succeeded by the next consecutive BB – i.e. there is no branch or jump at the end – or one ending with a direct or indirect jump or branch instruction. Typically, blocks ending with a direct jump or call will have one valid destination and conditional branches two, while indirect control transfers can have an arbitrary number of valid destinations. Call is set when the BB end with a call, in this case return address will be store inside a stack called Shadow Stack. Return mark the end of the function, in this case the value stored previously in the Shadow Stack will be used to validate the address of return. To finish VD flag indicated if there is ValidDest entry in these metadata. If it is set to zero there will and must be no ValidDest entry following.

ValidDest entry are use to store one valid destination address allowed to be reached/executed at the end of the BB, corresponding to an allowed edge in the CFG. Addr store the absolute address of the destination right shifted of two bit. This allow to keep the possibility to store a 32bit address, but it is only possible on fixed length instruction architecture.

Empty entries are used when there is no ValidDest to store or when all Valid-Dest have been already stored in previous entries. It also serve to match the size of metadata to the number of instruction of the Basic Block, in order to keep the memory alignment consistent.

Finally, the end of the BB is marked by an EndBB entry, which additionally contains a hash signature computed over all the instructions of the BB. Both EndBB header and NInstr are used to determine the end of the BB. This redundancy allow to detect metadata corruption.

Note that in some cases destination of indirect branch or jump cannot be computed at the compilation, in this case the VD bit is unset and there will be no verification of the destination address at the end of this BB. Not setting VD bit can leave an opportunity to an attacker to exploit this to hijack control flow to jump somewhere else. But considering the fact that the CCFI-Checker will automatically ensure that the next instruction is the beginning of an BB by checking the presence of a Start BB header, the possibility are widely reduced. In case of a BB ending with a Call without valid destination stored in its metadata, the Func flag in the header of the next BB is check to ensure this call is not diverted to a gadget.

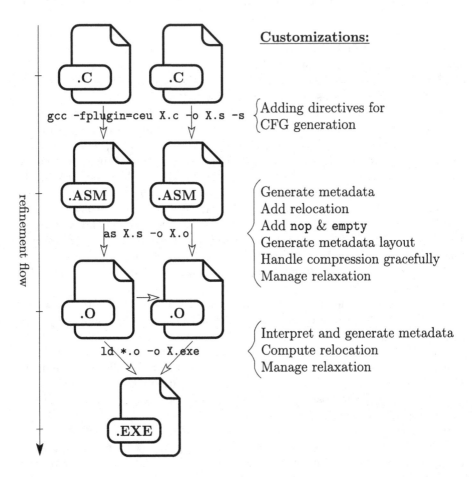

Fig. 4. Compilation flow

Toolchain. All metadata are computed during the compilation, by adding a plugin to GCC and modifying the linker. The creation of metadata is done in two phase during the assembly and the linkage. Figure 4 summarizes the compilation flow.

Firstly a GCC plugin is inserted to the compilation workflow to insert assembly directive in the assembly code generated to add metadata. For the compiler a BB can contain a call, this is not compatible with our approach. During this phase BB containing call are split up to be compatible with our solution.

When a BB is too small to contain all needed metadata a corresponding number of `nop` is added to extend it. This case happens generally when a BB is only one instruction long or when the end of the BB is a indirect jump with a lot of destination possible. At the end of this first phase memory space have been allocated to store metadata for each BB but there values are not yet set.

The second phase is done with the linker, when all relocation are done all `VD` in metadata can be filled. The signature `Hash` is also computed at this stage, after the relocation stage because the linker can modify some instruction like short jump and long jump.

5   Speculative Execution

Depending on the specific implementation of the CPU, there can be other situations that require adjustment of the solution. One such case is branch prediction and speculative execution, which leads to a mismatch between the *fetched* instructions and those that are effectively *executed*. Since the CFI-cache monitors the cache interface of the CPU, it needs to be aware of such features in order to correctly detect the destination of branches. This section describe how such feature is detected as an attack by a simple implementation and explain needed change on the `CCFI-Checker` to be able to protect processor using speculative execution. Section 8 explains how we have resolved this issue for the used RISC-V implementation.

Speculative execution is commonly used in modern processors, and even in some microcontrollers due to its benefits in term of performance improvement. From our CFI point of view speculative execution can be detected as CF violation since the processor actually begins to execute some instructions of the predicted jump destination. If the branch prediction appears to be incorrect, it will rollback all change induced by the speculative execution and jump to the right address. This behaviour is represented on Fig. 5, where the processor have predicted the that the branch will no be taken and execute speculatively the instruction at the address 133c. Prediction was wrong, and processor rollback and jump to address 1210. This impromptu jump is detected as violation of the CFG by the basic implementation presented in the previous Sect. 4. More advanced processor, in order to improve performance, can also have prefetch technique that make it impossible to follow the execution flow from instruction fetched.

To address this behaviour we have to make distinction between instruction fetched and instruction executed. Each instruction fetched is stored in a circular buffer along with its metadata. This circular buffer is as deep as needed to reproduce the latency of the pipeline between fetch stage and the stage of trace interface. For each fetched instruction by the processor, one line is stored in the `Buf` module. Each line contain the instruction, its address and the metadata associated. So when the trace interface output an address, this address is send to `Buf` module to select the corresponding line. By construction it is never possible for the processor to output an PC from the trace interface without having its corresponding metadata present in `Buf`. Once the line selected, `Buf`

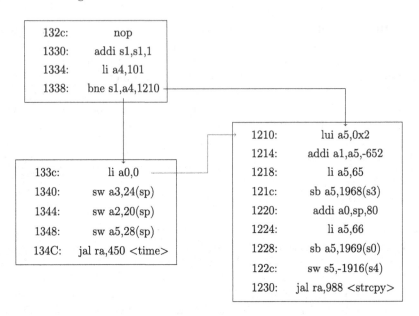

Fig. 5. Exemple of miss branch prediction

the related information (PC, instruction and metadata) to the CCFI-Checker. Doing so CCFI-Checker is able to follow the execution of the processor step by step without error even with an processor using speculative execution.

This solution for handling speculative execution is easily scalable on different sizes of processor pipeline and prediction mechanism by adjusting the maximum size of the cyclic buffer. This approach also has the advantage of not limiting the number of valid destination we can store for one BB.

6   Interruptions Management

In the literature of CFI, interruption and exception are rarely discussed due to the fact they can happen at any time and break the CFG of the current running program.

When an interruption occurs the processor determines the memory address of the interruption handler and jumps to it. There two major ways for a processor to execute the handler. The first one is to have static hard-coded address in the processor, regardless of the interruption the processor will execute the code at this address. The distinction of the type of interruption and the call of the right function handler is left to the programmer. The second method is to have a dedicated memory zone for an array of code pointer. For each one of interruption the processor fetches the corresponding code pointer and executes the pointed handler.

In all cases this results to jump directly on the interruption subroutine at any time and from anywhere. From outside of the processor this behaviour is viewed as a violation of the CFG. To be agnostic of the type of interruption our solution consists in adding an Int flag in the metadata header of the first and last BB of the handler function to detect start and end of handler function.

This allows to detect on-the-fly triggered interruptions, regardless of the processor implementation. Upon interruption, CCFI-checker detects the discontinuity of the control flow but metadata will indicate this is at the same time an Start BB end Int meaning this function is call because of an interruption. Figure 6 is a partial view of the CCFI-Checker FSM. From any state if the next instruction is the Start of a BB and also the beginning of an interruption procedure so CCFI-Checker save its current context of execution in an internal memory. The shadow stack is used to save the current PC. Once it is done the CCFI-Checker jumps to another FSM dedicated to follows the execution of the interruption handler (right FSM of the Fig. 6). This FSM is the same that the normal FSM except for the END BB where the flag ENDINT is checked. If the ENDINT flag is present in a ENDBB then the previous saved context is restored. Once the context have been restored CCFI-checker can continue verification of the BB where it has been interrupted.

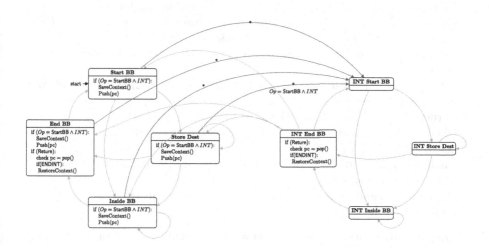

Fig. 6. Interruption FSM

This mechanism of saving and restoring context allows to be interrupted in the middle of a BB without triggering any false CFI alarms. In case of reentrancy a internal stack is used to save multiple contexts. Reentrance level is limited by the depth of this stack.

To overcome this limitation, next implementations this stack can trigger an alarm to flag when its full. This will allow the programmer to implement a routine to dump this stack in memory. This virtually allow to have unlimited interruption reentrancy. This technique will introduce a vulnerability in our design since data of the internal state of CCFI-checker will be exposed to the monitored program.

7   Attack Model and Security Guaranties

In this work, we address the protection of embedded platforms without DEP. We consider that the attacker is able to exploit programming bugs which allow buffer overflows. Such attacks can either modify the return address on the stack and/or inject malicious code. Note that this attack model is quite permissive in contrast to the classical CFI setting, which usually considers that code memory is immutable [1].

Additionally, we consider non-destructive physical attacks. This includes random changes in memory by either software-driven attacks (row-hammer) or hardware attacks (such as electromagnetic injection or glitches) leading to instruction skips. Since the successful demonstration of practical attacks such as row-hammer, physical attacks must be considered a realistic scenario, especially in the context of embedded and mobile devices.

Assuming that the main memory contains the code alongside with its correctly generated metadata, the CCFI-checker enables detection of the following attacks:

- Changing a return address on the stack (detected by shadow stack)
- Changing the target of a call, branch or jump outside of the static CFG (detected by destination address verification)
- Returning or jumping into the middle of a BB (detected by StartBB label check)
- Adding instructions at the end of a BB (detected by EndBB label check and instruction counter)
- Turning a branch into a nop (detected by signature check)
- Changing the pc to skip an instruction (detected by signature and instruction counter)
- Changing any instruction word in memory or up to the CPU interface (detected by signature)
- Deleting or manipulation metadata in any way inconsistent with the code (detected by signature)

One obvious limitation are physical attacks that directly affect the internal state of the CPU, such as the register state or skipping computations within the pipeline. Note that however such attacks will be caught if they directly or indirectly change the instruction address on the cache interface. We also do not consider advanced destructive attacks (such as focused ion beams) that could e.g. cut the interrupt line on the circuit die and thereby practically disable the CCFI-checker.

Furthermore, data only attacks that do not change the static control flow are not detected. An attacker that has full control over the memory could also forge metadata. A typical solution for this problem is to assume that the metadata (or the metadata and the code) reside in a protected read-only memory. Considering our proposed architecture in Fig. 1, such a solution can easily be implemented by having a completely separated memory bus for the CCFI-cache, thereby preventing any access to the metadata originating from the CPU.

Finally, special care needs to be taken for the treatment of the interrupt triggered by the CCFI-checker. Since interrupt mechanisms vary greatly on different target platforms, there is no system-independent solution. For instance, if interrupt target vectors are writable from user code, the interrupt service routine (ISR) itself needs to be protected. Any tampering with the ISR would then lead to a re-occurring violation, blocking the system in an infinite loop. In embedded platforms, watchdog counters are typically used to reset the system when it gets caught in a deadlock. Depending on the application, if recovery is considered less important, the interrupt line of the CCFI-checker can also be routed directly to the reset line, preventing any attack path via the ISR.

8 Implementation

In order to validate the CCFI architecture, we have implemented it on microcontroller platform based on industrial RISC-V processor [8]. The CPU core is a 5-stage pipeline processor with a two memory interfaces for accessing instructions and data (Harvard architecture). The platform uses a crossbar for memory access, with one ROM for code and metadata and one RAM for the execution.

As mentioned in Sect. 5, branch prediction can potentially pose a problem for the CCFI-checker, since the address seen on the memory interface (i.e. the program counter) may not coincide with the effective branch target address. The targeted processor have branch prediction and speculative execution capabilities. It also had a complex prefetch system which prevent us to directly use the PC from the instruction cache fetch to determine the execution flow of the program. We claim that the proposed architecture is suitable for complex prediction schemes, A detailed discussion of the required modifications is beyond the scope of this paper.

Table 2 shows an example with two BBs and the corresponding metadata. The upper BB ends with a conditional branch. There are two valid destinations stored in the metadata record. In the code, there are two additional nops, which are needed to match the size of the metadata, and – for the second one – to resolve the prefetch of the conditional branch.

Table 3. Hardware cost

Component	Cells	Cell area
CCFI-cache	2078	58728
CCFI-checker	8199	24812

Table 4. Hardware cost of caches

Component	Cells	Cell area	Net area	Total
Dcache ctrl	3808	63278	6194	69473
Icache ctrl	2114	58655	3511	62166

9   Performance

The interruption support has been tested in many benchmarks having predictable and random interruptions. Our implementation is able to save and restore context of execution without errors and significant impact on the performance level.

Tables 3 and 4 report the hardware cost of CCFI-cache module, CCFI-checker and caches on Intel's Cyclone V FPGA.

Table 5 presents the execution time in number of cycles when the code is running on a more powerful processor with speculative execution. Nominal run is the software without any modification and without the presence of CCFI. NOP only corresponds to the software modified by the toolchain but without the CCFI module. This test gives us the impact on performance when adding NOP to enlarge BB. CFI/NOP corresponds to the run fully protected by CCFI module. These benchmarks show an impact of 21% on average. Most of the overhead is due to the NOP added in the code to ensure metadata alignment (Table 6).

As we can see in Table 5 nearly all runtime overhead came from the added NOP. In total NOP added represent 25% of more code. Empty metadata represented the memory space allocated for metadatas not used. As we can see around 31% of memory space of metadata does not store useful information.

Table 5. Benchmark on A* processor in number of cycle

Run	Bubble sort	Drystone	AES
Nominal	1023533	420857	6342603
CFI/NOP	1289903	443337	8340834
NOP only	1289599	442644	8339606
Software overhead	25.99%	5.17%	31.48%
Hardware overhead	0.02%	0.15%	0.01%
Total overhead	26.02%	5.34%	31.50%

Table 6. Software modification

Run	Bubble Sort	Drystone	AES
Number total of instructions	989	1490	2944
Number total of BB	251	339	528
Number total of nop added	216	232	456
Number total of empty metadata	327	575	1127

10   Conclusion

Correct code execution is required by certification schemes, for instance the Protection Profile PP084. When the device is susceptible to fault injections and cyber-attacks, some hardware support helps maintain a tolerable throughput. However, modifying the processor would be error-prone since revalidation is costly, and legacy processors cannot be modified anyway.

We present in this paper a non-intrusive hardware-based protection able to effectively mitigate cyber and physical attacks. Our solution uses precomputed control flow information which are verified at runtime. The extracted information is stored as metadata in a dedicated code section. Profiling attest that this solution is very competitive regarding the hardware overhead and the performance penalty, which are minimal and affordable in most cases which make our technology practical and deployable.

The bottleneck of our solution is that the binary code shall be instrumented with some extract NOPs to match the size of basic blocks in respectively the code and the metadata. As a perspective, the compiler shall be involved actively to help produce basic blocks which are not too small, thereby reducing the overhead caused by such stuffing.

Acknowledgments. This work has been partly financed via TEAMPLAY, a project from European Union's Horizon 2020 research and innovation program, under grand agreement N° 779882 (https://teamplay-h2020.eu/). Also, this project has been transfered as "Cyber Escort Unit" protection to the "Securyzr" integrated Secure Element Product at Secure-IC S.A.S.

References

1. Abadi, M., Budiu, M., Erlingsson, Ú., Ligatti, J.: Control-flow integrity principles, implementations, and applications. ACM Trans. Inf. Syst. Secur. **13**(1) (2009)
2. Coudray, T., Fontaine, A., Chifflier, P.: PICON: control flow integrity on LLVM IR. In: Symposium sur la sécurité des technologies de l'information et des communications, Rennes, France, 3–5 June 2015 (2015)
3. de Clercq, R., et al.: SOFIA: software and control flow integrity architecture. In: Design, Automation & Test in Europe (DATE). Dresden, pp. 1172–1177 (2016)
4. Danger, J., Guilley, S., Porteboeuf, T., Praden, F., Timbert, M.: HCODE: hardware-enhanced real-time CFI. In: Proceedings of the 4th Program Protection and Reverse Engineering Workshop, PPREW@ACSAC, New Orleans (2014)
5. Karaklajić, D., Schmidt, J.M., Verbauwhede, I.: Hardware designer's guide to fault attacks. IEEE Trans. Very Large Scale Integration (VLSI) Syst. **21**(12), 2295–2306 (2013)
6. Werner, M., Wenger, E., Mangard, S.: Protecting the control flow of embedded processors against fault attacks. In: Smart Card Research and Advanced Applications (CARDIS), Bochum. Revised Selected Papers, pp. 161–176 (2015)
7. Kim, Y., et al.: Flipping bits in memory without accessing them: an experimental study of DRAM disturbance errors. SIGARCH Comput. Archit. News **42**(3), 361–372 (2014)

8. Asanović, K., Patterson, D.A.: Instruction sets should be free: the case for RISC-V. In: EECS Department, University of California, Berkeley, Technical report UCB/EECS-2014-146, August 2014
9. Carlini, N., Wagner, D.A.: ROP is still dangerous: breaking modern defenses. In: Proceedings of the 23rd USENIX Security Symposium, San Diego, pp. 385–399 (2014)
10. Szekeres, L., Payer, M., Wei, T., Sekar, R.: Eternal war in memory. IEEE Secur. Priv. **12**(3), 45–53 (2014)
11. Biham, E., Carmeli, Y., Shamir, A.: Bug attacks. In: Wagner, D. (ed.) CRYPTO 2008. LNCS, vol. 5157, pp. 221–240. Springer, Heidelberg (2008). https://doi.org/10.1007/978-3-540-85174-5_13
12. Aldaya, A.C., Sarmiento, A.C., Sánchez-Solano, S.: AES t-box tampering attack. J. Cryptographic Eng. **6**(1), 31–48 (2016). https://doi.org/10.1007/s13389-015-0103-4
13. Intel, Control-flow enforcement technology preview, revision 2.0, June 2017. https://software.intel.com/sites/default/files/managed/4d/2a/control-flow-enforcement-technology-preview.pdf
14. van der Veen, V., et al.: Practical context-sensitive CFI. In: Proceedings of the 22nd ACM SIGSAC Conference on Computer and Communications Security, Denver, 2015, pp. 927–940 (2015)
15. Christoulakis, N., Christou, G., Athanasopoulos, E., Ioannidis, S.: HCFI: hardware-enforced control-flow integrity. In: Proceedings of the Sixth ACM on Conference on Data and Application Security and Privacy, pp. 38–49. CODASPY, New Orleans (2016)

Integrating Side Channel Security in the FPGA Hardware Design Flow

Alessandro Barenghi$^{(\boxtimes)}$, Matteo Brevi, William Fornaciari ,
Gerardo Pelosi , and Davide Zoni

Department of Electronics Information and Bioengineering (DEIB),
Politecnico di Milano, Piazza Leonardo da Vinci, 32, 20133 Milan, Italy
{alessandro.barenghi,william.fornaciari,gerardo.pelosi,
davide.zoni}@polimi.it

Abstract. The design of digital systems has its mainstay in the electronic design automation flows which act as crucial instruments to reduce the effort to realize complex computing platforms. In this work, we investigate the possibility of integrating side channel security analyses within the existing FPGA design flow, to provide a feedback to the hardware designer in a prompt and effective way. To this end, we realize an analysis framework which detects side channel leakage on the power consumption side channel at two well established checkpoints in hardware design, i.e., post synthesis and post implementation. We report the results of the proposed framework when integrated within the commercial Xilinx Vivado design toolchain. As a case study, we employ an open source SoC running a software version of the AES block cipher and provide a taxonomy of the side channel information leakage. The reported results highlight how our approach is able to provide precise insights on the sources of information leakage in the hardware design at hand. In particular, we show that the results of the simulations at post synthesis and post implementation stages provide complementary sets of insights on the information leakage, which, thanks to our methodology, can be traced back to architectural components which are the culprits of the said leakage.

Keywords: Design automation and tools · FPGA design flow · Side channel analysis

1 Introduction

The Internet-of-Things (IoT) revolution is leading to a tightly connected world populated by millions of smart devices that, following the edge computing paradigm of externalize the processing onto leaf computing nodes, are collecting, computing, and exchanging data streams among them. The pervasiveness of these devices calls for technical means to provide privacy guarantees on the collected and processed data. This, in turn, points to the use of cryptographic building blocks to attain the said guarantees in a reliable and provable way.

© Springer Nature Switzerland AG 2021
G. M. Bertoni and F. Regazzoni (Eds.): COSADE 2020, LNCS 12244, pp. 275–290, 2021.
https://doi.org/10.1007/978-3-030-68773-1_13

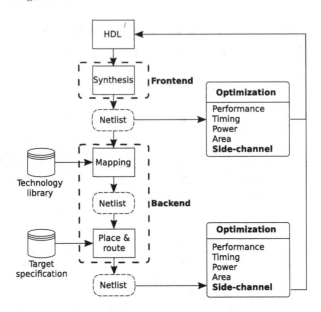

Fig. 1. Bird's-eye view of a hardware design flow enhanced with side channel analysis

A prominent attack avenue for IoT devices is represented by the so-called Side Channel Attacks (SCAs), which are able to recover the secret key of a cryptographic primitive exploiting the link between the data being processed by a computing device and an environmental parameter of the computing device such as its power consumption, electromagnetic emissions, or time taken to perform the computation. Indeed, a practical case of SCA being effective against a widely commercialized IoT device is the one of Philips smart bulbs [13], which were proven to be vulnerable to Correlation Power Analysis (CPA), in turn allowing an attacker to exploit them as a foothold to violate the security of home networks, or as a pawn to lead distributed denial of service attacks.

Digital design flows have been crucial for a long time in order to dominate the ever increasing complexity and diversity of designing digital devices with adequate performance and efficiency requirements, while fitting timing constraints imposed by the market. Indeed, they have arguably been one of the most significant enabling technologies for the IoT revolution, as they allowed to drastically shorten the time to design new, specialized computing platforms.

A natural consequence of the intrinsic need for security guarantees in IoT devices is the inclusion of security itself as a design metric. Such an inclusion points to the need of augmenting the current Electronic Design Automation (EDA) flows with stages that provide an evaluation of the security of the design itself with respect to a particular attack class. Concerning the security against SCAs, a pioneering effort in augmenting the traditional ASIC hardware design flow as well as in promoting the side channel security assessment as a standard design metric, was made in [12], where the authors propose a methodology to identify a side channel sensitive portion of a circuit and provide a secured re-implementation of the portion itself employing a SCA-resistant logic style. Another work in the direction of providing security-oriented features within a well established EDA flow is the one in [15], where the authors augment an EDA flow targeting ASIC with a set of modules performing side channel analyses based on the power consumption at the different stages of the EDA flow, i.e., synthesis, place-and-route, implementation. The work validates its approach on the design of an ASIC accelerator for the execution of the Advanced Encryption Standard (AES) block cipher with a 128-bit cryptographic key (a.k.a. AES-128), and on an SCA protected S-Box for the PRESENT cipher. A further motivating point for the need of integrating SCA awareness in the EDA toolchain is represented by the increasing complexity of the CPUs employed in IoT platforms, leading to a side channel information leakage which is tightly coupled with the microarchitectural features of the CPU itself [1–6,18].

Contributions. In this work, we tackle the augmentation of an industry-grade FPGA design flow with a software-only analysis of the side channel vulnerability of a design. Our intent is to reduce the delay in the feedback loop to the designer when it comes to the understanding of whether or not a given design may be vulnerable to power-consumption-based SCAs. Our objective is to augment the FPGA design flow, as depicted in Fig. 1 with side channel security analyses after the synthesis stage, providing a preliminary analysis, and after the entire backend of the EDA flow has been run, obtaining a more close-to-deployment analysis. As a case-study, we employ a full System-On-Chip (SoC) based on an implementation of the open OpenRISC Instruction Set Architecture (ISA), which is analyzed when running a software implementation of AES-128. Our experimental validation highlights the advantages of performing side channel analyses in both stages, as some of the leaking points detected by each one of them are not observable by the other. Moreover, our analysis framework allows the designer to trace back the leakage to the microarchitectural components that are the source of the said leakage, helping him to effectively remove potential security issues.

The rest of this manuscript is organized as follows. The proposed enhanced FPGA design flow to support side channel vulnerability analyses is discussed in Sect. 2, considering the augmentation of the widely adopted commercial Xilinx Vivado toolchain. Section 3 presents a taxonomy of the side channel leakage detected, employing as a statistical instrument a *specific t-test* [8] to detect it. Conclusions and directions for future investigations are drawn in Sect. 4.

2   Augmenting the Xilinx Vivado FPGA Design Flow

In this section, we detail the augmentation to the hardware design flow to support the SCA vulnerability analysis considering the power consumption side channel. The proposed augmentation of the design flow is depicted in Fig. 2, and stems from the typical two stages approach of EDA tools, represented by clear boxes in the figure. The typical EDA design flow is traditionally split in a set of stages

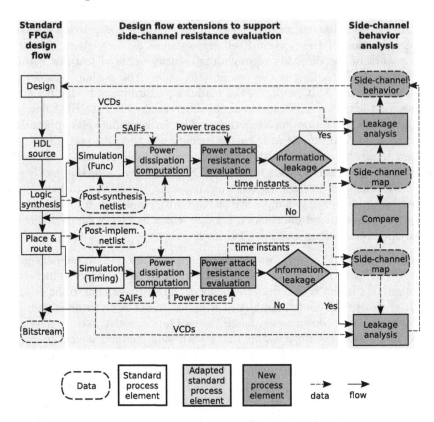

Fig. 2. Proposed SCA-aware design flow for FPGA targets. Newly added elements are depicted as orange blocks, while existing enhanced elements are depicted in yellow (Color figure online)

which translate a high-level Hardware Definition Language (HDL) description of the design into a low-level technology independent description. This description, which is in the form of a *netlist*, i.e., a set of elementary components such as Boolean gates and muxes, is used to run a first pass of functional simulations, which are able to detect mismatches between the desired design behavior and the actual one pertaining to incorrectly computed values. The netlist representation does not yet take into account the actual components of the target platform which will be realizing the functionalities of the elementary components. The step following the logic synthesis are the ones of the design implementation and they take the gate-level netlist and map its components onto the ones available on the target platform (in the FPGA design flow case) or onto the ones available with the provided technology library (in an ASIC design flow). After performing the mapping onto the platform components, the resulting set of design parts is placed onto the available resources and the inter-component connections are routed. The outcome of this step is ready to be deployed onto the target FPGA, after a semantic preserving translation from a post place-and-route netlist onto a bitstream file. The post place-and-route netlist, which is output by the implementation passes, can be employed to perform accurate simulations of the design at hand, as it takes into account the actual components which will be implementing it, together with the signal propagation delays induced by the routed interconnections. We note that the post implementation synthesis represents the most accurate netlist in terms of timing, area and power characteristics, while the post synthesis one provides only an estimates of such metrics, allowing only an initial coarse grained evaluation of the said metrics.

We augmented the FPGA design flow by adding the analysis to detect the side channel leakage after both the logic synthesis stage, and the implementation stage (see *Simulation (func)* and *Simulation (timing)* blocks in Fig. 2). While this choice may appear counter-intuitive, as the simulations at the post implementation stage take into account a more accurate circuit model, our findings (reported in Sect. 3) show that complementary insights are obtained from pre and post place-and-route results.

We follow the well established convention of simulating the design at a functional level on the post synthesis netlist, thus obtaining a corresponding Value Change Dump (VCD) file which represents the switching activity of an ideal circuit where no signal propagation delays in the wirings are considered. Similarly, following a well established best practice, we perform a complete timing simulation exploiting the information coming from the place-and-route stages on the post implementation netlist.

Any FPGA design flow includes a power consumption estimation stage, which aims at providing to the designer a reasonable estimate of the expected energy requirements of the circuit (see *Power dissipation computation* blocks in Fig. 2. Such a power estimation requires as an input the Switching Activity Interchange File (SAIF) file, together with the netlist of the design to be simulated. Currently, the FPGA design flow provided by Xilinx, which is the one we are augmenting, only yields the average power consumption estimate coming from the switching activity described in the entire SAIF. While this is sufficient to obtain a reasonable estimate of the power consumption for functional purposes, a single-valued average estimate of the behavior of the circuit during the execution of an entire cryptographic primitive does not provide enough time resolution to assess the source of a potential side channel leakage.

To this end, we enhanced the power estimation stage, realizing an automated framework to slice time-wise the SAIF representation of the switching activity of the circuit executing the entire cryptographic primitive into arbitrarily small portions. Our framework exploits the availability of the VCD file to perform a slicing which is synchronous with the clock signal, allowing to obtain a sequence of SAIF files including the switching activity of the target design during a time interval of a single clock cycle, or a portion of a clock cycle. The sequence of obtained SAIF files is then fed to the Xilinx `power report` tool, which derives the power consumption of each one of them. Recombining in the appropriate chronological order the obtained power estimates, we build our simulated power traces. We chose a time interval of half a clock cycle in our experimentation, i.e., two simulated power samples are collected for each simulated clock cycle.

Starting once the synthetic power traces have been generated by the power dissipation computation blocks, we realized the power consumption side channel evaluation stage of the flow which is in charge of assessing the information leakage of the design (see *Power attack resistance evaluation* and *Information leakage* blocks in Fig. 2). To this end, several statistical tests have been suggested in the public literature, ranging from performing an actual side channel attack, to leakage model agnostic tests [7,8].

Since our aim is to be able to provide meaningful suggestions to the designer on which component may be the cause of an information leakage in a given time instant, we chose to employ the *specific t-test*, as proposed in the same work as its *non-specific* variant [8]. Our choice of the *t*-test is mutuated by the absence of noise in the simulated environment, which allows to employ such a test without implicit assumptions on the distribution of the noise [16]. The specific *t*-test partitions in two sets the power traces obtained from the repeated execution of the cipher primitive at hand with a fixed value of the cryptographic key and different, randomly chosen input plaintexts (encryption primitive) or ciphertexts, (decryption primitive). The partitioning of the traces is driven by the value of an intermediate variable in the computation of the primitive itself (e.g..., a bit being asserted or not in the inner state of a block cipher). Once the partition is completed, a statistical *t*-test (hence the name) is employed to compare the average power consumption over each one of the two trace sets, analyzing one time instant at a time. This results in the computation of as many *t* statistics as the time instants in the simulated power traces, which are then evaluated to affirm or reject the null hypothesis that the average power consumptions of the traces in the two sets are the same in a given time instant. We note that, while a high value of a *t* statistic computed for a given time instant points to a very likely difference in the behavior of the design being caused by a data dependent event, this may not directly lead to an exploitable leakage [9], namely due to false positives such as the ones highlighted in [18]. We note that the proposed design flow can be easily configured to apply any other evaluation metric different from the statistical test chosen in this work.

The *Leakage analysis* processing block (on the right-hand pane of Fig. 2) aggregates all the generated information to deliver the side channel behavior of the circuit under investigation. In particular, we pair the results of the *t*-test with the data available from the simulation VCD. Our leakage analysis stage scans the logical transitions contained in the VCD file, in the time intervals corresponding to the detection of a possible leakage by the specific *t*-test. The *leakage analysis* stage collects a list of all the signals where a logic transition matches the partitioning criterion of the *t*-test and traces back to the signals the potential leakage, exploiting the information contained in the netlist corresponding to the appropriate EDA flow stage (i.e., the Netlist at post synthesis or post implementation).

The final result of the analysis provides the designer with a side-by-side signal waveform and *t*-test result view, allowing the designer to audit and, if needed, amend the design on the side channel information leaking components.

Table 1. Taxonomy of highlighted side channel information leakage. For each identified information leakage type we associated its observability in the two considered hardware design flow stages, i.e., post synthesis and post implementation, and one snapshot reporting an instance of it

Scenario	Leakage detected		Figure no.
	Post synthesis	Post implementation	
Spreading signals	✓	✓	3
Time shift	✓	✓	4
Zero variance (post impl.)	✓		5
Signal domination	✓		6
Zero variance (post synt.)		✓	7
Signal isolation		✓	8

3 Experimental Validation

To validate our proposed augmentation of the FPGA design flow, we pick as our case study the OpenRISC Platform System on Chip (ORPSoC) [10], which implements the OpenRISC 1000 architectural specification. The ORPSoC features a single-issue, in-order OpenRISC 1000 CPU with a 5 stages pipeline, and a main memory module connected to it via a Wishbone compliant bus. We synthesized the ORPSoC targeting a clock frequency of 50 MHz, and employing a Xilinx Artix 7 XC7A200 device as our target platform. We employed the Vivado 2017.4 Xilinx toolchain to perform the synthesis and implementation, while obtaining the switching activity files with Xilinx XSim 2017.4.

The synthesized SoC is running a software implementation of the Advanced Encryption Standard (AES) symmetric block cipher, employing its variant with a 128-bit key. The software is obtained compiling a standard-abiding, memory optimized (S-Box) implementation written in C. We computed the power traces corresponding to 700 AES executions on independent, uniformly drawn, random plaintexts while keeping a fixed secret key. The overall data collection took 45 days on 4 servers equipped with legacy Intel Xeon E5620 processors (launched on 2010) clocked at 2.40 GHz with 32 GiB of DDR3. The significant computation time required is due to the need of restarting the *Vivado Report Power* tool each time a power estimate for a SAIF containing the switching activity of half a clock cycle must be computed. While this computational bottleneck is currently significant, we still chose to employ the Xilinx Power Report tool as it is currently the one containing the most reliable characterization of the Xilinx FPGA target chips. We were able to determine that this current computational bottleneck can be removed, observing how the computation time is spent by Xilinx Power Report, via the consolidated Linux time accounting subsytem. Indeed, we found out that the actual userspace computation load is less than 0.1% of the actual running time (i.e., $\approx$1 h), while the 99.9% of the wall-clock time is taken by reading the input files and by the operating system overhead.

A. Barenghi et al.

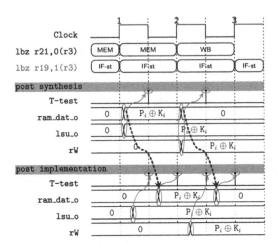

Fig. 3. Spreading signals information leakage scenario reported in Table 1

We collected two energy measurements per clock cycle, i.e., at the first and second half of the target clock period, as the minimum number of samples to allow the detection of the effects of the network delays introduced in the map and place-and-route stages on the power consumption, while keeping the computational requirements for the data collection within acceptable range.

In our leakage assessment, we present the result of running a specific t-test with the parameters suggested in [8]. In particular, we employed the value of the first bit of the AES cipher state after the first AddRoundKey primitive is computed as the labeling criterion to partition the collected traces into two sets. We computed the value of the t statistic point-wise in time for the two set of traces and considered that the t test rejects the null hypothesis, stating that the means of the power consumptions of the two sets are not distinguishable if the value of the t-statistic is below 4.5 as suggested in [8]. This, in turn, implies that, if the t-test rejects the null hypothesis, there is no detectable side channel leakage with this amount of measurements with a confidence of 99.99%.

We report in Table 1 the complete taxonomy of the side channel information leakage emerged from the evaluation of our case study platform, classified according to whether post synthesis or post implementation power traces exhibit a leakage or not. For each identified information leakage scenario, the corresponding figure indexed in Table 1 details a representative example of the class as obtained as the output of our tool. For the sake of clarity, we will represent the outcome of the t-test instead of the t-statistic itself, simply depicting whether, for a given time instant, the t-test detects potential side channel leakage or not.

Spreading Signals. The first scenario we consider is the one where information leakage is detected both on post synthesis traces and post implementation traces, while the time instants where the leakage is detected on post synthesis traces are a subset of the ones where a leakage is also detected on post

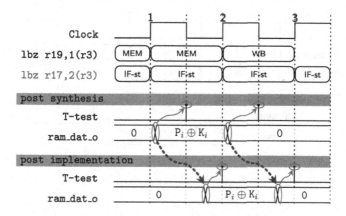

Fig. 4. Time shift information leakage scenario reported in Table 1

implementation traces. A practical case of such scenario, reported in Fig. 3, allows us to provide further insight on the reasons behind such a difference. First of all, our framework traced back the potential leakage origin to a transition on the ram_dat_o, lsu_dat_o signals (two signals involving the storage of the result of the AddRoundKey primitive by the load-store unit). While the logic transitions take place exactly on the raising clock edge in post synthesis, leading to a leakage in the corresponding (first) half of the clock cycle, the post implementation simulation shows delayed transitions causing leakage in both clock cycle halves. This fact confirms that common intuition that taking into account more accurately the network delays will result in a more accurate picture of the exact time instants where the information leakage takes place.

Time Shift. The Time Shift scenario emerges whenever the *t*-test reports that the possible information leakage in the post implementation analysis is shifted forward in time, with respect to the one detected by the post synthesis analysis. Analogously to the case of Spreading Signals, we are able to ascribe this fact to the more accurate evaluation of the network delays allowed by the information contained in the post implementation netlist. We report an instance of such a scenario in Fig. 4, where a transition from the sensitive value represented by the output of the AddRoundKey primitive to zero, taking place on the load-data signal of the load-store unit, gives rise to a leakage which is time-locked to the first half of the clock cycle in post synthesis simulations, while it appears in the second half of the clock cycle when post implementation traces are considered.

Zero Variance (Post Impl.). The Zero variance in post implementation traces is an interesting scenario where we observed a lack of leakage being detected on post implementation traces, while the post synthesis analysis shows distinct leakage. An instance of such a scenario is reported in Fig. 5, where the leakage is caused by the sensitive value transiting on a forwarding path for the first operand. Indeed, carrying out the side channel leakage analysis on post synthesis traces shows the expected information leakage in the first half of the clock

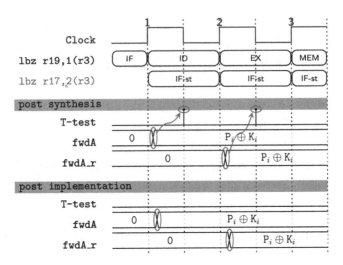

Fig. 5. Zero variance (on post implementation traces) scenario as in Table 1

cycle where the aforementioned transitions take place. By contrast, no leakage is detected on post implementation traces and the variance of the post implementation power consumption traces in the instant where leakage is detected on the post synthesis ones is null. While we cannot ascertain the reason for such a behaviour of the Xilinx `power report` output, we posit as a reasonable justification the fact that the signal routing optimization performed in the place-and-route stage may bring the power consumption of some signal drivers below the minimum power simulation resolution. Indeed, such a fact would result in a net cancellation of the data dependent contribution to the overall power consumption, and the consequent zero variance in the post implementation traces. This highlights the counter-intuitive fact that, despite the higher accuracy of the design model provided by a post implementation netlist, some information leakage may be missed if the analysis is not performed on post synthesis traces too.

Signal Domination. Another scenario where an information leakage is detected only on post synthesis traces, but not on post implementation traces is the Signal Domination one. Differently from the Zero variance (on post implementation traces) scenario, in this case the variance of the post implementation simulated traces is not null, however, no leakage is detected. Figure 6, reports an instance of this scenario where a transition from zero to the sensitive value constituted by one byte of the output of the `AddRoundKey` primitive is taking place on the `dbus_o` signal, while another transition, from a different output byte of the same primitive to zero is taking place on the `lsu_o` signal. In the post synthesis power traces, no interference between the two transitions takes place, as the first one concludes before the raising edge of the clock signal at the beginning of the second clock cycle, giving rise to a distinguishable leakage by the t-test.

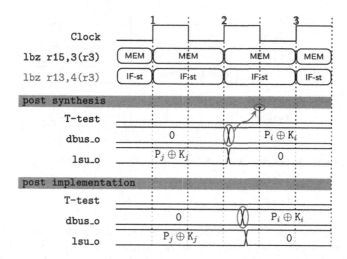

Fig. 6. Signal domination example for each one of the side channel information leakage classes identified in Table 1. We attack the i-th bit of the secret key. P_i, P_j are two bits of the plaintext, while K_i and K_j are two bits of the secret key

Note that, in this case, no relation exists between the values of the transition taking place on lsu_o and the partitioning of the traces into two sets exists, as the said partitioning depends on the values transiting on dbus_o. Analyzing the post implementation traces we have that the t-test fails to detect any leakage, despite the transition on dbus_o is taking place within the same clock cycle. We ascribe this effect to the delayed transition happening on lsu_o, which is likely to be the dominant factor in the power consumption in the first half of the second clock cycle. Indeed, such a dominant power consumption caused by an unrelated value effectively adds a significant amount of noise to an otherwise perfectly distinguishable information leaking power consumption. Therefore, the signal domination scenario highlights another significant case where the post synthesis traces offer a clearer picture of the potential information leakage of the design with respect to a post implementation analysis.

We note that, in this scenario, a higher number of simulated traces may allow the t-test to overcome the empasse caused by the additional noise.

Zero Variance (in Post Synthesis Traces). This scenario represent the dual scenario with respect to the Zero variance (in post implementation traces). In particular, it considers the case where a leakage is detected only in the post implementation traces, where it is not detected in the corresponding time instants in the post synthesis ones, which have zero variance in the said time instant. While arguably more expectable than the Zero variance (in post implementation traces), as the design model provided by the post implementation netlist is closer to the actual design, this scenario also highlight the need to analyze the potential information leakage both post synthesis and post implementation. We report in Fig. 7, an instance of such a scenario, which is reported by our

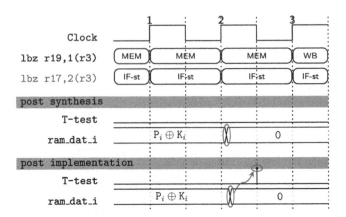

Fig. 7. Zero variance (post synt.) example for each one of the side channel information leakage classes identified in Table 1. We attack the i-th of the secret key and P_i, P_j are two bits of the plaintext while K_i and K_j are two bits of the secret key

framework when the sensitive value is transiting on the data line of the memory bus, i.e., ram_dat_i. Indeed, in this case, it is quite likely that the post synthesis model of the circuit, which neglects the effects on the power dissipation caused by the capacity load of long signal lines underestimates the power required to charge the memory bus. By contrast, the post implementation traces, leveraging the more accurate description of the memory bus connections, provide a more fitting report on the power consumption, which allows the t test to successfully detect the information leakage.

Signal Isolation. The signal isolation scenario, where information leakage is detected only in the analysis of post implementation traces, is essentially the dual case of the signal domination scenario. An occurrence of this scenario is reported in Fig. 8, where the output signals of two different bytes of the data bus carrying the second operand into the ALU toggle at the same moment in the post synthesis simulation, having their value change from zero to a byte of the output of the AddRoundKey primitive. While the byte contained in rB[i] is the one actually related to the t-test partitioning criterion, the one in rB[j] is unrelated to the said criterion. As a result, the post synthesis power simulation does not yield a detectable leakage, as the relevant power consumption caused by the transition on rB[i] is shadowed by the unrelated, and at least equally strong power consumption due to the transition of rB[j]. Analyzing the result of the post implementation power simulation we have that, thanks to the more accurate estimate of the network delays, the aforementioned signal transitions take place in slightly different time instants, with the information leaking one taking place in the second half of the clock cycle. As a consequence, the information leaking power consumption is isolated from the non relevant one. This in turn results in the t-test detecting leakage in the corresponding time interval.

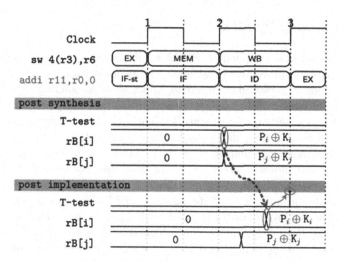

Fig. 8. Signal isolation example for each one of the side channel information leakage classes identified in Table 1. We attack the i-th of the secret key and P_i, P_j are two bits of the plaintext while K_i and K_j are two bits of the secret key

We note that, similarly to the signal domination scenario, a higher number of power consumption traces may lead to a detection of the information leakage during the post synthesis analysis.

Summary. Summing up the results obtained analyzing in detail the taxonomy of information leakage detected by our approach, we can state the following:

(1) performing a post implementation simulation effectively provides a higher timing accuracy to the side channel leakage detection. The Spreading Signals and Time Shift scenarios exemplify the effects of such an increased precision allowing to detect sequences of leakages.

(2) Performing post synthesis side channel analysis yields complementary insights to the ones provided by post implementation analysis. Indeed the Signal Domination scenario highlights a potential side channel leakage which may be visible or hidden depending on the device targeted for implementation. This in turn may lead a designer, relying only on post implementation simulations, to ship an IP block that indeed may exhibit a side channel leakage when implemented on a different target.

(3) Performing post implementation simulations is still advised as they may highlight, as expected, side channel leakages which can only be modeled effectively with accurate timing information on the implemented design.

(4) The current resolution of the power simulation tools in the FPGA design flows may not be sufficient to highlight all the information leakages via power consumption, as shown in the Zero variance scenarios.

4   Concluding Remarks

This work presented an augmented FPGA hardware design flow to assess power-based side channel information leakages. The proposed framework is currently built on the widely employed commercial Xilinx Vivado toolchain. Starting from the complete OpenRISC SoC design, running a software implementation of the AES-128 block cipher as representative use-case, our investigation provides a complete taxonomy of the side channel information leakage scenarios which are made evident from a simulation-time side channel evaluation. Our toolchain augmentation also allows us to trace back the plausible sources of the side channel information leakage, when employing a *specific t*-test on an intermediate value of the algorithm, or any intermediate value specific leakage assessment test. This feature is achieved through an automated analysis of the value logical transitions taking place at the same time as the information leakage. The results of our automated analysis highlight that it is worthwhile to perform a simulated power analysis both at the post synthesis level (to detect issues with the IP design which may not be evident unless implemented on a different target device) and at the post implementation level (to benefit from the network delay modeling).

Currently, the computational requirements for our analysis are significant, mainly due to the significant overheads (estimated to be greater than three orders of magnitude), imposed by the current lack of a per-cycle power estimation in the existing EDA flows for FPGA. Since we were able to validate the report of consistent results with the current Xilinx Vivado toolchain, showcasing the effectiveness of the augmented toolchain in detecting side channel leakage, we consider the removal of such a computational bottleneck as a pressing need for furher developments. Indeed, we maintain that such a performance bottleneck is removable, as most of the time (>99.9%) in our current power consumption simulations is spent in bootstrapping a fresh instance of the power simulator for each time interval, corresponding to a bootstrap per each sample of a trace. We note that, as viable alternative to the industry-dependent integration of a per-cycle power estimation in Xilinx Vivado, the availability of effective power estimation models for open EDA flows such as Symbiflow and Yosys [11,14,17] would allow them to output the desired power simulations in significantly reduced timeframes. Indeed, such an evolution would further foster a fully auditable design and side channel security analysis for FPGA targets.

Finally, we foresee the validation of the leakage detection made by our augmented toolchain through comparison with a physical target as an interesting avenue to be pursued. Indeed, while we confirmed the existence of a potential side channel leakage analyzing the values of the logic transitions, practically gauging the extent of the leaked information and its measurability would allow a further confirmation of the effectiveness of the methodology itself.

References

1. Agosta, G., Barenghi, A., Pelosi, G.: Compiler-based techniques to secure cryptographic embedded software against side channel attacks. IEEE Trans. CAD Integr. Circ. Syst. **39**(8), 1550–1554 (2020). https://doi.org/10.1109/TCAD.2019.2912924

2. Agosta, G., Barenghi, A., Pelosi, G., Scandale, M.: A multiple equivalent execution trace approach to secure cryptographic embedded software. In: 2014 The 51st Annual Design Automation Conference, DAC 2014, San Francisco, CA, USA, 1–5 June 2014, pp. 210:1–210:6. ACM (2014). https://doi.org/10.1145/2593069. 2593073

3. Agosta, G., Barenghi, A., Pelosi, G., Scandale, M.: The MEET approach: securing cryptographic embedded software against side channel Attacks. IEEE Trans. CAD Integr. Circ. Syst. **34**(8), 1320–1333 (2015). https://doi.org/10.1109/TCAD.2015. 2430320

4. Barenghi, A., Fornaciari, W., Pelosi, G., Zoni, D.: Scramble suit: a profile differentiation countermeasure to prevent template attacks. IEEE Trans. CAD Integr. Circ. Syst. **39**(9), 1778–1791 (2020). https://doi.org/10.1109/TCAD.2019.2926389

5. Barenghi, A., Pelosi, G.: Side-channel security of superscalar CPUs: evaluating the impact of micro-architectural features. In: Proceedings of the 55th Annual Design Automation Conference, DAC 2018, San Francisco, CA, USA, 24–29 June 2018, pp. 120:1–120:6. ACM (2018). https://doi.org/10.1145/3195970.3196112

6. Barenghi, A., Pelosi, G., Teglia, Y.: Information leakage discovery techniques to enhance secure chip design. In: Ardagna, C.A., Zhou, J. (eds.) WISTP 2011. LNCS, vol. 6633, pp. 128–143. Springer, Heidelberg (2011). https://doi.org/10.1007/978-3-642-21040-2_9

7. Batina, L., Gierlichs, B., Prouff, E., Rivain, M., Standaert, F.-X., Veyrat-Charvillon, N.: Mutual information analysis: a comprehensive study. J. Cryptol. **24**(2), 269–291 (2010). https://doi.org/10.1007/s00145-010-9084-8

8. Becker, G.C., et al.: Test vector leakage assessment (TVLA) methodology in practice. In: International Cryptographic Module Conference, vol. 1001 (2013)

9. Coron, J., Naccache, D., Kocher, P.C.: Statistics and secret leakage. ACM Trans. Embed. Comput. Syst. **3**(3), 492–508 (2004). https://doi.org/10.1145/1015047. 1015050

10. Jullien, F., et al.: Open RISC Platform SoC (ORPSoC) Version 3 (2018). https://github.com/openrisc

11. Krieg, C., Wolf, C., Jantsch, A.: Malicious LUT: a stealthy FPGA trojan injected and triggered by the design flow. In: Liu, F. (ed.) Proceedings of the 35th International Conference on Computer-Aided Design, ICCAD 2016, Austin, TX, USA, 7–10 November 2016, p. 43. ACM (2016). https://doi.org/10.1145/2966986.2967054

12. Regazzoni, F., et al.: A design flow and evaluation framework for DPA-resistant instruction set extensions. In: Clavier, C., Gaj, K. (eds.) CHES 2009. LNCS, vol. 5747, pp. 205–219. Springer, Heidelberg (2009). https://doi.org/10.1007/978-3-642-04138-9_15

13. Ronen, E., Shamir, A., Weingarten, A., O'Flynn, C.: IoT goes nuclear: creating a ZigBee chain reaction. IEEE Secur. Priv. **16**(1), 54–62 (2018). https://doi.org/10. 1109/MSP.2018.1331033

14. Shah, D., Hung, E., Wolf, C., Bazanski, S., Gisselquist, D., Milanovic, M.: Yosys+nextpnr: an open source framework from verilog to bitstream for commercial FPGAs. In: 27th IEEE Annual International Symposium on Field-Programmable Custom Computing Machines, FCCM 2019, San Diego, CA, USA, 28 April – 1 May 2019, pp. 1–4. IEEE (2019). https://doi.org/10.1109/FCCM.2019.00010

15. Sijacic, D., Balasch, J., Yang, B., Ghosh, S., Verbauwhede, I.: Towards efficient and automated side channel evaluations at design time. In: Batina, L., Kühne, U., Mentens, N. (eds.) PROOFS 2018, 7th International Workshop on Security Proofs for Embedded Systems, colocated with CHES 2018, Amsterdam, The Netherlands, 13 September 2018. Kalpa Publications in Computing, vol. 7, pp. 16–31. EasyChair (2018), http://www.easychair.org/publications/paper/xPnF

16. Standaert, F.-X.: How (not) to use Welch's T-test in side-channel security evaluations. In: Bilgin, B., Fischer, J.-B. (eds.) CARDIS 2018. LNCS, vol. 11389, pp. 65–79. Springer, Cham (2019). https://doi.org/10.1007/978-3-030-15462-2_5

17. Wolf, C.: SymbiFlow, an open source FPGA tooling for rapid innovation. https://symbiflow.github.io/

18. Zoni, D., Barenghi, A., Pelosi, G., Fornaciari, W.: A comprehensive side-channel information leakage analysis of an in-order RISC CPU microarchitecture. ACM Trans. Des. Autom. Electron. Syst. **23**(5), 57:1–57:30 (2018). https://doi.org/10.1145/3212719

Side-Channel Countermeasures

Self-secured PUF: Protecting the Loop PUF by Masking

Lars Tebelmann[1][(✉)] ⓘ, Jean-Luc Danger[2] ⓘ, and Michael Pehl[1] ⓘ

[1] TUM Department of Electrical and Computer Engineering, Chair of Security in Information Technology, Technical University Munich, Munich, Germany
{lars.tebelmann,m.pehl}@tum.de
[2] Télécom Paristech, Paris, France
jean-luc.danger@telecom-paris.fr

Abstract. Physical Unclonable Functions (PUFs) provide means to generate chip individual keys, especially for low-cost applications such as the Internet of Things (IoT). They are intrinsically robust against reverse engineering, and more cost-effective than non-volatile memory (NVM). For several PUF primitives, countermeasures have been proposed to mitigate side-channel weaknesses. However, most mitigation techniques require substantial design effort and/or complexity overhead, which cannot be tolerated in low-cost IoT scenarios. In this paper, we first analyze side-channel vulnerabilities of the Loop PUF, an area efficient PUF implementation with a configurable delay path based on a single ring oscillator (RO). We provide side-channel analysis (SCA) results from power and electromagnetic measurements. We confirm that oscillation frequencies are easily observable and distinguishable, breaking the security of unprotected Loop PUF implementations. Second, we present a low-cost countermeasure based on temporal masking to thwart SCA that requires only one bit of randomness per PUF response bit. The randomness is extracted from the PUF itself creating a *self-secured PUF*. The concept is highly effective regarding security, low complexity, and low design constraints making it ideal for applications like IoT. Finally, we discuss trade-offs of side-channel resistance, reliability, and latency as well as the transfer of the countermeasure to other RO-based PUFs.

Keywords: Physically unclonable function · Side-channel analysis · RO PUF · Loop PUF · Masking · Countermeasure · IoT

1 Introduction

In an increasingly interconnected world, hardware trust anchors play an important role to avoid that vulnerabilities in single nodes break security of

This work was partly funded by the German Ministry of Education and Research in the project SecForCARs under grant number 01KIS0795 and under the SPARTA project, which has received funding from the European Union's Horizon 2020 research and innovation programme under grant agreement number 830892.

ⓒ Springer Nature Switzerland AG 2021
G. M. Bertoni and F. Regazzoni (Eds.): COSADE 2020, LNCS 12244, pp. 293–314, 2021.
https://doi.org/10.1007/978-3-030-68773-1_14

entire systems. Especially low-cost devices used in the Internet of Things (IoT) are physically accessible and may serve as an entry point for attacks. While such devices require decent security mechanisms, their low-cost nature limits the acceptable cost overhead. One major issue is secure key storage to provide the credentials for e.g., secure firmware updates or authenticated communication. However, secured non-volatile memory (NVM) is frequently not affordable. Also, NVM protection mechanisms, needed to store the key securely, require permanent power, draining the limited energy resources of the IoT device.

Physical Unclonable Functions (PUFs) provide a solution by deriving a secret from manufacturing variation that are unique, unpredictable, and individual for every chip. A PUF measures a property related to the variations, such as the delay, and derives secret bits from the measurement when the device is powered on. Due to noise, the secret bits are not perfectly stable and are typically processed by an error correction algorithm to derive a stable key. As soon as the chip is powered off, the secret vanishes from volatile memory and can no longer be attacked. The conjunction with the fact that PUFs are readily built from standard cells, makes them an ideal low-cost solution for the IoT.

In this work, we focus on PUFs based on ring oscillators (ROs) that measure the delay at a certain position of the chip through the oscillation frequency of an RO [18]. Specifically, we consider the Loop PUF [3,4], a configurable RO PUF based on a single configurable RO. In general, other configurable PUFs are primarily used in challenge-response protocols, and are therefore subject to machine learning attacks [1,6,15]. In contrast, the Loop PUF is used for key generation and the configuration by challenges is only used to maximize the entropy extracted from a certain chip area. As an attacker does not have access to the responses of the key generation and the challenges are generated online from a Hadamard matrix [14], i.e., linearly independent, machine learning attacks are out of the scope for the Loop PUF.

Since machine learning attacks and key retrieval during power off are out of scope for the Loop PUF, physical attacks during runtime have to be considered. Regarding the IoT scenario the most relevant case are non-invasive attacks with affordable equipment, i.e., capable of performing power and global EM measurements. We consider in this work side-channel analysis (SCA) attacks on the PUF primitive itself. Other attack vectors for SCA are at the postprocessing stage of the PUF to get a reliable key [12,21] but they are not addressed in this study.

Related Work. Several SCA attacks on PUF primitives have been proposed in literature, most of them being semi-invasive attacks. For some attacks, dedicated countermeasures have been suggested. However, existing countermeasures come with a high design overhead or require a large amount of random numbers.

For SRAM PUFs a cloning attack was proposed that measures near infrared photonic emissions of the SRAM cells to characterize the PUF and subsequently clone it using a focused ion beam [7]. Furthermore, an attack is proposed that exploits the remanesence decay effect of SRAM cells if an attacker is able to overwrite the SRAM used for the PUF [13,22]. The Arbiter PUF is characterized by analyzing the photonic emissions of the different delay stages in order to deduce a linear model for the Arbiter PUF that can be solved with little effort [19]. For the transient effect ring oscillator (TERO) PUF, EM-based SCA allows for determining the oscillation duration of single instances by using a Short-Time Fourier Transform (STFT). Knowledge of the oscillation duration allows for reducing the PUF's entropy. The leakage stems from counters that are placed in an interleaved manner [20].

Most relevant to this work, several attacks have been carried out on RO PUFs: (*i*) Using Laser Voltage Probing exposing the backside of a die to an near-infrared laser beam [8]: The intensity of the reflected beam is altered through absorption or interference effects and allows for the recovery of the RO frequencies. (*ii*) Using localized electromagnetic emissions of the ROs over a decapsulated die [11]: Frequencies from simultaneously activated ROs can be identified and exploited if ROs are used in several comparisons, i.e., are activated more than once. Consequently, a possible countermeasures consists in limiting the use of each RO to a single comparison. Additionally, it is suggested to measure multiple, i.e., more than two, ROs in parallel to increase the number of frequencies an attacker has to distinguish. (*iii*) Using localized EM measurement over a decapsulated FPGA die, single ROs can be resolved if placed far from each other [10]: However, for ROs placed in proximity to each other, separation of single ROs is deemed unlikely. Yet, multiplexers and counters exhibit leakage about the RO frequencies that can be resolved spatially. To impede the attack on counters and multiplexers, measurement path randomization, i.e., using different counters or multiplexers for each evaluation, and interleaved placement of the components are proposed. *(iv)* Geometric leaks in the EM spectrum of an ASIC enable the resolution of adjacently placed counters [17]: The RO PUF under attack follows a low-power design to reduce SCA leaks. However, depending on the measurement position on the decapsulated die, the counter frequencies have different amplitudes and can be distinguished. The authors conclude that interleaved placement of components is therefore not sufficient. Parallel comparison of multiple ROs, as proposed by [11], increases the number of possibilities, but does not protect from brute force attacks. Ultra-low-power counters are proposed as a possible hiding countermeasure.

Contributions. In this work, we propose a hardened, yet low complexity, implementation of a PUF primitive, that is based on the Loop PUF [3,4]. In most other oscillation-based PUF primitives, such as the RO PUF or the TERO PUF, multiple instances of an oscillator are implemented and compared in parallel. In contrast, the Loop PUF implements a single instance of the primitive, that is evaluated sequentially. We take advantage of the sequential evaluation method by randomizing the order of the challenges used to generate PUF bits. In particular, the randomness to determine the order is derived from the Loop PUF itself, making our proposed design a self-secured PUF primitive. The contributions of this work include:

1. Side-channel analysis of the Loop PUF using a single measurement.
2. Temporal masking countermeasure for the Loop PUF that benefits from the sequential evaluation method.
3. Proposal of a self-secured PUF by drawing the randomness from the PUF itself.

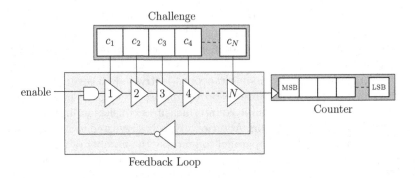

Fig. 1. Schematic of the Loop PUF structure.

Structure. The rest of this work is structured as follows: Sect. 2 recapitulates the functional principle of the Loop PUF and introduces our implementation used for the experiments. Section 3 performs a practical side-channel attack on the Loop PUF and analyzes the results. The countermeasure against the SCA as well as the concept of the self-secured PUF is provided in Sect. 4. Subsequently, Sect. 5 discusses the application of the scheme to RO PUFs and the impact of measurement time, before we draw our conclusion in Sect. 6.

2   The Loop PUF

This work mainly analyzes and improves a simple PUF based on a ring oscillator, the Loop PUF, w.r.t. side channel attacks. One goal of this study is to check if the low complexity property of this PUF can be kept when inserting countermeasures against SCA. Another interest is the potential transfer of security solutions to other RO PUFs. In this section the working principle of the Loop PUF as well as its implementation on Xilinx Artix-7 FPGAs is presented.

2.1   Architecture

The Loop PUF is a delay PUF introduced by Cherif et al. [3,4]. Its main component is a delay chain composed of N identical controllable delay stages. A ring oscillator (RO) is formed when the output of the delay chain is feedback to the chain's input through an inverting gate. An *enable* signal allows for starting and stopping the oscillation. Figure 1 illustrates the Loop PUF schematic.

Each of the N delay stages of the PUF contains two delay elements such as inverters or buffers, as depicted in Fig. 2a. A challenge bit c_i applied to the ith stage selects, e.g., via a multiplexer, one of the two elements that is included in the RO path. The challenge C applied to the PUF is the N-bit word composed of the c_i. The frequency of the RO depends on the sum of selected delays. Neglecting noise and aging, it is constant for given environmental conditions but unique for each hardware realization of a Loop PUF due to local process variations of the individual delay elements during the device fabrication.

2.2 Operating Mode

The Loop PUF requires an operating mode to derive secret bits from the oscillation frequencies obtained for given challenges. The basic operating mode is presented in Algorithm 1. It consists of two subsequent measurements: The first using the challenge C and the second with the complementary challenge $\neg C$ applied (Lines 1, 3). In other words, the frequencies of the RO with different delay elements in the ring are measured.

Algorithm 1. Basic Loop PUF Operation

Input: Challenge C (a word of N bits)
Input: Measurement time in terms of periods n_{acq} of the reference clock
Output: Response δ_C (a signed integer whose sign is mapped to the secret bit k_C)
1: Set current challenge to C
2: Count oscillations of Loop PUF for n_{acq} cycles of reference clock $\Rightarrow v_C$
3: Set current challenge $\neg C$
4: Count oscillations of Loop PUF for n_{acq} cycles of reference clock $\Rightarrow v_{\neg C}$
5: Compute $\delta_C = v_C - v_{\neg C}$
6: **return** δ_C with $k_C = \text{MSB}(\delta_C) \in \{0, 1\}$

The challenge dependent frequency of the RO is the underlying secret to be observed. It is measured by counting the number of oscillations of the loop for a fixed predefined measurement time (Lines 2, 4). For this purpose, the N-bit challenge C is applied to the Loop PUF. Then, the *enable* signal is set to logical 1 while a reference counter counts a predefined number n_{acq} of periods of a reference clock oscillating with frequency f_{clk}. After the acquisition time T_{acq} is finished, the oscillation frequency is approximated from the counter value v_C as

$$f_C \approx f_{clk} \cdot \frac{v_C}{n_{acq}} = \frac{v_C}{T_{acq}}. \tag{1}$$

Note that due to the discrete counter values, f_C is subject to quantization noise. After deriving f_C the respective counter value $v_{\neg C}$ and frequency $f(\neg C)$ for the complementary challenge $\neg C$ are derived accordingly. The sign of the frequency difference $\Delta f = f(C) - f(\neg C)$ is the secret response bit k_C obtained from the

Loop PUF. The secret PUF response bit k_C is therefore derived from the most significant bit (MSB) of the counter differences $\delta_C = v_C - v_{\neg C}$ (Line 6):

$$k_C = \text{MSB}(\delta_C) = \begin{cases} 1 \text{ if } \text{sign}(\Delta f) \geq 0 \\ 0 \text{ otherwise.} \end{cases} \tag{2}$$

The differential measurement process compensates for a large amount of influences through environmental conditions and aging effects. Since these effects happen on a larger time scale than the measurement time, subsequently measured frequencies are affected similarly. Therefore, the most significant bit of δ_C and, thus, the response bit k_C has high stability if the oscillation frequency for challenges C and $\neg C$ are sufficiently distinct. Compared to other oscillation based PUF primitives, such as the RO and TERO PUF, spatial biases are avoided by using the same oscillator sequentially.

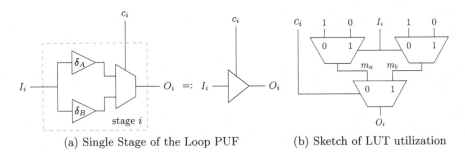

(a) Single Stage of the Loop PUF   (b) Sketch of LUT utilization

Fig. 2. Schematic and LUT utilization of stage i of a Loop PUF

2.3   Loop PUF Challenges for Maximum Entropy

It was shown by Rioul et al. [14], that one solution to get an entropy of N_{key} bits out of the Loop PUF, is to compose it of $N = N_{\text{key}}$ delay stages and challenge it by N_{key} *Hadamard codewords* [2] from a $N \times N$ *Hadamard Matrix*. Hadamard codewords are pairwise orthogonal; They have a minimum Hamming distance of $N/2$ from each other and share a Hamming weight of $N/2$, except for the null codeword. Hadamard codewords can be constructed on chip with low effort, preserving the low-complexity property of the design as there is no need of memory to store the challenges.

As the PUF is natively unreliable, it is necessary to have a sufficiently high number of challenges to run postprocessing based on error correcting codes or to filter out unreliable challenges as shown in [16]. This implies that the required number N of delay stages and *Hadamard codewords* has to be bigger than the number of key bits. Alternatively, multiple Loop PUFs can be instantiated.

2.4 Loop PUF Implementation

The most sophisticated part of a Loop PUF design is the implementation of the delay chain. Ideally, the expected delay of the Loop PUF is independent of the challenge and a difference in the delay is only due to process variations affecting the delay elements. I.e., wiring should have no influence and the delay elements in a delay stage according to Fig. 2a should be as similar as possible.

To reach this goal, the Loop PUF implementation in this work utilizes the multiplexer structure of the FPGA in accordance to the suggestions for a ring-oscillator PUF design in [5]: Every slice of the Xilinx Artix-7 FPGA used in this work contains four 6-input-2-output LUTs. The inputs to a LUT select a path from functionality dependent initialized SRAM cells through a multiplexer tree to the LUT output. Figure 2b sketches the concept for a delay element implemented in a 2-input-1-output LUT. To implement two distinct inverter gates as the basic delay elements (alternatively buffers can be realized) of a delay stage in one LUT, the SRAM at the input of two multiplexers in the same hierarchy level is initialized so that their outputs (m_a, m_b) correspond to the inverse of a certain input (I_i). An additional challenge input (c_i) selects if the LUT output O_i is $O_i = m_a$ or $O_i = m_b$. Consequently, the routing between delay stages, i.e., from O_i to I_{i+1} etc., is independent from the challenges and does not influence the delay differences.

For c_i and I_i, inputs of the LUT are selected such that the *expected* delay is independent from the challenge bit. Still, due to the FPGA internal routing and implementation of the path from SRAM cells through multiplexers to the output, a certain challenge dependent systematic delay bias might be caused. This corresponds to delay elements in Fig. 2a, which are faster or slower on all devices and would result in a reduced entropy of the Loop PUF. If the same amount of fast and slow paths are active for the challenges which are compared, i.e., for C and $\neg C$, the effect is mitigated assuming all LUTs are affected by the same systematic effect. Challenges $C/\neg C$, which are selected correspondingly, have the same Hamming weight. For challenges that are Hadamard codewords, this property is inherently fulfilled if the null challenge $C_0 = \mathbf{0}$ is discarded.

From the described delay elements, we realize a 64-stage Loop PUF that is implemented in only 17 slices in 8 CLBs. The Loop PUF is realized within a closed domain with fixed placement and routing such that it does not interfere with other parts of the design. The other parts of the design are placed in a separate area but without additional constraints regarding placement and routing.

Using Hadamard codewords and discarding C_0, the design suffices to generate 63 bits. For a key-storage scenario, either more stages in the delay path or multiple Loop PUFs are required on a chip. A longer delay chain causes, however, lower frequency and therefore longer measurement time. A shorter delay chain is less efficient in terms of challenges due to discarding C_0. Thus, we consider a length of 64 delay stages a realistic size.

We decided having a single Loop PUF on the device since it corresponds to the best case for an attacker. Using multiple Loop PUFs in parallel, the attacker faces the additional obstacle of spatially resolving different counters, which has been shown to be feasible using localized EM measurements [17]. The additional barrier of localized measurements does, however, not change the overall results and is deemed out of the scope of this work. To further support the analysis, the design supports supplying challenges externally and reading back the measured counter values allowing for validation of leakage observed in the side-channel. Responses are computed on a PC receiving the counter values from the device, since the analysis in Sect. 3 does not consider the potential leakage in the comparison step. Note however, that in a practical scenario the attacker is not required to have access to any of the internal counter values or being able to apply challenges.

3   Side-Channel Analysis of the Loop PUF

This section provides the methodology and results for the SCA of the Loop PUF. First, the experimental setup is described in Sect. 3.1. Subsequently, methods to detect the Frequencies of Interest at which the Loop PUF oscillates are proposed in Sect. 3.2 and a side-channel attack is conducted in Sect. 3.3. Finally in Sect. 3.4, the results are generalized regarding limitations and constraints of the attack and possible countermeasures.

3.1   Experimental Setup

The experimental setup for the SCA evaluation of the Loop PUF consists of a Chip Whisperer 305, that features an Artix-7 (XC7A100TFTG256) running at $f_{clk} = 100\,\text{MHz}$. A PicoScope 6402D USB oscilloscope performs the acquisition at a sampling frequency of $f_s = 1.25\,\text{GHz}$. The input bandwidth of the scope is 250 MHz, which is sufficient regarding the oscillations frequencies of the Loop PUF and their harmonics that are in the range from 15 MHz to 65 MHz as shown in Sect. 3.2. Measurements are performed in parallel for both, power and EM side-channel as depicted in Fig. 3. Power measurements are acquired using the SMA jack X4 of the CW305, which outputs the voltage drop of the FPGA's internal supply voltage VCC_{int} over a 100 mΩ shunt amplified by a 20 dB low-noise amplifier. EM measurements are taken using a Langer EMV RF-R 50-1 near field probe with a diameter of approximately 10 mm. A 30 dB Langer EMV PA303 pre-amplifier is used to enhance the signal amplitudes in order to benefit from the oscilloscope's dynamic range.

The EM probe is placed on the front-side about 1 mm above the package to capture field lines that are orthogonal to the package surface. A coarse positioning procedure is applied to find the location of interest above the package: For each quadrant on the package measurements are taken and the procedure in Sect. 3.2 is used to determine whether the relevant frequencies are present. The position providing the highest peak at the frequency of interest, depicted in Fig. 3, is chosen for all further evaluations.

Fig. 3. CW305 measurement setup. The *RF-R 50-1* EM probe position and the power jack are depicted.

3.2 Frequency of Interest Detection

In order to attack the Loop PUF, an attacker has to determine the frequencies of the oscillation termed as Frequency of Interest (FoI) in the following. In Fig. 4 the spectral representation of different detection methods are depicted. All figures are based on a single measurement per challenge, where the Loop PUF is activated for $T_{acq} \approx 5.24\,\text{ms}$. The first 5.2 ms are transformed into the frequency domain using a Fast Fourier Transform (FFT) of $N_{FFT} = 2,684,359$ frequency bins and a Hanning window to minimize aliasing effects. The resulting spectra exhibit various spikes which makes automatic evaluation difficult. Thus, low-pass filtering is applied along the frequencies to smooth the spectrum. Using the filtering technique, single frequency noise form perturbations and artifacts are reduced, while Loop PUF frequencies, that have a small fluctuation, remain.

Figures 4a and b show the spectra $X(f)$ of two challenges C and $\neg C$ for power and EM measurements respectively. The Loop PUF frequency $f_0 \approx 15.77\,\text{MHz}$, verified by Eq. (1), is indicated as well as the multiples $f_1, \ldots, f_3$. In the power side-channel, the frequencies show notable peaks, while in the EM side-channel, peaks are partly covered by other signals. Furthermore, in both side-channels, frequency peaks unrelated to the Loop PUF show up. While some frequency components can be attributed to expected sources such as the system clock $f_{clk} = 100\,\text{MHz}$, other frequencies are a priori indistinguishable from the Loop PUF frequency. Therefore, two methods for reliable Frequency of Interest (FoI) detection are proposed.

FoI Based on Signal-to-Noise Ratio. The first method subtracts an estimated noise floor $N(f)$ from the spectra $X(f)$, generating a Signal-to-Noise Ratio. $\text{SNR}(f) = X(f)/N(f)$. Results are depicted in Figs. 4c and d. The noise floor is estimated from measurements with inactive Loop PUF, eliminating certain irrelevant frequencies, such as the clock frequency. In Figs. 4c and d the noise floor estimate $N(f)$ is based on averaging over the frequency spectra of

128 measurements, where the Loop PUF was not active. Compared to the spectra $X(f)$ in Figs. 4a and b the frequencies f_1, f_2, f_3 show up more clearly in $SNR(f)$ and other frequency components are canceled out. The basic frequency f_0 is covered by other signals in the EM side-channel. The peaks at 68.6 MHz and it multiple at 137.2 MHz are unrelated to the Loop PUF, yet the candidate frequencies for an attacker are reduced.

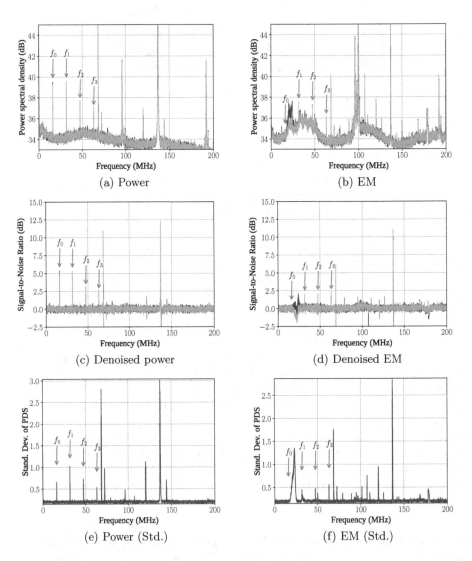

Fig. 4. FoI detection methods for the Loop PUF frequency. (a)–(b): power spectral density (PSD) of exemplary side-channel measurements for C and $\neg C$. (c)–(d): PSD subtracted by PSD from noise measurement. (e)–(f): FoI method using the standard deviation of the PSD among all challenges.

FoI Based on Standard Deviation. An attacker may not be able to estimate the noise floor reliably by idle measurements, e.g., if other operations, which are not active in the idle measurements, run in parallel to the Loop PUF. Thus, a second FoI detection method is proposed based on the standard deviation over frequency spectra of all challenges. The basic idea is that frequency components present in all measurements, such as the clock frequency, show a low standard deviation, while frequencies that vary for different measurements produce a higher standard deviation. In Figs. 4e and f the standard deviation of the frequency spectrum among the different challenges is depicted for power and EM measurements. Indeed, the FoI detection in the power side-channel in Fig. 4e reveals the Loop PUF frequency f_0 as well as multiples f_1, f_2, f_3. In the EM side-channel, Figs. 4e and f a frequency ramp is visible between 15 MHz and 24 MHz, that partly covers f_0. Thus, the fundamental Loop PUF frequency of f_0 can still be sensed with priory knowledge, but is hardly identifiable for an attacker. Only f_1, f_2, f_3 are clearly visible. Similar to the Signal-to-Noise Ratio (SNR)-based method, additional frequencies are detected around 68.6 MHz and 72 MHz that are unrelated to the Loop PUF. Overall, more unrelated peaks occur compared to the SNR-based method, but FOIs can be more clearly distinguished compared to the raw spectra in Figs. 4a and b.

Concluding, two methods to detect the FOIs are proposed that allow an attacker to determine the frequencies related to the Loop PUF. If possible, the SNR-based method is preferable, otherwise calculating the standard deviations across challenges provides sufficient information.

3.3 Side-Channel Analysis of the Loop PUF

The frequencies in range of the FOIs determined in Sect. 3.2, are evaluated regarding the possibility of extracting information about the Loop PUF. The following evaluations focus on a spectral range from 31.4 MHz to 31.7 MHz, because a frequency around 31.54 MHz is identified as a FoI in the EM side-channel. The same frequency range is used for power side-channel to ease comparison.

As noted in Algorithm 1, the counter value v_C that results from the challenge C is compared to the counter value $v_{\neg C}$ that results from the complementary challenge $\neg C$. The challenges are applied sequentially, thus an attacker can observe the resulting frequencies f_C and $f_{\neg C}$ separately. If the order in which C and $\neg C$ are applied is known, as is the case for the design presented in Sect. 2.2, the attacker can guess the PUF bit k_C by comparing the frequency spectra of the challenges.

In Fig. 5 the typically observed spectra for challenge C and its complement $\neg C$ are depicted. The peaks $\hat{f}_C$ and $\hat{f}_{\neg C}$ are clearly different and can be distinguished by an attacker. The sign of the comparison $\Delta\hat{f} = \hat{f}_C - \hat{f}_{\neg C}$ is used as the guess for the PUF response bit, i.e.,

$$\hat{k}_C = \begin{cases} 1 \text{ if } \operatorname{sign}(\Delta\hat{f}_C) \geq 0 \\ 0 \text{ if } \operatorname{sign}(\Delta\hat{f}_C) < 0. \end{cases} \tag{3}$$

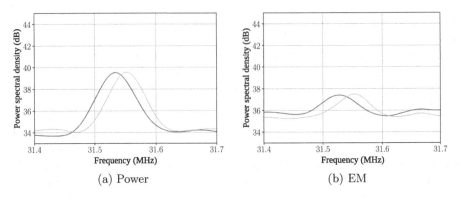

(a) Power   (b) EM

Fig. 5. Zoom of the power spectral density for a challenge C (blue) and its complement $\neg C$ (orange). (Color figure online)

In order to determine the success of an attack on all Loop PUF bits, the actual
counter difference $\Delta v_C = v_C - v_{\neg C}$ is compared to its estimate

$$\Delta \hat{v}_C = \left\lfloor \hat{f}_C \cdot T_{acq} \right\rfloor - \left\lfloor \hat{f}_{\neg C} \cdot T_{acq} \right\rfloor \tag{4}$$

determined by the side-channel observations. The floor operator reflects the
assumption that the counter value is incremented after every Loop PUF oscillation.

Figure 6 depicts the match between Δv_C and $\Delta \hat{v}_C$. Estimated differences
$\Delta \hat{v}_C$ with $\mathrm{sign}(\Delta \hat{v}_C) \neq \mathrm{sign}(\Delta v_C)$ are depicted as filled red squares. Using the
method in Eq. (3), from 63 Loop PUF bits, only two and, respectively, three
bits result in a wrong guess for the power/EM side-channel. Notably, the wrong
guesses correspond to smaller frequency differences that are more difficult to
resolve by the attack. However, smaller frequency differences also correspond
to unstable PUF bits that are compensated by an error-correcting step in key
generation or even discarded. I.e., an attacker can afford a certain number of
wrong bit guesses since also on the device not all 63 bits might be derived
correctly[1].

Summing up, the response of the Loop PUF can be recovered from non-
invasive power and EM measurements using a single measurement per challenge
for all but a few unstable bits. Thus, the unprotected Loop PUF design is broken
by side-channel attacks.

---

[1] An additional attack vector is the enhancement of the frequency leakage by leakage
of the helper data and the error-correcting code that would allow for setting up a
system of linear equations to retain the individual delays of the Loop PUF. However,
the entire attack surface could only be considered, if the complete PUF architecture
was evaluated and we focus on the primitive only.

3.4 Limitations and Constraints: Frequency Resolution

In order to understand general limitations of both, the SCA presented in Sect. 3.3 as well as the countermeasures proposed in Sect. 4, this section provides constraints regarding the possible frequency resolution of observations.

The smallest frequency f_{min}, which can be resolved by measurement, is the frequency where exactly one complete period of the oscillation fits into the observation window. In case of the Loop PUF, the maximum observation time is the acquisition time T_{acq}, i.e.,

$$f_{min} := \frac{1}{T_{acq}} = \frac{f_{clk}}{n_{acq}}. \tag{5}$$

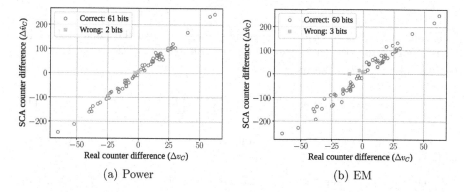

Fig. 6. Attack results from SCA on the Loop PUF: Match of real counter differences and estimated counter differences from frequency measurements using maxima around 31.55 MHz.

For measurements with an oscilloscope in the time domain, the maximum frequency f_{max} that can be resolved, is determined by the Shannon-Nyquist sampling theorem as $f_{max} = f_s/2$ for the sampling frequency f_s. Thus, the observable frequency range[2] is bounded to

$$\frac{1}{T_{acq}} = f_{min} \leq f \leq f_{max} = \frac{f_s}{2}. \tag{6}$$

An attacker is expected to get the best result if the entire acquisition time T_{acq} is measured. For a measurement period of T_{acq}, the number of sampling points, i.e., the length of the applied FFT is

$$N_{FFT} = f_s \cdot T_{acq}. \tag{7}$$

---

[2] Note that technically, the smallest frequency that can be resolved is 0 Hz, i.e., the DC component. However, in Eq. (6) we are concerned with the *observable* frequencies.

For real valued time domain signals, the spectrum is symmetric. Therefore, an FFT of length N_{FFT} maps the signal into $N_{FFT}/2+1$ frequency bins ranging from DC to f_{max}. The frequency resolution of the FFT frequency bins is

$$\Delta_{FFT} = \frac{f_{max}}{N_{FFT}/2} = \frac{f_s}{N_{FFT}} = \frac{1}{T_{acq}}. \tag{8}$$

In other words, a longer acquisition time T_{acq} allows the attacker to obtain a better resolution of the frequency differences.

From an attackers perspective, the observed bin center frequency $\hat{f}$ corresponds to some real oscillation frequency f_{real} of the Loop PUF. From Eq. (8), f_{real} is bounded by the width of the frequency bins to

$$\hat{f} - \frac{1}{2 \cdot T_{acq}} \leq f_{real} \leq \hat{f} + \frac{1}{2 \cdot T_{acq}}. \tag{9}$$

Assuming all frequencies within a specific bin appear with the same probability, the best guess an attacker can make for the counter value according to Eq. (4) from the observed $\hat{f}$ is therefore

$$\hat{v}_C = \left\lfloor \left(\hat{f} \pm \frac{1}{2 \cdot T_{acq}} \right) \cdot T_{acq} \right\rfloor = \left\lfloor \hat{f} \cdot T_{acq} \right\rfloor \pm 1. \tag{10}$$

Regarding limitations and constraints for shown attacks and countermeasure below, from Eqs. (9) and (10) we conclude that:

1. If the frequency difference of two challenges C and $\neg C$ is $|f_C - f_{\neg C}| > \Delta_{FFT}$, the resulting PUF response bit k_C is always revealed by an attack.
2. If $|f_C - f_{\neg C}| \leq \Delta_{FFT}$, the probability that both f_C and $f_{\neg C}$ are in the same FFT bin, i.e., indistinguishable for an attacker, increases with decreasing distance of the frequencies. The attack will succeed for small frequency differences only with a certain probability.
3. While the sign of the counter difference can be revealed, an attacker will fail in deriving the least significant bit (LSB) of the counters.

Note that regarding Item 2, intentionally designing a Loop PUF with closeby frequencies does not serve as a countermeasure: The comparison of frequencies close to each other is not desirable from a PUF perspective, because bits derived from such a comparison are less robust against noise. The conclusions in Items 1 and 2 emphasize the necessity for countermeasures to protect the Loop PUF. Additionally, Item 3 substantiates that the LSB of a counter cannot be revealed by the attack. Consequently, the LSB is used in the next section as a random bit to protect the Loop PUF.

4   Securing the Loop PUF

To thwart the SCA on the Loop PUF presented in Sect. 3, a masking countermeasure is introduced in this section. We first present the general concept of the temporal masking scheme in Sect. 4.1 and show in Sect. 4.2 how it can be used to make the Loop PUF self-secured by using the counter LSB as random bit. In Sects. 4.3 and 4.4 we evaluate the mask quality and provide results for SCA for the proposed countermeasure.

4.1   Temporal Masking

The measurement of the Loop PUF is performed sequentially: Measurement for challenge C is followed by measurement for its complement $\neg C$. The order of the frequency measurements is important since it determines the secret bit according to Eq. (2). At the same time, the ordered sequential measurement is exploited by the SCA in Sect. 3.3. To protect the sequential measurements against SCA, the order of measurements to derive a certain PUF response bit k_C is randomized by a 1-bit mask m in Algorithm 2[3]. The algorithm requires as input a mask bit that is unpredictable for an attacker.

Algorithm 2. Protected Loop PUF Operation

Input: Challenge C (a word of N bits)
Input: Measurement time in terms of periods n_{acq} of the reference clock
Input: mask m (1-bit random variable)
Output: Response δ_C (a signed integer whose sign is mapped to the secret bit k_C)
  1: Set current challenge $C' = m \; ? \; C : \neg C$
  2: Count oscillations of Loop PUF for n_{acq} cycles of reference clock $\Rightarrow v_{C'}$
  3: Set current challenge $\neg C'$
  4: Count oscillations of Loop PUF for n_{acq} cycles of reference clock $\Rightarrow v_{\neg C'}$
  5: Compute $\delta_C = m \; ? \; v_{C'} - v_{\neg C'} : v_{\neg C'} - v_{C'}$
  6: **return** δ_C with $k_C = \mathrm{MSB}(\delta_C) \in \{0, 1\}$

Comparing Algorithm 2 to Algorithm 1, the mask bit m determines if C or $\neg C$ is applied first (Lines 1, 3). If m is logically 0, the sequence of challenges is $C \prec \neg C$; Otherwise, if m is logically 1, the order is $\neg C \prec C$. Since m is – by definition – unknown to an attacker, he/she cannot determine the order of frequency measurement. Consequently the described SCA does no longer succeed.

Without further modification, a changed order of measurements leads to a wrong sign derived from the frequency difference on-chip. The sign is corrected by considering the order of measurement also in the subtraction (Line 5). The mask bit m determines the order in which the frequencies are subtracted such that the final result is independent from m but still cannot be observed by an attacker.

---

[3] Note, that the reordering of measurements does not affect PUF quality metrics as it has not effect on the oscillation frequency.

4.2 Self-secured Loop PUF Using 1-Bit RNG from LSB

The question how to efficiently implement the masking scheme from Sect. 4.1 without the effort of an additional Random Number Generator (RNG) remains. We suggest to use the LSB of the frequency counter $m = \text{LSB}(v)$ for this purpose and discuss the quality of the mask in Sect. 4.3.

Algorithm 3 describes the key generation with masking to avoid side-channel leakages. The algorithm takes the acquisition time n_{acq} in clock cycles of a reference clock as an input during design time. When executed, it derives all Hadamard codewords except of the null challenge $C_0 = \mathbf{0}$ (Line 1). Note that the Hadamard codewords can be computed during runtime and do not require additional memory. The succesive codeword can be computed parallel to applying the current codeword to the PUF.

The null challenge cannot be used to extract a key bit as it is a source of bias if the delay stage is imbalanced (cf. Section 2.4). However, it can be used to derive a mask bit (Lines 2 to 4) for the generation of the first response bit. The oscillations of the Loop PUF for C_0 are measured for a fixed time and the LSB of the resulting counter value is taken as m.

Algorithm 3. Protected Loop PUF

Input: Measurement time in terms of periods n_{acq} of the reference clock
Output: $k = [k_{N-1}, \ldots, k_1]$ = key of $(N-1)$ bits
 1: Compute the Hadamard codewords set $\mathcal{C} = \{C_1, \ldots, C_{N-1}\}$ with $\text{HW}(C_i) = N/2$
 2: Set current challenge $C' = C_0 = \mathbf{0}$
 3: Count oscillations of Loop PUF for n_{acq} cycles of reference clock $\Rightarrow v_{C'}$
 4: Set mask $m = \text{LSB}(v_{C'})$
 5: **for all** $i = N - 1$ down to and including 1 **do**
 6:     Set current challenge $C' = m\ ?\ C_i : \neg C_i$
 7:     Count oscillations of Loop PUF for n_{acq} cycles of reference clock $\Rightarrow v_{C_i'}$
 8:     Set current challenge $\neg C_i'$
 9:     Count oscillations of Loop PUF for n_{acq} cycles of reference clock $\Rightarrow v_{\neg C_i'}$
10:     Compute $\delta_C = m\ ?\ v_{C_i'} - v_{\neg C_i'} : v_{\neg C_i'} - v_{C_i'}$
11:     Set $k_i = \text{MSB}(\delta_C) \in \{0, 1\}$
12:     Set mask $m = \text{LSB}(v_{C_i'})$
13: **end for**

Subsequently, all other $i = 1, \ldots, N - 1$ Hadamard codewords C_i and their complements $\neg C_i$ are applied to the Loop PUF. The measurement order of C_i and $\neg C_i$ is randomized by the current mask bit m (Line 6 to 10) reflecting the steps from Algorithm 2. A secret PUF bit k_i is derived from the MSB of the counter difference. Finally, the mask bit is updated to the random LSB of the counter value $v_{C_i'}$ protecting the next measurement.

Figure 7 sketches a possible hardware implementation of the self-secured Loop PUF omitting generation of the Hadamard codewords, reference counter, state machine, output registers, and reset tree. In an actual design, the state machine

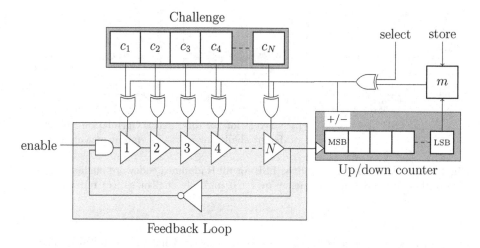

Fig. 7. Schematic of the protected Loop PUF structure.

would cause generation of Hadamard codewords and loading of codewords to the challenge register while resetting the counter. An up/down counter might be used for counting the periods of the Loop PUF.

Starting with the null challenge, $m = 0$ and $select = 0$, the number of Loop PUF oscillations within the acquisition time are measured. Without loss of generality, it can be assumed that the counter is counting upwards in this mode. Setting $store = 1$ for one cycle after n_{acq} clock cycles, the LSB of the resulting counter value is buffered as the first mask bit.

Subsequently, four main states are repeated until all $N - 1$ challenges have been applied to the Loop PUF: *(i)* The mask bit from the buffer is applied to the input of the XOR tree, another challenge is loaded, and the counter is reset. *(ii)* The *select* signal in the design is set to logical 0 and *enable* is set to logical 1. *(iii)* After n_{acq} cycles of the reference clock, the LSB is buffered but not yet used as m, *select* is switched to logical 1. *(iv)* After another n_{acq} cycles of the reference clock, the MSB is taken as a secret bit.

The structure of the design causes that if $m \oplus select = 0$, the counter counts upwards and C is applied to the PUF. If $m \oplus select = 1$, $\neg C$ is used while counting downwards. I.e. if $m = 0$, first C is applied while counting upwards before $\neg C$ is applied while counting downwards; If $m = 1$ the order of C and $\neg C$ as well as the counting direction in state *(ii)* and *(iii)* is reversed, so that after the complete sequence of states the up/down counter always contains the correct frequency difference and no inversion of the MSB is required.

4.3 Empirical Analysis of the LSB-Mask

Temporal masking is effective, if the attacker cannot predict the mask bit m. Section 3.3 shows that the LSB is not resolvable by the suggested measurement strategy. Hence, the question remains if the attacker can predict the LSB by some

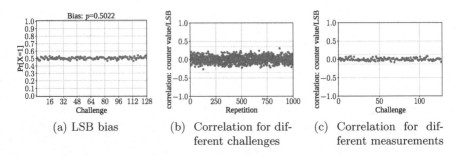

(a) LSB bias

(b) Correlation for different challenges

(c) Correlation for different measurements

Fig. 8. (a) Relative frequency of the LSB for all Hadamard codeword challenges. Correlation between LSB and frequency over (b) multiple challenges, (c) repeated measurements.

other means. This would be the case if *(i)* the LSB has an exploitable bias or *(ii)* is correlated to some observable property, namely the oscillation frequency.

Bias. A bias is considered exploitable if $LSB(v)$ for the same challenge is equal for all devices or if $LSB(v)$ exhibits a global bias w.r.t. all challenges. We exclude the former case from further analysis, since a bias over devices implies the same frequencies for a challenge over all devices. Consequently the PUF quality is low and some redesign is required. To rule out a bias on the device that influences the quality of the mask bit, Fig. 8a depicts the relative frequencies of the LSB for different challenges, where each challenge is measured $1,000$ times. It is evident that no apparent bias exists among challenges. The global bias of all LSBs from all challenges is 0.5022, which is within the expected range. Note that the counter values of all 128 challenges are used to increase the sample size and to evaluate all possible LSBs as the 63 challenges used to produce the random bits are not known a priori.

Correlations with Frequency. Regarding correlations to the oscillation frequency, two cases are considered: First, the attacker might take advantage from correlation between the LSB and the frequency over multiple repeated measurements for a fixed challenge. This would indicate that a certain guessed frequency corresponds to a certain LSB. Second, the attacker might take advantage of a correlation between the LSB and the frequency over multiple challenges, which would indicate a general dependency between frequency and the LSB. Figures 8b and c refute the existence of both kinds of correlations in our design. Both figures show the respective correlation values between frequency and LSB along with a threshold depicted in dashed red. Values below the threshold, given by $\pm 4/\sqrt{n}$, are not significantly different from zero with a confidence of 99.99% [9]. The number of observations n used to calculate the correlation is $n = 128$, i.e., the number of different challenges, and the experiment is repeated for 1,000 measurements in Fig. 8b. In Fig. 8c, $n = 1,000$ different measurements are correlated and the experiment is repeated for each challenge. In neither case is the significance threshold exceeded indicating no correlations between LSB and frequency.

To sum up, the LSB of the Loop PUF counter is suited for the use as a masking bit. It does not show significant bias, nor is the LSB correlated to the frequency of the oscillation, which an attacker could observe. Establishing these properties makes the self-secured Loop PUF a low-complexity and secure design.

4.4   Side-Channel Analysis of the Self-secured Loop PUF

Finally, we evaluate the effectiveness of the self-secured PUF design on practical measurements. In order to assure a fair comparison, the exact same measurements as in Sect. 3.3 are used, but the order of measurements for C and $\neg C$ presented to the attacker is modified according to Algorithm 3. The random bit m is determined from the counter values obtained from the device.

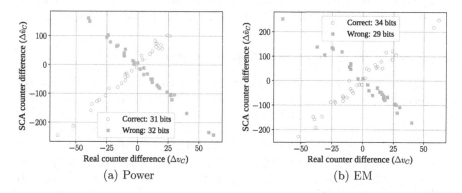

Fig. 9. Attack results from SCA on the self-secured Loop PUF: Match of real counter differences and estimated counter differences.

In Fig. 9, the attacker's capability to estimate the counter difference is depicted. Note, that the attacker tries to guess the MSB as well as the LSB. From the remarks from Sect. 3.4 it is evident that the LSB cannot be retrieved, which is reflected in Fig. 9. Due to the randomized acquisition order, the relationship between real counter differences and SCA-based counter difference estimates is broken and the self-secured Loop PUF is effectively hardened against SCA.

5   Remarks on the Proposed Solution

Previous sections show strong benefits of the temporal masking scheme when applied to the Loop PUF. In Sect. 5.1, we show that the naïve reduction of the measurement time is not sufficient to protect against SCA. In Sect. 5.2, we elaborate the application of temporal masking to other RO PUFs.

5.1 Impact of Measurement Time

The frequency measurement depends largely on the measurement window T_{acq}. From Sect. 3.4 the attack becomes more difficult with the reduction of T_{acq}, as the FFT accuracy decreases. Thus, a naïve countermeasure would be the reduction of the measurement time. Additionally, the latency is proportional to T_{acq} making a design with smaller T_{acq} more efficient. However, a small T_{acq} significantly reduces the reliability because the quantization noise of the counting process is increased. Hence, the best compromise depends on different factors such as the required latency and reliability of the key generation.

Neglecting latency, a large T_{acq} provides a higher reliability of the PUF response bits. As a larger T_{acq} comes at the cost of leakages for SCA attacks, a countermeasure like temporal masking is inevitable. Yet, temporal masking provides security benefits independent of the measurement time, since it impedes attacks independent of the capability of the attacker to resolve frequencies. It is, e.g., still effective against fault attacks where an attacker is able to extend the measurement time by decreasing the frequency of the reference counter.

5.2 Application of Temporal Masking to RO PUFs

Temporal masking is a simple, yet secure countermeasure for Loop PUFs based on sequential measurement of delays. Classical RO PUFs require parallel frequency measurement of two ROs connected to separate counters. However, the countermeasure can be applied if the frequency of the two selected ROs is measured sequentially by the same counter, as for the Loop PUF.

Temporal masking of RO PUFs renders attacks infeasible that spatially resolve the counters, like [10,17], as long as the ROs itself cannot be spatially resolved. As multiple RO pairs are measured to derive a sufficient number of bits from an RO PUF, different design trade-offs are possible: *(i)* For sequential measurements using the same counter, the latency to get the PUF response is doubled while the number of counters is halved. *(ii)* Keeping the number of counters constant allows measurement of the same amount of ROs in parallel as in the classical RO PUF design. But in order to avoid side-channel leakages, the measured ROs must belong to different RO pairs. Otherwise the same attacks as for classical RO PUFs would be possible. As only the way of parallelization is changed, the latency stays the same in this second case. Additional overhead may be required, e.g., in form of additional memory to cache measured frequencies and required random bits for the first activated ROs.

Summarizing, in terms of complexity, the number of counters can be reduced down to a single counter. However, the area required for the large number of ROs in a typical RO PUF design is much larger than the area of a single counter. Hence, the number of counters is not limited by area constraints but rather by the latency requirement as outlined above. More interestingly, there is no specific design effort required for the protection, contrary to the path randomization method proposed by Merli et al. [10,11].

6 Conclusion

In this work, we showed that SCA of the Loop PUF poses an imminent threat to its security. We proposed detection methods for the oscillation frequencies of the configurable RO and exploited non-invasive power and EM side-channels to break the unprotected Loop PUF. In order to mitigate the attacks, we introduced a low-cost yet secure and robust countermeasure suitable for IoT applications. *Temporal masking* randomly alters the order of challenges retaining the security subject to physical attacks. An implementation of the Loop PUF was introduced that leverages the low reliability of the LSB by using it as a random bit for masking. The dual use as PUF and random number generator enables a low-complexity and efficient integration, making the protected Loop PUF self-secured. Measurement results verified the high level of security provided by the protection mechanism. Finally, we indicated that the low-cost protection is easily ported to other RO PUFs avoiding additional complexity or design effort unlike existing countermeasures. Future work includes the study of fault injection attacks on RO-based PUFs and further analysis of the SCA protection.

References

1. Becker, G.T.: The gap between promise and reality: on the insecurity of XOR Arbiter PUFs. In: Güneysu, T., Handschuh, H. (eds.) CHES 2015. LNCS, vol. 9293, pp. 535–555. Springer, Heidelberg (2015). https://doi.org/10.1007/978-3-662-48324-4_27

2. Bossert, M.: Hadamard Matrices and Codes, chap. American Cancer Society, Wiley Encyclopedia of Telecommunications (2003)

3. Cherif, Z., Danger, J., Guilley, S., Bossuet, L.: An easy-to-design PUF based on a single oscillator: the loop PUF. In: 2012 15th Euromicro Conference on Digital System Design, pp. 156–162, September 2012

4. Cherif, Z., Danger, J., Lozach, F., Mathieu, Y., Bossuet, L.: Evaluation of delay PUFs on CMOS 65 nm technology: ASIC vs FPGA. In: HASP 2013, p. 4. Tel-Aviv, Israel (2013)

5. Feiten, L., Scheibler, K., Becker, B., Sauer, M.: Using different LUT paths to increase area efficiency of RO-PUFs on Altera FPGAs. In: TRUDEVICE Workshop, Dresden (2018)

6. Ganji, F., Tajik, S., Fäßler, F., Seifert, J.-P.: Strong machine learning attack against PUFs with no mathematical model. In: Gierlichs, B., Poschmann, A.Y. (eds.) CHES 2016. LNCS, vol. 9813, pp. 391–411. Springer, Heidelberg (2016). https://doi.org/10.1007/978-3-662-53140-2_19

7. Helfmeier, C., Boit, C., Nedospasov, D., Seifert, J.: Cloning physically unclonable functions. In: 2013 IEEE International Symposium on Hardware-Oriented Security and Trust (HOST), pp. 1–6, June 2013

8. Lohrke, H., Tajik, S., Boit, C., Seifert, J.-P.: No place to hide: contactless probing of secret data on FPGAs. In: Gierlichs, B., Poschmann, A.Y. (eds.) CHES 2016. LNCS, vol. 9813, pp. 147–167. Springer, Heidelberg (2016). https://doi.org/10.1007/978-3-662-53140-2_8

9. Mangard, S., Oswald, E., Popp, T.: Power Analysis Attacks. Springer, Boston (2007). https://doi.org/10.1007/978-0-387-38162-6

10. Merli, D., Heyszl, J., Heinz, B., Schuster, D., Stumpf, F., Sigl, G.: Localized electromagnetic analysis of RO PUFs. In: 2013 IEEE International Symposium on Hardware-Oriented Security and Trust (HOST). pp. 19–24, June 2013

11. Merli, D., Schuster, D., Stumpf, F., Sigl, G.: Semi-invasive EM attack on FPGA RO PUFs and countermeasures. In: 6th Workshop on Embedded Systems Security (WESS 2011). ACM, March 2011

12. Merli, D., Stumpf, F., Sigl, G.: Protecting PUF error correction by codeword masking. Cryptology ePrint Archive, Report 2013/334 (2013). http://eprint.iacr.org/2013/334

13. Oren, Y., Sadeghi, A.-R., Wachsmann, C.: On the effectiveness of the remanence decay side-channel to clone memory-based PUFs. In: Bertoni, G., Coron, J.-S. (eds.) CHES 2013. LNCS, vol. 8086, pp. 107–125. Springer, Heidelberg (2013). https://doi.org/10.1007/978-3-642-40349-1_7

14. Rioul, O., Solé, P., Guilley, S., Danger, J.: On the entropy of physically unclonable functions. In: 2016 IEEE International Symposium on Information Theory (ISIT), pp. 2928–2932, July 2016

15. Rührmair, U., et al.: PUF modeling attacks on simulated and silicon data. IEEE Trans. Inf. Forensics Secur. 8(11), 1876–1891 (2013)

16. Schaub, A., Danger, J.L., Guilley, S., Rioul, O.: An improved analysis of reliability and entropy for delay PUFs. In: 2018 21st Euromicro Conference on Digital System Design (DSD), pp. 553–560. IEEE (2018)

17. Shiozaki, M., Fujino, T.: Simple electromagnetic analysis attacks based on geometric leak on an ASIC implementation of ring-oscillator PUF. In: Proceedings of the 3rd ACM Workshop on Attacks and Solutions in Hardware Security Workshop, ASHES 2019, pp. 13–21. ACM, New York (2019)

18. Suh, G.E., Devadas, S.: Physical unclonable functions for device authentication and secret key generation. In: 2007 44th ACM/IEEE Design Automation Conference, DAC 2007, pp. 9–14 (2007)

19. Tajik, S., et al.: Physical characterization of arbiter PUFs. In: Batina, L., Robshaw, M. (eds.) CHES 2014. LNCS, vol. 8731, pp. 493–509. Springer, Heidelberg (2014). https://doi.org/10.1007/978-3-662-44709-3_27

20. Tebelmann, L., Pehl, M., Immler, V.: Side-channel analysis of the TERO PUF. In: Polian, I., Stöttinger, M. (eds.) COSADE 2019. LNCS, vol. 11421, pp. 43–60. Springer, Cham (2019). https://doi.org/10.1007/978-3-030-16350-1_4

21. Tebelmann, L., Pehl, M., Sigl, G.: EM side-channel analysis of BCH-based error correction for PUF-based key generation. In: Proceedings of the 2017 Workshop on Attacks and Solutions in Hardware Security, ASHES 2017, pp. 43–52. ACM, New York (2017)

22. Zeitouni, S., Oren, Y., Wachsmann, C., Koeberl, P., Sadeghi, A.: Remanence decay side-channel: the PUF case. IEEE Trans. Inf. Forensics Secur. 11(6), 1106–1116 (2016)

Leakage-Resilient Authenticated Encryption from Leakage-Resilient Pseudorandom Functions

Juliane Krämer and Patrick Struck[✉]

Technische Universität Darmstadt, Darmstadt, Germany
{juliane,patrick}@qpc.tu-darmstadt.de

Abstract. In this work we study the leakage resilience of authenticated encryption schemes. We show that, if one settles for non-adaptive leakage, leakage-resilient authenticated encryption schemes can be built from leakage-resilient pseudorandom functions.

Degabriele et al. (ASIACRYPT 2019) introduce the FGHF′ construction which allows to build leakage-resilient authenticated encryption schemes from functions which, under leakage, retain both pseudorandomness and unpredictability. We revisit their construction and show the following. First, pseudorandomness and unpredictability do not imply one another in the leakage setting. Unfortunately, this entails that any instantiation of the FGHF′ construction indeed seems to require a function that is proven both pseudorandom and unpredictable under leakage. Second, however, we show that the unpredictability requirement is an artefact that stems from the underlying composition theorem of the N2 construction given by Barwell et al. (ASIACRYPT 2017). By recasting this composition theorem, we show that the unpredictability requirement is unnecessary for the FGHF′ construction. Thus, leakage-resilient AEAD schemes can be obtained by instantiating the FGHF′ construction with functions that are solely pseudorandom under leakage.

Keywords: AEAD · Leakage resilience · Side channels · FGHF′

1 Introduction

Authenticated encryption schemes with associated data (AEAD) are fundamental cryptographic primitives which enable Alice to send a ciphertext to Bob such that (1) Eve does not learn anything about the underlying message and (2) Bob can detect any manipulation of the ciphertext. In recent years, the study of AEAD schemes has received a lot of attention, for instance through the recent CAESAR competition [7] or the ongoing NIST standardization process on lightweight cryptography [26].

Recently, several AEAD schemes which are designed to be secure in the presence of leakage have been proposed [3,9,11,13–15,22]. Barwell et al. [3] show that the Encrypt-then-MAC paradigm [5] yields a leakage-resilient AEAD scheme if

© Springer Nature Switzerland AG 2021
G. M. Bertoni and F. Regazzoni (Eds.): COSADE 2020, LNCS 12244, pp. 315–337, 2021.
https://doi.org/10.1007/978-3-030-68773-1_15

both the encryption scheme and the MAC are leakage-resilient. They also introduce the corresponding security notions. Recently, Degabriele et al. [13] refined this result by introducing the FGHF' construction, showing that leakage-resilient encryption schemes and MACs can be built from fixed-input-length functions which are both pseudorandom and unpredictable under leakage. While leakage-resilient pseudorandomness is well established in the literature, leakage-resilient unpredictability has been defined by Degabriele et al. specifically for the FGHF' construction. This security notion allows the adversary to obtain leakage for the input of which it predicts the output.[1] This raises the natural question:

What is the relation of pseudorandomness and unpredictability under leakage?

While pseudorandomness and unpredictability imply one another in the leak-free setting, Degabriele et al. claim that the notions are incomparable under leakage. We confirm their claim by providing two constructions, each being secure with respect to one notion while being insecure with respect to the other. This seems to entail that any instantiation of the FGHF' construction indeed requires a function that is proven both pseudorandom and unpredictable under leakage. Given that leakage-resilient unpredictability is a new security notion, our separation result gives rise to another question:

Can leakage-resilient AEAD schemes be built from
leakage-resilient pseudorandom functions?

Surprisingly, we answer this question in the affirmative. We demonstrate that the necessity of leakage-resilient unpredictability stems from the composition theorem of Barwell et al. [3]. As observed in [13], this composition theorem imposes a security notion towards the MAC that prohibits constructing it from a leakage-resilient pseudorandom function. However, the composition theorem aims for arbitrary encryption schemes and MACs, while the encryption scheme and the MAC of the FGHF' construction [13] exhibit a special structure. Thus, we show that recasting the composition theorem from [3] for these encryption schemes and MACs, allows to relax the security notion of the MAC such that it can be constructed from a leakage-resilient pseudorandom function. This comes at the cost of imposing a stronger security notion for the encryption scheme. However, it turns out that the encryption scheme underlying the FGHF' construction— without any modification— achieves this stronger notion.

1.1   Our Contribution

Our contribution is threefold.

1) We show that, in contrast to the leak-free setting, pseudorandomness and unpredictability are not equivalent under leakage, thereby confirming a conjecture made in [13].

---

[1] Note that the same does not work for pseudorandomness. Leakage of a single output bit allows to easily distinguish the function from a random function.

2) We recast the N2 composition theorem in the leakage setting by Barwell et al. [3], for a certain class of encryption schemes and MACs. We show that, in this case, other security notions for the encryption scheme and the MAC are sufficient to build leakage-resilient AEAD schemes. More precisely, we can weaken the security notion for the MAC at the cost of strengthening the security notion for the encryption scheme.

3) We revisit the FGHF' construction [13] with respect to our recast composition theorem. We show that the encryption part (without any modification) achieves this stronger security notion. Regarding the MAC, we show that leakage-resilient pseudorandomness is sufficient to achieve the weaker security notion imposed by our recast composition theorem. This completely removes the necessity of leakage-resilient unpredictability to instantiate the FGHF' construction, as opposed to the initial work [13]. Since proving leakage-resilient unpredictability turned out to be a main challenge for SLAE [13] (a sponge-based instantiation of FGHF'), this is an important contribution towards building leakage-resilient AEAD schemes from simpler building blocks.

1.2   Related Work

Leakage-resilient cryptographic primitives, ranging from (authenticated) encryption to MACs, have been proposed in [8,10,11,19,21,27]. In contrast to our setting, these works allow leakage on the challenge queries. However, some of underlying components are assumed to be leak-free, which is typically achieved using techniques such as masking [12]. A subset of these works also assume that the leakage is simulatable, an assumption that is not beyond dispute [24,29]. Functions and permutations which are pseudorandom under leakage have been proposed for instance in [13,16,18,30,31]. Functions which are unpredictable under leakage have only been studied in [13] which also defined this notion.

1.3   Organization of the Paper

Section 2 provides the necessary background required for this work. In Sect. 3 we provide the motivation for our work by showing that, in the leakage setting, pseudorandomness and unpredictability of functions do not imply one another. We recast the composition theorem for the N2 construction by Barwell et al. [3] in Sect. 4. In Sect. 5, we show that the FGHF' construction [13] achieves the security notions demanded by our recast composition theorem.

2   Preliminaries

2.1   Notation

We use the game-playing framework [6]. In a game, the adversary gets access to one or more oracles which is represented as superscripts, e.g., $\mathcal{A}^{\mathcal{O}}$. In this work we mainly use distinguishing games, in which the adversary has to determine a secret bit b. The output of the game is 1, i.e., the adversary wins, if the adversary guesses the bit b correctly. Otherwise, the output of the game is 0, i.e., the adversary looses. For an adversary $\mathcal{A}$ and a game G, we write $G^{\mathcal{A}} \Rightarrow x$ to denote that the output of G, when interacting with $\mathcal{A}$, is x. Likewise, we write $\mathcal{A}^{G} \Rightarrow x$ to denote that $\mathcal{A}$, when playing G, outputs x.

2.2 Primitives

An *authenticated encryption scheme with associated data* AEAD consists of two algorithm Enc and Dec. The encryption algorithm Enc : $\mathcal{K} \times \mathcal{N} \times \mathcal{A} \times \mathcal{M} \rightarrow \{0,1\}^*$ maps from key space $\mathcal{K}$, nonce space $\mathcal{N}$, associated data space $\mathcal{A}$, and message space $\mathcal{M}$ to the ciphertext space $\mathcal{C}$. The decryption algorithm maps from the key space $\mathcal{K}$, nonce space m, associated data space $\mathcal{A}$, and ciphertext space C to the message space $\mathcal{M}$. In case of an invalid ciphertext, Dec returns a special symbol $\perp$. Symmetric encryption schemes are defined analogously, except that the algorithms do not take associated data as input. In this work we focus on a specific class of encryption schemes, which we call *mirror-like*. These are encryption schemes where the encryption algorithm is an involution. Such schemes are fully determined by their encryption algorithm. Examples for mirror-like encryption schemes are the generic encryption scheme underlying the FGHF' construction [13] as well as the sponge-based encryption schemes used in the AEAD schemes SLAE [13] and ISAP [14]. Besides these concrete schemes, instantiating block ciphers with encryption modes like CFB, OFB, and CTR also yield mirror-like encryption schemes.

A message authentication code MAC consists of two algorithms Tag and Ver. The tagging algorithm Tag : $\mathcal{K} \times \mathcal{X} \rightarrow \{0,1\}^t$ maps a key $K \in \mathcal{K}$ and a message $X \in \mathcal{X}$ to a tag $T \in \{0,1\}^t$. The verification algorithm Ver : $\mathcal{K} \times \mathcal{X} \times \{0,1\}^t \rightarrow \{\top, \perp\}$ maps a keys $K \in \mathcal{K}$, a message $X \in \mathcal{X}$, and a tag $T \in \{0,1\}^t$ to either $\top$, indicating that the tag is valid, or $\perp$, indicating that the tag is invalid. Within this work we only consider *canonical* MACs which are implicitly defined by the tagging algorithm Tag, i.e., the verification algorithm recomputes the tag of the message and accepts if the given tag equals the recomputed tag. We write MAC[$\mathcal{F}$] to denote the canonical MAC built from a function $\mathcal{F}$.

2.3 Leakage Model

Our leakage model is the same as in [13], which follows [3], building on *leakage resilience* as defined in [17]. It follows the *only computation leaks information* assumption [25], i.e., only data that is processed during computation can leak information. For instance, encrypting a message with a certain key can not leak information about another (unused) key. Leakage is modelled by (deterministic and efficiently computable) functions from some predetermined set $\mathcal{L}$. Leakage of composite constructions is the composition of the underlying leakage functions. Thus, if primitive C is a composition of primitives A and B with leakage sets $\mathcal{L}_A$ and $\mathcal{L}_B$, then $\mathcal{L}_C = \mathcal{L}_A \times \mathcal{L}_B$ is the leakage set of C. In this work we focus on non-adaptive leakage, which we model by restricting $\mathcal{L}$ to be a singleton. Since the leakage depends entirely on the concrete device, the non-adaptive leakage model is suitable in practice, also argued by several works [1,16,18,30,32].

We recall the leakage resilience security notions that we need throughout this work. Following the blueprint by Barwell et al. [3], all notions are defined via security games where the adversary has access to one or more leakage oracle(s) which leak and one or more challenge oracle(s) which do not leak. According to [4], the former represent the power of the adversary while the latter model its goals in breaking the security of the scheme. Regarding the queries by the adversary, we follow [3] and say that an adversary *forwards* and *repeats* a query if it repeats a query across different oracles and the same oracle, respectively. For instance, querying the same tuple to the leakage encryption and challenge encryption is considered forwarding as is querying the output of an encryption oracle to a decryption oracle.

Non-adaptive Leakage. All security notions below are defined following the style put forth in [13] which in turn is based on [3]. In particular, the permitted leakage functions are given by a set of leakage functions $\mathcal{L}$.

While all the proofs hold in the general setting of adaptive leakage, just as in [13], we emphasise that we focus on non-adaptive leakage, i.e., any leakage set should be thought of as a singleton. This stems from the fact that an instantiation of the $FGHF'$ construction requires a leakage-resilient pseudorandom function which is unachievable in the adaptive leakage setting as discussed in [32], unless further restrictions are imposed on the leakage.

2.4 Security Notions

Regarding the restrictions of nonce selection by the adversary, we define *semi-nonce-respecting* adversaries. These are adversaries which are nonce-respecting, i.e., they never repeat a nonce, with respect to the challenge encryption oracle, but not with respect to the leakage encryption oracle. This follows the recent definition of misuse-resilience given in [2] and used for instance in [20]. Regarding the decryption oracles, note that there is no restriction imposed on how the nonces are selected.

In the following we recall the (leakage) security notions from [3,13] for authenticated encryption schemes, symmetric encryption schemes, MACs, function families, pseudorandom generators, and hash functions.

For authenticated encryption schemes with associated data, we define leakage-resilient authenticated encryption (LAE) security. It is the counterpart of the security notion given by Rogaway [28], recast in the leakage setting by Barwell et al. [3]. We use the code-based variant given by Degabriele et al. [13].

Definition 1 (LAE Security [13]). *Let* $\text{AEAD} = (\text{Enc}, \text{Dec})$ *be an authenticated encryption scheme with associated data and the game* LAE *be as defined in Fig. 1. For any nonce-respecting adversary* $\mathcal{A}$ *that never forwards or repeats queries to or from the oracles* Enc *and* Dec *and only makes encryption and decryption queries containing leakage functions in the respective sets* $\mathcal{L}_{AE}$ *and* $\mathcal{L}_{VD}$, *describing the leakage sets for authenticated encryption and verified decryption, its corresponding* LAE *advantage is given by:*

$$\mathbf{Adv}_{\mathrm{AEAD}}^{\mathsf{LAE}}(\mathcal{A}, \mathcal{L}_{AE}, \mathcal{L}_{VD}) = 2 \Pr\left[\mathsf{LAE}^{\mathcal{A}} \Rightarrow \mathrm{true}\right] - 1.$$

Game LAE	oracle Enc(N, A, M)	oracle Dec(N, A, C)
$b \leftarrow_{\$} \{0,1\}$	$C \leftarrow \mathrm{Enc}(K,N,A,M)$	if $b = 0$
$K \leftarrow_{\$} \mathcal{K}$	if $b = 0$	$\quad$ return $\perp$
$b' \leftarrow \mathcal{A}^{\mathsf{Enc},\mathsf{LEnc},\mathsf{Dec},\mathsf{LDec}}()$	$\quad$ return $C' \leftarrow_{\$} \{0,1\}^{|C|}$	return $M \leftarrow \mathrm{Dec}(K,N,A,C)$
return $(b' = b)$	else	
	$\quad$ return C	oracle LDec(N, A, C, L)
		$\Lambda \leftarrow L(K,N,A,C)$
	oracle LEnc(N, A, M, L)	$M \leftarrow \mathrm{Dec}(K,N,A,C)$
	$\Lambda \leftarrow L(K,N,A,M)$	return (M, Λ)
	$C \leftarrow \mathrm{Enc}(K,N,A,M)$	
	return (C, Λ)	

Fig. 1. LAE security game.

For symmetric encryption schemes we define IND-CPLA security as defined in [3], which corresponds to the classical notion of IND-CPA security enhanced with leakage.

Definition 2 (IND-CPLA Security [13]). *Let* $\mathrm{SE} = (\mathrm{Enc}, \mathrm{Dec})$ *be a symmetric encryption scheme and the game* INDCPLA *be as defined in Fig. 2. For any semi-nonce-respecting adversary* $\mathcal{A}$ *that never forwards or repeats queries to or from the oracle* Enc *and only makes encryption queries containing leakage functions in the set* $\mathcal{L}_E$, *its corresponding* IND-CPLA *advantage is given by:*

$$\mathbf{Adv}_{\mathrm{SE}}^{\mathsf{INDCPLA}}(\mathcal{A}, \mathcal{L}_E) = 2 \Pr\left[\mathsf{INDCPLA}^{\mathcal{A}} \Rightarrow \mathrm{true}\right] - 1.$$

The N2 composition theorem in [3] requires a stronger variant called IND-aCPLA, where the 'a' stands for *augmented*. In this notion, the adversary also gets access to a leakage decryption oracle. The queries, however, are heavily restricted as it can only be queried on queries forwarded from the leakage encryption oracle LEnc.

For MACs we deviate slightly from the security notion given in [3,13]. The difference is that we allow the adversary to forward queries between its leakage oracles but not between its challenge oracle and its leakage oracles. In [3,13] the adversary is not allowed to forward queries between its leakage tagging oracle and any of its verification oracles, however, forwarding between its leakage verification oracle and challenge verification oracle is permitted. Since the notions are very much akin, we write SUF-CMLA for our notion and SUF-CMLA* for the one from [3,13].

Game INDCPLA	oracle $\mathsf{Enc}(N, M)$	oracle $\mathsf{LEnc}(N, M, L)$
$b \leftarrow_\$ \{0,1\}$	$C \leftarrow \mathrm{Enc}(K, N, M)$	$\Lambda \leftarrow L(N, M, L)$
$K \leftarrow_\$ \mathcal{K}$	if $b = 0$	$C \leftarrow \mathrm{Enc}(K, N, M)$
$b' \leftarrow \mathcal{A}^{\mathsf{Enc},\mathsf{LEnc}}()$	$\quad$ return $C' \leftarrow_\$ \{0,1\}^{|C|}$	return (C, Λ)
return $(b' = b)$	else	
	$\quad$ return C	

Fig. 2. IND-CPLA security game.

Definition 3 (SUF-CMLA Security [13]). *Let* $\mathrm{MAC} = (\mathsf{Tag}, \mathsf{Ver})$ *be a message authentication code and the game* SUFCMLA *be as defined in Fig. 3. For any adversary* $\mathcal{A}$ *that never forwards queries to or from the oracle* Vfy, *and only queries leakage functions to its oracles* LTag *and* LVfy *in the respective sets* $\mathcal{L}_T$ *and* $\mathcal{L}_V$, *its corresponding* SUF-CMLA *advantage is given by:*

$$\mathbf{Adv}_{\mathrm{MAC}}^{\mathsf{SUFCMLA}}(\mathcal{A}, \mathcal{L}_T, \mathcal{L}_V) = 2\Pr\left[\mathsf{SUFCMLA}^{\mathcal{A}} \Rightarrow \mathrm{true}\right] - 1.$$

Game SUFCMLA	oracle $\mathsf{Vfy}(X, T)$	oracle $\mathsf{LTag}(X, L)$
$b \leftarrow_\$ \{0,1\}$	if $b = 0$	$\Lambda \leftarrow L(K, X)$
$K \leftarrow_\$ \mathcal{K}$	$\quad$ return $\bot$	$T \leftarrow \mathrm{Tag}(K, X)$
$b' \leftarrow \mathcal{A}^{\mathsf{Vfy},\mathsf{LTag},\mathsf{LVfy}}()$	else	return (T, Λ)
return $(b' = b)$	$\quad v \leftarrow \mathrm{Ver}(K, X, T)$	
	$\quad$ return v	oracle $\mathsf{LVfy}(X, T, L)$
		$\Lambda \leftarrow L(K, X, T)$
		$v \leftarrow \mathrm{Ver}(K, X, T)$
		return (v, Λ)

Fig. 3. SUF-CMLA security game.

For function families, we define both pseudorandomness and unpredictability under leakage. The former is well established in the literature, the latter was only recently introduced [13].

Definition 4 (LPRF Security [13]). *Let* $\mathcal{F}: \mathcal{K} \times \mathcal{X} \to \{0,1\}^t$ *be a function family over the domain* $\mathcal{X}$ *and indexed by* $\mathcal{K}$, *and the game* LPRF *be as defined in Fig. 4. For any adversary* $\mathcal{A}$ *that never forwards or repeats queries to or from the oracle* F *and only queries leakage functions in the set* $\mathcal{L}_F$, *its corresponding* LPRF *advantage is given by:*

$$\mathbf{Adv}_{\mathcal{F}}^{\mathsf{LPRF}}(\mathcal{A}, \mathcal{L}_F) = 2\Pr\left[\mathsf{LPRF}^{\mathcal{A}} \Rightarrow \mathrm{true}\right] - 1.$$

Removing the leakage oracle LF restores the classical notion of PRF security. We denote the corresponding game analogously to the other games by PRF (dropping the L for 'leakage'). We will use this game for our separation example in Sect. 3.

Game LPRF	oracle $F(X)$	oracle $LF(X, L)$
$b \leftarrow_\$ \{0,1\}$	if $b = 0$	$y \leftarrow F(K, X)$
$K \leftarrow_\$ \mathcal{K}$	return $y \leftarrow_\$ \{0,1\}^t$	$\Lambda \leftarrow L(K, X)$
$b' \leftarrow \mathcal{A}^{F,LF}()$	else	return (y, Λ)
return $(b' = b)$	return $F(K, X)$	

Fig. 4. LPRF security game.

Definition 5 (LUF Security [13]). *Let* $\mathcal{F}: \mathcal{K} \times \mathcal{X} \to \{0,1\}^t$ *be a function family over the domain* $\mathcal{X}$ *and indexed by* $\mathcal{K}$*, and the* LUF *game be as defined in Fig. 5. Then for any adversary* $\mathcal{A}$ *its corresponding* LUF *advantage is given by:*

$$\mathbf{Adv}_{\mathcal{F}}^{\mathsf{LUF}}(\mathcal{A}, \mathcal{L}_F) = \Pr\left[\mathsf{LUF}^{\mathcal{A}} \Rightarrow \mathrm{true}\right].$$

A crucial difference between LUF and LPRF is that the former allows the adversary to obtain leakage for an input and still being able to win the game by predicting the output for this input while the latter does not allow such queries. This is exactly the difference that we exploit in our separation example.

Game LUF	oracle $\mathrm{Guess}(X, Y')$	oracle $F(X)$
win $\leftarrow$ false	$Y \leftarrow \mathcal{F}(K, X)$	$\mathcal{S} \leftarrow_\cup X$
$\mathcal{S} \leftarrow \emptyset$	if $X \notin \mathcal{S} \wedge Y = Y'$	$Y \leftarrow \mathcal{F}(K, X)$
$K \leftarrow_\$ \mathcal{K}$	win $\leftarrow$ true	return Y
$b' \leftarrow \mathcal{A}^{\mathrm{Guess},F,\mathrm{Lkg}}()$	return $(Y = Y')$	oracle $\mathrm{Lkg}(X, L)$
return win		$\Lambda \leftarrow L(K, X)$
		return Λ

Fig. 5. LUF security game.

We make use of the following definition of a pseudorandom generator which enables the adversary to specify the output length (in bits) by querying it to the challenge oracle. The difference to [13] is that we stick to the single challenge case as opposed to their notion of multiple challenges.

Definition 6 (Pseudorandom Generators [13]**).** *Let* $\mathcal{G}\colon \mathcal{S} \times \mathbb{N} \to \{0,1\}^*$ *be a pseudorandom generator with an associated seed space* $\mathcal{S}$*, and let the* PRG *game be as defined in Fig. 6. Then for any adversary* $\mathcal{A}$*, making exactly one query to* G*, its corresponding* PRG *advantage is given by:*

$$\mathbf{Adv}_{\mathcal{G}}^{\mathsf{PRG}}(\mathcal{A}) = 2\Pr\left[\mathsf{PRG}^{\mathcal{A}} \Rightarrow \mathsf{true}\right] - 1.$$

Game PRG	oracle G(L)
$b \leftarrow\!\!{\scriptstyle\$}\ \{0,1\}$	if $b = 0$
$b' \leftarrow \mathcal{A}^{\mathsf{G}}()$	$\quad R \leftarrow\!\!{\scriptstyle\$}\ \{0,1\}^L$
return $(b' = b)$	else
	$\quad S \leftarrow\!\!{\scriptstyle\$}\ \mathcal{S}$
	$\quad R \leftarrow \mathcal{G}(S, L)$
	return R

Fig. 6. PRG security game.

For a hash function $\mathcal{H}$ over a generic domain $\mathcal{X}$, we define its collision resistance below.

Definition 7 (Collision Resistance [13]**).** *Let* $\mathcal{H}\colon \mathcal{X} \to \{0,1\}^w$ *be a hash function. Then for any adversary* $\mathcal{A}$ *its corresponding advantage is given by:*

$$\mathbf{Adv}_{\mathcal{H}}^{\mathsf{CR}}(\mathcal{A}) = \Pr\left[\mathcal{H}(X_0) = \mathcal{H}(X_1) \wedge X_0 \neq X_1 \wedge X_0, X_1 \in \mathcal{X} \mid (X_0, X_1) \leftarrow \mathcal{A}\right].$$

2.5 The FGHF′ Construction

Degabriele et al. [13] developed the FGHF′ construction, which allows to build a leakage-resilient AEAD scheme from four simple building blocks: two fixed-input-length functions $\mathcal{F}$ and $\mathcal{F}'$, a pseudorandom generator $\mathcal{G}$, and a hash function $\mathcal{H}$. The function $\mathcal{F}$ and the pseudorandom generator $\mathcal{G}$ build the encryption scheme $\mathrm{SE}[\mathcal{F},\mathcal{G}]$ while the hash function $\mathcal{H}$ and the function $\mathcal{F}'$ build the MAC $\mathrm{MAC}[\mathcal{H},\mathcal{F}']$. The construction is illustrated in Fig. 7 while the pseudocode is given in Fig. 8.

The notable feature of the construction is that only the fixed-input-length functions have to be leakage-resilient, while the pseudorandom generator and the hash function can be instantiated with off-the-shelf primitives from the literature. The security implications, which illustrate one of the main results from [13], are displayed in Fig. 9. Note the special structure of the FGHF′ construction, that is, $\mathrm{SE}[\mathcal{F},\mathcal{G}]$ being a mirror-like encryption scheme and $\mathrm{MAC}[\mathcal{H},\mathcal{F}']$ being a canonical MAC (considering the composition of $\mathcal{H}$ and $\mathcal{F}'$ a function with variable-input-length). Combined with the leakage model, we conclude that the leakage sets $\mathcal{L}_E$ and $\mathcal{L}_D$ for $\mathrm{SE}[\mathcal{F},\mathcal{G}]$ are equal as are the leakage sets $\mathcal{L}_T$ and

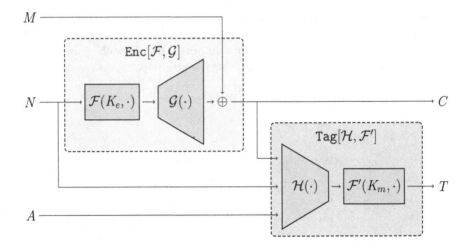

Fig. 7. Graphical illustration of the FGHF' construction [13]. It consists of an encryption scheme $\mathrm{SE}[\mathcal{F}, \mathcal{G}]$ and a MAC $\mathrm{MAC}[\mathcal{H}, \mathcal{F}']$ composed via the N2 composition. The encryption scheme consists of a fixed-input-length LPRF $\mathcal{F}$ and a PRG $\mathcal{G}$. The MAC consists of a vector hash $\mathcal{H}$ and a fixed-input-length function $\mathcal{F}'$ that is both a LUF and an LPRF. The encryption and tagging algorithm of $\mathrm{SE}[\mathcal{F}, \mathcal{G}]$ and $\mathrm{MAC}[\mathcal{H}, \mathcal{F}']$ are $\mathrm{Enc}[\mathcal{F}, \mathcal{G}]$ and $\mathrm{Tag}[\mathcal{H}, \mathcal{F}']$, respectively.

algorithm $\mathrm{Enc}((K_e, K_m), N, A, M)$	**algorithm** $\mathrm{Dec}((K_e, K_m), N, A, (C_e, T))$
// Compute ciphertext using $\mathrm{SE}[\mathcal{F}, \mathcal{G}]$	$H \leftarrow \mathcal{H}(N, A, C_e)$
$S \leftarrow \mathcal{F}(K_e, N)$	$T' \leftarrow \mathcal{F}'(K_m, H)$
$C_e \leftarrow \mathcal{G}(S, |M|) \oplus M$	**if** $T' = T$
// Compute tag using $\mathrm{MAC}[\mathcal{H}, \mathcal{F}']$	$\quad S \leftarrow \mathcal{F}(K_e, N)$
$H \leftarrow \mathcal{H}(N, A, C_e)$	$\quad M \leftarrow \mathcal{G}(S, |C_e|) \oplus C_e$
$T \leftarrow \mathcal{F}'(K_m, H)$	$\quad$ **return** M
return $C \leftarrow (C_e, T)$	**return** $\perp$

Fig. 8. Pseudocode of the FGHF' construction [13].

$\mathcal{L}_V$ for $\mathrm{MAC}[\mathcal{H}, \mathcal{F}']$, i.e., $\mathcal{L}_E = \mathcal{L}_D = \mathcal{L}_F \times \mathcal{L}_G$ and $\mathcal{L}_T = \mathcal{L}_V = \mathcal{L}_H \times \mathcal{L}_{F'}$. Here, $\mathcal{L}_F$, $\mathcal{L}_G$, $\mathcal{L}_H$, and $\mathcal{L}_{F'}$ are the leakage sets of the underlying components $\mathcal{F}$, $\mathcal{G}$, $\mathcal{H}$, and $\mathcal{F}'$. The very same is implicitly assumed in [13]. Likewise, we obtain the leakage sets $\mathcal{L}_{AE} = \mathcal{L}_E \times \mathcal{L}_T = \mathcal{L}_F \times \mathcal{L}_G \times \mathcal{L}_H \times \mathcal{L}_{F'} = \mathcal{L}_D \times \mathcal{L}_V = \mathcal{L}_{VD}$ for the resulting AEAD scheme.

3 Unpredictability and Pseudorandomness Under Leakage

Along with the FGHF' construction, Degabriele et al. [13] introduce a security notion for unpredictability of functions under leakage. They prove the existence

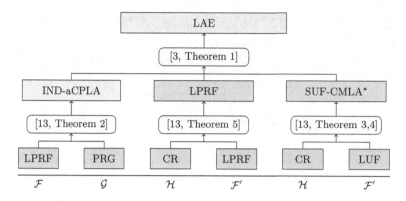

Fig. 9. Security implications for the FGHF′ construction from [13, Theorem 6]. Note that we do not give the formal definition of IND-aCPLA and SUF-CMLA* as we use slightly different notions.

of functions that achieve both unpredictability and pseudorandomness under leakage. Regarding the relation between these notions, they claim them to be incomparable, without giving a clear justification or a proof for this statement. We confirm this by providing a separation example which proves that the notions do not imply one another. Therefore, we give two functions: under leakage, the first function is unpredictable but not pseudorandom, while the second function is pseudorandom but not unpredictable. For both functions, we assume a function which, under leakage, is both unpredictable and pseudorandom. Note that this assumption is valid as the existence of such functions has been shown in [13] for the sponge-based instantiation SLAE of the FGHF′ construction.

3.1 Under Leakage: Unpredictability $\nRightarrow$ Pseudorandomness

We start with the simple case, that is, a function which is unpredictable but not pseudorandom under leakage.

Construction 8. *Let* $\mathcal{F}_* \colon \{0,1\}^k \times \{0,1\}^n \to \{0,1\}^t$ *be a function. Define the function*

$$\mathcal{F} \colon \{0,1\}^k \times \{0,1\}^n \to \{0,1\}^{t+1}$$
$$\mathcal{F}(K, X) \mapsto 0 \parallel \mathcal{F}_*(K, X).$$

Lemma 9. *Let* $\mathcal{F}_*$ *be a function that is both a* LUF *and an* LPRF *and* $\mathcal{F}$ *be the function constructed from* $\mathcal{F}_*$ *according to Construction 8. It holds that* $\mathcal{F}$ *is a* LUF *but not an* LPRF.

Proof. The function $\mathcal{F}$ is LUF as any LUF adversary against $\mathcal{F}$ can easily be transformed into a LUF adversary against $\mathcal{F}_*$. On the other hand, the leading 0 of any output makes it easy to distinguish the function from a random function. If, after several queries, an output starting with 1 is observed, the adversary outputs 0 (indicating ideal), otherwise, it outputs 1 (indicating real). $\qquad\square$

Games G_0, G_1, G_2	oracle $F(X)$ in G_0	oracle $LF(X, (L_O, L_I))$
$b \leftarrow_\$ \{0,1\}$	$K_s \leftarrow \mathcal{F}_I(K, X)$	$K_s \leftarrow \mathcal{F}_I(K, X)$
$K \leftarrow_\$ \mathcal{K}$	return $Y \leftarrow \mathcal{F}_O(K_s, X)$	$\Lambda_I \leftarrow L_I(K, X)$
$b' \leftarrow \mathcal{A}^{F,LF}()$		$Y \leftarrow \mathcal{F}_O(K_s, X)$
	oracle $F(X)$ in G_1	$\Lambda_O \leftarrow L_O(K_s, X)$
	$K_s \leftarrow_\$ \{0,1\}^s$	return $(Y, (\Lambda_O, \Lambda_I))$
	return $Y \leftarrow \mathcal{F}_O(K_s, X)$	
	oracle $F(X)$ in G_2	
	return $Y \leftarrow_\$ \{0,1\}^t$	

Fig. 10. Games G_0, G_1, and G_2 used in the proof of Lemma 11. The games share the leakage oracle LF, while each game uses its own challenge oracle as described.

3.2   Under Leakage: Pseudorandomness $\not\Rightarrow$ Unpredictability

Now we address the complex part of the separation example and show that there are functions which are pseudorandom but not unpredictable under leakage.

Construction 10. Let $\mathcal{F}_O \colon \{0,1\}^s \times \{0,1\}^n \to \{0,1\}^t$ and $\mathcal{F}_I \colon \{0,1\}^k \times \{0,1\}^n \to \{0,1\}^s$ be functions. The subscripts O and I indicate the outer and inner function, respectively. Define the function

$$\mathcal{F} \colon \{0,1\}^k \times \{0,1\}^n \to \{0,1\}^t$$
$$\mathcal{F}(K, X) \mapsto \mathcal{F}_O(\mathcal{F}_I(K, X), X).$$

The idea of Construction 10 is as follows. It uses some *master key* K and, for each input X, it derives a *session key* using the inner function $\mathcal{F}_I$, i.e., $K_s = \mathcal{F}_I(K, X)$. The output Y is generated by the outer function $\mathcal{F}_O$ using the session key K_s and input X. The lemma below shows that the construction is pseudorandom but not unpredictable under leakage.

Lemma 11. Let $\mathcal{F}_O$ and $\mathcal{F}_I$ be two functions and $\mathcal{F}$ be the function constructed from $\mathcal{F}_O$ and $\mathcal{F}_I$ according to Construction 10. Suppose $\mathcal{F}_I$ is both a LUF and an LPRF and $\mathcal{F}_O$ is PRF. Then $\mathcal{F}$ is an LPRF but not a LUF.

Proof. We first show that $\mathcal{F}$ is an LPRF. For simplicity, we restrict the adversary to a single challenge query and argue at the end how it can be lifted to multiple challenge queries. We make use of the games G_0, G_1, and G_2 displayed in Fig. 10. The games are constructed such that G_0 is equal to LPRF with secret bit $b = 1$ and G_2 is equal to LPRF with secret bit $b = 0$. Recall that the leakage set $\mathcal{L}_F$ of $\mathcal{F}$ is the Cartesian product of the leakage sets $\mathcal{L}_O$ of $\mathcal{F}_O$ and $\mathcal{L}_I$ of $\mathcal{F}_I$. Using a simple reformulation to the adversarial advantage yields

$$\mathbf{Adv}_{\mathcal{F}}^{LPRF}(\mathcal{A}, \mathcal{L}_F) = \Pr\left[\mathcal{A}^{LPRF} \Rightarrow 1 \mid b = 1\right] - \Pr\left[\mathcal{A}^{LPRF} \Rightarrow 1 \mid b = 0\right]$$
$$= \Pr\left[\mathcal{A}^{G_0} \Rightarrow 1\right] - \Pr\left[\mathcal{A}^{G_2} \Rightarrow 1\right]. \tag{1}$$

For the game hop between G_0 and G_1, we construct an LPRF adversary $\mathcal{A}_{lprf}$ against $\mathcal{F}_I$ as follows. When $\mathcal{A}$ makes its query X to F, $\mathcal{A}_{lprf}$ queries X to its own challenge oracle to obtain the session key K_s, computes $Y \leftarrow \mathcal{F}_O(K_s, X)$, and sends Y back to $\mathcal{A}$. For leakage queries $(X, (L_O, L_I))$ by $\mathcal{A}$, $\mathcal{A}_{lprf}$ queries its own leakage oracle on (X, L_I) to obtain (K_s, Λ_I), computes $Y \leftarrow \mathcal{F}_O(K_s, X)$ and $\Lambda_O \leftarrow L_O(K_s, X)$, and sends $(Y, (\Lambda_O, \Lambda_I))$ back to $\mathcal{A}$. It is easy to see that $\mathcal{A}_{lprf}$ perfectly simulates G_0 or G_1 for $\mathcal{A}$ depending on its own challenge. Also all queries by $\mathcal{A}_{lprf}$ are permitted as it queries exactly the same values as $\mathcal{A}$. Hence we conclude with

$$\Pr\left[\mathcal{A}^{\mathsf{G}_0} \Rightarrow 1\right] - \Pr\left[\mathcal{A}^{\mathsf{G}_1} \Rightarrow 1\right] \leq \mathbf{Adv}_{\mathcal{F}_I}^{\mathsf{LPRF}}(\mathcal{A}_{lprf}, \mathcal{L}_I). \tag{2}$$

For the game hop between G_1 and G_2, we construct the following PRF adversary $\mathcal{A}_{prf}$ against $\mathcal{F}_O$. At the start, $\mathcal{A}_{prf}$ samples a random master key K which it will use for the leakage queries by $\mathcal{A}$. Whenever $\mathcal{A}$ queries $(X, (L_O, L_I))$ to its leakage oracle, $\mathcal{A}_{prf}$ (locally) computes $K_s \leftarrow \mathcal{F}_I(K, X)$, $\Lambda_I \leftarrow L_I(K, X)$, $Y \leftarrow \mathcal{F}_O(K_s, X)$, and $\Lambda_O \leftarrow L_O(K_s, X)$, and sends $(Y, (\Lambda_O, \Lambda_I))$ to $\mathcal{A}$. For the challenge query X by $\mathcal{A}$, $\mathcal{A}_{prf}$ forwards the query to its own challenge oracle and the response back to $\mathcal{A}$. It is again easy to see that $\mathcal{A}_{prf}$ perfectly simulates the games G_1 and G_2 for $\mathcal{A}$ depending on its own challenge. The significant feature is that $\mathcal{A}_{prf}$ can simulate the leakage oracle for $\mathcal{A}$ locally, which is why we only need PRF security as opposed to LPRF security. We conclude with

$$\Pr\left[\mathcal{A}^{\mathsf{G}_1} \Rightarrow 1\right] - \Pr\left[\mathcal{A}^{\mathsf{G}_2} \Rightarrow 1\right] \leq \mathbf{Adv}_{\mathcal{F}_O}^{\mathsf{PRF}}(\mathcal{A}_{prf}). \tag{3}$$

Inserting (2) and (3) in (1) yields

$$\mathbf{Adv}_{\mathcal{F}}^{\mathsf{LPRF}}(\mathcal{A}, \mathcal{L}_F) = \Pr\left[\mathcal{A}^{\mathsf{G}_0} \Rightarrow 1\right] - \Pr\left[\mathcal{A}^{\mathsf{G}_2} \Rightarrow 1\right]$$
$$\leq \mathbf{Adv}_{\mathcal{F}_I}^{\mathsf{LPRF}}(\mathcal{A}_{lprf}, \mathcal{L}_I) + \mathbf{Adv}_{\mathcal{F}_O}^{\mathsf{PRF}}(\mathcal{A}_{prf}).$$

We briefly discuss how the proof can be adapted if $\mathcal{A}$ is allowed to make multiple challenge queries. The first part works exactly the same, that is, $\mathcal{A}_{lprf}$ forwards the query X to get the session key K_s and computes $Y \leftarrow \mathcal{F}_O(K_s, X)$. For the second part, there is a subtle issue why the same reduction does not work if $\mathcal{A}$ makes multiple challenge queries. In G_1, $\mathcal{A}$ expects that every query uses a fresh session key sampled uniformly at random, while the key used in the game PRF is fixed, thus it can not simulate the correct game for $\mathcal{A}$. Instead, the game hop can be lifted to multiple challenge queries via a straightforward hybrid argument, where $\mathcal{A}_{prf}$ answers the first $i - 1$ queries with random values, the i-th query using its own challenge oracle just as described for the single challenge case, and the last $q - i$ queries with $\mathcal{F}_O(K_s, X)$ for a randomly chosen session key K_s. This induces a factor q, the number of challenge queries, into the bound above.

It remains to show that $\mathcal{F}$ is not a LUF. We construct the following LUF adversary. It queries its leakage oracle Lkg on a randomly chosen input X, leaking the session key K_s. Given the session key, it computes $Y \leftarrow \mathcal{F}_O(K_s, X)$ and sends (X, Y) to its challenge oracle Guess, which will set the winning flag to true. $\quad\square$

Our LUF adversary exploits the fact that the game LUF allows to obtain leakage for the input for which the output is predicted. Hence, the adversary leaks the session key K_s for some input X, which enables it to perfectly predict the output. Note that this does not enable the adversary to predict an output for a different input. Our LUF adversary bypasses the LUF security of the inner function $\mathcal{F}_I$ and attacks the outer function $\mathcal{F}_O$ instead. Regarding the LPRF security, observe the following. The LPRF adversary is also able to obtain a session key K_s through its leakage oracle. However, this session key is only valid for the queried input and the game LPRF does not allow to query this input to the challenge oracle, which would make the notion unachievable anyway. We essentially show that it is sufficient to secure the master key K by deriving the session keys using an inner function with strong security guarantees (LPRF and LUF in our case).

We believe this result to be of independent interest as it shows that extra caution is judicious in the leakage setting. Our constructions show how well-known and established results from the leak-free setting, like the equivalence between pseudorandomness and unpredictability, do not necessarily remain valid in the leakage setting.

4   Leakage Resilience of the N2 Construction

In the previous section we established that the security notions LUF and LPRF are incomparable. This entails that any instantiation of the FGHF′ construction has to prove LPRF and LUF security separately. Considering the instantiation SLAE [13], proving these notions is the most complex part of the work. Thus, we now turn our attention towards removing the requirement of LUF security. As argued in [13], LUF security is required to build a secure MAC according to the composition theorem for the N2 construction [3] (see also Fig. 9). Recall that Degabriele et al. [13] prove that the encryption scheme SE[$\mathcal{F}, \mathcal{G}$] and the MAC MAC[$\mathcal{H}, \mathcal{F}'$], underlying the FGHF′ construction, achieve the security notion required by the N2 composition theorem by Barwell et al. [3]. However, Barwell et al. prove their composition for arbitrary encryption schemes and MACs, while Degabriele et al. focus on a mirror-like encryption scheme and a canonical MAC. In this section, we recast the composition theorem for the N2 construction to the case of mirror-like encryption schemes and canonical MACs.

The theorem below shows that the N2 composition of a mirror-like encryption scheme and a canonical MAC is LAE-secure if the underlying components are. For ease of exposition, we give the full proof for our setting. Subsequently, we discuss how our proof differs from the one given in [3].

Theorem 12 (LAE Security of the N2 Construction). *Let* SE $=$ (Enc, Dec) *be a mirror-like symmetric encryption scheme and* MAC $=$ (Tag, Ver) *be a canonical MAC with associated leakage sets* $(\mathcal{L}_E, \mathcal{L}_D)$ *and* $(\mathcal{L}_T, \mathcal{L}_V)$, *respectively. Let* N2 *be the composition of* SE *and* MAC *as displayed in Fig. 7 with associated leakage sets* $\mathcal{L}_{AE} = \mathcal{L}_E \times \mathcal{L}_T$ *and* $\mathcal{L}_{VD} = \mathcal{L}_D \times \mathcal{L}_V$. *For any nonce-respecting adversary* $\mathcal{A}_{ae}$ *against* N2 *there exists a semi-nonce-respecting* IND-CPLA *adversary*

$\mathcal{A}_{se}$ *against* SE, *an* LPRF *adversary* $\mathcal{A}_{lprf}$ *against* Tag, *and a* SUF-CMLA *adversary* $\mathcal{A}_{mac}$ *against* MAC *such that:*

$$\mathbf{Adv}_{N2}^{LAE}(\mathcal{A}_{ae}, \mathcal{L}_{AE}, \mathcal{L}_{VD}) \leq \mathbf{Adv}_{SE}^{INDCPLA}(\mathcal{A}_{se}, \mathcal{L}_{E}) + \mathbf{Adv}_{Tag}^{LPRF}(\mathcal{A}_{lprf}, \mathcal{L}_{T})$$
$$+ \mathbf{Adv}_{MAC}^{SUFCMLA}(\mathcal{A}_{mac}, \mathcal{L}_{T}, \mathcal{L}_{V}).$$

Proof. Since SE is a mirror-like encryption scheme and MAC is a canonical MAC, it holds that $\mathcal{L}_{E} = \mathcal{L}_{D}$ and $\mathcal{L}_{T} = \mathcal{L}_{V}$. This immediately implies that the leakage sets $\mathcal{L}_{AE}$ and $\mathcal{L}_{VD}$ of N2 are identical. We us a sequence of games $G_0, \ldots, G_3$ shown in Fig. 11. Game G_0 is the game LAE instantiated with N2 with secret bit fixed to 1. In game G_1, the decryption oracle is changed to reject any queried ciphertext. Game G_2 and G_3 are like G_1, except for the following differences. Game G_2 generates challenge ciphertext by sampling it at random while but still computing the real tag of this ciphertext. In game G_3 both the ciphertext and the tag are sampled at random. Hence G_3 equals the game LAE instantiated with N2 with secret bit fixed to 0. Using a simple reformulation to the adversarial advantage yields

$$\mathbf{Adv}_{N2}^{LAE}(\mathcal{A}_{ae}, \mathcal{L}_{AE}, \mathcal{L}_{VD}) = \Pr\left[\mathcal{A}_{ae}^{LAE} \Rightarrow 1 \mid b = 1\right] - \Pr\left[\mathcal{A}_{ae}^{LAE} \Rightarrow 1 \mid b = 0\right]$$
$$= \Pr\left[\mathcal{A}_{ae}^{G_0} \Rightarrow 1\right] - \Pr\left[\mathcal{A}_{ae}^{G_3} \Rightarrow 1\right]$$
$$= \sum_{i=1}^{3} \left(\Pr\left[\mathcal{A}_{ae}^{G_{i-1}} \Rightarrow 1\right] - \Pr\left[\mathcal{A}_{ae}^{G_i} \Rightarrow 1\right]\right). \qquad (4)$$

Below we bound each of the game hops. The hop from G_0 to G_1 is bound by the SUF-CMLA security of the underlying MAC MAC, the hop from G_1 to G_2 by the IND-CPLA security of the underlying encryption scheme SE, and the hop from G_2 to G_3 by the LPRF security of the tagging algorithm Tag.

Let us start with the adversarial advantage between games G_0 and G_1. We construct the following SUF-CMLA adversary $\mathcal{A}_{mac}$. It samples a random key K_e for the encryption scheme SE. Queries (N, A, M) to Enc are answered by $\mathcal{A}_{mac}$ as follows. It computes the ciphertext $C_e \leftarrow \text{Enc}(K_e, N, M)$, obtains the tag T by invoking its oracle LTag on $((N, A, C_e), \emptyset)^2$, and sends the ciphertext $C \leftarrow (C_e, T)$ back to $\mathcal{A}_{ae}$. Leakage encryption queries $(N, A, M, (L_e, L_t))$ are processed as follows. The ciphertext $C_e \leftarrow \text{Enc}(K_e, N, M)$ and corresponding leakage $\Lambda_e \leftarrow L_e(K_e, N, M)$ are computed locally by $\mathcal{A}_{mac}$. Subsequently, it queries its leakage oracle LTag on $((N, A, C_e), L_t)$ to obtain (T, Λ_t) and sends back $C \leftarrow (C_e, T)$ and $\Lambda \leftarrow (\Lambda_e, \Lambda_t)$ to $\mathcal{A}_{ae}$. For any leakage decryption query $(N, A, (C_e, T), (L_d, L_v))$, $\mathcal{A}_{mac}$ forwards $((N, A, C_e), T, L_v)$ to its leakage oracle LVfy to obtain (V, Λ_v), which it forwards to $\mathcal{A}_{ae}$ if $V = \bot$. Otherwise, i.e., $V = \top$, $\mathcal{A}_{mac}$ computes $M \leftarrow \text{Dec}(K_e, N, C_e)$ and $\Lambda_d \leftarrow L_e(K_e, N, C_e)$, and sends back $(M, \Lambda_d, \Lambda_v)$ to $\mathcal{A}_{ae}$. Whenever $\mathcal{A}_{ae}$ queries its oracle Dec on $(N, A, (C_e, T))$, $\mathcal{A}_{mac}$ forwards $((N, A, C_e), T)$ to its oracle Vfy. If the response of Vfy is $\bot$, it forwards it to $\mathcal{A}_{ae}$, otherwise, it computes $M \leftarrow \text{Dec}(K_e, N, C_e)$ and sends it to $\mathcal{A}_{ae}$.

---

^{2} $\mathcal{A}_{mac}$ does not submit a leakage function, as it simulates a challenge oracle for $\mathcal{A}_{ae}$.

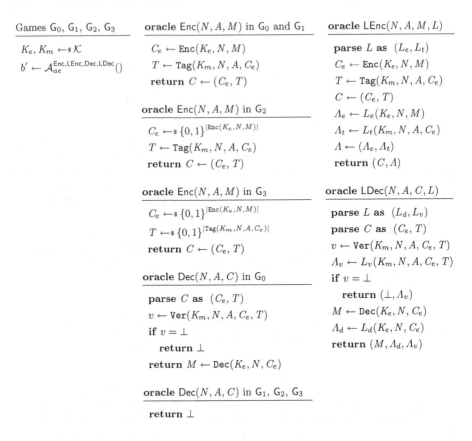

Games G_0, G_1, G_2, G_3

$K_e, K_m \leftarrow_\$ \mathcal{K}$
$b' \leftarrow \mathcal{A}_{ae}^{\mathsf{Enc,LEnc,Dec,LDec}}()$

oracle $\mathsf{Enc}(N, A, M)$ in G_0 and G_1

$C_e \leftarrow \mathsf{Enc}(K_e, N, M)$
$T \leftarrow \mathsf{Tag}(K_m, N, A, C_e)$
return $C \leftarrow (C_e, T)$

oracle $\mathsf{Enc}(N, A, M)$ in G_2

$C_e \leftarrow_\$ \{0,1\}^{|\mathsf{Enc}(K_e,N,M)|}$
$T \leftarrow \mathsf{Tag}(K_m, N, A, C_e)$
return $C \leftarrow (C_e, T)$

oracle $\mathsf{Enc}(N, A, M)$ in G_3

$C_e \leftarrow_\$ \{0,1\}^{|\mathsf{Enc}(K_e,N,M)|}$
$T \leftarrow_\$ \{0,1\}^{|\mathsf{Tag}(K_m,N,A,C_e)|}$
return $C \leftarrow (C_e, T)$

oracle $\mathsf{Dec}(N, A, C)$ in G_0

parse C **as** (C_e, T)
$v \leftarrow \mathsf{Ver}(K_m, N, A, C_e, T)$
if $v = \bot$
  return $\bot$
return $M \leftarrow \mathsf{Dec}(K_e, N, C_e)$

oracle $\mathsf{Dec}(N, A, C)$ in G_1, G_2, G_3

return $\bot$

oracle $\mathsf{LEnc}(N, A, M, L)$

parse L **as** (L_e, L_t)
$C_e \leftarrow \mathsf{Enc}(K_e, N, M)$
$T \leftarrow \mathsf{Tag}(K_m, N, A, C_e)$
$C \leftarrow (C_e, T)$
$\Lambda_e \leftarrow L_e(K_e, N, M)$
$\Lambda_t \leftarrow L_t(K_m, N, A, C_e)$
$\Lambda \leftarrow (\Lambda_e, \Lambda_t)$
return (C, Λ)

oracle $\mathsf{LDec}(N, A, C, L)$

parse L **as** (L_d, L_v)
parse C **as** (C_e, T)
$v \leftarrow \mathsf{Ver}(K_m, N, A, C_e, T)$
$\Lambda_v \leftarrow L_v(K_m, N, A, C_e, T)$
if $v = \bot$
  return $(\bot, \Lambda_v)$
$M \leftarrow \mathsf{Dec}(K_e, N, C_e)$
$\Lambda_d \leftarrow L_d(K_e, N, C_e)$
return $(M, \Lambda_d, \Lambda_v)$

Fig. 11. Games $G_0, \ldots, G_3$ used in the proof of Theorem 12. The oracles LEnc and LDec are identical across the games. Each game uses the oracles Enc and Dec as specified.

Clearly, $\mathcal{A}_{mac}$ queries its leakage oracles LTag and LVfy only on the permissive functions, as $\mathcal{A}_{ae}$ does. $\mathcal{A}_{mac}$ does also not make any prohibited query, as it invokes its challenge oracle Vfy if and only if $\mathcal{A}_{ae}$ makes a query to its challenge decryption oracle Dec which never forwards any query to or from it.

Recall that the difference between G_0 and G_1 is that the former implements the real decryption oracle while the latter rejects any decryption query. Conditioned on the secret bit b of SUFCMLA being 0, $\mathcal{A}_{mac}$ never decrypts C_e, hence it perfectly simulates G_1 for $\mathcal{A}_{ae}$. Likewise, if $b = 1$, $\mathcal{A}_{mac}$ only decrypts if the tag T is valid, thus it perfectly simulates G_0 for $\mathcal{A}_{ae}$. Hence we conclude with

$$\Pr\left[\mathcal{A}_{ae}^{G_0} \Rightarrow 1\right] - \Pr\left[\mathcal{A}_{ae}^{G_1} \Rightarrow 1\right] \leq \mathbf{Adv}_{\mathrm{MAC}}^{\mathsf{SUFCMLA}}(\mathcal{A}_{mac}, \mathcal{L}_T, \mathcal{L}_V). \quad (5)$$

For the remaining game hops, note that the oracle Dec rejects any ciphertext irrespective of the validity of the tag which is why we omit it in the description as every reduction simply responds with $\bot$.

For the game hop between G_1 and G_2, we construct an IND-CPLA adversary $\mathcal{A}_{se}$ as follows. It generates a key K_m for MAC and runs the adversary $\mathcal{A}_{ae}$ answering its queries as follows. For leakage queries $(N, A, M, (L_e, L_t))$ to LEnc it passes (N, M, L_e) to its own oracle LEnc and obtains (C_e, Λ_e) in return. It computes the tag $T \leftarrow \mathsf{Tag}(K_m, N, A, C_e)$, corresponding leakage $\Lambda_t \leftarrow L_t(K_m, N, A, C_e)$, and sends $((C_e, T), (\Lambda_e, \Lambda_t))$ back to $\mathcal{A}_{ae}$. For leakage queries $(N, A, (C_e, T), (L_d, L_v))$ to LDec, $\mathcal{A}_{se}$ first computes $V \leftarrow \mathsf{Ver}(K_m, (N, A, C_e), T)$ and $\Lambda_v \leftarrow L_v(K_m, N, A, C_e, T)$. If $V = \bot$, it sends $(\bot, \Lambda_v)$ back to $\mathcal{A}_{ae}$. If $V = \top$, it forwards (N, M, L_e) to its own leakage encryption oracle LEnc to obtain $(M, \Lambda_d)^3$ and sends $(M, (\Lambda_d, \Lambda_v))$ back to $\mathcal{A}_{ae}$. Queries (N, A, M) to Enc are handled by obtaining C_e from its own challenge encryption oracle invoked with (N, M), computing the tag $T \leftarrow \mathsf{Tag}(K_m, N, A, C_e)$, and sending (C_e, T) back to $\mathcal{A}_{ae}$.

Since $\mathcal{A}_{ae}$ queries its leakage oracles only on functions in the corresponding leakage set, so does $\mathcal{A}_{se}$. Every challenge encryption query by $\mathcal{A}_{ae}$ entails that $\mathcal{A}_{se}$ invokes its challenge encryption query. Likewise, every leakage query, either encryption or decryption, leads to a leakage encryption query by $\mathcal{A}_{se}$. As a valid LAE adversary, $\mathcal{A}_{ae}$ does not forward queries from challenge to leakage oracles or vice versa, as does $\mathcal{A}_{se}$. Note further that $\mathcal{A}_{se}$ is semi-nonce-respecting. This follows from $\mathcal{A}_{se}$ simulating both leakage oracles of $\mathcal{A}_{ae}$ using its leakage encryption oracle and $\mathcal{A}_{ae}$ being nonce-respecting.

It is easy to see that $\mathcal{A}_{se}$ perfectly simulates either G_1 or G_2 for $\mathcal{A}_{se}$. The games differ in the ciphertext part C_e generated by Enc. In G_1 it is the encryption of the message M, while it is a random bit string in G_2. By setting C_e to the output of its own challenge oracle, $\mathcal{A}_{se}$ simulates G_1 and G_2 for $\mathcal{A}_{ae}$ conditioned on the secret bit b of the game INDCPLA being 1 and 0, respectively. It holds that

$$\Pr\left[\mathcal{A}_{ae}^{G_1} \Rightarrow 1\right] - \Pr\left[\mathcal{A}_{ae}^{G_2} \Rightarrow 1\right] \le \mathbf{Adv}_{\mathrm{SE}}^{\mathsf{INDCPLA}}(\mathcal{A}_{se}, \mathcal{L}_E). \qquad (6)$$

Finally, we construct the following LPRF adversary $\mathcal{A}_{lprf}$ to bound the adversarial advantage between G_2 and G_3. It generates a key K_e for the underlying encryption scheme. Leakage encryption queries $(N, A, M, (L_e, L_t))$ are processed by locally computing $C_e \leftarrow \mathsf{Enc}(K_e, N, M)$ and $\Lambda_e \leftarrow L_e(K_e, N, M)$, invoking LF on $((N, A, C_e), L_t)$ to obtain (T, Λ_t), and sending $((C_e, T), (\Lambda_e, \Lambda_t))$ back to $\mathcal{A}_{ae}$. For leakage decryption queries $(N, A, (C_e, T), (L_d, L_v))$, $\mathcal{A}_{lprf}$ sends $((N, A, C_e), L_v)$ to its leakage oracle LF to obtain (T', Λ_v). If $T \ne T'$, $\mathcal{A}_{lprf}$ sends $(\bot, \Lambda_v)$ to $\mathcal{A}_{ae}$. Otherwise, $\mathcal{A}_{lprf}$ computes locally $M \leftarrow \mathsf{Dec}(K_e, N, C_e)$ and $\Lambda_d \leftarrow L_d(K_e, N, C_e)$, and sends $(M, (\Lambda_d, \Lambda_v))$ to $\mathcal{A}_{ae}$. For queries (N, A, M) that $\mathcal{A}_{ae}$ makes to its challenge encryption oracle Enc, $\mathcal{A}_{lprf}$ samples a random bit string C_e of appropriate length, invokes its challenge oracle F on (N, A, C_e) to obtain T, and sends (C_e, T) back to $\mathcal{A}_{ae}$.

Recall that the difference between G_2 and G_3 is how the tag T is generated. In G_2 it is the real tag computed on a random ciphertext, in G_3 it is a random bit

---

^{3} Note that $\mathsf{Enc}(K, N, C) = \mathsf{Dec}(K, N, C)$.

string. By construction, $\mathcal{A}_{lprf}$ perfectly simulates G_2 and G_3 if its own challenge bit b (from the game LPRF) is equal to 1 and 0, respectively.

Every challenge (leakage) query by $\mathcal{A}_{lprf}$ stems from a challenge (leakage) query by $\mathcal{A}_{ae}$. As $\mathcal{A}_{ae}$ does not forward queries between its challenge and leakage oracles neither does $\mathcal{A}_{lprf}$. Hence we conclude that $\mathcal{A}_{lprf}$ is a valid LPRF adversary against Tag, which yields

$$\Pr\left[\mathcal{A}_{ae}^{G_2} \Rightarrow 1\right] - \Pr\left[\mathcal{A}_{ae}^{G_3} \Rightarrow 1\right] \leq \mathbf{Adv}_{\mathsf{Tag}}^{\mathsf{LPRF}}(\mathcal{A}_{lprf}, \mathcal{L}_T). \qquad (7)$$

Inserting (5), (6), and (7) in (4) proves the statement.   □

We will now go into the differences between our proof and the proof from [3]. In [3], the first game hop differs in that it also changes the leakage decryption oracle LDec. The change is such that any leakage decryption query which are not forwarded from the leakage encryption oracle is rejected by returning ⊥. In [3], this change is necessary in order to bound the second game hop with the security of the underlying encryption scheme. To detect the difference, the LAE adversary $\mathcal{A}_{ae}$ has to submit a (fresh) valid ciphertext to LDec as an invalid ciphertext would be rejected anyway. This entails that $\mathcal{A}_{ae}$ has generated a (fresh) valid tag for this ciphertext, which the reduction will use to distinguish whether its challenge oracle implements the verification algorithm or ⊥. Since the leakage decryption oracle is simulated via the leakage verification oracle, the reduction has to forward this leakage query to its own challenge oracle to distinguish between the real and the ideal world. This is exactly the query which prevents building such a MAC from a function which is pseudorandom and ultimately led to the introduction of LUF security by Degabriele et al. [13].

The next two game hops are the same as in our proof, except that the leakage decryption oracle does not decrypt any fresh ciphertext due to the change in the first game hop. This restriction allows to bound the second game hop by the IND-aCPLA security of the underlying encryption scheme, as the only queries that can not be answered with the oracle from the game INDaCPLA (decryption of fresh ciphertext) are answered with ⊥. In our case of mirror-like encryption schemes, this issue does not arise if the scheme is secure with respect to semi-nonce-respecting adversaries in which case we only need IND-CPLA security as forwarded leakage decryption queries are answered like fresh queries.

The third game hop is essentially the same, again only differing in the leakage decryption oracle. Since the LPRF adversary simulates the encryption-related part of the game locally, this difference is trivial.

Finally, Barwell et al. [3] have a fourth game hop. In this game hop, where the challenge oracles are already idealised, they merely revert the change of the leakage decryption oracle from the first game hop in order to end up with the idealised game, that is LAE with secret bit 0. Since we never change any leakage oracle throughout our proof, we do not need this additional game hop.

5   Leakage Resilience of the FGHF′ Construction

Having established the leakage resilience of the N2 composition for mirror-like encryption schemes and canonical MACs, we turn our attention towards the

FGHF' construction. Since our recast composition theorem imposes different security notions for the encryption scheme and the MAC, it remains to show that the encryption scheme $\mathrm{SE}[\mathcal{F}, \mathcal{G}]$ and the MAC $\mathrm{MAC}[\mathcal{H}, \mathcal{F}']$ of the FGHF' construction achieve these notions. In Sect. 5.1 we show that we can build a SUF-CMLA-secure MAC from a function which is pseudorandom under leakage. Combined with a result of Degabriele et al. [13] we obtain the SUF-CMLA security of $\mathrm{MAC}[\mathcal{H}, \mathcal{F}']$. In Sect. 5.2, we show that the encryption scheme $\mathrm{SE}[\mathcal{F}, \mathcal{G}]$ (proven IND-aCPLA-secure against nonce-respecting adversaries by Degabriele et al. [13]) achieves IND-CPLA security against semi-nonce-respecting adversaries.

5.1   Leakage-Resilient MACs from LPRFs

The following theorem shows that we can construct a SUF-CMLA-secure MAC from a function that is an LPRF. The difference to [13] is that our security notion does not allow the adversary to forward queries from its leakage oracle to its challenge oracle. The proof is given in the full version of this paper [23].

Theorem 13. *Let $\mathcal{F} \colon \mathcal{K} \times \mathcal{X} \to \{0,1\}^t$ be a function family with associated leakage set $\mathcal{L}_F$, and let $\mathrm{MAC}[\mathcal{F}]$ be the corresponding canonical MAC with associated leakage sets $\mathcal{L}_T$, $\mathcal{L}_V$ where $\mathcal{L}_F = \mathcal{L}_T = \mathcal{L}_V$. Then, for any SUF-CMLA adversary $\mathcal{A}_{mac}$ against $\mathrm{MAC}[\mathcal{F}]$ which makes q queries to Vfy, there exists an adversary $\mathcal{A}_{lprf}$ against $\mathcal{F}$ such that:*

$$\mathbf{Adv}_{\mathrm{MAC}[\mathcal{F}]}^{\mathrm{SUFCMLA}}(\mathcal{A}_{mac}, \mathcal{L}_T, \mathcal{L}_V) \leq \mathbf{Adv}_{\mathcal{F}}^{\mathrm{LPRF}}(\mathcal{A}_{lprf}, \mathcal{L}_F) + \frac{q}{2^t - q}.$$

Note that the above theorem states that for any LPRF $\mathcal{F}$ the canonical MAC $\mathrm{MAC}[\mathcal{F}]$ is SUF-CMLA-secure with the same message space as $\mathcal{F}$. In order to let the MAC handle arbitrarily long inputs, we need $\mathcal{F}$ to handle arbitrarily long inputs. This is achieved by first hashing the (arbitrarily long) input using a collision-resistant hash function and then applying the function $\mathcal{F}$. The resulting construction yields an LPRF with arbitrary input length as has been shown by Degabriele et al. [13, Theorem 5].

5.2   Leakage-Resilient Encryption from LPRFs

The theorem below states that the encryption scheme $\mathrm{SE}[\mathcal{F}, \mathcal{G}]$ constructed from a fixed-input-length function $\mathcal{F}$ and a PRG $\mathcal{G}$ (cf. Figure 7) is IND-CPLA-secure against semi-nonce-respecting adversaries if $\mathcal{F}$ is an LPRF and $\mathcal{G}$ is a secure PRG. We essentially show that the proof from [13] also holds for semi-nonce-respecting adversaries. Since we only need IND-CPLA security, we prove it for this case, adaptation to IND-aCPLA is straightforward. The proof is given in the full version of this paper [23].

Theorem 14. *Let $\mathrm{SE}[\mathcal{F}, \mathcal{G}]$ be the mirror-like encryption scheme depicted in Fig. 7, composed of a fixed-input-length function family $\mathcal{F}$ and a PRG $\mathcal{G}$*

with respective associated leakage sets $\mathcal{L}_F$ and $\mathcal{L}_G$. Then, for any semi-nonce-respecting IND-CPLA adversary $\mathcal{A}_{se}$ against $\text{SE}[\mathcal{F}, \mathcal{G}]$, making q queries to Enc, and associated leakage sets $\mathcal{L}_E = \mathcal{L}_F \times \mathcal{L}_G$, there exist an LPRF adversary $\mathcal{A}_{lprf}$ against $\mathcal{F}$ and a PRG adversary $\mathcal{A}_{prg}$ against $\mathcal{G}$ such that:

$$\mathbf{Adv}_{\text{SE}[\mathcal{F},\mathcal{G}]}^{\text{INDCPLA}}(\mathcal{A}_{se}, \mathcal{L}_E) \leq \mathbf{Adv}_{\mathcal{F}}^{\text{LPRF}}(\mathcal{A}_{lprf}, \mathcal{L}_F) + q\,\mathbf{Adv}_{\mathcal{G}}^{\text{PRG}}(\mathcal{A}_{prg}).$$

The difference to [13] is that they consider PRGs which can be queried multiple times while we stick to the single query case. This entails that we need a hybrid argument over the q encryption queries by $\mathcal{A}_{se}$, which induces the factor q. In [13], the hybrid argument appears in the proof of the sponge-based PRG.

5.3   Security of the FGHF' Construction

We can now state our main result, the following theorem, which states that the FGHF' construction yields an LAE-secure AEAD scheme, if the underlying functions $\mathcal{F}$ and $\mathcal{F}'$ are leakage-resilient pseudorandom, $\mathcal{G}$ is a secure PRG, and $\mathcal{H}$ is a collision-resistant hash function. The theorem follows directly from Theorem 12, Theorem 13, and Theorem 14 combined with [13, Theorem 5]. The implications are also illustrated in Fig. 12.

Theorem 15 (LAE Security of the FGHF' Construction). Let $\mathcal{F}$ be a fixed-input-length LPRF, $\mathcal{G}$ a PRG, $\mathcal{H}$ a vector hash function, and $\mathcal{F}'$ be a fixed-input-length LPRF with associated leakage sets $\mathcal{L}_F$, $\mathcal{L}_G$, $\mathcal{L}_H$, and $\mathcal{L}_{F'}$, respectively. Let FGHF' be the composition of $\mathcal{F}$, $\mathcal{G}$, $\mathcal{H}$, and $\mathcal{F}'$ (see Fig. 7) with associated leakage sets $\mathcal{L}_{AE} = \mathcal{L}_{VD} = \mathcal{L}_F \times \mathcal{L}_G \times \mathcal{L}_H \times \mathcal{L}_{F'}$. Then for any nonce-respecting LAE adversary $\mathcal{A}_{ae}$ against FGHF', making q_E and q_D queries to Enc and Dec, respectively, there exist adversaries $\mathcal{A}_{lprf}$, $\overline{\mathcal{A}}_{lprf}$, $\mathcal{A}_{prg}$, and $\mathcal{A}_{hash}$ such that:

$$\mathbf{Adv}_{\text{FGHF}'}^{\text{LAE}}(\mathcal{A}_{ae}, \mathcal{L}_{AE}, \mathcal{L}_{VD}) \leq \mathbf{Adv}_{\mathcal{F}}^{\text{LPRF}}(\mathcal{A}_{lprf}, \mathcal{L}_F) + 2\,\mathbf{Adv}_{\mathcal{F}'}^{\text{LPRF}}(\overline{\mathcal{A}}_{lprf}, \mathcal{L}_{F'})$$
$$+ q_E\,\mathbf{Adv}_{\mathcal{G}}^{\text{PRG}}(\mathcal{A}_{prg}) + 2\,\mathbf{Adv}_{\mathcal{H}}^{\text{CR}}(\mathcal{A}_{hash}) + \frac{q_D}{2^t - q_D}.$$

Theorem 15 improves [13, Theorem 6] by removing the additional requirement of unpredictability under leakage imposed on $\mathcal{F}'$. This entails that any instantiation of the FGHF' construction can rely on the same function to instantiate $\mathcal{F}$ and $\mathcal{F}'$, thus one could name it FGHF instead. Indeed, the sponge-based instantiation SLAE [13] uses the same function to instantiate $\mathcal{F}$ and $\mathcal{F}'$, however, pseudorandomness and unpredictability under leakage were proven separately.

Acknowledgements. We thank Jean Paul Degabriele and Christian Janson for helpful discussions. This work was funded by the Deutsche Forschungsgemeinschaft (DFG) – SFB 1119 – 236615297.

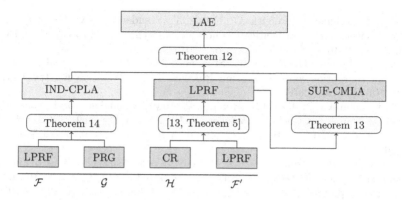

Fig. 12. Our security implications of the FGHF' construction (cf. Theorem 15).

References

1. Abdalla, M., Belaïd, S., Fouque, P.-A.: Leakage-resilient symmetric encryption via re-keying. In: Bertoni, G., Coron, J.-S. (eds.) CHES 2013. LNCS, vol. 8086, pp. 471–488. Springer, Heidelberg (2013). https://doi.org/10.1007/978-3-642-40349-1_27

2. Ashur, T., Dunkelman, O., Luykx, A.: Boosting authenticated encryption robustness with minimal modifications. In: Katz, J., Shacham, H. (eds.) CRYPTO 2017. LNCS, vol. 10403, pp. 3–33. Springer, Cham (2017). https://doi.org/10.1007/978-3-319-63697-9_1

3. Barwell, G., Martin, D.P., Oswald, E., Stam, M.: Authenticated encryption in the face of protocol and side channel leakage. In: Takagi, T., Peyrin, T. (eds.) ASIACRYPT 2017. LNCS, vol. 10624, pp. 693–723. Springer, Cham (2017). https://doi.org/10.1007/978-3-319-70694-8_24

4. Barwell, G., Page, D., Stam, M.: Rogue decryption failures: reconciling AE robustness notions. In: Groth, J. (ed.) IMACC 2015. LNCS, vol. 9496, pp. 94–111. Springer, Cham (2015). https://doi.org/10.1007/978-3-319-27239-9_6

5. Bellare, M., Namprempre, C.: Authenticated encryption: relations among notions and analysis of the generic composition paradigm. In: Okamoto, T. (ed.) ASIACRYPT 2000. LNCS, vol. 1976, pp. 531–545. Springer, Heidelberg (2000). https://doi.org/10.1007/3-540-44448-3_41

6. Bellare, M., Rogaway, P.: The security of triple encryption and a framework for code-based game-playing proofs. In: Vaudenay, S. (ed.) EUROCRYPT 2006. LNCS, vol. 4004, pp. 409–426. Springer, Heidelberg (2006). https://doi.org/10.1007/11761679_25

7. Bernstein, D.J.: CAESAR: Competition for Authenticated Encryption: Security, Applicability, and Robustness (2014)

8. Berti, F., Guo, C., Pereira, O., Peters, T., Standaert, F.-X.: TEDT, a leakage-resilient AEAD mode for high (physical) security applications. IACR Cryptol. ePrint Arch. **2019**, 137 (2019)

9. Berti, F., Guo, C., Pereira, O., Peters, T., Standaert, F.-X.: TEDT, a leakage-resist AEAD mode for high physical security applications. IACR Trans. Cryptogr. Hardware Embed. Syst. **2020**(1), 256–320 (2020)

10. Berti, F., Koeune, F., Pereira, O., Peters, T., Standaert, F.-X.: Leakage-resilient and misuse-resistant authenticated encryption. Cryptology ePrint Archive, Report 2016/996 (2016). http://eprint.iacr.org/2016/996
11. Berti, F., Pereira, O., Peters, T., Standaert, F.-X.: On leakage-resilient authenticated encryption with decryption leakages. IACR Trans. Symmetric Cryptol. **2017**(3), 271–293 (2017)
12. Chari, S., Jutla, C.S., Rao, J.R., Rohatgi, P.: Towards sound approaches to counteract power-analysis attacks. In: Wiener, M. (ed.) CRYPTO 1999. LNCS, vol. 1666, pp. 398–412. Springer, Heidelberg (1999). https://doi.org/10.1007/3-540-48405-1_26
13. Degabriele, J.P., Janson, C., Struck, P.: Sponges resist leakage: the case of authenticated encryption. In: Galbraith, S.D., Moriai, S. (eds.) ASIACRYPT 2019. LNCS, vol. 11922, pp. 209–240. Springer, Cham (2019). https://doi.org/10.1007/978-3-030-34621-8_8
14. Dobraunig, C., Eichlseder, M., Mangard, S., Mendel, F., Unterluggauer, T.: ISAP - towards side-channel secure authenticated encryption. IACR Trans. Symmetric Cryptol. **2017**(1), 80–105 (2017)
15. Dobraunig, C., Mennink, B.: Leakage resilience of the duplex construction. In: Galbraith, S.D., Moriai, S. (eds.) ASIACRYPT 2019. LNCS, vol. 11923, pp. 225–255. Springer, Cham (2019). https://doi.org/10.1007/978-3-030-34618-8_8
16. Dodis, Y., Pietrzak, K.: Leakage-resilient pseudorandom functions and side-channel attacks on Feistel networks. In: Rabin, T. (ed.) CRYPTO 2010. LNCS, vol. 6223, pp. 21–40. Springer, Heidelberg (2010). https://doi.org/10.1007/978-3-642-14623-7_2
17. Dziembowski, S., Pietrzak, K.: Leakage-resilient cryptography. In: 49th FOCS, pp. 293–302. IEEE Computer Society Press, October 2008
18. Faust, S., Pietrzak, K., Schipper, J.: Practical leakage-resilient symmetric cryptography. In: Prouff, E., Schaumont, P. (eds.) CHES 2012. LNCS, vol. 7428, pp. 213–232. Springer, Heidelberg (2012). https://doi.org/10.1007/978-3-642-33027-8_13
19. Guo, C., Pereira, O., Peters, T., Standaert, F.-X.: Leakage-resilient authenticated encryption with misuse in the leveled leakage setting: definitions, separation results, and constructions. Cryptology ePrint Archive, Report 2018/484 (2018). https://eprint.iacr.org/2018/484
20. Guo, C., Pereira, O., Peters, T., Standaert, F.-X.: Authenticated encryption with nonce misuse and physical leakage: definitions, separation results and first construction. In: Schwabe, P., Thériault, N. (eds.) LATINCRYPT 2019. LNCS, vol. 11774, pp. 150–172. Springer, Cham (2019). https://doi.org/10.1007/978-3-030-30530-7_8
21. Guo, C., Pereira, O., Peters, T., Standaert, F.-X.: Towards lightweight side-channel security and the leakage-resilience of the duplex sponge. IACR Cryptol. ePrint Arch. **2019**, 193 (2019)
22. Guo, C., Pereira, O., Peters, T., Standaert, F.-X.: Towards low-energy leakage-resistant authenticated encryption from the duplex sponge construction. IACR Trans. Symmetric Cryptol. **2020**(1), 6–42 (2020)
23. Krämer, J., Struck, P.: Leakage-resilient authenticated encryption from leakage-resilient pseudorandom functions. IACR Cryptol. ePrint Arch. **2020**, 280 (2020)
24. Longo, J., Martin, D.P., Oswald, E., Page, D., Stam, M., Tunstall, M.: Simulatable leakage: analysis, pitfalls, and new constructions. In: Sarkar, P., Iwata, T. (eds.) ASIACRYPT 2014. Part I, volume 8873 of LNCS, pp. 223–242. Springer, Heidelberg (2014)

25. Micali, S., Reyzin, L.: Physically observable cryptography. In: Naor, M. (ed.) TCC 2004. LNCS, vol. 2951, pp. 278–296. Springer, Heidelberg (2004). https://doi.org/10.1007/978-3-540-24638-1_16

26. National Institute of Standards and Technology. Lightweight cryptography standardization process (2015)

27. Pereira, O., Standaert, F.-X. and Vivek, S.: Leakage-resilient authentication and encryption from symmetric cryptographic primitives. In: Ray, I., Li, N., Kruegel, C. (eds.) ACM CCS 2015, pp. 96–108. ACM Press, October 2015

28. Rogaway, P.: Authenticated-encryption with associated-data. In: Atluri, V. (ed.) ACM CCS 2002, pp. 98–107. ACM Press, November 2002

29. Standaert, F.-X., Pereira, O., Yu, Yu.: Leakage-resilient symmetric cryptography under empirically verifiable assumptions. In: Canetti, R., Garay, J.A. (eds.) CRYPTO 2013. LNCS, vol. 8042, pp. 335–352. Springer, Heidelberg (2013). https://doi.org/10.1007/978-3-642-40041-4_19

30. Standaert, F.-X., Pereira, O., Yu, Y., Quisquater, J.J., Yung, M., Oswald, E.: Leakage resilient cryptography in practice. In: Sadeghi, A.R., Naccache, D. (eds.) Towards Hardware-Intrinsic Security - Foundations and Practice, Information Security and Cryptography, pp. 99–134. Springer, Heidelberg (2010). https://doi.org/10.1007/978-3-642-14452-3_5

31. Yu, Yu., Standaert, F.-X.: Practical leakage-resilient pseudorandom objects with minimum public randomness. In: Dawson, E. (ed.) CT-RSA 2013. LNCS, vol. 7779, pp. 223–238. Springer, Heidelberg (2013). https://doi.org/10.1007/978-3-642-36095-4_15

32. Yu, Y., Standaert, F.-X., Pereira, O., Yung, M.: Practical leakage-resilient pseudorandom generators. In: Al-Shaer, E., Keromytis, A.D., Shmatikov, V. (eds.) ACM CCS 2010, pp. 141–151. ACM Press, October 2010

Author Index

Printed in the United States
By Bookmasters